Congo
Democratic Republic • Republic

the Bradt Travel Guide

Sean Rorison

edition
I

www.bradtguides.com

Bradt Travel Guides Ltd, UK
The Globe Pequot Press Inc, USA

Congo
Don't
miss…

Congo River
An aerial view
(RK) page 3

Virunga National Park
Home to mountain gorillas
(AVZ) page 185

Diosso Gorge
(SR) page 268

Wagenia fishermen
Kisangani
(MWS/ALAMY) page 166

Ndoki-Nouabalé National Park
(TB) page 284

above **Women selling caterpillars — a nutricious local delicacy** (KE) page 47

left **Ba'aka woman collecting bananas for her family, Mindzoukou** (KE) page 126

above   *Tchukudu* (homemade bicycle), Goma (SR)

below   Travelling by boat down the Congo River (KE) page 43

Libinza tribe children going to school by canoe,
Ngiri River, DRC (JJ/ALAMY) page 79

AUTHOR

Sean Rorison is a freelance writer from Vancouver, British Columbia, who has made his way to nearly 80 countries. His range of travel interests is broad, including some of the most contentious regions of the world – from Afghanistan to Iraq, Colombia to Somalia; he has also indulged his love for more mainstream destinations like Liechtenstein, Malta and Japan. He has written numerous articles on the political and social situations in Somalia, Algeria, Pakistan and the Republic of Congo as well as operated his own website, Sean's Travel Stories, since 1998. In 2002, he helped start the popular travel journal site Polo's  Bastards, which focuses primarily on difficult destinations. While his readers revel in his journeys to the Congos, they still haven't warmed up to his visits to Malta.

AUTHOR STORY

Months of debate preceded the writing of this book. Was it feasible to combine the Democratic Republic of Congo and the Republic of Congo? Did the parks listed on maps even exist? Were there any animals left? Could one safely traverse the country? Luckily, Bradt Guides gave me the room to write what was needed and the opportunity to update information at a moment's notice. The culmination of five-years worth of visits to both countries, the writing more often than not also involved keeping an eye on news updates, and praying things didn't change overnight. Indeed, twice when I visited Kinshasa combat broke out within a week of my departure, and advisories on where was safe to visit in Virunga park were being updated relentlessly, as fighting swept over regions around Goma.

Despite a taxi driver calling me 'crazy' for visiting the Congos simply for 'tourism' – it's thought too unstable to merit a visit by neighbouring countries – I can see tell-tale signs of a tourist industry in the exciting stages of its infancy. Backpackers are cropping up regularly in Goma these days, and though they may rarely go further afield, it's a sure sign that travellers are slowly coming back to the region. At the moment groups are small and often independently organised, but hopefully in a few years larger companies will have the confidence to visit as well. As always, I'll be watching with fingers crossed.

PUBLISHER'S FOREWORD   *Hilary Bradt*

The first Bradt travel guide was written in 1974 by George and Hilary Bradt on a river barge floating down a tributary of the Amazon. It was followed by *Backpacker's Africa*, published in 1979. In the 1980s and '90s the focus shifted away from hiking to broader-based guides to new destinations – usually the first to be published on those places. In the 21st century Bradt continues to publish these ground-breaking guides, along with guides to established holiday destinations, incorporating in-depth information on culture and natural history alongside the nuts and bolts of where to stay and what to see.

Bradt authors support responsible travel, with advice not only on minimum impact but also on how to give something back through local charities. Thus a true synergy is achieved between the traveller and local communities.

* * *

I've wanted to publish a guide to this geographically magnificent but politically chaotic region ever since the BBC's wonderful wildlife programme: Congo. I was already a convert 30 years ago when I visited eastern Zaire, as it was then, and saw my first gorillas as well as the dramatic volcanic eruptions of Nyiragongo. Finding an author to take on this Herculean task was a challenge, but who better than Sean Rorison, who helped start up my favourite travel website, Polo's Bastards ('Going where we ain't supposed to'). He's done a great job. The Congos need and deserve more tourists, and this book should help start the ball rolling.

Reprinted July 2010   First published March 2008
Bradt Travel Guides Ltd, 23 High Street, Chalfont St Peter, Bucks SL9 9QE, England
www.bradtguides.com
Published in the USA by The Globe Pequot Press Inc, 246 Goose Lane,
PO Box 480, Guilford, Connecticut 06475-0480

Text copyright © 2008 Sean Rorison Maps copyright © 2008 Bradt Travel Guides Ltd
Illustrations © 2008 Individual photographers and artists
Editorial Project Manager: Emma Thomson

ISBN-10: 1 84162 233 8   ISBN-13: 978 1 84162 233 0
British Library Cataloguing in Publication Data
A catalogue record for this book is available from the British Library

Photographs Ariadne Van Zandbergen (AVZ), David Tipling (DT), Gerry Ellis/Minden Pictures/FLPA (GE/MP/FLPA), Jacques Jangoux/Alamy (JJ/Alamy), Kate Eshelby (KE), Marcus Wilson-Smith/Alamy (MWS/Alamy), Reto Kuster (RK), Sean Rorison (SR), Thomas Brever (TB), Thomas Furst (TF)
Front cover Mount Mikeno (GE/MP/FLPA)
Back cover Mountain gorilla *Gorilla gorilla berengi* (ANZ), Ba'aka pygmy woman (RK)
Title page Early morning mist in the Ituri rainforest (RK), Mbuti pygmy woman (RK), Okapi *Okapia johnstoni* (RK)
Illustrations Carole Vincer   **Maps** Dave Priestley, Malcolm Barnes (colour map)
Typeset from the author's disc by Wakewing
Production managed by Jellyfish Print Solutions and manufactured in India by Replika Press Pvt. Ltd.

Acknowledgements

Writing a guidebook on the Congos is a project somewhere between difficult and foolish even at the best of times, which is certainly why I need to extend many thanks to those who went out of their way to assist me in this effort. Initial thanks go to Graham Chisholm and Augustin Nduwa Kakwata of Industrial Copper Systems in Likasi and Lubumbashi for their assistance there. Thanks also to Albutin Ilunga Shimbi for all of the excellent information on Kalemie as well as Emmanuel Kakesa and Arthur Kalunga for their help in rounding out Katanga.

Thanks to Paul Clammer for some great initial advice and encouragement – good luck with Afghanistan. Thanks to Nikolaus Grubeck for regaling me with chaotic Congo stories a year before my first visit. In Kinshasa, thanks to Claude Jibidar of the World Food Programme for information on infrastructure improvements across the country. Thanks also to Derek Weiss for that Kituba dictionary. Much gratitude goes to the staff at Go Congo Tours: Michel Van Roten, Judith Opinga, Ernest Obe and others, who went out of their way to help me when I was wandering around the western end of DR Congo. And a big thanks to Kennedy Nari Ndayisenga for taking that road trip with me from Goma to Bunia. Also thanks to Alex Muja of Jambo Safaris. In Bukavu, my appreciation goes to Robert Mbarushimana, for putting up with all my persistent questions.

At the ICCN appreciation goes to Vitale Katembo in Goma, who helped to pave the way for an easy time traversing all of Virunga; also Malingane Ntabiruba in Kisangani for lending me his private motorcycle chauffeur (with the fancy Parc National de Maïko licence plate) while running around the city's environs. Also my gratitude goes out to the ICCN staff at the main office in Kinshasa, specifically Gérard Ipantua Iba-Yung for filling in many of the gaps surrounding all of the DR Congo's parks.

At the DRC's Office National de Tourisme, thanks to Jean Joseph Matete in Kisangani for happily listing everything there was to see in Equateur to me. And a big thank you to Raph for spending so much time running around Matadi with me and piling into that crowded shared taxi to Boma.

I should extend my thanks to the numerous police officers, immigration officials and other random folks with badges in both countries for the forced pleasantries and intentional delays that are par for the course when visiting. And I'd like to thank all of them for not throwing me in jail, only asking for modest amounts of money, and eventually sending me on my way. I'm not a spy, just a writer, and thanks for understanding that.

Thanks to Sara Evans for her contribution on rangers in Virunga and Philip Briggs an Janice Booth for their box on Batwa pygmies. Finally, last but not least, thanks to Tricia Hayne and Hilary Bradt, who helped get this project rolling, and who believed that I could write this book. I hope the final product meets your expectations. As well, I express my greatest appreciation to everyone else at Bradt Travel Guides.

Contents

LIST OF MAPS

A NOTE ABOUT TELEPHONE NUMBERS

Telephone codes and mobile numbers vary widely (and wildly!) throughout the Congos. As a general rule, though, mobile numbers in the DR Congo have ten digits, including the zero at the beginning of them, though this is not a hard and fast rule – some have only nine digits. Land lines tend to have seven digits and do not require a zero to dial them. For more information see page 87.

FEEDBACK REQUEST

Every effort has been made to ensure that the details contained within this book are as accurate and up to date as possible. Inevitably, however, things move on. Any information regarding such changes, or relating to your experiences in the Congos – good or bad – would be very gratefully received. Such feedback is invaluable when compiling further editions. Send your comments to Bradt Travel Guides Ltd, 23 High Street, Chalfont St Peter, Bucks SL9 9QE, England; e info@bradtguides.com.

Introduction

Given how vast the Congos are, and how important they are to the African continent, it is a wonder that so few people have managed to visit even in the best of times. Yet given how bad the infrastructure is, how famously unstable their governments are, and how volatile sweeping regions of these already massive countries can be, it is a wonder that anyone has bothered to visit in the past decade at all.

The Congos are the proverbial elephants in the middle of the living room. They occupy a huge space not only geographically but also psychologically to the Africans – the famous river that stretches all the way from the Atlantic Ocean to the Great Lakes of east Africa; the massive mineral deposits that have yielded untold riches for most of the wrong people; huge reserves of wildlife and rainforest; animals found nowhere else on the planet; vast, undeveloped stretches where most foreigners only dream of exploring. And yet for those few who try to get in, millions are desperate to get out.

History in these countries has never been boring, and it has rarely, if ever, not been brutal. The Democratic Republic of Congo has had its name changed four times since its inception as Congo Free State in 1884. Tribal wars and massacres have persisted from time immemorial up to the present day. Brutal dictators have come and gone. A massive multi-national war, killing millions, came and went. Riots and looting, coup attempts and assassinations, the spectre of Ebola and cannibalism have all existed in a frighteningly short timespan within the Congos. The four horsemen arrived together and never really left, though these days they are taking a breather – we can hope they stay that way.

It is hard to say one can really know Africa without knowing the Congos. For all their importance, they are so easily overlooked because of their problems, but as their situations stabilise, their role in the continent and the world will grow to where it should be. It is far more than just their own countries at stake, for their prosperity will mean the prosperity of all Africa. Those who make the effort to visit will be surprised at a genuinely hospitable group of people who have adapted to life in difficult situations. Optimism is easy to find, and foreigners arriving with the same attitude will not be disappointed.

This book will focus primarily on the parks and reserves that are currently accessible, as well as the major cities and towns near the parks. However, I have made many attempts to include various other aspects of my research and experience in the countries and you will find useful information for towns out of the way – though I do advise that a visitor to the DR Congo should have a specific purpose there and stick to it. Wandering around without the appropriate contacts and permits can be problematic. Nonetheless, for those of you with reasons to visit certain areas out of the way, I have provided information.

Time will tell if the old days of Zairian overlanding, extended wilderness trekking, and wild nights in Kinshasa will return. The Congolese are resilient, a cultural power in their own right, and have responded to renewed stability by trying to move on. An increase in tourism will help this, and it is my hope that this book will point those of you who visit in the right direction.

Part One

GENERAL INFORMATION

Background Information

The lungs of Africa and the middle of the continent, the Congos are the wild in-between that few manage to visit. Its towns are scattered across a vast area with little infrastructure, and a lack of development has allowed this region to remain one of the most untamed on the planet. This is a huge area of dark corners, both geographically and mentally. It is the quintessential African experience, but also the harshest one out there. It is not a place where things are done halfway, or done timidly – it is a region where man has fought continuously against his own demons and the elements of nature at large. And unlike the rest of the world, for the most part mankind is still very much caught in the throes of this battle – wilderness still dominates, even in its most developed areas.

It is unlike the other jurisdictions of Africa where animals are given their own space while man claims his: they are all still battling for their own territory. It is still very much a story of outposts and great unknowns. There is no other place in Africa where one will find the same level of adventure, or the same level of natural variety. It is also the Petri dish of the world, a melting pot of germs and plants still only half discovered by scientists – it is the source of the phrase 'Mysterious African Disease'.

It is the sole occupier of the continent's second-largest river. It is a region of vast riches and resources that other countries could only dream of owning. It is a region of politics that are sprawling and complicated to even the most attentive. It is the maelstrom in the centre, the vortex around which all other countries in Africa revolve. It is a looming presence in all senses of the word, a land to be revered and respected, a place which can easily devour the unsuspecting. It is the true heart of Africa – it always has been, and will undoubtedly continue to be.

GEOGRAPHY

Occupying most of the equatorial region in Africa, both Congos have some of the most varied landscapes in the continent. Broadly speaking, the north of both countries is covered in dense tropical rainforest, still largely undeveloped, and subject to long periods of rain and cloud. This rainforest, next to the Amazon in South America, is the world's largest and most significant.

Stretching from the Atlantic Ocean and slowly winding its way in a lazy coil eastward is the Congo River, bisecting both countries and a lifeline for the deep interior of central Africa. Second longest on the continent at over 4,300km, it stretches from the hills near Lake Tanganyika northward, then eases west and then south again to drain into the Atlantic. Two sets of rapids make the river impossible to navigate directly from source to sea, and the widest section is between the almost-lake formation of Malebo Pool and the falls near Kisangani. The bays along the ocean have made excellent harbours and are home to a vibrant variety of fish and resources.

On the eastern edge of the Congos are the Great Lakes of Africa in the Great Rift Valley, using the borders of lakes Tanganyika, Albert, Kivu and Edward. The frontier of the DR Congo is marked by volcanoes and highlands in the east. This area is geologically active to an incredible extent, with several volcanoes erupting on a regular basis. The highlands also host some of Africa's highest peaks in the Ruwenzori and Virunga mountains.

Westward from these towering peaks is, generally speaking, the Congo Basin. It is like a bowl, between the two altitude extremes of the Great Rift Valley and the hills that divide the Congos from Gabon. The central plains of the DR Congo are fertile and marshy in the north, with extensive drainage patterns for hundreds of estuaries from the main Congo River.

Further south in the DR Congo, the equatorial jungles give way to the rolling plains that are more typical of southern Africa. Fertile grasslands with hot summers and a short rainy season create a much drier atmosphere than the northern rainforests. On a high plateau easing slowly downward into the Congo Basin, there is less humidity here than in the deep jungle. The plateau also hosts incredibly rich land, with intense fertility and vast deposits of underground mineral wealth.

CLIMATE

There are only two seasons across the Congos: dry and rainy, though depending on where you are, the times for these will change. In the rainforest the rainy season arrives like clockwork in the winter, from about October to April; frequent downpours and scattered clouds will greet the traveller, and could heed movement across the moist and muddy lowlands. In general, through the northern belt of equatorial rainforest the rainy season runs from October to April, and in the Katanga region the rains come from December to March.

Monsoon rains are the norm, meaning short outbursts of rain that will last one or two hours and drench everything in sight. These tend to occur in the afternoon and early evening.

Temperatures in the plains of the south of DR Congo can be as much as 35°C in the summer, but averaging about 25°C across the rainforest, with heavy humidity. In the mountains along the east it can get cooler in the day and evening, sometimes going as low as 10°C.

HISTORY TO THE MID-19TH CENTURY

The history of the two Congos is inextricably tied to that of sub-Saharan Africa as a whole; as the convergence of the continent, it can initially be overwhelming due to its numerous interacting elements. There has been little study on the earliest millennia in the Congos, and early kingdoms that dominated the area are only known through oral traditions before the arrival of Europeans. Archaeological excavations in the area have been either minute or non-existent.

Early European historical texts focused on a primitive and decentralised group of tribes that were encountered upon their arrival in the area, though even their own explorers would disagree with this notion as they were in regular contact with what were royalty of the region for trading. However, this attitude would persist for centuries, almost until the present day, and would further justify partitioning of the continent by colonial powers.

When we discuss the specifics of the two countries now both known as Congo, we only arrive at these designations relatively late. Tribal politics and mass migration into the region formed nation-states long before the arrival of Europeans, and the middle centuries of the 2nd millennium AD would be marked by the interaction between these kingdoms and European traders. Therefore a great deal of simultaneity occurs when discussing the history of the region as numerous countries interact, and their interests and histories collide.

EARLIEST HISTORY The first arrivals to the central African landscape were pygmy tribes who settled in the area – the Twa, Baka and Aka pygmy peoples lived nomadic lives across the rainforests of central Africa as hunter-gatherer societies. There is some prehistory documentation on what are believed to be this part of Africa's first human inhabitants – the Egyptians are noted to have made contact with them, and reliefs of pygmies can be found on the tombs in Sakkara's pyramid at Giza. In ancient Greece, Herodotus's *Histories* discusses the first contact of ancient civilisations with what are believed to be pygmy peoples:

> After journeying for many days over a wide extent of sand, they came at last to a plain where they observed trees growing; approaching them, and seeing fruit on them, they proceeded to gather it. While they were thus engaged, there came upon them some dwarfish men, under the middle height, who seized them and carried them off. The Nasamonians could not understand a word of their language, nor had they any acquaintance with the language of the Nasamonians. They were led across extensive marshes, and finally came to a town, where all the men were of the height of their conductors, and black-complexioned. A great river flowed by the town, running from west to east, and containing crocodiles.
>
> The *Histories* of Herodotus, written 440BCE,
> translated by George Rawlinson, 1858

Herodotus goes on to speculate that the city they had encountered beyond the sand was a 'nation of sorcerers' and was nearing the source of the Nile.

The pygmies would not be alone for too long, as the region was further inhabited by various Bantu tribes who are thought to have originated near Lake Chad several thousand years ago. They eventually moved south into the equatorial rainforests, initially only coming into limited contact with pygmies, though would be at odds with each other ever since.

Numerous fracturings occurred in the 1st millennium of the Common Era as villages and smaller kingdoms emerged. These kingdoms and people displaced other tribes that had migrated north from southern Africa, those being descendants of the Khoisan tribe, who settled amongst the savannas of what is modern-day Katanga and points further south.

Complex societies formed across central Africa during this time, with various trade routes slowly established. Nations had arisen by the end of the 1st millennium, and central Africa was dominated by the Kongo, Loango and Ndongo kingdoms along the Atlantic coast, as well as the Luba and Lunda kingdoms deeper inland. These were sophisticated organisations with clear hierarchies of royalty, subjects, tradespeople, farmers, and yes – even slaves.

THE LOANGO KINGDOM Loango was founded around the 12th century AD with its full establishment sometime in the mid 14th century. It had a very pronounced monarchy in its capital city of Loango, a town slightly inland from the Atlantic coast and quite near to present-day Pointe Noire. They also had a large trading centre at the mouth of the Congo River – then known as the Nzadi River. The city was a meeting point for tradesmen and artisans, a large market that tied the regions of the kingdom together. The King of Loango, the Maloango, lived here and made appearances in the centre of the city when fields were being cultivated or when vassals would pay tribute. Loango was itself a vassal state of its larger neighbour Kongo, and would answer to their rule throughout its existence.

The kingdom had a structure of provinces with governors, with a governor succeeding the king upon his death. The governor was then rotated so that the next province in line would see its governor promoted to king in succession.

The kingdom was also a gatherer of ivory and slaves for export, which was a principal source of its prosperity upon contact with Europeans in the 17th century. Taxes and duties were excised on European traders arriving in the area, and Loango merchants were very active in exploring the deeper regions of central Africa for slaves and other resources to sell to Europeans.

Once the practice of slavery was abolished, the power and influence of the Loango Kingdom waned as one of its principal exports was no longer in demand. Another theory of the decline of the Loango Kingdom was that its highly decentralised power structure created an oligarchy of nobles and as the higher figure of the Maloango was no longer needed, it was thus unable to hold the various Loango provinces together as a nation.

THE NDONGO KINGDOM South of the Nzadi River formed the Ndongo Kingdom, sometimes known as the Mbundu Kingdom as its members were of the Mbundu tribe. It too had a monarchy, with a line of kings known as Ngolas. The earliest history of the Ndongo speculates that they migrated west to the sea from deeper inland, somewhere near the Luba and Lunda kingdoms, and settled throughout the coastal region. Contact with other tribes introduced their society, which had existed in a hunter-gatherer state, to techniques in blacksmithing and pottery.

The larger and more powerful Kingdom of Kongo to the north had stated originally to Europeans that Ndongo was a vassal state under their control; however, in practice this could never be confirmed, and they had no real interaction with the Kongo Kingdom on a regular basis.

With the arrival of Europeans, Ndongo and Kongo became at odds with each other. Portuguese slave traders established another port of call at Luanda, and the loss of Kongo's monopoly on slave exports in the region put the two nations at war. A critical battle at Caxito, along the Dande River, effectively severed ties between the two kingdoms in 1556. This would remain their border until the eventual dissolution of both states.

THE LUBA AND LUNDA KINGDOMS Discovering where the Luba and Lunda kingdoms divide, merge and divide again is something inexact, but we do know their histories are intertwined.

Coalescing as a people in the 1st millennium AD, the Lunda and Luba peoples lived in almost the middle of the continent. They had already established trade routes east to the Indian Ocean and were working metals for many centuries before merging together in the 16th century to create the Luba and Lunda kingdoms.

Luba's ruler would be appointed by spiritual leaders, the Balopwe, who would speak to ancestors for guidance on whom to appoint to Mulopwe, King of the Luba. Because of his appointment by spiritual leaders, the Mulopwe held significant power over lesser governing subjects in the Luba hierarchy.

The Luba Kingdom was divided amongst governors as well as village leaders, all of whom belonged to a secret society named Bambudye, and the Luba king was the head of this society. The kingdom expanded quickly from its formation and established mines for copper, organised fishing operations, and extracted oil from palm trees.

The Lunda had consolidated power by treaty across village chiefs in the region between the Luba to the north and Kongo to the west, and managed trade caravans throughout the area. Their knowledge of nation-building is usually attributed to a

Luba king being married to a Lunda chief, which created enormous disdain amongst Lunda peoples – who then migrated outside their traditional regions and expanded Lunda territory significantly, but also established a very similar social order in the Lunda nation-state. Lunda were considered a sort of vassal state of the Luba, though this is not entirely accurate either – they were separate states, with the Luba being the stronger and more organised of the two.

THE KONGO KINGDOM Of largest importance to the western region of central Africa is the Kongo Kingdom. It was, in its time, an economic and cultural powerhouse and the first nation to have regular contact with European explorers, meaning that there is more history known as to its existence than other African nations of the time.

Its beginnings stretch back to around 1100AD, north of the Nzadi River in a kingdom called Bungu, with the marauding son of a local leader, Motinobene. Motinobene used his men to charge tolls along the river to traders, attacked local villages and forced their population into speaking the Kongo language. Motinobene's men married the daughters of local chiefs, and in this way began to spread their culture and ethnicity. Eventually Motinobene settled in an area near present-day Matadi in the Kwilu Valley, founding a town called Mpemba Ksai. A line of rulers would be buried in the valley, and Kongo tradition would remember this place as an area of sacred beginnings for the Kongo Kingdom. With Motinobene marrying the daughter of a spiritual leader named Manikabunga, he set in place a line of dynastic succession; a subsequent treaty with his neighbours called the Mbata set up a line of royalty. All of his successors would marry the daughters of Mbata, and in this way the royal line of Kongo was born – the ruler of the Kongo Kingdom would be known as the Manikongo.

Manikongo would move his capital south to a densely populated region called Mbanza Kongo, though Mpemba Ksai would remain a sacred burial ground for royalty. Mbanza Kongo was a large town settled in a fertile area, and had a highly centralised political structure. Further trade and political alliances put the neighbouring kingdoms of Loango and Ndongo under the Manikongo as vassal states, and upon first contact with Europeans, Kongo was a formidable nation in its own right.

It was under this established monarchy that first contact with Portuguese explorers would occur in 1482, as Diego Cão arrived at the mouth of a massive river.

ARRIVAL OF THE EUROPEANS The arrival of King John II in Portugal saw numerous changes in the monarchy and aristocracy in the seafaring European country, and one of the king's central interests was reigniting the oceanic explorations that would further expand the trade routes and influence of Portugal. With the blessing of King John II, the explorer Diego Cão set out to chart the southern Atlantic coasts of Africa. Hoping to find a fast shipping route to Asia, he was known to have stopped at the Gold Coast (modern-day Ghana). Further south he eventually encountered the mouth of a massive river. In 1482, he set anchor in the bay of Loango (present-day Cabinda) and asked local people what the name of the river was. They said 'Nzadi', but he misunderstood them and recorded the river's name as 'Zaire'.

Cão and his men erected a stone pillar in honour of St George on the southern banks of the Zaire River and sailed upriver for a while before deciding to send some local messengers out on foot in search of a ruler, and then continuing south along the African coast. Upon returning to pick up his messengers they had not yet returned, and in light of this took four prominent local men and returned to

Portugal. Cão was ennobled for his discoveries and would make further explorations along the southern African coast.

It was not until his second voyage southward in 1485, returning with the same local men, that contact with the Kongo's leader occurred. Nzinga Nkuwu was Manikongo at the time and welcomed contact with the Portuguese explorer, and being sufficiently impressed by his culture, permitted Catholic missionaries to arrive six years later. Nzinga himself took a European name after this contact, calling himself John after the Portuguese king of the time. Manikongo John of Kongo's successor was even more enamoured with the Catholic religion: he was baptised, given the European name of Alfonso, and began creating a tax structure to support the Church. The Kongo Church incorporated European religious ceremonies with local animist ones, and would remain an important part of the kingdom's culture for the remainder of its existence.

INTERCONTINENTAL TRADE AND THE FIRST EUROPEAN COLONIES Slavery was a practice that had existed for quite some time in the Kongo Kingdom, usually with captured prisoners of war being sold or traded. European missionaries helped establish schools and churches in the kingdom, and the successor to Manikongo Alfonso, Manikongo Alvaro, enacted further Westernisation of his upper classes by assigning European titles such as Duke and Marquis to their names. Kongo also established embassies in several European nations as relations developed between the two continents.

European contact, though, would be overshadowed by the slave trade. Portugal's own king was looking for labour to be used at farms in nearby São Tomé, and Kongo was willing to trade for them. Their own presence in the region was also growing: the Portuguese had settled in Luanda after a conflict with the Ndongo Kingdom in 1579, managing this with partial help from the Kongo, and would create a larger footprint of foreigners on their own continent. Further agitation was created when the King of Portugal won the right to nominate bishops to a new cathedral in Mbanza Kongo, renamed to São Salvador.

THE DECLINE OF THE KONGO KINGDOM Slaves were being exported at increasing rates throughout the 16th century while other Portuguese governors, now with a foothold in Luanda, began to hire mercenaries to conduct raids deeper into the territories of both Kongo and Ndongo. The Imbangala were a barbaric group of local Africans who kidnapped children to serve in their army and engaged in cannibalism, and were set forth by the Governor of Portuguese Angola to invade the southern provinces of Kongo in 1622. Kongo and Portugal from this point on, then, had become enemies with each other – though their trading relationship continued as more people were captured from deeper inside the African interior and shipped out for slavery.

Tension continued between Kongo and Portuguese Angola for nearly 50 years. Kongo itself was being torn apart by internal rivalries. Luanda was captured by the Dutch and recaptured by Portugal during this period, and a fracturing of the Kongo Kingdom saw the vassal state of Mbwila sign a treaty with Portugal acceding its authority to them. Kongo sent an army into Mbwila to take back what they thought was rightfully theirs, and Portugal met Kongo's army in Ulanga, Mbwila's capital.

The Battle of Ambuila in 1556 was a critical moment in the downfall of the Kongo Kingdom. The Manikongo of the time, Antonio I, was killed along with many other Kongo nobles. With no clear leadership plan in place Kongo became further fractured, and civil war ensued. São Salvador was razed in 1678 and its population fled into the hills, where rival factions built fortresses and lived in solitude.

The last gasp of a unified Kongo Kingdom occured in 1700; peasants across the former Kongolese Empire lived under constant threat of war and combat, yet were still inundated with the preachings of European missionaries. This created a situation ideal for one woman, who in 1702 would proclaim herself to be the new embodiment of St Anthony. The Kongolese would call her Kimpa Vita, while European texts would call her Dona Beatriz, also referred to as the 'Kongolese Joan of Arc'.

Her claims of direct contact with the spiritual world were believed by the peasants. Born of noble blood some 25 years earlier, Kimpa Vita already had experience in the religious cult of *isimbi* early in her life. This gave her knowledge of how to operate a religious sect, and she would use this knowledge to its full potential. Telling her followers to cast off the Christian practices of marriage, confession and baptism, she was already gaining ire amongst European missionaries. Then, she stated that the Holy Cross was fetishism and ordered them all burned. She said she died every Friday, travelled to the heavens to communicate with the spirits there, and returned on Monday to convey their message. She also proclaimed herself the religious leader that would reunify the Kongo Kingdom, and implored the nobles scattered across the land's territory to allow her to appoint a new king.

São Salvador had been sacked by the Portuguese and armies loyal to them some decades before. Kimpa Vita requested that the old capital be reoccupied. Kongo noble Pedro IV had already arrived in the former town, and she appointed him the new ruler of Kongo. It was her leadership that brought several splintered factions together under the Kongo banner and under Pedro IV specifically, allowing the kingdom to gel into a nominally cohesive force for a few more decades.

Kimpa Vita, though, would meet an unfortunate fate. Claiming to have possession of a Papal Bull (a charter from the Vatican Church), she travelled between the strongholds of nobility hoping to get them rallying under Pedro IV; but her boasting of having a Papal Bull in her possession, and refusing to show it to anyone, would have her arrested. King Pedro IV, and the European Church, were not kind to her: they declared her a heretic, and in 1706 she was burned at the stake.

For further information, consult *The Kongolese Saint Anthony: Dona Beatriz, Kimpa Vita and the Antonian Movement, 1684–1706* by John Kelly Thornton.

Continued battles between groups in this region, along with the constant export of slaves, had depleted the kingdom of a cohesive authority. Portuguese Angola still existed as a colonial power along the coast, though, and agitated the actions of local rulers throughout this period. They also commissioned the Lunda Kingdom to raid the eastern edges of the former Kongo, all but eliminating their authority as a singular nation in the mid 18th century. However, the Kongo Kingdom continued to exist in various incarnations until the European nations formally divided the African continent amongst themselves in the late 19th century. During this period, the lack of a centralised authority helped European trading interests, pulling more slaves out of the jungles and onto boats headed for farms and plantations in Brazil and São Tomé.

Other kingdoms began to emerge from the dissipating ancient territories of Kongo and Luba: slaves who had managed to flee from Portuguese traders began forming a society inland from the coast in 1568, giving rise to the Kuba Kingdom. The Lubas as a whole were being whittled away, and in the mid 19th century

Ngelengwa Msiri would form the Kingdom of Garengaze along the western shores of Lake Tanganyika in 1858. He would eventually settle in the town of Bunkeya, and run an important nation there until 1892.

RENEWED EUROPEAN INTEREST By the 19th century, European missionaries had long since departed any establishments inland, and their presence would be almost non-existent aside from port towns along the coast. Central Africa was an impenetrable rainforest, and European traders relied upon the merchants of local tribes to bring them the slaves and ivory they desired.

One brave British man would change all of this, though. James Kingston Tuckey, a sailor and explorer born in Ireland, had the first steam-powered sloop on his side. Christened the HMS *Congo*, it was destined to finally navigate into the heart of central Africa with its state-of-the-art paddlewheels, swivelling guns, and 30-tonne steam engine bearing the power of 20 horses. Tuckey wanted to prove that the Congo and Niger rivers linked up, thereby opening the heart of the continent to the new technology of paddlewheelers, and to discover what lurked deep inside the jungles of the continent.

Tuckey's luck was not good. The steam engine did not work properly, and the crew had to resort to using backup sails to arrive at the mouth of the Congo River in 1816. They persisted upriver from there, but malaria and yellow fever were wearing down his crew. His mighty vessel reached impassable rapids. His men would continue out on foot, trying to find the end of the rapids and what lay ahead; the terrain was mountainous and difficult to navigate, and he continued losing men to diseases they had not encountered before. On 9 September 1816, he would reach his furthest point:

> We perceived the river winding again to the SE but our view did not extend above three miles of the reach; the water clear of rocks, and, according to the information of all the people, there is no impediment whatever, as far as they know, above this place.

He would turn back and die of exhaustion on the Atlantic coast, near modern-day Moanda, later that same year, with three-quarters of his expedition crew having perished on the journey. Little did he know that the river was actually navigable inland from this seemingly impenetrable point, and it would not be for several decades until another European returned to make an attempt at continuing this journey.

Tuckey's diaries and observations would prove to be a catalyst for major change in Africa, and especially the Congos. He had a book published posthumously, *Narrative of an Expedition to Explore the River Zaire*. It would, at the very least, provide valuable insight to European explorers of what lay further inland into what was still an empty spot on the map.

Tuckey revelled in the magnitude of the Congo River, as all other explorers who came after him would also do:

> The river now, for the first time, bore a majestic appearance, having the land on each side moderately elevated, with little hills of lime-stone further back, but still almost without wood.

FURTHER EFFORTS AT MAPPING THE RIVER Increased exploration across the continent persisted in the following decades. In 1826, English Captain William F W Owen commandeered two ships, the *Leven* and *Barracouta*, to create the most detailed survey of the Congo River from its mouth to 25 miles inward, halfway between Moanda and Boma. A French captain would be next, Jean-Baptiste Douville, who from 1828 to 1830 made several attempts at navigating up the Zaire

River – though did not realise until late in a sprawling account of his journey that he was navigating the Cuanza River in Angola. His proclamation of navigating the Congo (or 'Fleuve Couango dit Zaire' on his maps, as published in *Atlas du voyage au Congo et dans l'intérieur de l'Afrique équinoxiale* in 1832) to 25°E, made the mystery of the Congo River all the more intriguing for future exploration.

Doctor David Livingstone would depart the western shores of Africa in 1852, initially exploring the interior. He made countless adjustments to previous maps of the rivers and their drainage patterns in southern and central Africa. He debunked Douville's claims of the 'Couango' river, encountered the Zambezi River, and gained notoriety across the world for his explorations.

In 1855, another steam sloop, the *Alecto*, led by Commander J Hunt, attempted to succeed Tuckey, but failed in ascending the falls. Sir Richard Francis Burton in 1863 would follow Tuckey's maps and ascend to the same point on the rapids, but go no further. Three years later David Livingstone would return to southern Africa, searching for the source of the Nile – and along with numerous accomplishments on the trip, would fail to find the famed river's origin. He would, however, be haunted by the notion that a large river he was exploring just west of Lake Tanganyika was not the Nile as he had hoped, but the Lualuba. The Lualuba River would later be discovered to be an estuary of the Congo River. This information would remain buried for an extended period of time, though, as the outside world lost contact with Livingstone and his expedition.

The continued mysteries of the Congo River, the disappearance of Livingstone and intense public curiosity of his status, and growing European interest in the recolonisation of the continent would bring a whole new cast of characters to the region in the 1870s. A Belgian monarch, a journalist for an American newspaper, and an eager Italian-cum-Frenchman would begin to write a new chapter in the history of central Africa.

The histories of the Republic of Congo and the DR Congo from the mid 19th century to the present day are continued in the *History* sections of the respective country chapters.

LANGUAGE

There is one language that dominates both the Congos, and that is **French**. Belgium, though a bilingual country itself, only exported the francophone language to its massive old colony. Congo-Brazzaville (see box, page 16) has always been a centrepoint of French culture, though as it departed from its close ties to Paris it maintained a distinct francophone nature to itself. Everyone in the region speaks French, without exception. Knowing just a little will get a traveller much further than otherwise, and outside of major towns will be the primary method of interacting with locals.

The French spoken across both Congos can be difficult to understand as not only do locals speak with heavy accents, but they also throw in their own tribal words on occasion. Therefore while almost every person across both Congos will be able to communicate with a traveller in French, don't expect to understand the response right off the bat – asking them to slow down (*parlez lentement*) when confronted with a barrage of hard-to-understand French will help you get a grasp of what someone may be saying. The good news is that most locals will understand a large variety of spoken French from a foreigner, and thus perfection in the language is not necessary for ease of communication.

The DR Congo, however, is making inroads into the **English** world. With MONUC and its bilingual staff arriving, fixers and concierges of major cities are beginning to learn the language. In Lubumbashi and other places in the provinces

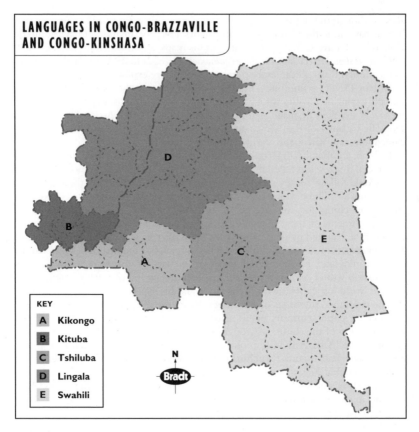

of Katanga there is plenty of English spoken as migration from Zambia has brought the language across. In the east of the country, there is a small amount of English available amongst the more educated. It is not impossible, then, to find English-speaking people in major towns across the DR Congo. In the other Congo, the language is practically non-existent.

Of the non-European languages used, four dominate across the Congos. The capital cities are melting pots to be sure, but **Lingala** is the language primarily spoken. The dialect differs even in the short distance between Kinshasa and Brazzaville, but there is a standardised version that is used in media and education circles. Lingala also dominates in northern Congo-Brazzaville and the northwest regions of Congo-Kinshasa (see box, page 16).

Katanga Province is dominated by **Swahili**, and travellers who have visited other east African countries will find that the language is very much the same. It is also spoken across much of the eastern DR Congo, up to southern parts of Ituri Province. Near the Rwandan border and amongst the Banyamulenge peoples and other groups in the Kivu provinces the national language of Rwanda, Kinyarwanda, is spoken and understood. **Tshiluba** is spoken in the Kasai provinces, the middle of the DR Congo, a language descended from the ancient Luba Kingdom that existed in the same region over a millennium ago.

In Congo-Brazzaville, aside from Lingala in the capital and north, **Kituba** is spoken across the southern region and is the dominant language in Pointe Noire. An offshoot of the Kikongo language, Kituba is spoken widely in Congo-

Brazzaville and the western regions of the DR Congo. The original **Kikongo** language, descended from the original linguistic patterns of the Kongo Kingdom, is still used in the DR Congo province of Bas-Congo and as far east as Kikwit. French, Kituba and Lingala are the official languages of the Congo. French, Kikongo, Lingala, Tshiluba and Swahili make up the DR Congo's official languages.

I have provided glossaries for all of these languages in *Appendix 2*, as well as some tips on speaking French for those unfamiliar with it.

RELIGION

CHRISTIANITY The arrival of the Portuguese at the end of the 15th century saw missionaries preach the Gospel in the Kingdom of Kongo, and it would become immensely important to the first nations of the region, as well as play an important role in shaping their future. The king of the time embraced the religion wholeheartedly, and his successor would even adopt a Christian name – Alfonso. Alfonso would be baptised, and communications between Kongo and Europe would be frequent. The Catholic Church recognised Kongo as a Christian nation, and religious schools in Portugal accepted citizens from Kongo for religious training.

Missionary work, then, has been important to the makeup of the region for centuries. For the most part, Christian teachings have been followed enthusiastically by local tribes – though the exact application of Christianity may sometimes seem to differ from what missionaries brought with them. Indeed, the Christian faith across the Congos has always lived side by side with the original animist practices, and people do not seem to believe that either one is exclusive of the other.

The Bible was translated into Kikongo some centuries ago, though research in the 18th century revealed that people did not know the name of this singular 'God' that Christianity preached.

Missionaries voluntarily departed the region sometime in the late 18th century as the Kongo Kingdom dissolved. Yet in their wake they left numerous small churches, and a century later as a new generation of European explorers arrived on the banks of the Congo River, missionaries would return. It would be missionary work again that revealed untold horrors perpetrated due to the rubber trade, in letters from William Henry Sheppard, as he worked his way deep into the territory of Congo Free State.

Mobutu's Zaire would ban much of what the Catholic Church had aspired to for centuries. Christian names were discarded for Congolese names, and dissent in the Church was met with expulsion for any bishops who opposed these measures. Christian universities were nationalised and Africanised. Mobutu's regime admitted it had gone too far in 1976, two years after he had banned celebrations of Christmas.

Pope John Paul II visited the DR Congo twice in his lifetime, in 1980 and 1985. Catholic bishops in the era of Mobutu were also outspoken opponents of his one-party regime, making their presence in the country unpopular with the authorities.

Protestantism is also prominent, and gained ground in the era of Zaire. While Catholicism opposed much of what Mobutu was aiming for in his religious reforms, the Protestant Churches sided with these policies as it gave the Protestant Church an equal stance with Catholicism. The various Protestant groups that spanned across Zaire were merged into a singular unit, the Eglise du Christ au Zaire, or ECZ, and they gained political clout from this merger. In 1990, the ECZ, who had more or less acquiesced to Mobutu's requests, were in a position to lobby his government for democratic reforms.

Most Congolese on either side of the river still aspire to some sort of Catholicism. Every small town has at least one European church, and there are impressive cathedrals in the larger cities such as Kinshasa, Brazzaville and Lubumbashi. Roughly half of all people in the Congos are Roman Catholic, attesting to the lengthy history of conversion in the region.

Other Christian faiths are also present, especially in the DR Congo – in Katanga and around Lubumbashi there are small groups of Jehovah's Witnesses. With war and strife plaguing the eastern half of the country, missionary groups have found an opportunity to capitalise on their problems by offering aid as well as preaching their own version of the Gospel. Their numbers are still very minor, though they also have a small presence across Congo-Brazzaville.

ISLAM Zanzibari slave traders brought Islam with them as they delved deeper and deeper into central Africa seeking slaves. Thus, the majority of Muslims across the DR Congo can be found in the east. Descendants of Muslims who had been employed in various colonial armies have also migrated over the years into the east, bringing Muslim practices from Sudan, Uganda and Tanzania into the DR Congo's eastern provinces. Ancient slave routes possess the largest number of Muslims, even to this day: the towns of Maniema, and villages near Ujiji, still are the strongest centres of Islam in the country.

Islam subjugated animist practices, but did not eliminate them – much the same as what happened with Christianity. Many traditional practices of the east still continue, though under the name of Islam.

Immigrants from west Africa brought Islam into Congo-Brazzaville around 1916, and their numbers remain very small – perhaps fewer than 50,000 Congolese are Muslim. Marien Ngouabi permitted Muslims to practise their religion in the open, and Denis Sassou-Nguesso permitted the creation of an Islamic council in 1988. The Islamic footprint is therefore barely noticeable, and mosques are a definite rarity across the country. Brazzaville has the country's largest mosque.

JUDAISM Jewish families emigrated with Europeans to the major cities of Kinshasa and Lubumbashi in the DR Congo; Lubumbashi even had a synagogue built in 1930. Europeans seeking to flee the wars on their continent came to the Belgian Congo, and many arrived between 1915 and 1950. It was a common place for European Jews to reside before Israel was created in 1948 – the Association Zioniste du Congo Belge organised a country-wide Jewish organisation that kept all worshippers of the religion more or less in touch with each other.

The number of true Jewish people in the Congo now is incredibly minuscule. There has been little to no crossover to the indigenous population. A few hundred Jewish people remain, mostly in Lubumbashi, as the town still has the country's only existing synagogue and Jewish cemetery.

KIMBANGUISM Founded by Simon Kimbangu in the early 20th century, when he reported beginning to have visions calling for him to become a healer and apostle. He began a ministry around 1921, preaching faith healing, and soon a personality cult developed around him. Kimbangu successfully engineered a mass protest in 1921, and Belgian authorities, worried by Kimbangu's power over a large portion of the population, imprisoned him near Elisabethville (present-day Lubumbashi). He spent three decades there before perishing. Fellow Kimbanguists, hunted by the authorities, fled to Brazzaville and may have been of assistance in founding their own locally grown hybrid Christian sect, the Matsouanists.

Just prior to independence, in 1959, the Kimbanguist Church was recognised as an official religious organisation and allowed to practise openly. The Church would not have nearly as much clout as it did in the first half of the century, but would still garner a large following of people in the DR Congo.

Kimbanguism is non-political and puritan. It preaches pacifism, and teaches its followers to abandon many animist practices as well as avoid alcohol, tobacco, as well as dancing. The general structure surrounds the preachings of the Baptist Church, and Kimbanguists joined the World Council of Churches in 1970. Much myth and legend surrounds the life of Simon Kimbangu, though his followers rarely congregate into large organised areas of worship. It is said that roughly 10% of people in the DR Congo are Kimbanguists.

MATSOUANISM In contrast to the apolitical Kimbanguist movement that emerged in the Belgian Congo, the Matsouanist movement has had a deep interrelation with the other Congo's affairs.

It was founded by André Matsoua, who originally trained as a priest but left to become an army officer in 1919. He departed soon after, seeing combat in north Africa before fleeing and settling in Paris around 1926. He quickly became embroiled in the affairs of unions and formed Amicale there, a pro-union support network. The movement became hugely popular with the Congolese – so much so that he was tracked down by officials from French Congo, arrested, and sent back to Brazzaville. He was sentenced to exile in Chad for deserting his duties, but escaped and fled to Nigeria. A year later he was captured as he travelled to Oubangui-Chari, the modern-day Central African Republic; he fled again, enlisted in the French army in World War II, and was subsequently wounded in combat. He was later arrested again while in hospital, and sent back to Congo. He died while being punished with hard labour.

His legacy would be influential on Congo. Leaders of the Lari tribe refused to believe he was dead, and used his teachings to rally their own people to political action. It was the belief of the Matsouanists that accelerated the process for change to independence in Congo. Fulburt Youlou proclaimed himself the successor to André Matsoua, and ascended to the presidency, yet hardline Matsouanists oppose any form of government, and Youlou needed to be careful to appeal to moderate Matsouanists as well as hardliners. Matsouanists had great political clout in Congo during the 1960s, as governments and politicians they disapproved of could lose popularity quickly as a result of their influence.

Contemporary Matsouanism is a combination of political activism and religious appreciation of its founder. Other political leaders have used the Matsouanist's sentiment to further their own needs, including Bernard Kolelas, who successfully rallied many of them to his side during the turbulent factional conflicts of the 1990s.

ANIMISM, SORCERY AND WITCHCRAFT Spiritual practices indigenous to the tribes that comprise both Congos in contemporary times have existed since time immemorial, and continue to exist: even with the organised religions of the world having a heavy footprint in every populated area, locals still believe strongly in the otherworld of spirits, superstitions and sorcery.

These beliefs have been used to great effect throughout the recent war – rebels have indulged in cannibalism to gain strength and become invincible in battle; politicians may blame their opposing candidates of appealing to evil spirits to win, and gain favour from voters; children have been cast out of families for practising 'witchcraft' or 'sorcery'. These things are taken deadly seriously in the Congos, and understanding a bit about them can go a long way into understanding local behaviours.

Following the name changes of the two Congos can be confusing to say the least, and frustrating if you're new to all of this. Broadly speaking, Congo could refer to either country, whether French Brazzaville-governed Congo or Belgian Kinshasa-governed Congo; it has also incorporated Rwanda and Burundi, parts of Angola, at one time was the catch-all for French African territory stretching from Brazzaville to the upper limits of Chad, and is the current name for the large river that divides the two nations (the river originally was referred to by locals as the Nzadi, though this name has long been relegated to the dustbin of history). To make matters even harder, People's Republic of Congo referred to Congo- Léopoldville from 1964 to 1971, and Congo-Brazzaville from 1970 to 1991 (it also was briefly the name of the Simba-run rebel government established in Stanleyville in 1967). Republic of the Congo was the name for Congo-Léopoldville from 1960 to 1964, and has been the current name for Congo-Brazzaville since 1991. It doesn't end there, though: another People's Republic of Congo existed as a rebel government in Kisangani during the civil war of 1964 to 1965, and some in Kisangani might refer to their city as once being the capital of the People's Republic of Congo. The province of Bas-Congo also seceded from Congo-Kinshasa for a brief period during 1960.

Moyen Congo, or Middle Congo, was the French name for the Congo-Brazzaville-governed colony in various incarnations from 1900 until independence in 1960. However, Moyen Congo was also the colonial name for a Congo-Léopoldville-era province that stretched north along the Congo River to just south of present-day Mbandaka and southwest to near the border with Portuguese Angola.

Kongo with a 'K', when used in the English language, refers to the ancient Kingdom of Kongo that was the largest African state upon contact with Europeans in the 1400s. It is also the name of the new western province of Congo-Kinshasa, Kongo Central. Kongo is also the direct German translation for Congo, and could refer to any of the above when written in that language.

Dates, as well, only go so far in clarifying this arrangement as both countries became independent in 1960 and both renamed their countries to some sort of Congo in that year.

Until Mobutu Sésé Seko renamed his country to Zaire, both countries were often referred to much in the same manner as they are now: Congo-Brazzaville for French Congo, and Congo-Léopoldville for the former Belgian Congo.

The larger problem is that there are a wide-ranging number of practices in the Congos relating to animist traditions, and simplification is not straightforward. Generally speaking, the dead are revered and so are their bodies; evil spirits are perceived to be real and haunt the living, and they need to be treated with some level of respect. Some people have offered potions to locals offering to ward off evil spirits – in December 2005, 64 people died after drinking one of these potions.

Children are believed to have close ties with the spiritual world, and in an unfortunate twist of fate, a family will cast a child out onto the street if they are suspected of practising sorcery. 'Sorcery' may, in fact, simply be bad luck – when there is a death in the family, or when someone loses their job. A family will cast out their most vulnerable member as atonement for this unfortunate turn of events – which, in recent times, has led to an increase in the numbers of street children – especially in Kinshasa. Some Churches will offer to 'exorcise' the evil spirits from the child accused of sorcery, and put them through various forms of torture to cleanse their souls, before they are permitted to take refuge in their building.

There is a lack of any centralised history with regard to customs relating to animist traditions. The hundreds of tribes that have lived in the region for centuries, not to mention rebel groups, pygmies, and swindlers taking advantage of

Thus, in current practice, differentiation between the two countries these days is simplified by referring to its capital after the word Congo: Congo-Kinshasa being the former Zaire, and Congo-Brazzaville being French Congo. A traveller may also hear the Congolese of Congo-Brazzaville refer to their larger neighbour as Zaïrois, though the country name of Zaire is now defunct. People in Congo-Kinshasa will refer to their neighbour, usually, as Congo-Brazzaville and the people as Congolais Français.

Another use for the word Congo (if your head wasn't spinning enough) is with reference to Cabinda, the Angolan-controlled exclave. After 1885 and until independence in 1975 it was known as Portuguese Congo, or Congo Portuguis.

Appendix 3 lists the current and obsolete names for both countries. When discussing the history of either country, consider the context to avoid excessive confusion. Throughout this book I use the names in their historical contexts – for example when discussing Congo-Kinshasa throughout Mobutu's regime I will use Zaire, and after the takeover by Kabila I will change to DR Congo. In the confusing times of the 1960s I use Congo-Léopoldville and Congo-Brazzaville. Note that Congo-Léopoldville was briefly called the Democratic Republic of Congo in the 1960s as well. The same goes for cities – before Kinshasa's name change in 1966, I use Léopoldville, as well as Stanleyville when discussing Kisangani, and Elisabethville for Lubumbashi.

City names changed across Congo-Léopoldville starting in 1966 and completing in 1971 as the country was renamed Zaire. Even as Mobutu Sésé Seko's regime collapsed, the names remained in place. Here is a cheat sheet to assist in any brief confusions:

Albertville	– Kalemie	Lusambo	– Kasai
Bakwanga	– Mbuji-Mayi	Nouvelle-Anvers	– Makanza
Coquilhatville	– Mbandaka	Paulis	– Isiro
Costermansville	– Bukavu	Ponthierville	– Ubundu
Elisabethville	– Lubumbashi	Port Francqui	– Ilebo
Jadotville	– Likasi	Shaba	– Katanga
Lac Léopold II	– Lac Mai-Ndombe	Stanleyville	– Kisangani
Léopoldville	– Kinshasa	Thysville	– Mbanza-Ngungu

people, has led to a complicated and muddy understanding by both anthropologists and locals alike. Many often pray to the Christian God to absolve their child of witchcraft or sorcery.

NATURAL HISTORY AND WILDLIFE

The Congos have had nature reserves and protected parks for longer than any other part of Africa. Yes, believe it or not, but this certainly does not mean that these areas have enjoyed the same level of protection that other parks across the continent have. King Léopold II created the first African nature reserves in 1889, concerned for the long-term survival of the elephant. While his Belgian officials were ruthlessly destroying whole communities to increase the volume of rubber extracted from Congo Free State, the king would be paying more attention to the well-being of elephants across his private nation.

The first official park that still exists was created in 1925 by King Albert, and unsurprisingly called Albert National Park – which was renamed later to Virunga National Park, and to this day has remained in a similar form along the shores of Lake Albert in eastern DR Congo. Other parks and reserves would follow: Kagera in 1934 (modern-day Kahuzi-Biega), Garamba in 1938, Kundelungu in 1939. The Belgian administration handled the parks separately from the rest of the colony, and they were well protected from exploitation during the period prior to independence. Mobutu Sésé Seko added more parks: Salonga North and South, L'Upemba Parks North and South, the Okapi Reserve, and Maiko National Park.

These parks still exist, in spite of continued troubles. Numerous anti-poaching teams, charities and park rangers do their best to protect the most vulnerable regions of these parks. The hidden war that has persisted across the DR Congo is the hundreds of rangers killed protecting wildlife from rebels, invading armies and poachers.

Conversely, the other Congo has had national parks for almost as long, and they have not seen any interference with their wildlife populations. Two parks are most accessible: Lefini Reserve is just north of Brazzaville, and only a half-day's journey from Pointe Noire is Conkouati-Douli National Park. In the far north on the border with the Central African Republic is the Ndoki-Nouabalé National Park, which is readily accessible by aircraft or boat. However, the region east of Ouesso and north of Impfondo is a truly wild place by any stretch of the imagination, and some say one of the least-explored regions on the face of the earth.

2

Practical Information

WHEN TO VISIT

The Congos have two seasons: dry and rainy. In the dry season the roads tend to be better for overlanding, though it can get hot and dusty at times. In the rainy season some roads may be impassable due to mud and flooding, so visits into the deep rainforest are usually done in the dry months. There is an exception to this as the southern reaches of DR Congo are in the African savanna belt and experience a later rainy season, but can be oppressively hot in the summer (see *Chapter 1*, page 4).

HIGHLIGHTS

There are many high points across the region, mostly natural – such as the towering Ruwenzori Mountains in the east, which are climbable along a trail of guesthouses to the peaks. The Congo River is a sight to behold anywhere along its banks, and the history of central Africa's largest river is a great one (see *Chapter 1*, page 10). For sworn urbanites who don't mind a little squalor the opposing cities of Kinshasa and Brazzaville are unique – no other capitals exist so closely to each other, and no other neighbouring cities so close could be so different. Pointe Noire has developed into a small expatriate enclave with fine restaurants and fishing tours for the francophone world, but there's no reason that the English-speaking world can't join in. For the truly adventurous there is always the possibility of overlanding through the DR Congo, something rarely done but sure to give a dedicated traveller some serious bragging rights.

The vast majority of people visiting the Congos these days do so for the wildlife, and specifically the gorillas. Most people will go with a noted tour group as obtaining permits and transport to these areas is still not simple for a solo traveller. I would also highly recommend sticking with one certain region if you will be visiting for only a few weeks, as traversing the Congos from place to place can be a lengthy endeavour. While gorillas do make their homes near the borders of Rwanda and Uganda it is on the DR Congo side that they reside in larger populations. Arriving in Rwanda and Uganda and taking a tour into the parks along the eastern border is a great option for some short-term wildlife viewing.

Brazzaville can also be a good base from which to explore the wildlife of northern Congo, and taking a tour through the Lefini Reserve or further north in the Ndoki-Nouabalé National Park will be rewarding.

SUGGESTED ITINERARIES

DR CONGO From Rwanda, a great circuit would begin in Goma with a hike to the top of Mount Nyiragongo, followed by a visit to the mountain gorillas near Djombe. Then travel south by a fast boat (*canôt rapide*) to Bukavu, visit the eastern lowland gorillas in Kahuzi-Biega National Park, and then leave through the Ruzizi border crossing to Cyangugu. This would take roughly a week, and you would see some of the best sites the DR Congo has to offer.

Likewise, a visit from Uganda could begin in Bunagana with a visit to the mountain gorillas of Djombe. Then, continue north to visit the Rwindi Plains, the gorillas of Tshiaberimu, then continue east from Beni to see the hippos at Ishango and climb the Ruwenzoris at Mutwanga before departing at Kasindi. I'd recommend two weeks for this programme.

CONGO Arriving and departing from Pointe Noire would give the opportunity to visit Point Indienne and Diosso, the Jane Goodall Chimpanzee Sanctuary and Conkouati-Douli National Park over a week. For a two–three-week journey, head north from Brazzaville to begin with the Lefini Reserve and Odzala Park. Or conversely, join a tour and visit Ndoki-Nouabalé National Park by plane.

From Lubumbashi, if you can rent a vehicle, both L'Upemba parks and Kundelungu could be visited over two weeks as well as the town of Likasi. From Kinshasa with your own vehicle, heading southwest to Bas-Congo to visit Zongo Falls, the caves at Mbanza-Ngungu, Matadi, Boma, and Moanda would make a good two-week trip.

✚ HEALTH with Dr Felicity Nicholson

People new to exotic travel often worry about tropical diseases, but it is accidents that are most likely to carry you off. Road accidents are very common in many parts of the Congos so be aware and do what you can to reduce risks: try to travel during daylight hours, always wear a seatbelt and refuse to be driven by anyone who has been drinking. Listen to local advice about areas where violent crime is rife too.

PREPARATIONS Preparations to ensure a healthy trip to either the DR Congo or Congo require checks on your immunisation status: it is wise to be up to date on **tetanus, polio** and **diphtheria** (now given as an all-in-one vaccine, Revaxis, that lasts for ten years), and **hepatitis A**. Immunisations against **meningococcus** and **rabies** may also be recommended. Proof of vaccination against **yellow fever** is mandatory for entry into the Congos. The World Health Organization (WHO) recommends that this vaccine should be taken by everyone over nine months of age, although proof of entry is only officially required for those over one year of age. If the vaccine is not suitable for you then obtain an exemption certificate from your GP or a travel clinic. Immunisation against **cholera** may be advised for longer visits, especially if you are intending to stay in poorer areas. The oral cholera vaccine (Dukoral) gives about 75% protection and for adults and children over six years of age the course consists of two doses given between one and six weeks apart and at least one week before entering the area. Coverage is said to last for about two years. For those aged between two and six, then three doses are needed, which requires a boost after six months.

Hepatitis A vaccine (Havrix Monodose or Avaxim) comprises two injections given about a year apart. The course costs about £100 but may be available on the NHS, protects for 25 years and can be administered even close to the time of departure. **Hepatitis B** vaccination should be considered for longer trips (two months or more) or for those working with children or in situations where contact with blood is likely. Three injections are needed for the best protection and can be given over a three-week period if time is short for those aged 16 or over. Longer schedules give more sustained protection and are therefore preferred if time allows and have to be used for those under 16. Hepatitis A vaccine can also be given as a combination with hepatitis B as 'Twinrix', though two doses are needed at least seven days apart to be effective for the hepatitis A component, and three doses are needed for the hepatitis B.

The newer, injectable **typhoid** vaccines (eg: Typhim Vi) last for three years and are about 85% effective. Oral capsules (Vivotif) are currently available in the US (and soon in the UK); if four capsules are taken over seven days it will last for five years. They should be encouraged unless the traveller is leaving within a few days for a trip of a week or less, when the vaccine would not be effective in time. **Meningitis** vaccine (ideally containing strains A, C, W and Y, but if this is not available then A+C vaccine is better than nothing) is recommended for all travellers, especially for trips of more than four weeks (see *Meningitis*, page 31). Vaccinations for rabies are ideally advised for everyone, but are especially important for travellers visiting more remote areas, especially if you are more than 24 hours from medical help and definitely if you will be working with animals (see *Rabies*, page 32).

Experts differ over whether a BCG vaccination against **tuberculosis** (TB) is useful in adults: discuss this with your travel clinic.

In addition to the various vaccinations recommended above, it is important that travellers should be properly protected against malaria. For detailed advice, see below.

Ideally you should visit your own doctor or a specialist travel clinic (see page 23) to discuss your requirements if possible at least eight weeks before you plan to travel.

Malaria Along with road accidents, malaria poses the single biggest serious threat to the health of travellers in most parts of tropical Africa, the Congos included. It is unwise to travel in malarial parts of Africa whilst pregnant or with children: the risk of malaria in many parts is considerable and these travellers are likely to succumb rapidly to the disease. The risk of malaria at altitudes above 1,800m is low.

Malaria in the Congos The *Anopheles* mosquito that transmits the parasite is found throughout both countries both in the cities and the jungle areas and there is no specific region that is more affected than another. It is important therefore to do everything you can not to get bitten and to take the appropriate malaria prophylaxis as discussed in the relevant sections.

Malaria prevention There is not yet a vaccine against malaria that gives enough protection to be useful for travellers, but there are other ways to avoid it; since most of Africa is very high risk for malaria, travellers must plan their malaria protection properly. Seek current advice on the best antimalarials to take: usually mefloquine, Malarone or doxycycline. If mefloquine (Lariam) is suggested, start this two-and-a-half weeks (three doses) before departure to check that it suits you; stop it immediately if it seems to cause depression or anxiety, visual or hearing disturbances, severe headaches, fits or changes in heart rhythm. Side effects such as nightmares or dizziness are not medical reasons for stopping unless they are sufficiently debilitating or annoying. Anyone who has been treated for depression or psychiatric problems, has diabetes controlled by oral therapy or who is epileptic (or who has suffered fits in the past) or has a close blood relative who is epileptic, should probably avoid mefloquine.

In the past doctors were nervous about prescribing mefloquine to pregnant women, but experience has shown that it is relatively safe and certainly safer than the risk of malaria. That said, there are other issues, so if you are travelling to the Congos whilst pregnant, seek expert advice before departure.

Malarone (proguanil and atovaquone) is as effective as mefloquine. It has the advantage of having few side effects and need be continued for only one week after returning. However, it is expensive and because of this tends to be reserved for shorter trips. Malarone may not be suitable for everybody, so advice should be taken from a doctor. The licence in the UK has been extended for up to three months' use and a paediatric form of tablet is also available, prescribed on a weight basis.

Another alternative is the antibiotic doxycycline (100mg daily). Like Malarone it can be started just one day before arrival. Unlike mefloquine, it may also be used in travellers with epilepsy, although certain anti-epileptic medication may make it less effective. In perhaps 1–3% of people there is the possibility of allergic skin reactions developing in sunlight; the drug should be stopped if this happens. Women using the oral contraceptive should use an additional method of protection for the first four weeks when using doxycycline. It is also unsuitable in pregnancy or for children under 12 years.

Chloroquine and proguanil are no longer considered to be effective enough for the Congos, but may be considered as a last resort if nothing else is deemed suitable.

All tablets should be taken with or after the evening meal, washed down with plenty of fluid and, with the exception of Malarone (see above), continued for four weeks after leaving.

Despite all these precautions, it is important to be aware that no antimalarial drug is 100% effective, although those on prophylactics who are unlucky enough to catch malaria are less likely to get rapidly into serious trouble. In addition to taking antimalarials, it is therefore important to avoid mosquito bites between dusk and dawn (see *Avoiding insect bites*, page 30).

There is unfortunately the occasional traveller who prefers to 'acquire resistance' to malaria rather than take preventive tablets, or who takes homoeopathic prophylactics, thinking these are effective against killer disease. Homoeopathy theory dictates treating like with like so there is no place for prophylaxis or immunisation in a well person; bona fide homoeopathists do not advocate it. Travellers to Africa cannot acquire any effective resistance to malaria, and those who don't make use of prophylactic drugs risk their life in a manner that is both foolish and unnecessary.

Malaria diagnosis and treatment Even those who take their malaria tablets meticulously and do everything possible to avoid mosquito bites may contract a strain of malaria that is resistant to prophylactic drugs. Untreated malaria is likely to be fatal, but even strains resistant to prophylaxis respond well to prompt treatment. Because of this, your immediate priority upon displaying possible malaria symptoms – including a rapid rise in temperature (over 38°C), and any combination of a headache, flu-like aches and pains, a general sense of disorientation, and possibly even nausea and diarrhoea – is to establish whether you have malaria, ideally by visiting a clinic.

Diagnosing malaria is not easy, which is why consulting a doctor is sensible: there are other dangerous causes of fever in Africa, which require different treatments. Even if you test negative, it would be wise to stay within reach of a laboratory until the symptoms clear up, and to test again after a day or two if they don't. It's worth noting that if you have a fever and the malaria test is negative, you may have typhoid or paratyphoid, which should also receive immediate treatment.

Travellers to remote parts of either country would be wise to carry a course of treatment to cure malaria, and a rapid test kit. With malaria, it is normal enough to go from feeling healthy to having a high fever in the space of a few hours (and it is possible to die from falciparum malaria within 24 hours of the first symptoms). In such circumstances, assume that you have malaria and act accordingly – whatever risks are attached to taking an unnecessary cure are outweighed by the dangers of untreated malaria. Experts differ on the costs and benefits of self-treatment, but agree that it leads to over-treatment and to many people taking drugs they do not need, yet treatment may save your life. There is also some division about the best treatment for malaria, but either Malarone or Coarthemeter is the current treatment of choice. Discuss your trip with a specialist either at home or in Kinshasa or Brazzaville.

Heatstroke and protection from the sun In the hot southern savanna of DR Congo and even in the open lowlands along the Congo River, heatstroke can be a serious concern for those who have not adjusted to the equatorial climate. It can be caused by both hot, dry weather as well as hot, humid conditions; both extremes are found in the Congos. It is very important to try and stay out of direct sunlight for long periods of time, especially in the middle of the day, and drink plenty of water. Symptoms of heatstroke can vary but it is usually indicated by confusion, dizziness, a fast pulse, fatigue, headache and a lack of sweating. Quick treatment is imperative as heatstroke can be fatal. Get out of direct sunlight, wet the skin with water and place the person under a fan and try to rehydrate them. If in doubt get medical help as soon as possible.

Also give some thought to packing suncream. The incidence of skin cancer is rocketing as Caucasians are travelling more and spending more time exposing themselves to the sun. If you must expose yourself to the sun, build up gradually from 20 minutes per day. Be especially careful of the sun reflected off water, and wear a T-shirt and lots of waterproof suncream (at least SPF15) when swimming. Sun exposure ages the skin, makes people prematurely wrinkly, and increases the risk of skin cancer. Cover up with long, loose clothes and wear a hat when you can. The glare and the dust can be hard on the eyes, too, so bring UV-protecting sunglasses and, perhaps, a soothing eyebath.

Water sterilisation You can fall ill from drinking contaminated water so try to drink from safe sources, eg: bottled water, where available. If you are away from shops such as halfway up the Ruwenzori and your bottled water runs out, make tea, pour the remaining boiled water into a clean container and use it for drinking. Alternatively, water should be passed through a good bacteriological filter or purified with iodine or the less effective chlorine tablets (eg: Puritabs).

TRAVEL CLINICS AND HEALTH INFORMATION A full list of current travel clinic websites worldwide is available from the International Society of Travel Medicine on www.istm.org. For other journey preparation information, consult www.tripprep.com. Information about various medications may be found on www.emedicine.com. For information on malaria prevention, see www.preventingmalaria.info.

UK

Berkeley Travel Clinic 32 Berkeley St, London W1J 8EL (near Green Park tube station); ☏ 020 7629 6233
Cambridge Travel Clinic 48a Mill Rd, Cambridge CB1 2AS; ☏ 01223 367362; e enquiries@ travelcliniccambridge.co.uk; www.travelcliniccambridge.co.uk; ⊕ 12.00–19.00 Tue–Fri, 10.00–16.00 Sat
Edinburgh Travel Clinic Regional Infectious Diseases Unit, Ward 41 OPD, Western General Hospital, Crewe

Rd South, Edinburgh EH4 2UX; ☏ 0131 537 2822; www.mvm.ed.ac.uk. Travel helpline (☏ 0906 589 0380) ⊕ 09.00–12.00 Mon–Fri. Provides inoculations & antimalarial prophylaxis, & advises on travel-related health risks.
Fleet Street Travel Clinic 29 Fleet St, London EC4Y 1AA; ☏ 020 7353 5678; www.fleetstreetclinic.com. Vaccinations, travel products & latest advice.

Dr Jane Wilson-Howarth

Long-haul air travel increases the risk of deep-vein thrombosis. Although recent research has suggested that many of us develop clots when immobilised, most resolve without us ever having been aware of them. In certain susceptible individuals, though, clots form on clots and when large ones break away and lodge in the lungs this is potentially dangerous. Fortunately this happens in only a tiny minority of passengers. Studies have shown that flights of over five-and-a-half hours are significant, and that people who take lots of shorter flights over a short space of time can also form clots. People at highest risk are:

- Those who have had a clot before – unless they are now taking warfarin
- People over 80 years of age
- Anyone who has recently undergone a major operation or surgery for varicose veins
- Someone who has had a hip or knee replacement in the last three months
- Cancer sufferers
- Those who have ever had a stroke
- People with heart disease
- Those with a close blood relative who has had a clot

Those with a slightly increased risk:

- People over 40
- Women who are pregnant or have had a baby in the last couple of weeks
- People taking female hormones, the combined contraceptive pill or other oestrogen therapy
- Heavy smokers
- Those who have very severe varicose veins
- The very obese
- People who are very tall (over 6ft/1.8m) or short (under 5ft/1.5m)

Hospital for Tropical Diseases Travel Clinic Mortimer Market Bldg, Capper St (off Tottenham Ct Rd), London WC1E 6AU; ☎ 020 7388 9600; www.thehtd.org. Offers consultations & advice, & is able to provide all necessary drugs & vaccines for travellers. Runs a healthline (☎ 0906 133 7733) for country-specific information & health hazards. Also stocks nets, water purification equipment & personal protection measures.

Interhealth Worldwide Partnership Hse, 157 Waterloo Rd, London SE1 8US; ☎ 020 7902 9000; www.interhealth.org.uk. Competitively priced, one-stop travel-health service. All profits go to their affiliated company, InterHealth, which provides health care for overseas workers on Christian projects.

Liverpool School of Medicine Pembroke Pl, Liverpool L3 5QA; ☎ 0151 708 9393; f 0151 705 3370; www.liv.ac.uk/lstm

MASTA (Medical Advisory Service for Travellers Abroad) Moorfield Rd, Yeadon, Leeds, West Yorkshire LS19 7BN; ☎ 0113 238 7500; www.masta-travel-health.com. Provides travel-health advice, antimalarials & vaccinations. There are over 25 MASTA pre-travel clinics in Britain; call or check online for the nearest. Clinics also sell mosquito nets, medical kits, insect protection & travel hygiene products.

NHS travel website www.fitfortravel.scot.nhs.uk. Provides country-by-country advice on immunisation & malaria, plus details of recent developments, & a list of relevant health organisations.

Nomad Travel Store/Clinic 3–4 Wellington Terrace, Turnpike Lane, London N8 0PX; ☎ 020 8889 7014; travel-health line (☎ 0906 863 3414 – office hrs only); e sales@nomadtravel.co.uk; www.nomadtravel.co.uk. Also at 40 Bernard St, London WC1N 1LJ; ☎ 020 7833 4114; 52 Grosvenor Gardens, London SW1W 0AG; ☎ 020 7823 5823; & 43 Queens Rd, Bristol BS8 1QH; ☎ 0117 922 6567. For health advice, equipment such as mosquito nets & other anti-bug devices, & an excellent range of adventure travel gear. Clinics also in Southampton.

A deep-vein thrombosis (DVT) is a blood clot that forms in the deep leg veins. This is very different from irritating but harmless superficial phlebitis. DVT causes swelling and redness of one leg, usually with heat and pain in one calf and sometimes the thigh. A DVT is only dangerous if a clot breaks away and travels to the lungs (pulmonary embolus). Symptoms of a pulmonary embolus (PE) include chest pain that is worse on breathing in deeply, shortness of breath, and sometimes coughing up small amounts of blood. The symptoms commonly start three to ten days after a long flight. Anyone who thinks that they might have a DVT needs to see a doctor immediately who will arrange a scan. Warfarin tablets (to thin the blood) are then taken for at least six months.

PREVENTION OF DVT Several conditions make the problem more likely. Immobility is the key, and factors like reduced oxygen in cabin air and dehydration may also contribute. To reduce the risk of thrombosis on a long journey:

- Exercise before and after the flight
- Keep mobile before and during the flight; move around every couple of hours
- Drink plenty of water or juices during the flight
- Avoid taking sleeping pills and excessive tea, coffee and alcohol
- Perform exercises that mimic walking and tense the calf muscles
- Consider wearing flight socks or support stockings (see www.legshealth.com)
- Ideally take a meal each week of oily fish (mackerel, trout, salmon, sardines, etc) ahead of your departure. This reduces the blood's ability to clot and thus DVT risk. It may even be worth just taking a meal of oily fish 24 hours before departure if this is more practical.

If you think you are at increased risk of a clot, ask your doctor if it is safe to travel.

Trailfinders Travel Clinic 194 Kensington High St, London W8 7RG; ℡ 020 7938 3999; www.trailfinders.com/travelessentials/travelclinic.htm

Travelpharm The Travelpharm website, www.travelpharm.com, offers up-to-date guidance on travel-related health & has a range of medications available through their online mini-pharmacy.

Irish Republic
Tropical Medical Bureau Grafton St Medical Centre, Grafton Bldgs, 34 Grafton St, Dublin 2; ℡ 1 671 9200; www.tmb.ie. A useful website specific to

tropical destinations. Also check website for other bureaux locations throughout Ireland.

USA
Centers for Disease Control 1600 Clifton Rd, Atlanta, GA 30333; ℡ 800 311 3435; travellers' health hotline f 888 232 3299; www.cdc.gov/travel. The central source of travel information in the USA. The invaluable *Health Information for International Travel*, published annually, is available from the Division of Quarantine at this address.
Connaught Laboratories Pasteur Merieux Connaught, Route 611, PO Box 187, Swiftwater, PA 18370; ℡ 800 822 2463. They will send a free list of

specialist tropical-medicine physicians in your state.
IAMAT (International Association for Medical Assistance to Travelers) 1623 Military Rd, 279, Niagara Falls, NY 14304-1745; ℡ 716 754 4883; e info@iamat.org; www.iamat.org. A non-profit organisation that provides lists of English-speaking doctors abroad.
International Medicine Center 915 Gessner Rd, Suite 525, Houston, TX 77024; ℡ 713 550 2000; www.traveldoc.com

Canada

IAMAT Suite 1, 1287 St Clair Av W, Toronto, Ontario M6E 1B8; ☎ 416 652 0137; www.iamat.org
TMVC Suite 314, 1030 W Georgia St, Vancouver, BC, V6E 2Y3; ☎ 888 288 8682; www.tmvc.com. Private clinic with several outlets in Canada.

Australia, New Zealand, Singapore

IAMAT PO Box 5049, Christchurch 5, New Zealand; www.iamat.org
TMVC ☎ 1300 65 88 44; www.tmvc.com.au. Clinics in Australia, New Zealand & Singapore, including:
Auckland Canterbury Arcade, 170 Queen St; ☎ 9 373 3531

Brisbane 75a Astor Terrace, Spring Hill, QLD 4000; ☎ 7 3815 6900
Melbourne 393 Little Bourke St, 2nd Floor, VIC 3000; ☎ 3 9602 5788
Sydney Dymocks Bldg, 7th Floor, 428 George St, NSW 2000; ☎ 2 9221 7133

South Africa and Namibia

SAA-Netcare Travel Clinics Sanlam Bldg, 19, Fredman Dr, Sandton, P Bag X34, Benmore, JHB, Gauteng, 2010; www.travelclinic.co.za. Clinics throughout South Africa.

TMVC NHC Health Centre, Cnr Beyers Naude & Waugh Northcliff; PO Box 48499, Roosevelt Park, 2129 (Postal Address); ☎ 011 888 7488; www.tmvc.com.au. Consult website for details of other clinics in South Africa & Namibia.

Switzerland

IAMAT 57 Chemin des Voirets, 1212 Grand Lancy, Geneva; www.iamat.org

PERSONAL FIRST-AID KIT If you are planning on travelling outside of any major cities, a first-aid kit of some sort is absolutely essential. A minimal kit should contain the following items:

- A good drying antiseptic, eg: iodine or potassium permanganate (don't take antiseptic cream)
- A few small dressings (Band-Aids)
- Suncream
- Insect repellent; antimalarial tablets; impregnated bed-net or permethrin spray
- Aspirin or paracetamol
- Antifungal cream, eg: Canesten
- Ciprofloxacin or norfloxacin, for severe diarrhoea
- Tinidazole for giardia or amoebic dysentery (see box opposite for regime)
- Antibiotic eye drops, for sore, 'gritty', stuck-together eyes (conjunctivitis)
- A pair of fine-pointed tweezers (to remove hairy caterpillar hairs, thorns, splinters, coral, etc)
- Alcohol-based hand rub or bar of soap in plastic box
- Condoms or femidoms
- Malaria diagnostic kits (5) and a digital thermometer (for those going to remote areas)

Put things like Band-Aids and gauze in sealable bags, and pack all of these in a hard plastic case in a place that is easy to find in your luggage.

COMMON MEDICAL PROBLEMS

Travellers' diarrhoea Travelling in the Congos carries a fairly high risk of getting a dose of travellers' diarrhoea; perhaps half of all visitors will suffer and the newer you are to exotic travel, the more likely you will be to suffer. By taking precautions

Dr Jane Wilson-Howarth

It is dehydration that makes you feel awful during a bout of diarrhoea and the most important part of treatment is drinking lots of clear fluids. Sachets of oral rehydration salts give the perfect biochemical mix to replace all that is pouring out of your bottom but other recipes taste nicer. Any dilute mixture of sugar and salt in water will do you good: try Coke or orange squash with a three-finger pinch of salt added to each glass (if you are salt-depleted you won't taste the salt). Otherwise make a solution of a four-finger scoop of sugar with a three-finger pinch of salt in a 500ml glass. Or add eight level teaspoons of sugar (18g) and one level teaspoon of salt (3g) to one litre (five cups) of safe water. A squeeze of lemon or orange juice improves the taste and adds potassium, which is also lost in diarrhoea. Drink two large glasses after every bowel action, and more if you are thirsty. These solutions are still absorbed well if you are vomiting, but you will need to take sips at a time. If you are not eating you need to drink three litres a day plus whatever is pouring into the toilet. If you feel like eating, take a bland, high carbohydrate diet. Heavy greasy foods will probably give you cramps.

If the diarrhoea is bad, or you are passing blood or slime, or you have a fever, you will probably need antibiotics in addition to fluid replacement. A dose of norfloxacin or ciprofloxacin repeated twice a day until better may be appropriate (if you are planning to take an antibiotic with you, note that both norfloxacin and ciprofloxacin are available only on prescription in the UK). If the diarrhoea is greasy and bulky and is accompanied by sulphurous (eggy) burps, one likely cause is giardia. This is best treated with tinidazole (four x 500mg in one dose, repeated seven days later if symptoms persist).

against travellers' diarrhoea you will also avoid typhoid, paratyphoid, cholera, hepatitis, dysentery, worms, etc. Travellers' diarrhoea and the other faecal-oral diseases come from getting other people's faeces in your mouth. This most often happens from cooks not washing their hands after a trip to the toilet, but even if the restaurant cook does not understand basic hygiene you will be safe if your food has been properly cooked and arrives piping hot. The most important prevention strategy is to wash your hands before eating anything. You can pick up salmonella and shigella from toilet door handles and possibly bank notes. The maxim to remind you what you can safely eat is:

PEEL IT, BOIL IT, COOK IT OR FORGET IT.

This means that fruit you have washed and peeled yourself, and hot foods, should be safe but raw foods, cold cooked foods, salads, fruit salads which have been prepared by others, ice cream and ice are all risky, and foods kept lukewarm in hotel buffets are often dangerous. That said, plenty of travellers and expatriates enjoy fruit and vegetables, so do keep a sense of perspective: food served in a fairly decent hotel in a large town or a place regularly frequented by expatriates is likely to be safe. If you are struck, see the box above for treatment.

Eye problems Bacterial conjunctivitis (pink eye) is a common infection in Africa; people who wear contact lenses are most open to this irritating problem. The eyes feel sore and gritty and they will often be stuck together in the mornings. They will need treatment with antibiotic drops or ointment. Lesser eye irritation should settle with bathing in salt water and keeping the eyes shaded. If an insect flies into your eye, extract it with great care, ensuring you do not crush or damage it otherwise you may get a nastily inflamed eye from toxins secreted by the creature. Small elongated red-and-black blister beetles carry warning colouration to tell you not to crush them anywhere against your skin.

Prickly heat A fine pimply rash on the trunk is likely to be heat rash; cool showers, dabbing dry, and talc will help. Treat the problem by slowing down to a relaxed schedule, wearing only loose, baggy, 100%-cotton clothes and sleeping naked under a fan; if it's bad you may need to check into an air-conditioned hotel room for a while.

Skin infections Any mosquito bite or small nick in the skin gives an opportunity for bacteria to foil the body's usually excellent defences; it will surprise many travellers how quickly skin infections start in warm humid climates and it is essential to clean and cover even the slightest wound. Creams are not as effective as a good drying antiseptic such as dilute iodine, potassium permanganate (a few crystals in half a cup of water) or crystal (or gentian) violet. One of these should be available in most towns. If the wound starts to throb, or becomes red and the redness starts to spread, or the wound oozes, and especially if you develop a fever, antibiotics will probably be needed: flucloxacillin (250mg four times a day) or cloxacillin (500mg four times a day). For those allergic to penicillin, erythromycin (500mg twice a day) for five days should help. See a doctor if the symptoms do not start to improve within 48 hours.

Fungal infections also get a hold easily in hot, moist climates so wear 100%-cotton socks and underwear and shower frequently. An itchy rash in the groin or flaking between the toes is likely to be a fungal infection. This needs treatment with an antifungal cream such as Canesten (clotrimazole); if this is not available try Whitfield's ointment (compound benzoic acid ointment) or crystal violet (although this will turn you purple!).

Altitude sickness Along the eastern border of the DR Congo, in the Ruwenzori Mountains, mountain peaks range from 3,000–5,000m. Above 1,500m, it is possible to suffer from some sort of altitude sickness, and it is important to take a few precautions. The most common altitude-related illness is called AMS, or Acute Mountain Sickness, which bears symptoms of headaches, fatigue and confusion.

The most important factor to consider is the speed of ascent. It takes a certain period of time for a person to adjust to a new altitude, and therefore the faster you rise in altitude, the greater the chance you can come down with Acute Mountain Sickness. The key is to ascend slowly – and if you or anyone in your party has symptoms of AMS, do not ascend further.

Adjusting to altitude can take anywhere from one to four days, and it is critical not to continue if there are any indications of AMS. Descent is also a simple solution, and most people suffering from AMS will see it disappear as they descend. If after waiting, no progress in a person's condition can be seen, it is imperative to descend.

It is also important, due to the possibility of mental confusion, to assume that any headaches or dizziness at a high altitude is AMS, and to treat it as such. There are several medications available to treat AMS in critical situations, such as Diamox, but consult a doctor or mountaineering specialist to see if its use would be acceptable for your physiology.

Snakebite Snakes rarely attack unless provoked, and bites in travellers are unusual. You are less likely to get bitten if you wear stout shoes and long trousers when in the bush. Most snakes are harmless and even venomous species will dispense venom in only about half of their bites. If bitten, you are therefore unlikely to have received venom; keeping this fact in mind may help you to stay calm. Many so-called first-aid techniques do more harm than good: cutting into the wound is harmful; tourniquets are dangerous; suction and electrical inactivation devices do not work. The only treatment is antivenom. In case of a bite that you fear may have been from a venomous snake:

- Try to keep calm – it is likely that no venom has been dispensed
- Prevent movement of the bitten limb by applying a splint
- Keep the bitten limb BELOW heart height to slow the spread of any venom
- If you have a crêpe bandage, wrap it around the whole limb (eg: all the way from the toes to the thigh), as tight as you would for a sprained ankle or a muscle pull
- Evacuate to a hospital that has antivenom. At the time of writing this is only known to be available in Kampala and Libreville. Many centres have an Indian antivenom that does not include the most common biting snakes in the Congos.

And remember:

- NEVER give aspirin; you may take paracetamol, which is safe
- NEVER cut or suck the wound
- DO NOT apply ice packs
- DO NOT apply potassium permanganate

If the offending snake can be captured without risk of someone else being bitten, take this to show the doctor – but beware since even a decapitated head is able to bite.

Other insect-borne diseases Malaria is by no means the only insect-borne disease to which the traveller may succumb. Others include sleeping sickness and river blindness (see box, *Avoiding insect bites* below). Dengue fever is not as common in Africa as in other parts of the world, but there are many other similar arboviruses. These mosquito-borne diseases may mimic malaria but there is no prophylactic medication against them. The mosquitoes that carry the dengue fever virus bite during the daytime, so it is worth applying repellent if you see any mosquitoes around. Symptoms include strong headaches, rashes and excruciating joint and muscle pains and high fever. Viral fevers usually last about a week or so and are not usually fatal. Complete rest and paracetamol are the usual treatment; plenty of fluids also help. Some patients are given an intravenous drip to keep them from dehydrating. It is especially important to protect yourself if you have had dengue fever before, since a second infection with a different strain can result in the potentially fatal dengue haemorrhagic fever.

Bilharzia or schistosomiasis with thanks to Dr Vaughan Southgate of the Natural History Museum, London, and Dr Dick Stockley, The Surgery, Kampala
Bilharzia or schistosomiasis is a disease that commonly afflicts the rural poor of the tropics. Two types exist in sub-Saharan Africa – *Schistosoma mansoni* and *Schistosoma haematobium*. It is an unpleasant problem that is worth avoiding, though can be treated if you do get it. This parasite is common in almost all water sources, even places advertised as 'bilharzia free'. The most risky shores will be close to places where infected people use water, wash clothes, etc.

As the sun is going down, don long clothes and apply repellent on any exposed flesh. Pack an insect repellent ideally containing around 50–55% of the chemical DEET. This may also be used in children and pregnant women. You also need either a permethrin-impregnated bed-net or a permethrin spray so that you can 'treat' bednets in hotels. Permethrin treatment makes even very tatty nets protective and prevents mosquitoes from biting through the impregnated net when you roll against it; it also deters other biters. Otherwise retire to an air-conditioned room or burn mosquito coils or sleep under a fan. Coils and fans reduce rather than eliminate bites. Travel clinics usually sell a good range of nets, treatment kits and repellents.

Mosquitoes and many other insects are attracted to light. If you are camping, never put a lamp near the opening of your tent, or you will have a swarm of biters waiting to join you when you retire. In hotel rooms, be aware that the longer your light is on, the greater the number of insects will be sharing your accommodation.

Aside from avoiding mosquito bites between dusk and dawn, which will protect you from elephantiasis and a range of nasty insect-borne viruses, as well as malaria (see page 21), it is important to take precautions against other insect bites. During the day it is wise to wear long, loose (preferably 100% cotton) clothes if you are pushing through scrubby country; this will keep off ticks and also tsetse and day-biting *Aedes* mosquitoes which may spread viral fevers, including yellow fever.

Tsetse flies hurt when they bite and it is said that they are attracted to the colour blue; locals will advise on where they are a problem and where they transmit sleeping sickness.

Minute pestilential biting **blackflies** spread river blindness in some parts of Africa between 190°N and 170°S; the disease is caught close to fast-flowing rivers since flies breed there and the larvae live in rapids. The flies bite during the day but long trousers tucked into socks will help keep them off. Citronella-based natural repellents (eg: Mosi-guard) do not work against them.

Tumbu flies or *putsi* are a problem where the climate is hot and humid. The adult fly lays her eggs on the soil or on drying laundry and when the eggs come into contact with human flesh (when you put on clothes or lie on a bed) they hatch and bury themselves under the skin. Here they form a crop of 'boils' each with a maggot inside. Smear a little Vaseline over the hole, and they will push their noses out to breathe. It may be possible to squeeze them out but it depends if they are ready to do so as the larvae have spines that help them to hold on.

In *putsi* areas either dry your clothes and sheets within a screened house, or dry them in direct sunshine until they are crisp, or iron them.

Jiggers or **sandfleas** are another flesh-feaster, which can be best avoided by wearing shoes. They latch on if you walk barefoot in contaminated places, and set up home under the skin of the foot, usually at the side of a toenail where they cause a painful, boil-like swelling. They need picking out by a local expert.

It is easier to understand how to diagnose it, treat it and prevent it if you know a little about the life cycle. Contaminated faeces are washed into the lake, the eggs hatch and the larva infects certain species of snail. The snails then produce about 10,000 cercariae a day for the rest of their lives. The parasites can digest their way through your skin when you wade or bathe in infested fresh water.

Winds disperse the snails and cercariae. The snails in particular can drift a long way, especially on windblown weed, so nowhere is really safe. However, deep water and running water are safer, while shallow water presents the greatest risk. The cercariae penetrate intact skin, and find their way to the liver. There male and female meet and spend the rest of their lives in permanent copulation. No wonder you feel tired! Most finish up in the wall of the lower bowel, but others can get lost and can cause damage to many different organs. *Schistosoma haematobium* goes mostly to the bladder.

Although the adults do not cause any harm in themselves, after about four to six weeks they start to lay eggs, which cause an intense but usually ineffective immune reaction, including fever, cough, abdominal pain, and a fleeting, itching rash called 'safari itch'. The absence of early symptoms does not necessarily mean there is no infection. Later symptoms can be more localised and more severe, but the general symptoms settle down fairly quickly and eventually you are just tired. 'Tired all the time' is one of the most common symptoms among expats in Africa, and bilharzia, giardia, amoeba and intestinal yeast are the most common culprits.

Although bilharzia is difficult to diagnose, it can be tested at specialist travel clinics. Ideally tests need to be done at least six weeks after likely exposure and will determine whether you need treatment. Fortunately it is easy to treat at present.

Avoiding bilharzia If you are bathing, swimming, paddling or wading in fresh water which you think may carry a bilharzia risk, try to get out of the water within ten minutes.

- Avoid bathing or paddling on shores within 200m of villages or places where people use the water a great deal, especially reedy shores or where there is lots of water weed
- Dry off thoroughly with a towel; rub vigorously
- If your bathing water comes from a risky source try to ensure that the water is taken from the lake in the early morning and stored snail-free, otherwise it should be filtered or Dettol or Cresol added
- Bathing early in the morning is safer than bathing in the last half of the day
- Cover yourself with DEET insect repellent before swimming: it may offer some protection

HIV/AIDS The risks of sexually transmitted infection are extremely high in the Congos whether you sleep with fellow travellers or locals. About 80% of HIV infections in British heterosexuals are acquired abroad with an estimated three million people living with HIV/AIDS in the two countries. If you must indulge, use condoms or femidoms, which help reduce the risk of transmission. If you notice any genital ulcers or discharge, get treatment promptly since these increase the risk of acquiring HIV. If you do have unprotected sex, visit a clinic as soon as possible; this should be within 24 hours, or no later than 72 hours, for post-exposure prophylaxis.

Meningitis This is a particularly nasty disease as it can kill within hours of the first symptoms appearing. The telltale symptoms are a combination of a blinding headache (light sensitivity), a blotchy rash and a high fever. Immunisation protects against the most serious bacterial form of meningitis and the tetravalent vaccine ACWY is recommended for the Congos by British travel clinics, but if this is not available then A+C vaccine is better than nothing.

Although other forms of meningitis exist (usually viral), there are no vaccines for these. Local papers normally report localised outbreaks. A severe headache and fever should make you run to a doctor immediately. There are also other causes of headache and fever, one of which is typhoid, which occurs in travellers to the Congos. Seek medical help if you are ill for more than a few days.

Rabies Rabies is carried by all mammals (beware the village dogs and small monkeys that are used to being fed in the parks) and is passed on to man through a bite, scratch or a lick of an open wound. You must always assume any animal is rabid, and seek medical help as soon as possible. Meanwhile scrub the wound with soap under a running tap or while pouring water from a jug. Find a reasonably clear-looking source of water (but at this stage the quality of the water is not important), then pour on a strong iodine or alcohol solution of gin, whisky or rum. This helps stop the rabies virus entering the body and will guard against wound infections, including tetanus.

Pre-exposure vaccinations for rabies is ideally advised for everyone, but is particularly important if you intend to have contact with animals and/or are likely to be more than 24 hours away from medical help. Ideally three doses should be taken over a minimum of 21 days, though even taking one or two doses of vaccine is better than none at all. Contrary to popular belief these vaccinations are relatively painless.

If you are bitten, scratched or licked over an open wound by a sick animal, then post-exposure prophylaxis should be given as soon as possible, though it is never too late to seek help, as the incubation period for rabies can be very long. Those who have not been immunised will need a full course of injections. The vast majority of travel health advisors including WHO recommend rabies immunoglobulin (RIG), but this product is expensive (around US$800) and may be hard to come by – another reason why pre-exposure vaccination should be encouraged.

Tell the doctor if you have had pre-exposure vaccine, as this should change the treatment you receive. And remember that, if you do contract rabies, mortality is 100% and death from rabies is probably one of the worst ways to go.

Tickbite fever African ticks are not the rampant disease transmitters they are in the Americas, but they may spread tickbite fever and a few dangerous rarities. Tickbite fever is a flu-like illness that can easily be treated with doxycycline, but as there can be some serious complications it is important to visit a doctor.

Ticks should ideally be removed as soon as possible, as leaving them on the body increases the chance of infection. They should be removed with special tick tweezers that can be bought in good travel shops. Failing that you can use your fingernails: grasp the tick as close to your body as possible and pull steadily and firmly away at right angles to your skin. The tick will then come away complete, as long as you do not jerk or twist. If possible douse the wound with alcohol (any spirit will do) or iodine. Irritants (eg: Olbas oil) or lit cigarettes are to be discouraged since they can cause the ticks to regurgitate and therefore increase the risk of disease. It is best to get a travelling companion to check you for ticks; if you are travelling with small children, remember to check their heads, and particularly behind the ears.

Spreading redness around the bite and/or fever and/or aching joints after a tick bite imply that you have an infection that requires antibiotic treatment, so seek advice.

Ebola The spectre of Ebola looms over the Congos but it is highly unlikely that any traveller would come into contact with it. At least three subtypes exist across the equatorial region of Africa, and most cases of the virus have occurred in or near the Congo regions. The first outbreak was in Yambuku in northern Zaire in 1976, and the most recent in the countries on the Gabonese–Congolese border near Okoyo – three outbreaks in this region between 2001 and 2003 left 302 people infected. Of those 302, 254 died from the virus. An outbreak usually receives massive press coverage due to the infamy of the virus and it is therefore easy to track any occurrences of it in the world.

The main route of transmission is from person-to-person contact through infected bodily fluids, and from treatment with contaminated needles. Other ways of contracting the virus include handling or even eating contaminated meat from gorillas, chimpanzees, antelope and porcupines; airborne transmission between humans has not been proven. Many Africans have contracted Ebola during burial ceremonies from a dead relative, when handling the body in unsanitary conditions is common. It is almost always fatal within three weeks of transmission.

Outbreaks have occurred where hospital care has been substandard. Avoid hospitals in small towns – with your own medical kit, the chances are you will have better supplies than most hospitals in both countries.

Initial symptoms of the disease are high fever, headache, exhaustion, dizziness and a sore throat. It could easily be confused with malaria or typhoid, which are far more common. Further progression of the disease includes bleeding from every opening in the body, low blood pressure and a weak pulse. Victims die of organ failure or excessive blood loss.

Avoiding Ebola is simple enough – keep up to date on regions that have had outbreaks and avoid handling dead chimpanzees, gorillas or forest antelopes and avoid eating meat if you are travelling through the bush in these general areas. Avoid contact with blood and other bodily fluids, and use appropriate measures such as gloves and a mask whenever confronted with people who are ill. Since this disease is infamous and so insidious, regions which have outbreaks are quickly sealed off from visitors. Congo-Brazzaville's northwestern border with Gabon has seen numerous outbreaks of the virus and one needs to be especially vigilant in this area. In the DR Congo, a large outbreak occurred near Kikwit in 1995, but most recently outbreaks have occurred in the neighbouring countries of Uganda and Sudan, which suggests due diligence when in the northeastern districts of Haut Uele and Ituri.

Pneumonic plague Two countries in the world still see regular outbreaks of plague, and one of them is the Democratic Republic of Congo. Plague is a zoonotic disease transmitted mainly between small animals and their fleas. Humans can acquire infection from bites by infected fleas, direct contact, inhalation and rarely from eating infected material. The most common and infamous form is the bubonic plague resulting from the bite of an infected flea, and it is believed to have killed millions in Europe during the Middle Ages. In the DR Congo, a less common but more virulent form is pneumonic plague. Typically it is due to secondary spread from an advanced bubonic infection. It can also be transmitted from human to human by inhalation of infected droplets. It occurs regularly in isolated mining camps and jungle towns. Ituri is the most active plague region on the planet.

However, the likelihood of coming into contact with it is slim. Symptoms include chills, diarrhoea, fever, headaches and swollen lymph nodes. Any of these can occur from two to seven days from the date of infection, and, without treatment, death can occur within a week. Anyone who is suspected of contracting plague should be isolated immediately, and all contact with them should be done with masks and gloves.

The good news regarding plague in the DR Congo is that it tends to occur in isolated patches, far off the beaten track, and where there are horrendously bad sanitary conditions. The most recent outbreaks have occurred in illegal mining camps in Ituri Province, and death has been common due to the lack of facilities for treatment. Plague requires the immediate administration of antibiotics, and supportive therapy to eliminate from an infected person – and when this is done, most victims will survive. It is therefore critical that medical help is sought immediately if there is any indication that an individual is stricken with the disease.

HOSPITALS If you require immediate treatment, get evacuated to a neighbouring country or to Kinshasa or Brazzaville. Hospitals in the region are poorly supplied and poorly sanitised, and you may be exposing yourself to even more risk by visiting one.

If you are out in the small towns or the bush, enquiring at aid agencies might get you some emergency care, but I would advise against relying on these people to tend to your problems as they are not in the Congos for your interests. If you are genuinely planning on going out into the wilderness I recommend you bring your own equipment in the form of a medical kit as pharmacies are difficult to find. And once outside the main centres of population such as Pointe Noire, Brazzaville, Kinshasa and Lubumbashi, it is highly unlikely you will find even basic medical items.

Get medical evacuation to a neighbouring country if you need surgery or any procedure that requires a transfusion – Libreville in Gabon, Kampala in Uganda, or Lusaka in Zambia all have far higher standards and hospitals that adhere to international regulations. There are also regular flights to Johannesburg from Kinshasa. The Centre Privé d'Urgence in Kinshasa can stabilise your condition if it is critical, but under no circumstances should you receive a blood transfusion – unless the option, of course, is your own demise. Health-care standards in the Congos are unchecked and unreliable.

INSURANCE Getting travel insurance is essential. Make sure it covers hospital visits, and some sort of medical evacuation if you plan on travelling to out-of-the-way places in the Congos. Insure all of your electronic equipment against theft and damage as this can easily occur. In general a policy that reimburses you when you get home is better than a policy that might reimburse you while on the road – receiving cash or even contacting your insurance company while in the Congos can be problematic. Many insurance policies also include embargoes on all or part of the DR Congo especially so make absolutely sure that your travel insurance will cover you while travelling in the two countries. Note that if you are planning on visiting national parks in the east of the DR Congo, this area may still be considered as a region 'at war' by certain companies and your insurance could be further invalidated.

SAFETY

Poverty is rampant, but outright begging is generally only seen in the capitals Kinshasa and Brazzaville; though once a foreign face is seen anywhere across the region other beggars can quickly appear. Citizens of both Congos are less likely to beg than in other countries and are more likely to try and extract cash and gifts through other means – such as overcharging. Set prices in taxis beforehand, and if possible have someone else negotiate prices for long-distance travel for you and tip them afterwards.

When crossing frontiers, it is likely that your luggage will be searched by hand and things can easily go missing. Keep anything of value in your immediate possession, and be vigilant at all times with things you are carrying.

CORRUPTION The largest problem any visitor will encounter is corruption – it is endemic across the two countries, a veritable institution, and often the only way any officials receive money since when they do get paid it can be months behind schedule. Unfortunately when given a uniform and badge of some sort, people in the Congos will see this as licence to stop and harass anyone and everyone for money – and as a foreigner you can be guaranteed that you will be singled out.

Remember that you are primarily seen as an opportunity by people you encounter, and friendliness can go a long way. However, I recommend against offering anything to anyone initially – I do not condone bribery and extortion and this habit can only make matters worse. This is a central problem with the Congos, and unless you want to depart empty-handed, limiting your generosity to those you meet is absolutely necessary.

Corruption is becoming less of a concern as international companies move into the DR Congo especially, and demand some semblance of professionalism from government officials that they deal with. Having genuine money problems can, sometimes, get you through tight situations and you might even find these people doing you a favour for free (but don't count on it). However, knowing how to deal with these people is still critical to being able to move throughout the two countries without losing your sanity and every item of value in your possession.

Remain polite at all times – no-one in the Congos responds well to anger or threats and losing control will only make your situation worse. Realise that random arrests, being pulled aside, and constant poring over your various documents all comes down to a quest for cash. If you keep this in mind and aim to mitigate the amount you need to pay, your journey will be that much more enjoyable.

In fact, I recommend trying to have fun with these people – as much as possible. Being courteous, affable, but ultimately lacking as much money as they want to take from you will be your best approach. Carrying a wallet with a few dollars between checkpoints can get you through tough situations – bring small notes in American dollars, central African francs (CFA), or Congolese francs (Cf) and hand them a wad of bills and quickly be on your way. They will not count them in front of you – they will be happy that you complied.

Besides this, it should be obvious that you should have your paperwork in order at all times when confronted with the possibility of running into various officials. Giving these people a valid reason to extort money from you is a bad situation to be in, as they will be trying their hardest to find anything wrong with your paperwork already.

And as a general rule, unless an officer is standing right in front of your vehicle with his hands waving and blowing his whistle so hard a vein is going to pop – just drive around them. If they stop you later, simply apologise and say you didn't see them. It's like that in the Congos.

WOMEN TRAVELLERS Females travelling solo through the Congos are something of a rarity, but if you are obviously foreign, you should take the same precautions as males. However, women's rights have a very long way to go in these regions and I cannot recommend travelling outside of the main towns and cities on your own – make some friends, go with a tour, have someone you trust accompany you. Going around alone at night is simply asking for trouble.

Some women can be seen in Kinshasa with Congolese boyfriends and given the dichotomy between men and women it may be necessary to have some sort of male accompaniment help a foreign woman in her errands around the country. Venture further afield and a solo female traveller will be quite the novelty, but like any traveller who is too far from the radar it could appear as an opportunity too good to pass up for a group of local thieves. While a male might get away with fewer precautions when travelling around the countries alone, a female should make sure that her itinerary is known to someone inside the country. Make arrangements for people to meet you along the way, and involve others in the decision-making

Understanding the 'Article 15' ideology of the DR Congo can go a long way to understanding why corruption is so rampant. It began in the 1960s with refugees fleeing revolts in central Congo, and demanding some supplies and shelter in their refugee camps. A prominent Luba leader, Albert Kalonji, told the dispersed population that the country was theirs, and it was up to them to fend for themselves – leave the government alone.

It was widely popularised by Mobutu Sésé Seko around 1990 as multi-party elections and government reform were anticipating the fall of Zaire. He admitted in a famous quote that it would be OK to 'steal a little'; this was widely printed in international newspapers, and taken to heart by the already corrupt bureaucracy around the country.

While 'Article 15' was the popular name for this behaviour, there was no such real decree put in writing; it was Mobutu's comments, and the generally accepted behaviour that whatever is in the country is yours to have – not all of it, just a little. Take just a little. These words did a great deal to divert blame of the looming economic crash of the nation to other sources; no longer was the government obligated to pay its salaries on time to the vast public service, or even investigate petty theft. The dictator's popularity rose throughout these final years, at least until riots destroyed central Kinshasa. The writing was on the wall by this time, however, and people needed to continue the practice of 'Article 15' just to get some cash flowing in.

This mentality continues to this very day. It is a philosophy decades old, entrenched in the national psyche, and even though Mobutu was ousted in shame from the DR Congo, by many he is still looked upon as a popular figure. It is sometimes called the street economy in the DR Congo – the economy that works, where one finds an angle any which way to bring more money in, while they wait for their real job to deliver a month's overdue pay cheque. In some ways it is intended to be a sideways and covert method for robbing people blind, and when the theory of relativity comes into play – that all foreign visitors make at least 100 times as much as a local – it can mean ridiculous amounts of money are demanded.

I've heard of expatriates paying US$150 for a steak, and customs officers seizing passports and demanding US$500 simply to give them back. A note in a ledger book can cost US$5–10, or US$100 if you are there on corporate business. Get too uppity about it and they'll put you in jail for a while, until someone arrives with cash to bail you out. The arrival of MONUC saw prices shoot through the roof initially, as they were mandated to establish themselves in Kinshasa on huge expense accounts, and paid whatever was necessary. It was not until 2003 or 2004 that the entire notion of corruption being a bad thing was uttered.

Things can go missing from your bags and pockets (it's happened to me on several occasions) too easily. You may call the person a thief, but he or she may not even think twice about it. The notion of personal property is, therefore, a little blurred; perhaps they were 'taking just a little' to keep themselves going. And reporting these sorts of things to the police is just plain silly – you'll pay more to get it back than it's worth, if it's something minor. Prevention remains your best defence.

process of how to travel around. Hire motorbike and taxi drivers based on recommendations, not simply by flagging one down on the street.

DISABLED TRAVELLERS The wheelchair-bound will find their lives difficult in the Congos, as accessibility is not regulated in any form whatsoever. Your life will be easier with a private vehicle, naturally, though a half-decent taxi can also be of great use. The high-end hotels and some grocery stores in Kinshasa have flat level entrances where a wheelchair can enter, but this is severely limited. I would definitely seek local help in this case – stay at a decent hotel, and have them hire you a car and an assistant to go out on the town. Take organised tours to areas outside of the city, and expect to be lifted up and all over the place. The unfortunate fact is that going it alone with a disability in these countries is not really possible, but people will try to accommodate you in any way they can.

CRIME Overall, crime is as much an issue in the two Congos as it is anywhere else in Africa – take care of your belongings, even in your hotel room be careful with your money and anything of value. Do not dress too extravagantly when in public and do not carry too much money while out on the town. Be careful at night and secure private transport when out in any town after dark, especially in Kinshasa. Avoid public transport altogether after dark in any of the big cities. Never walk around at night in any major towns, though Congo-Brazzaville is a far safer country than the DR Congo in this respect. Remember that you are more than likely being watched at all times, and wandering alone into a quiet neighbourhood can easily be construed as an opportunity to those less fortunate.

RIOTS Various cities across both Congos have, in the past, had some rather nasty public uprisings that receive plenty of press coverage and plunge a city into more disarray than usual. I mention rioting because in large African cities where poverty is common, crowds can quickly accumulate from nowhere and large numbers of men in uniforms may be sent to disperse those crowds by any means necessary. It is helpful, then, to know how to handle oneself in these situations – and the best I can recommend is to seek shelter indoors at the nearest place with reasonable security such as a hotel, bank or restaurant. Foreigners in plain view during chaotic moments can be far too inviting a target for a few agitated locals, and observing these events from afar is the only way to observe them at all. It may be inviting to wait and see what may transpire, but you are truly playing with your life in these situations. Peaceful protest is something that does not really exist in the DR Congo on a spontaneous level, and it should be obvious if you are witnessing an organised march or an illegal manifestation from the general attitude of people in the streets – and the numbers of soldiers and police in the area. However, to someone unfamiliar with daily life in the Congo's big cities, knowing the difference between the two can be tricky and because of this I would advise avoiding any large public gatherings unless a local is with you to provide some advice.

MAGIC TRICKS I include this because of the general superstitions of every local in Congo: spirits, magic and sorcery are all taken very seriously and any indication that a foreigner might be 'possessed', or even communicating the notion that otherworldly elements are assisting you in your travels, could spell bad things of a physical sense happening to you – not to mention those associated with you, who will have to atone with answering to their community members of why they were dealing with someone who is obviously connected to demons and other unsavoury spirits of the otherworld.

I've run into a few travellers over the years who befriend the local population with some sleight of hand tricks, or other minor 'magic' practices to break the ice. This can be great for kids, and entertain the local population, but I implore a traveller to refrain from these things while in the Congos. The risks are simply too great, and the beliefs in sorcery, animism and witchcraft too well entrenched in local culture, for it to be simply passed off as idle entertainment.

Even if it seems harmless at the time, as mentioned, suspicions can arise surrounding anyone who comes into contact with you. Therefore tell a joke, wear a stupid grin, be polite, but don't practise common magic parlour tricks in the Congos out of the blue. A large number of street kids became homeless because their families thought they were sorcerers.

CONGO-BRAZZAVILLE'S POULE REGION Travel throughout Congo-Brazzaville is generally feasible, with the exception of the Poule Region – the area west of Brazzaville and east of Madingo is still controlled by the 'Ninjas', Poule rebels dressed in black, and you will have difficulty securing any transport through here. Even if you could, I would advise against it – one stop along the way and word will spread that someone is travelling through and these people will more than likely try to stage an attack. They will also more than likely kill you as a result, as well as your driver, and anyone else travelling with you.

The only land route through the region is via the train, though it is insecure and often raided by the Ninjas. Just as with hiring a vehicle, a similar thing can be said for travelling by train – if word gets out that a foreigner is travelling on the train, it is more likely that it will be robbed.

With all of this said, obviously I do not recommend visiting the region under any conditions. Frequent flights connect Dolisie to Brazzaville, so passing through this area is not required anyway. If you do decide to overland through here, get a local guide from the same tribe as the Ninjas. Have him arrange everything beforehand, including what costs are required along how many checkpoints. Hire a guard or two from the local population who knows all of the rebels who man the checkpoints, and get *them* to pay bribes at each stop. It's complicated and convoluted, obviously not advisable, but like everything else – of course it's possible.

EASTERN DR CONGO The fortunes of those in the DR Congo's turbulent east have gone from bad to worse, to awful, back again to bad, and can now best be described as 'getting better'. The entire region is still very much in flux, with continuing problems from numerous rebel groups and agitation from external forces such as foreign governments.

Major towns are generally secure, but going out into the countryside requires preparation, planning, and above all local advice. Ask at every opportunity about the road ahead if you are taking private transport – things change faster than a guidebook can advise. If possible, hire a local to come with you and negotiate with people along the way. You may even need to hire security along certain roads in the east if you are overlanding – large trucks that ply these roads will sometimes have ubiquitous gunmen on their cabs and roofs, and one vehicle slowly trundling along dirt roads without any sort of protection is a great opportunity for people from all over the region to take their chances at relieving you of everything.

Things are improving, though, as the electoral results have given new hope to the region's population. Fewer precautions are necessary and all-out combat and disarray is generally a thing of the past. It is far more likely that if there is a problem the region will be sealed off, and you will only have to deal with corrupt officials rather than open conflict.

LANDMINES Large fields of mines left over from the days of UNITA litter the border between the DR Congo and Angola. Furthermore, there are reports of landmines in Cabinda, and the frontier regions of Congo-Brazzaville. All of these are decades old and, while usually not well marked, are well known by locals. Some farmers in Congo-Brazzaville have refused to work on certain fields because of the landmine risk.

A more insidious and difficult aspect of the landmine problem across the Congos exists in the east: in the Kivus, new minefields were laid during the conflicts of 2003 and 2004. Some roads have been mined, and it was an active part of the conflict to plant mines around markets, hospitals, houses and footpaths, deliberately targeting civilians as they went about their daily lives.

The good news is that in conjunction with MONUC, mine-clearing firms have been working steadily around the country. Nonetheless, running off into the bush is a bad idea: if you are travelling deep into unknown territory, ask for a local's advice at the very least, and preferably bring a guide. Make the guide walk in front, and follow his or her footsteps exactly if the area has a history of mines.

Most major towns and their outlying areas have been cleared, but there is no way of totally confirming the safety of a region due to the ongoing conflict in some regions of eastern DR Congo. All of this means, again, that running far off the beaten track in the Congos can have serious consequences.

REGISTERING WITH YOUR EMBASSY In the Congos, things can change – and they can change quickly. The governments in place have been stable for a few years, but both countries have a less than stellar track record for any semblance of continuity. Revolutions and coups can occur out of the blue, and rebellions in remote areas can shut down whole regions. Usually, when absolute catastrophe strikes, a visitor can see the writing on the wall at least a few days beforehand. However, the spontaneity of being in the Congos should not be understated, and is an integral part of what makes the region unique.

With that said, I highly recommend registering with your embassy. If your home country does not have diplomatic relations with the Congo you're visiting, find the nearest embassy responsible for it and register. Registering will ensure that you're up to date on situations occurring with any diplomatic representation, if required, and it will also mean that if in the worst of scenarios you find yourself on the doorstep of their building they do not treat you with excessive suspicion. If some sort of evacuation takes place under dire circumstances, you will be entitled to repatriation yourself.

Note that all of this is unlikely, but keeping in touch with your embassy is the best hedge you have against any way out in the face of total disaster. They are in these countries to assist their citizens if and when they are in genuine need, and should be seen as a resource in that respect.

WHAT TO TAKE

Whatever you think you may need in the Congos, bring it. It is difficult to find even mundane things, let alone speciality items. Basic things we take for granted in the West like potato peelers, cutlery, bottle openers, and even toothbrushes and pens can be difficult or impossible to find outside of Kinshasa; even in major cities like Brazzaville and Lubumbashi you will have difficulty getting them. These are not the countries to pack lightly, or be lean on what you bring – the variables are wide, the terrain difficult, and you need to be prepared for all eventualities. Some writers advise taking half the stuff and twice the money when travelling; for the Congos, I advise bringing twice the stuff and three times the money.

I highly recommend that unless you have your own private transport, you travel with a large backpack. Transport can be difficult or non-existent around the Congos and it is likely you will need to walk distances between borders and towns, down footpaths, or ride on the back of motorbikes on bumpy dirt roads. Naturally, the more cash you have the less this applies – if you have arranged contacts and a tour ahead of time this is less of a concern, but I still recommend bringing a medium to large backpack for any excursions in the wilderness. When in the jungle I should stress that you should not be lean on what you bring – these are volatile areas in many ways and any problems you encounter will only be solvable by what you have in your possession. These are not the kinds of places where one can simply head to the next village and find a few basic necessities.

A GPS is recommended for any sort of internal travelling in the region, but the caveat is that it will be scrutinised and maybe even confiscated by officials upon entry. Keep it discreet if you decide to bring it – however, it will come in handy for pinpointing your location in conjunction with a map. Another essential is a can opener – in the vast number of general stores scattered across the Congos buried in the jungle you will find small shacks without electricity or water and the only food they have available will invariably be in the form of cans covered in dust. Do not rely on someone else to have the tools available to open these things. Sturdy hiking boots, a hat of some sort, and matches are also essential. Picture yourself as going on a camping trip, even you are only staying in the cities.

Bugs and malaria are always a concern in these areas. A mosquito net, a strong insect repellent (intended for tropical purposes, nothing less), and antimalarials as emergency treatment even if you do not take them for prevention are absolutely necessary. A sturdy knife, or even machete, can also be helpful – often even locals will not have the tools necessary to fix things and you can be a great help by offering a tool or two when one is needed. There are three things I also wish I had brought on my first few visits to the Congos – a doorstop (for those cheap hotel doors that won't close, and for some added security when sleeping at night), hot sauce (for making those meals of canned tuna and canned corned beef almost palatable) and earplugs (to drown out the armada of screaming children on those dreadfully long bus rides).

HOW TO LIGHT AN OIL LAMP

One of the skills lost to the modern world, amongst others, namely – the ability to make fire without a lighter, wash one's clothes without a laundromat, find one's way without a compass or GPS, build a home from sticks and mud – is perhaps that most pertinent to the visitor to either Congo – how to light an oil lamp.

If you're out of candles, or a flashlight, the obligatory oil lamp might be staring you down in a quickly darkening spartan room somewhere between nowhere and a bus out sometime next week. In this case, conserving your battery power and using the local tools provided can be quite handy – saving your own materials for when there is really no other choice.

So faced with the latest in portable lighting technology from the 18th century, the first thing to do is familiarise yourself – on one side is a lever that raises and lowers the glass casing that protects the wick (where the flame comes from). Below the wick is a knob, which one uses to increase or decrease the amount of fuel going to the wick – thereby creating a larger or smaller flame upon ignition. At the base is a lid, where the fuel goes in. Make sure you ask for the right fuel before refilling.

Lighting it, then, is simple enough – light a match, push down on the lever, and put the lit match to the wick. Adjust the knob to get the flame to the desired brightness. Carry around dark hallways at your discretion, or use it to light up your room. You may find it's not a bad way to get light after all.

Finally, a torch (flashlight) is essential. On my first trip to Congo-Brazzaville I had lost mine along the way and wandered blithely around in the dark, though found it rather frustrating – especially when I needed to open a locked door in a hotel that had no light whatsoever! There are torches out there that can be converted into small lamps and I recommend these for lighting up a room when the power cuts out. And it will.

ELECTRICITY/PLUGS Extra batteries are essential – bring far more than you need. Recharging items can be intermittent, difficult or impossible depending on the area; power cuts are frequent even in major towns, power surges just as frequent. There are universal power plugs available which I recommend if you have a number of rechargeable devices.

Congo-Brazzaville operates on a 230V current and the DR Congo operates on a 220V current. Normally this shouldn't be much of an issue and most items intended for use in continental Europe should function in the two countries, but I still recommend bringing a universal plug and power converter just in case you encounter something odd. There are no real standards prevalent across the two countries and exceptions are common. For the price of these things, and the fact that I recommend bringing as much as possible, they should be coming with you anyway.

The two round-pronged plug is most common in the Congos, but instances of the three round-pronged plug and three round-pronged plug with the ground protruding are also prevalent. There are universal plug conversion kits out there, and I highly recommend these if you will be doing any travelling with electronics in the Congos.

$ MONEY, CURRENCY AND BANKING

The currency in Congo-Brazzaville is the central African franc (CFA), the same CFA used in Gabon, Cameroon, Central African Republic, Equatorial Guinea and Chad, also referred to in trading as XAF. Though of the same value, it is not the same currency as the west African franc, often referred to as the XOF. It is pinned to the euro at 100 units, meaning that €1=655.957CFA or 1CFA=€0.152449.

There are precisely two banks with an ATM in Congo-Brazzaville: in Brazzaville and Pointe Noire. Cash advances are available at some banks, and Western Union is the only other method of receiving money. Generally speaking, expect to use Western Union if you need a cash advance outside of Brazzaville – phone connections are good enough that this is possible, though the premium charged is high.

In the DR Congo, the notorious Congolese franc (Fc) continues its battle to stabilise. It's a floating currency that can vary wildly, and I recommend only changing as much as you need at various junctures. The US dollar is widely traded for anything beyond minor transactions, and once you've had to haul around a satchel full of Congolese francs in Kinshasa you will soon switch over to paying people with US dollars. Money changers on the street abound in the DR Congo, and cash advances are usually available via an only-in-Congo method of showing up at the bank with your credit card and enduring a half hour of waiting while the officials confirm your name and address with the credit-card company. Even in this way, there are few banks that will do this – one in Kinshasa and one in Lubumbashi. The only reliable way to pay for what you need is with US dollars cash. Things are changing slowly, however – a German bank, ProCredit Bank, opened the first ATM in central Kinshasa at the end of 2006.

Be careful with your currency traders before you leave your home country – Western currency companies are not used to dealing with African standards for currency transactions and you need to be on your toes when money is handed to you. The bills must be new editions with no marks, no folds, and generally in denominations of US$10 and upward. Pick and choose your bills at your local currency trader and spend a few minutes scrutinising them for yourself. The last thing you want is to be a few hundred dollars short because a bank in the Congos would not accept your legal tender.

Credit cards are in general unreliable methods of paying for anything in the Congos. Major hotels in Kinshasa, Lubumbashi and Brazzaville will accept credit cards for payment, but outside these main cities cards are essentially useless. These are cash societies, made all the more difficult on account of the possibility of robbery. International airline offices will accept credit cards for payment of flight tickets, but for domestic flights cash is still required. In these cases I recommend trying to pay with your credit card and if they refuse, go to the nearest bank that allows a cash advance and request the money yourself. The insurance of not having to carry around cash for expensive flights is worth the advance fee.

In both Congos Western Union is the most reliable method of receiving money. They are ubiquitous and every major town has a branch, and are often the only method of getting extra cash when outside the major cities. Arranging someone to send you cash beforehand if necessary, or even sending it in advance and writing down the tracking numbers, can save you a lot of hassle if you plan on travelling on a route through several towns. For the record, in my travels across two dozen countries in Africa the Congos were the only countries where I absolutely needed to get money sent to me through Western Union. While their prices for wiring money are high, they are also the most reliable method of receiving cash fast. Keep in mind, though, that it still takes several hours for transactions to be processed overseas, so calling someone to send you money still requires about a day's notice.

Opening a bank account in either country can be done at select international banks. A letter and sponsorship from a local employer is usually required, along with an initial deposit.

BUDGETING

Prices vary wildly in the Congos, but some things are consistently high – such as domestic flights across the DR Congo, various permits, and visas. Other costs such as hotels and meals are generally inexpensive – the latter sometimes very cheap indeed – with the exception of Kinshasa, where there are very few options at the lower end for hotels. If you stay away from places geared towards the high-earning expatriates, most things in Kinshasa can be done inexpensively.

The biggest issue is transport. Public buses are simple enough, but to see anything off the beaten track – and everything in the Congos is off the beaten track – one requires either a 4x4 vehicle or a chartered aircraft. Neither is cheap; both will run into hundreds, or thousands, of dollars per day. Therefore if it is at all possible, bring a motorbike or vehicle, or hire one once in town. If you have time to spare, bring a bicycle – they can be checked into an aircraft hold without much of a problem – and when the roads run out, you will then have some reasonably quick transport across rough terrain.

The lowest budget I could recommend, not including high-cost items such as flights and park permits, would hover at around US$40 per day. This should get you a cheap bed anywhere outside of Kinshasa, and two modest meals or a few things from a grocery store. Local transport can be inexpensive, but keep in mind that random police checks are frequent when travelling between towns and you may be required to pay a nominal 'fee' to proceed – anywhere from US$5–10. To be comfortable, and to factor in costs that will undoubtedly appear out of nowhere, I recommend an average mid-range budget of about US$100 per day – this would include visits to various parks, a mid-range hotel room, various briberies foisted upon you by officials, and restaurant meals.

The high end in the Congos has no limits – the most expensive hotels, air tickets, park permits, car hire and guides can all run into several hundred dollars daily. If you are travelling with this much money I recommend sticking to a tour of some sort, arranging for locals to deal with officials for you.

TIME

Both Congos are GMT + 1, the same as west Africa, and do not use daylight saving time (DST). The DR Congo, however, has two time zones – from Kananga and Kisangani east all towns use the same time zone as east Africa, which is GMT + 2, again without any daylight savings.

Sunrise tends to be quite constant as a result of both countries straddling the Equator. Generally the sun will be up by 06.30 and set at 18.30, giving exactly 12 hours of daylight.

✈ GETTING AROUND

BY AIR Travel around the Congos enough and you will have no choice but to purchase a domestic flight – the roads, when they exist, are bad and certain regions are, as mentioned, still emerging from war. In Congo-Brazzaville domestic flights are generally inexpensive, starting at US$50 from Dolisie to Pointe Noire and generally no more than US$75 for the longest stretches such as Brazzaville to Impfondo.

The air network in the DR Congo is extensive, with numerous small operations running flights to most major towns. Their schedules can change quickly, and often their equipment is dangerously old. A flight on the DR Congo airline Hewa Bora Air will be more expensive, but there are unlikely to be significant delays.

However, the costs for flying across the country are extortionate – I paid US$421 for a one-way flight from Kinshasa to Lubumbashi. Other long-range flying is similarly high, such as Kinshasa to Goma at US$300 and Kinshasa to Kisangani at US$250. Even short flights such as Kinshasa to Boma will cost about US$100. The only reliable method of finding out which flights are leaving on a given day is to show up at the local airport and enquire – most of these airlines are not on international booking systems. In fact, many of them do not even keep computer records.

BY RIVER Good old Kisangani barges run from Kinshasa to Kisangani these days, sometimes, unreliably. At the time of writing the frequency was three times a year, with an estimated travel time of one month (this does not count the organised tour that does the route from Kisangani to Kinshasa, which takes two weeks). Further south, the adventurous can try their luck at local boat transport to Kindu, but this cannot be guaranteed even under the best conditions. There is usually some sort of transport along the waterways of the Congos, but this method of transport is often slow – though in some areas such as the central DR Congo, it may be the only real option available.

BY ROAD Roads in the Congos, when they exist, vary from bad to virtually non-existent. Road transport between major towns is frequent enough, often on massive trucks that you can see packing for long journeys in Kinshasa and Pointe Noire. In Katanga around Lubumbashi the roads are quickly improving from the border to Likasi, facilitating mining operations, but beyond that expect the worst when travelling by road in the DR Congo. If you have your own private transport, this is a good start, but you will need permits, local advice and nerves of steel to travel serious distances overland. For short journeys in the same region, for example Dolisie to Pointe Noire or Beni to Bukavu, road travel is tolerable. Other routes are quickly being opened up to meet the needs of construction companies across the east, and Kisangani to Bunia, as well as Kisangani to Bukavu, should be feasible by the time this book arrives in your lap.

A strange fact of traversing the DR Congo is that it is often easier to travel between towns outside the country – for example if one wanted to travel from Bukavu to Goma, doing so via the paved roads in Rwanda would be a far less difficult task than attempting the harsh road on the DR Congo side. Of course crossing frontiers frequently brings its own sets of problems in this respect – though if in the process of enquiring about the road up ahead there are stories of rebels and police harassing travellers then this is one way to get around them.

BY RAIL Congo-Brazzaville's famous rail line to the west coast runs intermittently, slowly, and often dangerously. It goes through the dodgy Poule Region (see page 38) once per week, usually, unless it has been raided by the 'Ninjas' the previous week and therefore down for repairs. The trains are slow, uncomfortable and crowded – but cheap. The risks of getting caught up in the conflict in the Poule Region are high, so for this reason I can only recommend a rail trip from Dolisie to Pointe Noire or Dolisie to Mbinda; however, these services run just once per week and on differing days.

In the DR Congo the rail service is slowly coming back on stream. From Likasi to Kalemie there is a passenger rail service available, and is accompanied by security through the volatile region of eastern Katanga. A comfortable first-class train service runs from Lubumbashi to Kananga, and from there one can change over to another decent train to Ilebo. There is also a very poor rail line from Kolwezi west to the border with Angola, but no way to cross into that country from there. Trains arrive and depart on a fluctuating schedule and you could be spending days waiting for the train's arrival and in general, it will depart the day after it arrives.

OVERLANDING The glorious old days of overlanding through Zaire have long since past, and even in those days crossing the country was something only the bravest would attempt. In the new era of the DR Congo the situation can best be described best as … worse.

However, it is not impossible. From my research it is quite possible to travel by road from Zambia to Lubumbashi, rail to Ilebo, and road again to Kinshasa. From Angola, Matadi to Kinshasa is also more than feasible, and for the truly patient a road connection from Bukavu to Kisangani, and by boat down the Congo River to Kinshasa, is possible. From the Central African Republic it should not be too difficult to reach Gemena and then Kisangani, which would link up with boat and nominal road services in the region.

Most major routes within the DR Congo are possible, and that's as far as it goes – *possible*. Whatever you do, you absolutely need excessive amounts of time to cross the country. Count on a bare minimum of one month to cross, and that is without stopping or making any detours. Road repair is happening quickly, turning major routes from horrible dirt roads into simply bad dirt roads. Actual paved highways only exist between Likasi and Kasumbalesa in Katanga, as well as between Boma and the edge of Kinshasa Province. This is unlikely to change anytime soon.

These recommendations come with a warning, though – enquire at major and minor towns along the way about checkpoints, insurgencies, permits and various other dangers as you continue. Regions can been sealed off by police and army forces for reasons that will likely always remain unclear. I would recommend that if you are considering crossing the DR Congo overland that you employ a local guide from town to town, and possibly even some security. If you are considering anything between Kikwit and Kindu, I strongly suggest this – show up at the local police station with a grin and a wad of money, and see if they can get someone with a machine gun to ride in the back of the vehicle if they think the road ahead might be hairy. This was how things were done in Ituri for many years.

In the other Congo, travelling north from Brazzaville is not at all difficult. There are a few beaten paths that head to Okoyo and Franceville in Gabon, but until the road to Ouesso is fixed, there is no overland route to Cameroon aside from by foot. West from Brazzaville is a different story, though, on account of the Poule Region. Unfortunately the only way around this would be to travel south into Cabinda from Pointe Noire, and then cross into the DR Congo. Make sure you have your permits in order, and even if you do, expect to pay some serious money for the privilege of passing through this area – for vehicles from either Congo, Angola requires export permits to be purchased, which can run into thousands of dollars. It is unclear whether this applies to vehicles registered outside Africa, but enquiries can be made at the Angolan consulates in Matadi or Pointe Noire.

Preparing your vehicle Whatever you think may be needed on your trip, bring it. There are almost no places to repair a vehicle through either Congo once leaving major urban centres. Bring at least an extra set of tyres (yes, that's four), enough fluids to replace everything in your vehicle twice, and a self-powered winch for some tight spots. Bring extra parts as well as the tools to fix them. If you're not a mechanic, take a basic course before setting out: if something breaks, there will be no-one around to fix it, and likely no parts to fix it with anywhere inside the countries. This is by no means a comprehensive list; for more detailed advice, Bradt Travel Guides publishes a guide specifically for overlanding the continent called *Africa Overland: 4x4 – Motorbike-Bicycle-Truck*, which includes plenty of good advice for getting ready.

The Congos require a little more attention than usual for an overlanding journey through Africa. Most people will try and steal items from your vehicle while you are not looking, which means leaving nothing in full view if you're ever away from your vehicle. I would also recommend having a few 'secret' compartments welded to the inside frame of your vehicle where valuables can be stored. The chance of losing your vehicle outright is possible, but not likely; it is more important to have all of your papers in order, as corruption is still the main problem. Soldiers and police can conduct searches, and things will likely go missing.

Much the same goes for motorbikes. They can be bought in the countries, but the cheap bikes seen in small towns are generally not great for long distances. You'd need to purchase a decent touring bike, which runs to at least US$3,000. Accordingly, there are no restrictions on foreigners buying vehicles in either Congo.

ACCOMMODATION

From a hut in a roadside village in the deepest tropical jungle to the sparkling Grand Hôtel in Kinshasa, your options are wide-ranging. In the DR Congo, most major towns will have one still-operating hotel from those old colonial days that will be high on character and usually price as well. Then again, it may be abandoned. Kinshasa has plenty of mid-range hotels but almost nothing at the lower end where a traveller can crash, and two places of international repute where all of those from the outside world are expected to spend their time: the Memling Hôtel and Grand Hôtel, which hover between US$160 and US$450 for a night. Value is not good for these high-end hotels – you are paying a premium for basic services that are taken for granted even in neighbouring countries.

Mid-range hotels offer little for your money in the DR Congo. Cold water or even no water, no private phone, and insecure rooms are what one can get for even US$50 per night. At the low end, anything is possible but most likely includes a bed and an oil lamp and the owner pointing you in the direction of a hole in the ground called the 'bathroom'.

By contrast, in Congo-Brazzaville the average quality of hotel rooms is good with running water, electricity, and reasonable prices that range from US$15 and top out at US$300 for the international chains in Brazzaville. Only at the highest end of places will you get hot running water; at the lower end in the cities, you will get cold running water and on the fringes of civilisation you may only get a bucket if you're lucky. Shared toilets, or no toilets at all, are common across small villages. Washing from a bucket by candlelight is still something that occurs in the remote stretches of the Congos.

Sleeping under the stars is inadvisable for security reasons; if you are short on cash, ask around in any given town where the cheapest bed is and you will no doubt find a place. Most bars and music clubs have a few rooms at the back for mere dollars a night on offer, if you can convince them to charge you the normal rate. These are usually intended for prostitution but will be rented out if you can make a case for it. If you are on a long road trip, you will no doubt be shepherded to a place deemed 'safe' by your roadmates and made to feel welcome. Make sure you secure the door against intrusion.

✖ EATING AND DRINKING

Congolese like their beer, and there is no shortage of it anywhere. In the DR Congo, Primus beer is a national institution and 750mm bottles can be bought cheaply at small bars and restaurants across the nation. Most towns have at least one small restaurant, often empty, but with food made to order on asking. Use common sense when presented with a menu – if you are nowhere near a river, ordering seafood would not be the best idea. Things like fridges and freezers may not exist, so seek out foods that will not spoil at room temperature if you decide on a prepared meal in any small town.

Because of the lack of refrigeration, non-perishable foods are most common outside the major cities. Several types of meat and fish can be found in cans, sitting idle on shelves for months or even years before you pick them up. Check their seals, make sure they have not been opened, and bring your own can opener. Biscuits with artificial flavours make good snacks, and are incredibly cheap –

LIQUOR IN THE CONGOS

While Primus is the alcoholic beverage of choice across both Congos there are numerous other good drinking products just waiting to be imbibed available from Bralima – the Congolese brewing company, named thus on either side of the river, although Primus from Congo-Brazzaville might taste slightly different from Primus in Congo-Kinshasa, or it may not. After another 750ml bottle, it becomes hard to tell – and since the vast majority of beers come in 750ml measures it's best to share or get used to consuming large quantities of liquor.

There are other great beers aside from Primus in the Congos. Congo-Brazzaville's second brew is N'Gok, with a big green alligator on the label, and it's a lighter beer than Primus. Alcohol content is 0.5% more than Primus' 5%, and as usual, it's only available in 750ml bottles. The equivalent in the DR Congo is Skol, though this has a lighter alcohol content and is better if you have any plans for standing up after a few of them.

Darker beers are also popular. The heavy stuff is Turbo King, only available in the DR Congo. Advertisements galore call it 'a man's business', and indeed it is, with 6% alcohol and only available in 750ml bottles. A German-style beer is Doppel, again with 6% but with a much better taste in my opinion – it's an amber ale with a fruitier taste, a little more complex, and an ideal complement to a good meal.

Mützig is the only beer available that's sold in smaller bottles, and is a lighter German-style beer with only around 5% alcohol. Maltina is a non-alcoholic beer and is becoming increasingly popular with those who have to work the next morning.

Finally if you need the hard stuff it's available all too often in small plastic pouches for only a few cents. Whiskies, rums, vodkas, and other cheap knock-off liquors are in abundance and perhaps it makes life a little more bearable for those less fortunate, but these are definitely not for connoisseurs. However, if you're short on petrol, they may get you to the next town.

though still not cheap enough for most locals. Across the Congos there are some surprisingly awful 'glucose biscuits', made from several petroleum products and a small bit of wheat to give it that edible flavour. If you're truly short on cash these are a good option to keep your stomach from eating itself.

So what do the locals of Congo-Brazzaville eat, if not the well-sealed items in general stores? Manioc, bananas and sometimes large prawns. If you're on a road trip there will be plenty of opportunities to try these things, especially manioc – a staple food of the region, an otherwise bland-tasting plant that is sold as a small log wrapped in leaves. Palm wine is the local beverage for those who cannot afford beer – it is the fermented sap of palm trees, and you'll see it loaded and unloaded amongst small villages in large plastic jerry cans. It has a taste of alcoholised coconut juice with a bit of a moonshine quality on account of its local production. Foreigners drinking it in social settings will no doubt be quite a sight to the locals, who are not used to seeing outsiders drink their beverage of choice.

In fact, alcohol is far too easy to find amongst the small shops in Congo-Brazzaville. Strong beers in large, warm cans, and whiskies are available everywhere. If you enjoy drinking cheap liquor, you will have no problems in this country.

In the DR Congo the variety is wider – manioc and palm wine are still staples in the wilderness, but since the trade and transportation network is more developed you'll be able to find Western foods more easily. In the large cities and towns, eg: Kinshasa, Lubumbashi, and even Goma and Kisangani, you'll have at least one or two decent restaurants where there should be no concern over the quality of your food. Only in Kinshasa, Lubumbashi, Goma and Bukavu can you find truly international cuisine, and often at very high prices. The same rule goes for groceries in the DR Congo – if it doesn't keep for several months on the shelf, you probably won't find it in the smaller towns. Powdered milk is incredibly common across the country in lieu of fresh milk. On the positive side, fresh fruits are easy to find – oranges and bananas being the most common. The vegetable markets are often the best places for good, fresh food, and if you show up in a town on market day, you'll wonder how anyone could starve.

Along the roadsides in both countries any manner of fish, vegetable or meat is available as the locals will hold out random animal carcasses or the catch of the day as vehicles pass. I wouldn't trust these, as eating bushmeat can give you any number of problems. If you can get some local advice from someone you trust, it can introduce you to various meats and fish that you may not otherwise try. If you find something truly exotic being sold, again I would advise against it as endorsing the random killing of non-domesticated animals is something visitors should not do – wildlife populations are still quite fragile in both countries and this unregulated hunting should be discouraged.

Restaurant closing times aren't listed in the where to eat sections because, on the whole, establishments tend to shut up around midnight.

SPORTS

HUNTING I should begin this section with the statement that I condone the hunting of wild animals, for a trophy but preferably for food, and always in co-operation with local authorities. Hunters who visit Africa generally spend a large amount of money, employ a large number of local people who are desperate for any kind of work, and are bound by tight regulations on the conservation of local wildlife. I believe legal hunting can inject amounts of cash that can maintain wildlife populations over the long term; conversely, poachers get the brunt of my ire as they are making a bad situation worse.

Perhaps one of the tragedies of the Congos being so unstable, and plundered so often throughout their history, is that visiting them is often not the best way to see centuries-old artefacts of the kingdoms that pre-date current nation-states in the region. While contemporary art and culture thrive, museums chronicling the rich history of the people who settled in the heart of Africa are quite thin on the ground in their homeland. One must visit their colonial forebears for the best insight into their past to see the best selection of artefacts.

The best museum overall is in Brussels: the **Royal Museum for Central Africa** (*Leuvensesteenweg 13, 3080 Tervuren; www.africamuseum.be*), also called the Tervuren Museum, houses an extensive selection of art and artefacts from the Congo. They also have an excellent selection of books and research spanning numerous decades of scientists, explorers, anthropologists and archaeologists in the region. One permanent exhibit has photographs of the old colonial Congo, bringing to light the complete history of the Belgian Congo from ancient times up until independence.

Paris as well has several smaller museums devoted to African artworks, the newest of which is **Musée du Quai Branly** (*37 Quai Branly, portail Debilly, 75007 Paris; www.quaibranly.fr*), housing a large collection of colonial artworks including numerous artefacts from the Congo. Also worth investigating is **Librairie Anibwe** (*52 rue Greneta, 75002 Paris; nearest Metro: Opéra/Pyramides;* ☏ *01 45 08 48 33*) which houses countless books on central Africa.

For contemporary art, a travelling exhibit called **Africa Remix** (*www.africaremix.org.uk*) has been displayed around the world over the past two years. It has numerous artists from the DR Congo – though none from Congo-Brazzaville.

With that said, hunters should take note that animal populations are currently very fragile in the DR Congo especially. It is less of a concern in Congo-Brazzaville as the northern regions where hunters visit have not seen any real active conflict, and wildlife numbers are better managed. It is important for a hunter considering large game in the eastern DR Congo to be especially sensitive, and I would advise holding off on this area for several more years to allow animal populations to recover and ICCN to figure out how to regulate it. Many reports indicate they are far too eager to sell permits to hunting domains that are still too unregulated to make sustainable sport hunting viable.

Inquire with local tour operators for more information on hunting in the DR Congo. Congo-Brazzaville has well-organised hunting laws, including licensing fees based on each animal, export laws for trophies, and restrictions on ivory. The season begins in May and ends in October. Several reserves permit hunting, including areas around Odzala and Lefini. One is required to purchase a hunting permit in Brazzaville – contact the **Secrétariat Général à l'Administration du Territoire** in Brazzaville, on Boulevard des Armées.

SCUBA DIVING The diving industry is undeveloped across both Congos, and several unique considerations exist for those wishing to do some scuba in the region. Most of the Great Lakes have a build-up of methane in the water from volcanic activity, and Lake Albert is home to a huge variety of hippos – not your friendliest diving partners. The Congo River has very little visibility, even in the Mangroves Park where one might hope to see a manatee. Lac Mai Ndombe is pitch-black.

Practical Information SPORTS

2

The best option for diving would be in Lake Tanganyika, from Kalemie. Some small diving operations exist here for the purpose of collecting exotic fish – don't count on them assisting your own diving excursions in any way. That said, if you have all of your own equipment, and are well experienced at diving in high-altitude lakes, Lake Tanganyika may be the challenge you've been looking for.

FISHING Pointe Noire's deep-water fishing is a popular pastime for expatriates situated on the Atlantic coast, and a few charter operations will take tourists out on request. Several large fish have been caught here, including tarpon, sparidae, barracuda and tuna. Similarily in Moanda, DR Congo, a smaller and less developed industry exists for sport fishers. There are no specific tours for fishermen; it is therefore primarily an ad hoc charter business. While boats are readily available, any other kind of decent fishing gear will undoubtedly be unavailable unless you bring it with you.

There are some huge species in the river – world-record-sized catfish and Nile perch have been caught, as well as the giant tigerfish. A unique fish to the central African region, the giant tigerfish is a huge carnivorous beast that hunts other fish. It has gigantic teeth that stick out of its maw, and it is common throughout the Congo River. It can grow to huge proportions – up to 2m long, and weigh 40kg. Fishing them is dangerous, as they tend to hide in depressions at the bottom of the he attempted to subvert Soviet influences over African tribes. **Drums of the Congo** depicted a group of American adventurers searching for a mysterious meteor in the jungle.

After the independence of both countries in 1960, the interest in Congo waned considerably. The continued revolutions there, as well as the fact that the great African colonial project had come to an end, saw the era of white adventurers and savage warriors become somewhat passé, if not yet entirely politically incorrect. Hollywood would approach the Congo again in the 1968 film **The Mercenaries**, an action-adventure yarn based on Mike Hoare and Bob Denard's exploits fighting the UN and everyone else during their time in the Congo. The year 1970 saw an English comedy called **Carry on up the Congo** reignite some good old stereotypes when their group of explorers was captured by jungle women. In 1977, Hong Kong's emerging film industry made a King Kong rip-off that came to be known as **Colossus of Congo** in some markets, though the country was never referred to specifically – nonetheless, this would be the last time that Congo was used as a backdrop for stereotypical Africa until almost two decades later.

In 1995, the huge-budget Hollywood film **Congo**, based on the bestselling novel by Michael Crichton, brought modern stereotypes of Congo to a wide audience – greedy multi-national companies intent on exploiting central Africa's mineral wealth at all costs. Diamonds buried in the jungle, missing researchers, and evil businessmen all figure prominently in what is essentially a throwback to the golden era of jungle movies that saw groups of white explorers delve deep into central Africa.

Big-budget non-fiction films surrounding Congo's history have, comparably, been few and far between. Many were made during the time of Belgian and French Congo, but after independence is another story altogether. Two of the most recent (and easy to find) are **When We Were Kings** from 1996, a detailed account of 'The Rumble in the Jungle', Muhammad Ali and George Foreman's Kinshasa fight in 1974. In 2000, a large-budget French film explored the life and death of Patrice Lumumba in **Lumumba**.

river and wait for other fish to come along. Still, it is a pastime from the yacht club in Kinshasa to head out once in a while for these creatures. A great book to learn about this fish, and the methods for catching it, is *The Largest Tigerfish in the World – Goliath*, by Dann Douglas.

BIRDWATCHING The DR Congo has the largest recorded number of unique bird species in Africa. The other Congo shares its bird species with both the DR Congo and other countries of French central Africa. Its one near-endemic species is the Damara tern.

Eighteen endemic species have been counted in the DR Congo – most importantly the Congo peacock, Bedford's paradise flycatcher, Congo bay owl, Rockefeller's sunbird and three types of weavers.

The best birding region, with one of the highest numbers worldwide of species unique to the area, is the Albertine Rift as it straddles the border of the DR Congo and Uganda. West of Lake Albert are the Itombwe Mountains, which have been a boon for researchers over the years, though numerous species have been forgotten during many decades of strife. The mountains around Butembo and Lubero are especially remarkable, with 43 species unique to the area. Some migrate to the Ugandan side of the border, some don't. Highlights in this region include Albertine's francolin, Grauer's roadbill, Oberlander's groundthrush, Sassi's greenbull, Neumann's warblers, Grant's bluebill, Turner's eremomela, and too

The Congos are both nations that love the sport of football, perhaps too much so – while local matches are played at Kinshasa's stadium, more critical matches tend to be played abroad. DR Congo versus France, for example, was not played in the Congo. Yet everyone in the country was watching as they fought valiantly against the European team, on their scratchy televisions.

The DR Congo plays regularly abroad, and has a 69th-place world ranking owing to this fact. Across the river, Congo-Brazzaville's team does not do nearly as well, currently placed well out of the top 100.

Competition between the Congo teams has had a long history – the Stanley Pool Cup was organised by the Fédération de Football Association du Poule in colonial days, and called an international competition. It also included Angola, known as Portuguese Congo in those times. The winners could, therefore, boast of having won an international cup. Congo-Léopoldville dominated the competition from 1928 to 1938, with Brazzaville winning only once.

Upon independence the competition was renamed to the Coupe du Congo, and involved competing teams from all regions of both countries. No competitions were held prior to 1974 as the various revolutions and chaos that swept across the region did their damage to international sporting events. The competition was renamed again in 1982 to Coupe du Congo de Football, and continues to this day. No tournaments were held between 1997 and 1999, another turbulent period for both countries. Two Brazzaville teams have won the cup the most times, being the Diables Noirs and Etoile du Congo.

The DR Congo has its own leagues across the country, given the large travel distances between major urban centres. There is a national championship called Linafoot, pitting the best teams from every league against each other. In 1974 Zaire's national team qualified for the World Cup finals in Germany, the first team from sub-Saharan Africa to do so.

Both countries also have recently begun women's football tournaments. A great resource for up-to-date information on football in the Congos is at the website (*www.tpmazembe.com*).

many more to list here. Many others could exist, or migrate through the Congos; however, little real research has been done outside the eastern corridors.

There are many other low-lying lakes and wetlands in the Congos where birding is an excellent option. Near Kinshasa is Lac Ma Vallée, once a popular birding site, which remains accessible. Mount Hoyo Reserve has numerous species unique to Ituri. The wetlands near Likasi and L'Upemba Park are also especially abundant.

GIVING SOMETHING BACK

In the first decade of the 21st century, the Congo colonial project has come full circle – what was originally seen as an escape from the continued quagmires of their African colonies became a point of blame for the European powers that carved up the continent in 1886. In those days, it may have been unclear as to what exactly the colonial future had in store for the Congos; yet, in many ways, their current existence is a direct by-product of the pretences from which they originated.

Congo Free State has become a true meeting of international organisations; King Léopold's vision of a free trade zone in the middle of Africa has, in a roundabout way, come true. It may not have manifested itself into the glorious semi-nation that the Belgian monarch had initially sold to those at the Berlin Conference; indeed, its purpose was obfuscated and manipulated deliberately by anyone who cared to be involved.

Yet nowhere else has there been such a continuous, perpetual and persistent meeting of international non-governmental organisations (NGOs) as in the DR Congo. This may extend from the fact that the 'nation', per se, was so badly managed by the Belgians. Or, it may extend from a sense of purpose by Western nations to correct the errors of the colonial agenda.

It is, nevertheless, ultimately a fitting present for the current DR Congo. Bad French is spoken as often as English in Kinshasa. The media broadcast in any number of tribal languages. French is still the current *lingua franca* of the nation, yet it is changing, slowly, surely, as the nation coalesces as a whole.

This may seem unlikely to the continued efforts of NGOs who have been in the region for decades, as it may be to the casual newsreader who observes that it all seems hopeless. Corruption is a by-product of poverty; the destruction of one's natural history, and disrespect for one's country, are the by-products of corruption. And corruption in itself is the by-product of an ineffective governmental system.

The DR Congo was never meant to exist into perpetuity as a national entity, yet we perceive it as such. This is the colonial legacy, and the Congolese must live it. Their duty is to make do, at least, with the institutions given to them while building new ones on their own. It is the obligation of Western governments, and aid organisations across the globe, to guide them along a path of order out of their current chaos.

The tourist also has a duty, one as critical to the nation's well-being as any other individual. The tourist can make known the great value that the DR Congo's cultural and natural institutions are to the world at large. Respect for their significance, in this case, must flow outward to inward. Only if the Congolese perceive their natural history and wildlife to be valuable will they ensure that they are protected while the rest of the nation develops. It is a parallel development that must take place – all the more critical, since once animal populations and wilderness are significantly decimated, they can never be fully recovered.

Much of this carries over to the Republic of Congo. Long a forgotten footnote in history, barely noticed as a nation with its own troubles when a monumental neighbour with the same name lives beside it, the Republic of Congo has a long road ahead of it. In some ways it is in a better position to promote tourism and development, and in other ways it is still far behind. Central African practices such as corruption and bribery for even the simplest tasks are tolerated far more than they deserve to be. Infrastructure is still a shambles. It is an incredible irony that in Pointe Noire, the oil town that it is, there can still be shortages of fuel that will bring the town to a halt for several days.

Somewhere in all of this madness and strife, majestic nations exist. It takes outside voices to tell these cultures that their current situations are not acceptable. It also takes outside voices to provide incentives, both financially and spiritually, to those within the Congos who are seeking to improve them.

None of this will be easy; none of it will be simple. We all play a part in the preservation of a global heritage, and the promotion of a global culture where one can respect their origins, their landscape and their language. Amidst the usual chaos and madness that can punctuate a visit to the Congos, try and envision these nations and people for what they could become; and, if you see a way in which you can assist them to that goal, then the world at large will be a better place for your participation.

CHILDREN AND FAMILIES

Action Against Hunger (*www.actionagainsthunger.org*) International organisation seeking to improve the health of families & eliminate hunger. Active in both Congos.

Congo Action (*www.congoaction.co.uk*) British charity working in Kivu Province that arranges child sponsorship, development of school facilities & livestock acquisition.

GOAL (*www.goal.ie*) Provides short- & long-term assistance to families. Assists in rebuilding infrastructure, training local workers, & providing tools & seeds.

ICS/Le Cep (*www.icscopper.com*) Operates a farm & orphanage in Likasi, DR Congo.

International Save the Children Alliance (*www.savethechildren.net*) Focuses on protecting children & rebuilding their living environments as affected by war.

Oxfam (*www.oxfam.org.uk*) Operates both short- & long-term development projects in the DR Congo.

War Child International (*www.warchild.org*) Helping to rehabilitate children affected by wars in the DR Congo.

Watchlist on Children and Armed Conflict (*www.watchlist.org*) Advocacy group reporting violations against the rights of children in armed conflict.

Women's Commission for Refugee Women and Children (*www.womenscommission.org*) Helps to defend the rights & livelihoods of refugee women & children.

GENERALIST AND OTHER GROUPS

Agency for Technical Co-operation and Development (ACTED) (*www.acted.org*) French organisation that assists with long-term economic development strategies. Active in both Congos.

Amnesty International (*www.amnesty.org*) Advocacy group that monitors & reports human rights violations worldwide.

Care International (*www.care.org*) Large organisation aimed at fighting poverty worldwide.

Concern (*www.concern.ie*) Provides long-term development work for communities to experience an increased quality of life.

Forum on Early Warning and Response (*www.fewer-international.org*) Provides analysis of the conflict & produces papers to advocate & effect shifts in policy, guided by local & regional initiatives.

Global Witness Limited (*www.globalwitness.org*) Conducts field research & trains monitors to expose the link between the exploitation of resources & human rights violations.

Helen Keller International (*www.hki.org*) Provides training & assistance for vision & nutrition programmes.

Human Rights Watch (*www.hrw.org*) Conducts field research to research & report on human rights violations. Active in both Congos.

International Crisis Group (*www.crisisgroup.org*) Conducts field research & political analysis to report on conflict regions & provide concrete advocacy plans to prevent, reduce or eliminate current or future conflicts.

Institute for War and Peace Reporting (*www.iwpr.net*) Trains local reporters to promote local journalistic efforts in covering conflicts.

Telecoms Sans Frontières (*www.tsfi.org*) Specialises in providing emergency telecommunications to regions in conflict.

Welthungerhilfe – German Agro Action (*www.welthungerhilfe.de/home_eng.html*) German group focusing on rebuilding agricultural lands, safe drinking water, crafts & small business training. Active in both Congos.

World Organisation Against Torture (*www.omct.org*) Coalition of organisations lobbying against detention & torture practices in the DR Congo. Provides assistance to victims & campaigns for the rights of women & children.

LANDMINES

Handicap International (*www.handicap-international.com*) Offers a support network in the DR Congo for victims of landmines.

Mines Advisory Group (*www.mag.org.uk*) Assists in mine clearance & safe detonation of mine & ammunition stockpiles.

MEDICAL ASSISTANCE

Aide Médicale Internationale (*www.amifrance.org*) French group that seeks to restore & expand access to health facilities.

Direct Relief International (*www.directrelief.org*) Provides medical aid & supplies to local hospitals & emergency relief to war & disaster victims.

Doctors Worldwide (*www.doctorsworldwide.org*) Provides aid & medical relief in regions where none exists & provides methods to prevent outbreaks of disease.

Medair (*www.medair.org*) Swiss-based medical organisation that provides emergency & long-term medical assistance in the DR Congo.

Médecins du Monde (*www.medecinsdumonde.org*) French-based group that provides medical assistance in the DR Congo.

PARKS AND ENVIRONMENT

Africa Wildlife Foundation (*www.awf.org*) Has initiatives in the DR Congo for creating new wildlife refuges & promoting sustainable land use.

Birdlife (*www.birdlife.org*) Provides assistance to ensure the conservation of bird species.

Dian Fossey Foundation (*www.gorillafund.org*) Dedicated to promoting the plight of the mountain gorilla.

Great Ape Survival Project (*www.unep.org/grasp*) UN-sponsored organisation dedicated to protecting the traditional habitat of primates.

Wildlife Conservation Society (WCS) (*www.wcs.org/drcongo-wcs.org*) The premier conservation group in Congo-Brazzaville, with extensive lobby efforts for parks, reserves & animal conservation in the country. Also has an effective programme in the DR Congo.

REFUGEES

Internal Displacement Monitoring Centre (*www.internal-displacement.org*) Conducts missions in the Congos to measure refugee numbers & provide advocacy to various aid organisations.

International Medical Corps (*www.imcworldwide.org*) Provides emergency medical assistance to disaster- & war-ravaged regions.

International Rescue Committee (*www.theirc.org*) Provides short-term relief to refugees & assists in long-term development projects.

RELIGIOUS AFFILIATED GROUPS

Action by Churches Together (ACT) (*www.act-intl.org*) Worldwide church organisation aimed at assisting those caught in emergencies & armed conflict.

Caritas (*www.caritas.org*) Catholic Church organisation that provides long-term assistance to developing regions.

Catholic Agency for Overseas Development (CAFOD) (*www.cafod.org*) Development wing of the Catholic Church in England & Wales. Provides a large variety of projects aimed at reducing poverty & improving health.

Catholic Relief Services (*www.crs.org*) American Catholic-based organisation that provides various assistance to local communities. Active in both Congos.

Christian Aid (*www.christian-aid.org.uk*) Aid agency of churches in the United Kingdom & Ireland, working primarily through local organisations.

Médecins Sans Frontières (*www.msf.org*) Provides emergency medical aid. Active in both Congos.

Jane Goodall Foundation (*www.totallywild.net/conservation.php*) Focused on rescuing chimpanzees from the bushmeat trade; runs a sanctuary in western Congo-Brazzaville.

HELP Congo (*www.panafricanprimates.org*) Runs a chimpanzee sanctuary in Conkouati-Douli National Park, rescuing live chimps found in bushmeat markets.

John Aspinall Foundation (*blog.aspinalls.com*) Has a rehabilitation site in Congo-Brazzaville for orphaned gorillas with the intention of reintroducing them into the wild.

The Bushmeat Project (*www.bushmeat.net*) Dedicated to raising awareness of bushmeat hunting across central Africa.

Norwegian Refugee Council (*www.nrc.no*) Helps protect internal refugees through food distribution, legal assistance & shelter construction.

Première Urgence (*www.premiere-urgence.org*) Multi-levelled aid organisation providing emergency relief & post-disaster & post-war development to affected regions. Active in northwestern DR Congo.

Refugees International (*www.refugeesinternational.org*) Provides assistance to refugees, active in the DR Congo.

Church World Service (*www.churchworldservice.org*) Relief wing of the Protestant, Orthodox & Anglican churches in the USA. Provides a wide variety of development projects to both Congos.

Dan Church Aid (*www.dca.dk*) Danish organisation that provides long-term aid to reduce poverty. Also active in landmine removal.

Development and Peace (*www.devp.org*) Development agency wing of the Canadian Catholic Church. Operates a wide variety of long-term development projects.

Jesuit Refugee Service (*www.jesref.org*) Catholic-based organisation that assists refugees. Active in both Congos.

Malteser International (*www.malteser.de*) Relief wing of the Order of Malta, based on Catholic principles.

Mennonite Central Committee (*www.mcc.org*) Provides a multitude of assistance initiatives to those affected by war in the DR Congo.

www.stuffyourrucksack.com is a website set up by TV's Kate Humble which enables travellers to give direct help to small charities, schools or other organisations in the country they are visiting. Maybe a local school needs books, a map or pencils, or an orphanage needs children's clothes or toys – all things that can easily be 'stuffed in a rucksack' before departure. The charities get exactly what they need and travellers have the chance to meet local people and see how and where their gifts will be used.

The website describes organisations that need your help and lists the items they most need. Check what's needed in the Congos, contact the organisation to say you're coming and bring not only the much-needed goods but an extra dimension to your travels and the knowledge that in a small way you have made a difference.

Norwegian Church Aid (*www.nca.no*) Promotes human rights & development in co-operation with local church organisations.

United Methodist Committee on Relief (*www.gbgm-umc.org/umcor*) Relief wing of the United Methodist Church.

World Relief (*www.wr.org*) Provides numerous services via empowering local Christian churches.

Part Two

DEMOCRATIC REPUBLIC OF CONGO

Name Democratic Republic of Congo

Location Central Africa – from the Atlantic coast eastward to the Great Lakes of east Africa

Size 2,345,410km²

Climate Tropical in the north, with rains from November to April. In the south, semi-dry savanna with rains from December to March.

Population 63 million (2007 estimate)

Life expectancy 52 years

Capital Kinshasa: population around eight million

Other major cities Lubumbashi, Kisangani, Goma, Mbuji-Mayi

Languages French (official), Lingala, Kikongo, Tshiluba, Swahili

Religion Christianity, Islam, Kimbanguism, traditional beliefs

Currency Congolese franc (Fc; trades as CDF): £1 = 1,077Fc; € 1 = 806Fc; US$1 = 549Fc (Feb 2008)

Airlines Hewa Bora, Wimbi Dira, Bravo Air Congo

International airports Kinshasa N'djili (FIH), Lubumbashi Luano (FBM)

International telephone code +243

Time GMT + 1 from the Atlantic coast to Kisangani; GMT + 2 from Kananga and Lubumbashi east

Electrical voltage 220V

Flag Bright blue with a five-pointed star in the upper left-hand corner, and a wide red stripe with yellow lining running diagonally from bottom left to top right

National sport Football (soccer)

Public holidays 1 January (New Year), 4 January (Martyrs of Independence Day), 1 May (Labour Day), 17 May (Liberation Day), 30 June (Independence Day), 17 November (Army Day)

3

Background Information

HISTORY

THE DECLINE OF THE LUBAS AND THE ARRIVAL OF TIPPU TIP In the east, trade routes were active with slave exports to Arab traders along the Indian Ocean – they had established their first fort in eastern Congo in 1860 at Nyangwe, on the shores of the Lualaba River. Contact with the Portuguese had also opened up trading along the Atlantic coast, and the Luba Kingdom was heavily active in managing a flow of goods into and out of their region. The Lubas as well had seen their territory shrink as a result of Garengaze expanding on its eastern edge, and its decentralised system of power sharing had reduced its influence across the region. With new African kingdoms emerging and slavery picking away at the most able bodied, the population was slowly being drained as the power of European and Arab slave traders increased.

Tippu Tip was a Swahili-Arab businessman and landowner who was employed by sultans in Zanzibar, and heavily involved in establishing trade routes from east Africa to the Indian Ocean coast. Half Arab and half African, he was already active in ivory and slave trading by the age of 18 and was a governor under the Zanzibari sultans early on in his life. His commercial exploits went from strength to strength as he moved further inland with a massive army (nearly 50,000 at its peak), searching for more resources to expand his own estate and those he worked for. Eventually Tip's army would collide with the Luba Kingdom, though only marginally at first, and some accounts state that they lived side by side for a period of time. Tippu Tip, though, was relentless in his business interests and conducted continuous raids throughout the region for more slaves and ivory. In 1875, he established a headquarters in the region at Kasongo, which would be the beginning of his own state within eastern Congo – nominally called Tippu Tip's State, though his personal kingdom was always considered an outpost of the Zanzibari sultans before 1885.

Tippu Tip's State, at its height, stretched from the northern shores of Lake Tanganyika to the northeast corner of the Congo River. It was fully in his control only briefly, between 1884 and 1887, though his power and influence would linger throughout the region for decades. It was during this peak that he would encounter a curious, and somewhat belligerent, American explorer.

STANLEY'S VOYAGE A Welsh orphan who emigrated to the USA, Henry Morton Stanley became a journalist later in life and served as the overseas correspondent for the *New York Herald*. There was great interest in the day, of what had happened to British doctor David Livingstone, who had disappeared into the hinterlands of southern Africa several years earlier. In 1874, with the backing of the *New York Herald*'s owner, Stanley travelled to Zanzibar in search of him, mostly as a publicity stunt for the newspaper. Stanley spared no expense in setting himself up for the voyage, and started moving west into the deeper stretches of African wilderness.

The discovery of David Livingstone on the shores of Lake Tanganyika was a triumph for Henry Morton Stanley, and also a call for action from Livingstone's friends and supporters back in England. No sooner had Stanley departed for his voyage down the Congo River than the compatriots of Livingstone began to plan expeditions to get him out of the dangerous corner of the dark continent that he had found himself in.

Two expeditions from the west and east coasts of Africa would set out to rescue Livingstone. Sir Henry Rawlinson would fund the expedition from the west coast entirely of his own accord, and employ Lieutenant W J Grandy to lead it. They would set out from the town of Ambriz, just north of Luanda; Grandy had planned to find the Congo River from there, based on Henry Morton Stanley's new mappings of the route, and arrive at the closest point to Livingstone as possible.

Even at the outset, there was doubt as to whether the river would bring them close enough to Livingstone, but the urgency for rescuing the doctor was palpable amongst English dignitaries, and so Grandy's expedition went ahead. They finally set out in 1874, but by then were far too late for Livingstone.

Grandy and his men pushed forward into unexplored and barely mapped territory inside the African continent. They wandered in circles looking for the Congo River – being too far south, and lacking any real maps or directions for where the river may be, the expedition became lost regularly. Finally a message was sent from the Royal Geographical Society in London – Livingstone was confirmed dead, and the eastern expedition was nearing his last-known position. They were ordered to turn back.

Grandy would not make it, though – he fell ill from malaria or yellow fever, and died somewhere east of Luanda. The expedition was not an entire waste, however – the general mapping of the region was helped extensively due to Grandy's sacrifice. The relationship between the mouth of the Congo River and Luanda was confirmed.

He found Livingstone on the shores of Lake Tanganyika, and became all the more famous for his success.

Stanley was a prototypical 19th-century adventurer of sorts, high on himself and his exploits with low opinions of local people and their cultures. His new-found fame brought his name to the steps of the *Daily Telegraph* in Britain, who commissioned him to trace the Congo River from its source to the sea.

Continuing on his journey, Stanley moved westward from Lake Tanganyika and deep into the unknown, and it was during this time that he met with Tippu Tip. Tip considered Stanley an interesting character who might be of some use, and indeed Tip had not used the Congo River as a navigable route until Stanley's arrival in the region. Henry Morton Stanley's expedition is recounted in his two-volume book *Through the Dark Continent*. Stanley was the first to document the river in its full length, including its pitfalls. The Congo River had two notorious sections of rapids that would make it difficult for a complete route to be feasible: at Boyoma Falls, near modern-day Kisangani, and Yalala Falls, after Malebo Pool and Kinshasa-Brazzaville – where James Kingston Tuckey had turned back 60 years earlier. Stanley's journey from Zanzibar to the Atlantic coast took 999 days, and confirmed that the Congo River could be used for large ships between the two sections of rapids. He returned to Europe triumphant in 1877, though his reckless manner of interacting with the local population was criticised.

KING LÉOPOLD II European interest in Africa was growing once again and, after centuries of continued trading along coastal outposts, conflicting claims between

European powers of territory on the continent were increasing. Léopold II saw his small kingdom of Belgium as requiring a colony of some sort to secure its position of power in the world, and made several initial attempts in more traditional methods of creating a Belgian colony abroad. The lack of success at these brought him to reconsider his approach at a government-to-colony solution, and instead moved in a different direction – he created a private holding company, the Association Internationale Africaine, or AIA, and sought to acquire territory as private property for his new enterprise.

The AIA was originally heralded as a humanitarian project aimed at shared learning, shared exploration, and the betterment of the African continent as a whole. Founded in 1876, Léopold invited several dozen geographers, explorers and other experts to a conference in Brussels to form the association. Léopold from the beginning had engineered the AIA in such a way that it would benefit him and his imperial goals, and centred the organisation primarily on the formation of a central African state. However the other members of the association also had similar goals, and what had originally (though perhaps not honestly) emerged as a method for furthering European knowledge of the continent had turned into a front for imperialist powers to further secure their own interests in Africa.

In 1878, Léopold began funding another organisation, the International Congo Society, or Comité d'Etudes du Haut-Congo (CEHC). In collaboration with a British shipping tycoon and Belgian banker, their interest was primarily in the colonisation of Congo. Other European nations, especially France and Portugal, were not so keen on seeing the colonisation of Congo by the Belgians and protested their alleged expansion and exploration into the region. By 1881, Pierre Savorgnan de Brazza had already made an expedition to the rapids at Stanley Pool from the Atlantic and founded Brazzaville, and Léopold's dream of a Congo colony was quickly losing ground.

In 1879, Léopold contacted Henry Morton Stanley regarding his returning to the Congo River under the auspices of exploration for the Belgian king. Stanley agreed, and the relationship between the two would punctuate the creation of a Belgian Congo. The CEHC was renamed the Association Internationale du Congo, or AIC.

While the front of the AIC was that of a humanitarian mission, its true intents were relayed to Stanley: he was requested by Léopold to secure treaties, purchase land, resources, and anything else that he could get his hands on in the Congo region. Any treaties signed were required to cede all power and authority over to the AIC. Léopold's method was unique in a way, in that he was acquiring personal property on his own behalf and removing his nation of Belgium from the situation entirely. He was also commissioning other expeditions from the east coast of Africa to the interior, though they were far less successful.

Léopold's public explanation of his exploits focused on how the AIC was to build hospitals and schools across the territory and enrich the lives of African people. As Stanley continued his own mission to secure the resources and territories of King Léopold II in central Africa, all suspicions were assuaged by these public explanations. Belgium itself and Léopold, having little history of imperialist atrocities, would be seen as an ideal neutral party that could bring civilisation to the African hinterlands. Aristocrats and philanthropists across Europe even donated to his cause, lauding his humanitarian interests in the region.

By 1884, Stanley had secured a massive stretch of land in the middle of the African continent in the name of King Léopold and the AIC. This was not Belgian territory, nor of any other nation. Léopold was astute, though, and had made an agreement with the US president of the time to recognise his Congo colony as Belgian territory. President Chester Arthur was impressed by the noble-sounding goals of the Congo territory, and Léopold's emissary to Arthur compared the project to the United States's own amicable goals in Liberia of freeing slaves to their home continent to improve their lives. With his territory formally recognised, Léopold was in a solid position to make a case for its continued existence as a unique and separate colony at the Berlin Conference of 1884.

THE CONGO FREE STATE Increased interest in the African continent saw a month-long meeting of European nations at the Berlin Conference of 1884, as decisions were made on how exactly to divide up the continent of Africa to satisfy everyone's interests. Léopold II and his emissaries were active behind the scenes, convincing the larger colonial powers of France and Germany to the importance of free trade zones across Africa: the Congo River would remain free for shipping, though this would rarely be useful as it could not be navigated too far inland. With the support of the United States, Léopold's pitch for a Belgian colony at the centre of the continent was well received. The Congo state itself would be considered a unique bastion amongst African colonies, and remain in possession of the AIC. It would be considered a free trade zone, a sort of middle point to keep colonial powers in check, where businesses could operate without crippling tariffs or other governmental intrusion. All of this was presented as a good thing. Because of this special status, and the fact that the new-found Congo state was in effect private property, Léopold could do what he liked with the region while being removed from any diplomatic pressures.

In May 1885, King Léopold renamed the AIC to recognise that his colony had been formally recognised and enshrined in treaty, and the Congo Free State was born. It stretched from the mouth of the Congo River all the way east to Lake Tanganyika. Tippu Tip had agreed to cede his territory to the Belgian king in exchange for acting as a governor of the eastern region, and from this point onward worked under Léopold II until 1890 when one of his sons took rule of the territory.

THE RUBBER TRADE A new invention changed the fortunes of the Congolese for ever – the pneumatic tyre. Demand for new inflatable rubber tyres in the 1890s was insatiable, and so was the demand for rubber to make them. While the rest of the world was trying to increase the capacity of rubber, Léopold's Congo was discovered to have a very valuable resource – the rubber tree.

The Belgians had begun ruling the Congo Free State with little regard for the local population, and the demand for rubber saw an entirely new method of resource extraction – since rubber trees were buried deep in the jungle, local men were threatened with death or mutilation to go into the forest and extract rubber from the trees. Rubber in the Congo was in fact a vine that needed to be tapped, and the liquid poured into a bucket. Tales of exploitation were many during this period, but it went generally unreported due to the inaccessibility of the Congo Free State. When death was no longer a significant motivator for local men to collect rubber for export, Belgian forces began holding families hostage and cutting off hands. A whip called the *chicotte* was used regularly against those who dared to oppose their masters.

Léopold, famously, never set foot in the Congo himself. The actions against local populations occurred through his Force Publique, Belgian officials and Africans recruited into a military system that was heavily regimented and as harsh as the terrain in which it operated. They were notoriously cruel, and interested strictly in profiting from whatever they could in the Congo Free State. What happened to their labourers, then, was mostly incidental.

While these deeds were not unique to the Congo Free State at the time, the scale of the operation and the damage done to the local population was enormous.

Léopold and his Congo Free State could get away with it in all cases, thanks to the nation being not really a nation but rather a piece of private property, a free-trade zone, with no significant infrastructure or authority over it. For much of the 1890s the rubber boom sent profits right back into Léopold's personal bank account, and not even the country of Belgium. It would take two African-Americans' voyages down the Congo River to discover what was going on, and report it to the world.

THE HUMANITARIAN DISASTER George Washington Williams was a historian who was born and raised in the United States. A journalist by trade, he had a large interest in the originating continent of freed slaves. He founded an African-American newspaper, and wrote the first history of African-Americans in the 19th century. He would also be the first person to notice that something was deeply wrong in Léopold's Congo.

With several interests surrounding his desire to visit the Congo Free State, he was granted an audience with Léopold in 1889 and received permission to visit, and indeed his blessing. He departed soon after for Stanley Pool, to the new settlement of Léopoldville on its banks, and began witnessing what had been hidden to the world. His six months in the Congo, travelling by steamboat from Léopoldville upriver to Stanleyville, allowed him to witness the atrocities inflicted on the Congolese as they were forced into labour.

This prompted him to write his famous 'Open Letter' to King Léopold, addressing to him all that he had seen in the Congo Free State, and demanding (though in the formal tone of the letter, closer to requesting) that something be done about continued abuses. The letter was published, distributed as a pamphlet in both the USA and Europe. He would also write 'A Report upon the Congo-State and Country to the President of the United States of America' which further documented what was occurring.

There had been increasing friction between Léopold's Congo and businesspeople around the world as they had effectively been shut out of doing any work in the so-called 'Free Trade Zone' of Africa. This disaster of epic proportions served their purposes well, by highlighting the Congo Free State's failure to live up to its original proposed intent.

As George Washington Williams was departing from the Congo another African-American arrived, William Henry Sheppard. Arriving as a Presbyterian missionary, he had similar interests as Williams in African-American history and saw contact with Africa as a chance to escape the deep racial divisions inherent in the USA. He picked up where George Washington Williams left off – he was not in the Congo for a brief period as a journalist, but spent two decades there. It was his persistence in bringing to light the continued atrocities that would finally prompt the world to action.

CONGO REFORM ASSOCIATION Inspired by George Washington Williams's 'Open Letter' and continued lobbying from William Henry Sheppard as he wrote countless articles and letters of protest to highlight the atrocities taking place, the Congo Reform Association was formed in 1904. Founded by two Englishmen, Edmund Dene Morel and Roger Casement, their cause was backed by many famous writers of the time including Joseph Conrad – who had travelled down the Congo River in 1898 and enshrined for ever the madness that was occurring in his novel *Heart of Darkness*. The Congo Reform Association was, in effect, the first human rights organisation the world had ever known and would be a precursor to future human rights groups the world over. Their actions yielded success with the creation of a Commission of Inquiry that would travel to Congo to see if the allegations of abuse were accurate. The resulting 150-page report confirmed everything that had been said by Casement and Morel, Williams and Sheppard, and countless others who had travelled to the Congo Free State over the previous 15 years. As this report became public and the Belgians' opinion of their king began to slip, Léopold's Congo Free State would soon see some transformations.

FROM CONGO FREE STATE TO BELGIAN CONGO The Commission of Inquiry was the death knell for Léopold's Congo Free State. He was 70 years old at the time of its publication and faced with overwhelming opposition in the private sphere and international pressure, he needed to blink. There were also local problems: the natives were restless so to speak, and rebellions were occurring simultaneously across Congo's interior. The authority of the Force Publique had always been nominal far away from European outposts but in the early 1900s the Shi, Luba and Katanga kingdoms, among others, rebelled and formed their own small states within the Congo. These rebellions would not be quelled until World War I.

It was in these dark days as the inquiry moved forward, as Léopold's popularity plummeted and with his advancing years, he agreed to cede the state from his AIC organisation to the Belgian government. However, Léopold did not simply hand the state over to Belgium: he sold it, and spent two years negotiating a fair price for the colony.

In 1908, with the negotiations complete, Congo Free State had become Belgian Congo. Belgium assumed the debts of Congo Free State as well as paying King Léopold a massive sum for the colony in itself. Belgium would also finish several building projects within the Congo, assume various loans that Léopold had drawn for 'infrastructure improvements' in the country, and pay 50 million francs to Léopold himself. Not only did Léopold take nearly every shred of profit that Congo Free State made during its existence, but even after he had parted with the money would come out far ahead of the game.

In Boma in 1908 a ceremony made the change official, though the effects of this would be, in many ways, nominal. There was continued international interest in how the Congolese people were faring and other Europeans, among them Wilfred Thesiger, visited the Belgian Congo to ensure that reforms were taking place. Others were madly extracting rubber for as long as they could, until whenever they were stopped and requested to leave. Missionaries continued to keep a close eye on what transpired in their regions of the Congo. And in 1909, King Léopold II of Belgium died at a summer home, possibly from cancer. His assets and vast sums of wealth gained from exploiting the Congo Free State would remain within the possession of his family. The Congo Reform Association, content with the outcomes of what had transpired in Congo Free State, dissolved in 1913.

BELGIAN CONGO AND THE WORLD WARS Since Léopold had taken the brunt of international pressure for abuses in Africa, the Belgian regime that emerged after his rule could only make matters better. And yet, only slightly – forced labour was still a fact of life, though the most insidious acts of the Léopold era such as corporal punishment and kidnapping were banned. The Belgian authority improved matters nominally, but not greatly, and Belgian Congo would remain a similar place to what it was as Congo Free State.

In 1906, a major Belgian company was founded after initial research revealed vast amounts of underground wealth in Congo: the Union Minière du Haut Katanga (UMHK) was Belgian owned and operated, and quickly set about establishing mines deeper into Congolese territory. The demand for minerals would be equal to, if not greater than the demand for rubber, and the Congolese found themselves again put into a situation of forced labour.

The Congolese were also conscripted into the military, and in World War I were tasked with fighting off German troops who had invaded German East Africa in 1916. Those who were left in eastern Congo were all engaged in the war effort in some way, and with this mobilisation several local rebellions were quelled.

The years after World War I were some of the best that the Congo state had known for decades – though still punctuated by poor working conditions and a merciless set of European companies, the Congolese were no longer stuck in a circle of forced labour and exploitation – or perhaps, not as harsh. UMHK expanded its operations and made them more sophisticated for the time being, creating large mining towns across the southern and eastern regions of the country and employing large amounts of the population. Léopoldville had expanded into a decent-sized town.

Yet anti-colonial attitudes were prominent and with the growing rights of locals, their empowerment led them to more bold displays of dissent. Hundreds of thousands in the west of Congo joined a religious cult called Kimbanguism, and its founder, Simon Kimbangu, was imprisoned as a result – the unified numbers scared the Belgian authorities and Kimbanguism was quickly banned. Strikes were occurring across numerous mines in Katanga, and UMHK on occasion used deadly force to quell them. Belgian Congo was still little more than a free-trade zone with resource-based companies coming in and using local labour for extraction. Anything resembling a cohesive state, or national identity, was still far away.

During World War II, Belgian Congo's resources would prove useful to the Allies in the manufacturing of their weapons. Famously, the US had bought uranium from Congo for use in its atomic bombs. World War II saw several social changes in Congo as migration moved large populations away from rural lives and into cities; urbanisation and the notion of a national identity were beginning to form.

INDEPENDENCE FOR BELGIAN CONGO In the early 1950s the Congolese finally became citizens: they were allowed to own land, were put on equal ground with Europeans, were given access to public services, including the same courts used by foreigners. They were also given the right to vote at a local level, while their country would remain a colony of Belgium. Nonetheless there were rewards for becoming less African and more European with a programme of 'matriculation'. These évolués were heralded by the Belgian government for their personal advancements to becoming more 'sophisticated' per se, and given fine jobs in the public sector. While segregation by race was dwindling, segregation due to cultural assimilation was rising.

Attitudes like this were the catalyst for organisations calling for outright independence from Belgium; this was also the era of other African states lobbying for their own independence, and inspiration for one Joseph Kasa-Vubu to form the political party of Abako, or Association des Bakongo. The Belgians as well were considering the notion of an independent Congolese state, though some 30 years into the future. Abako famously demanded immediate independence – and might have been more careful for what they wished.

Abako gained instant popularity amongst voters across the Congo and did well in local elections. In 1958, Kasa-Vubu was voted in as leader of the Dendale commune, a small sector of Léopoldville, and began to make speeches demanding that Congo be recognised as its own nation. A large-scale revolt across Léopoldville in January 1959 had changed the Belgian attitude towards independence, and the government stated that it could occur sooner than later.

This, in fact, was not a good thing for the Congo. The country itself was still very much a disconnected stretch of wilderness with a few outposts of cities interspersed with small towns. A few meagre road and rail connections existed, but Congo was still mostly a thick wilderness. There was one other national political party aside from Abako, the Mouvement Nationale Congolais or MNC, headed by Patrice Lumumba. The mention of Belgium's government planning independence paved the way for several revolts and secessions in 1959: in Kasai, Luba and Baluba tribes fought while in Stanleyville another revolt resulted in the arrest of Lumumba and his subsequent imprisonment in Shaba Province (modern-day Katanga). The MNC would experience numerous fractures and Lumumba would remain in prison until independence.

Belgium's interest in putting all of these pieces back together in time for an independence ceremony that could be seen as honourable was quite slim. It was better, then, to cut and run altogether and escape the mess of their Congo colony entirely, and on 30 June 1960 that is exactly what occurred: Belgian Congo would be known as the Republic of Congo, with its capital remaining at Léopoldville. The symbolic head of state would be Joseph Kasa-Vubu and prime ministerial duties would be handled by Patrice Lumumba. The flag would remain the same at independence, and Belgium would at last be free of their colonial obligations. For the new state of the Republic of Congo-Léopoldville, though, their difficulties were only beginning.

FROM INDEPENDENCE TO CHAOS Less than two weeks after the Republic of Congo became its own nation, it began tearing itself apart. A mutiny in the army on 4 July 1960 pitted its European officers against its African soldiers. The officers were deposed and a native Congolese man, Joseph Désiré Mobutu, would rise to be named chief of staff. The mutiny spread across Katanga and the northeast; Patrice Lumumba urged for calm and restructured the army into a national entity, the Armée Nationale Congolaise, or ANC.

Belgium was back before it could really leave. On 10 July, it sent paratroopers to Léopoldville and ships to the mouth of the Congo River. A man by the name of Moise Tshombe, on the advice of the Belgians, engineered the secession of Katanga from Congo. Kasa-Vubu and Lumumba appealed to the United Nations for intervention in their country, and the UN in turn condemned the military action of Belgium in Congo. By 15 July, UN troops were in Congo and beginning to restore order.

This would not be the end of a critical year in Congo: South Kasai Province would secede as well, though it would hardly be as pertinent or difficult a struggle to reintegrate South Kasai as it would be to regain Katanga. Katanga had the majority of Belgium's UMHK-owned mining operations, a large number of Belgian expats, and scads of money to keep their dream of independence alive. Katanga's government, led by Tshombe, also hired white mercenaries to defend the province against Congo and UN soldiers.

Meanwhile, at the top of Congo's new government were divides as well: Joseph Kasa-Vubu decided to dismiss Patrice Lumumba from his position as prime minister in September, though he did not have the power to do so. Lumumba was under UN protection, essentially house arrest, in Léopoldville when the ANC, led by Mobutu, flexed their muscle and assumed power over the country's government. Kasa-Vubu was allowed to remain as a nominal figurehead, but all other government posts would be filled with friends and allies of Mobutu.

Lumumba managed to escape from Léopoldville and was heading for Stanleyville, where he had popular support, but was captured in the process by ANC soldiers and imprisoned. He was displayed on television as a traitor, humiliated for his opposition to Kasa-Vubu and Mobutu, and beaten. Belgium's long arms intervened again and demanded he be imprisoned in independent

Katanga, and Mobutu complied. Lumumba was moved, incarcerated, and eventually executed in Katanga – with the complicity of Tshombe and the Belgians, though who in fact was responsible for his execution still remains unclear.

THE UN IN CONGO: TAKE ONE ONUC, or Operations Nations-Unie au Congo, was the largest UN operation undertaken since its inception and as a result the UN became a major player in gluing together the fractured bits of Congo and tackling the continued problem of secessionist Katanga. A rival national government had formed in Stanleyville in November 1960 under the leadership of Antoine Gizenga with Cyrille Adoula as his second in command, drawing from the popular support of Patrice Lumumba. Speculation exists that this government was being funded by communist entities hoping to establish a government in the Congo sympathetic to the USSR. Their party would be instrumental in calling together a UN summit on resolving the continued conflicts across the nation, and in July 1961 plans for a reunified Congo were established. Kasa-Vubu would remain president while Gizenga and Adoula would be given positions in his new government. South Kasai would end its secession, and Cyrille Adoula would be appointed as new prime minister in August.

Katanga, though, would continue to rebel against a Léopoldville-operated government. Large battles occurred almost continuously between UN troops and aircraft, against Katangese fighter planes and soldiers, for over two years. Tshombe was well equipped to combat highly trained UN soldiers from Sweden, Ireland, the Philippines, and others. An air war also ensued during this time against Avikat, Katanga's own air force. Receiving side support from the Belgians, along with his private mercenaries, combat across Katanga was frequent during this time.

Tshombe's power began to slip however, and after a final fierce month of combat at the beginning of 1963 he conceded defeat to the UN forces. Tshombe would flee to Zambia and then Spain, and then return to Congo to participate in a new government and the only free elections Congo would know for quite some time.

ONUC would officially come to an end in 1964, five years after arriving in the Congo, and its actions heralded as a job well done. A new age of internationalist intervention would arrive, using the Congo as proof of the UN's relevance as a stabilising body in the world – though how it was done, with international troops engaging in open combat, would be debated for decades.

THE RISE OF MOBUTU Rebellions persisted across Congo between 1964 and 1965, and the ANC had their hands full; yet more importantly, Mobutu's army was expanding its zones of control across the entire nation and creating a level of authority that the Congo had never previously seen. Moise Tshombe had been instituted as prime minister in 1964 by Joseph Kasa-Vubu and elections were planned for 1965. Belgian paratroopers and mercenaries were being used against leftist rebels active in Stanleyville, and Tshombe's experience in operating mercenary companies would prove invaluable to Kasa-Vubu as he tried to bring his country under control. Rebels loyal to the assassinated Patrice Lumumba were by far the most significant threat to the government at this time, and a small front in the Cold War between Soviet- and Cuban-backed Lumumbist rebels and the US-backed government in Léopoldville was being fought out in the far reaches of eastern Congo.

There were further rifts, though, between Kasa-Vubu and Tshombe. Tshombe himself was gaining in popularity, perhaps too much so, and his attitudes towards maintaining white mercenaries in the Congo led to disagreements between the two men over Congo's direction in the world: Kasa-Vubu was local in his focus while

Tshombe seemed to be firm in his opinion that Western forces should remain in the Congo.

A free and fair election did occur in Congo, in May 1965, with Moise Tshombe emerging as prime minister, though his victory would be short-lived: on 24 November, citing the rift of opinion between Tshombe and Kasa-Vubu, Joseph Désiré Mobutu and his army staged a coup and took power.

Mobutu's life was slowly re-engineered as a legend, and he was hugely popular in his early years. He began to change the names of colonial towns: Léopoldville to Kinshasa, Stanleyville to Kisangani, and Elisabethville to Lubumbashi. Katanga Province would be known as Shaba. He nationalised the UMHK, which became Gécamines. He would also introduce a new flag, finally demonstrating a departure from the old flag of the country that had remained essentially the same since King Léopold engineered his massive private colony of Congo Free State.

A new constitution was created, allowing the President of Congo to rule almost uninhibited by any internal dissent. Uprisings which occurred were put down quickly, and the authority of the ANC remained firm. New elections were to take place in November 1970, and Mobutu was in a solid position to win them.

FROM CONGO TO ZAIRE There would be little doubt as to the ruler of Congo's elections in 1970: not only did he control the army, he was also the favoured man of Western governments – and given eastern Congo's history of leftist uprisings which could possibly institute a communist-friendly government in Congo, Mobutu's strong-arm tactics of keeping the country on the capitalist side of the Iron Curtain were undoubtedly desirable.

To say that the elections were fair would be, in effect, unfair: Mobutu won them handily, and his authority over Congo would be complete. During this time his first order of business would be to eliminate all other political parties, and his second was to completely thrust off the colonial past of his nation: from October 1971 onward, the Republic of Congo would be known as Zaire. The Armée Nationale Congolais became the Forces Armée Zaïroise, or FAZ. He also changed his own European name to become Mobutu Sésé Seko. All other people he was affiliated with did the same thing; Belgium's old plan of *évolué* had come full circle to a nearly total elimination of European influences in the country.

It would go further, though, as all foreign property was nationalised and European businesses taken over. Mobutu's rule over Zaire would be absolute, and all trade and commerce would be funnelled through the state. Most of that trade would then be channelled into his personal bank accounts.

This may have been slightly alarming for the Western governments who were happy to see a head of state from their side of the curtain running a vast stretch of wealth in central Africa, given the Cold War situation of the time his activities were given little attention. The extreme Marxist governments that were operating on the other side of the Congo River were truly disconcerting – the domino theory of communist revolution across Africa was still very much a real threat.

Mobutu's policy of expropriating private property was rescinded in 1975, though by then the damage had been done: there were few foreigners left doing business in Zaire, and the nation's commerce had been turned over to locals. Mobutu would not help matters much in this respect, though, by giving all expropriated businesses to friends and colleagues who may not have been in a position to run a business: numerous companies were bankrupted or run into the ground, and the only method to true financial security in Zaire would be via handouts from its head of state.

Mobutu secured his position as friend of the West by sending his army into Angola on the request of South Africa and the USA, though the FAZ was soundly defeated and sent scurrying back into Shaba. The help of the international community on his own soil would be required again when the Angolan rebels UNITA invaded and occupied western points of the province, and local rebels occupied the town of Kolwezi. It would take the assistance of the Belgians, French, Americans and Moroccans to put down the insurrection and drive the UNITA rebels out of Zaire's territory, but Shaba Province, later named back to Katanga Province, would remain an outpost for UNITA until its dissolution in 2003.

ELECTORAL REFORMS AND THE DECLINE OF MOBUTU Mobutu held another election in 1977, and unsurprisingly running unopposed, remained Zaire's head of state. A coup plot was unfolded in the military and heads of the army were executed. Intervention in Shaba would give the West some more leverage in adjusting Zaire to their liking, though, and parliamentarians requested that Mobutu institute electoral reforms. Another election took place in September 1982 with other parties running, though chaos would overshadow the electoral process. An official opposition group had formed under the Kinshasa politician and lawyer Etienne Tshisekedi, Union pour la Démocratie et le Progrès Social, or UDPS. Through much confusion and obfuscation Mobutu remained in control and opposition parties, while no longer banned, would remain unable to assume any power.

Throughout the 1980s there was continuing pressure on Mobutu to institute some kind of adjustments to his one-party state. Tshisekedi engineered a mass protest in Kinshasa in 1988, and student protests in 1989 were repelled with violence from the police forces. Mobutu's grip on Zaire, while still firm, was also being agitated by rebels who occupied Moba in Shaba Province briefly.

The collapse of the Soviet Union was an important point in Zaire's history. Mobutu must have seen the writing on the wall for his less than stellar methods of running his country, and without the fear of communist influence in Zaire the West could put more pressure on him to reform the nation. With his support evaporating from the West, he put his well-honed survival skills to work. In April 1990, Mobutu promised to create a new constitution for Zaire and proclaimed a 'Third Republic' with multi-party elections scheduled for the following year. A month later, his FAZ would kill hundreds of students in Lubumbashi. His popularity as head of state was taking a beating. He would appoint Tshisekedi prime minister, veto the decision, and then reappoint him as their ideas and opinions conflicted.

Protests and clashes continued into 1991 as a national assembly was convened to create a new constitution for Zaire, called the Sovereign National Conference. However, it would quickly be suspended as unpaid soldiers staged mutinies in Kinshasa and began a full-scale riot in the city: it would be the capital's first major riot in decades, and far from its last. French and Belgian soldiers were called in again to stabilise the city, but rioting would continue across Zaire for two months. Protests to reconvene the Sovereign National Conference would occur in Kinshasa but be put down violently by the FAZ. It would restart several months later, and in that time it was agreed that the country should be named back to Congo.

Mobutu, though, managed to obstruct the conference and shut out Tshisekedi's ministers – his political machinations were expert, having played his own game in Zaire for decades, and it would not be so simple to remove the reins on Mobutu's power. Tshisekedi would resign in disgust in 1993 and the conference would be suspended indefinitely.

Rioting would continue across Zaire in spurts, started mostly by soldiers, as Mobutu's grip on his country was slowly slipping. Other parliamentary reforms were run through government, accelerating an excruciatingly slow process towards change. The process, though, would be accelerated enormously as a result of a catastrophe occurring in a much smaller neighbour.

FROM MOBUTU'S ZAIRE TO KABILA'S CONGO A critical moment in the history of east Africa was in 1994 with the Rwandan genocide. This event did not occur in a vacuum, and as could only be expected, its implications for the region as a whole were vast. With the failure of the UN in Rwanda to halt the mass killing of Tutsis by Hutus, refugees flowed from Rwanda into the DR Congo at the onset of the genocide.

However, this would not be the catalyst for major change in Mobutu's Zaire. The rebel army in Rwanda, the Rwandan Patriotic Front, eventually halted the genocide and drove Hutu genocidaires into Zaire – Interahamwe militias, extremist Hutus who were primarily responsible for the massacre. While no longer having a presence in Rwanda, Interahamwe continued their attacks on the Tutsis in Rwanda and began to attack Tutsis resident in South Kivu Province – also referred to as Banyamulenge. While ethnically the same as Rwandan Tutsis they considered themselves Zaïrois, or Zairian, first and foremost. Yet Interahamwe did not differentiate between Banyamulenge and Rwandan Tutsis – the Tutsi group as a whole was being targeted.

The Vice-Governor of South Kivu, witnessing further massacres on his own soil, issued an edict in 1996 calling for all Banyamulenge to leave the province. Rebellion ensued, and while chaos reigned in the province the government of Rwanda found a chance to spearhead its own incursion into South Kivu under the figure of one Laurent Kabila – a failed commander of sorts who had seen many chances at power during his life in the Great Lakes region, and had long opposed the regime of Mobutu and fought against his forces during popular uprisings of the mid 1960s. Several rebel groups operating within South Kivu were merged under his leadership. Backed by the Rwandan government, the Rwandan army, as well as receiving further support from Uganda, Kabila and his entourage began a march west from the Rwandan border to Kinshasa under the acronym of AFDL – the Alliance of Democratic Forces for the Liberation of Congo-Zaire.

This was, of course, done originally under the pretence of ousting the Interahamwe from South Kivu to eliminate attacks on Rwandan Tutsis. Uganda had its own rebel problem that had been hiding out in eastern Zaire with the ADF, the Allied Democratic Front, and their presence in Zaire's eastern provinces was enough of a reason for their own armies to march into a much larger neighbour. The ulterior motive here was the vast resources of Zaire, and an aim at territorial expansion. Using the pretext of hunting down rebel groups placated international concern, and no intervention from any Western power was forthcoming to stop what had become, in effect, a full-scale invasion of eastern Zaire.

This long march to Kinshasa saw very little opposition, though several token battles were fought across the country as Kabila's army moved west. Mobutu's power was at its nadir, him suffering from ill health, and his formerly formidable network of officials and army generals were as much opposed to his rule as Kabila during his final days in the country. Already rioting against bad pay for years, the FAZ were primarily responsible for much of the looting that occurred while Kabila moved west – while his army was disciplined and focused, the FAZ were in disarray and used a chaos of their own making to further personal gains.

Kabila's arrival in Kinshasa ushered in a new era of the Congo Free State, now to be called the Democratic Republic of Congo. The old era of Zaire, under Mobutu, had fled to Morocco – where the former strongman would die a few years later, and remain buried at a cemetery in Casablanca.

Kabila's succession as the head of state of what would now be called the Democratic Republic of Congo was only the beginning of a long and protracted conflict that would be the largest, most complicated and deadliest war the world had seen in half a century.

AFRICA'S 'WORLD WAR' The arrival of Laurent Kabila as head of state in the now Democratic Republic of Congo was far less of a drastic change than many had hoped – he immediately began setting up a network of cronies and strongmen who answered to him in much the way that Mobutu ran the nation before him. More importantly for Kabila was that the nations who had engineered his march into Kinshasa, Rwanda and Uganda, no longer saw him as being beneficial to their greater cause of partition and plunder in the eastern regions of the country. And therefore almost as quickly as Kabila was put into power, a plan was formed to take him out.

A new rebel group emerged in the east based in Goma, called RCD or Rassemblement Congolais pour la Démocratie. Again backed by Rwanda and Uganda, the group was portrayed as a strictly home-grown affair that was seeking the overthrow of Kabila – while it was called a civil war, Rwanda and Uganda could use this veneer to divert attention away from their goals of establishing spheres of influence in their much larger neighbour. The group would fight against itself, though, and after a critical battle in Kisangani would split into two: RCD-Goma, Rwanda's rebel wing, and RCD-ML, Uganda's rebel wing. To make things even more confusing, another Ugandan-backed faction of this group would form in the northwest of the DR Congo and call itself RCD-National after disagreements within the RCD-ML faction.

These groups were mostly at odds with each other, but broadly speaking fighting for the same goal of again marching on Kinshasa to install a new head of state. Yet Kabila would have his own allies, fighting for their own interests: Angola, Zimbabwe, Namibia and Chad all sent troops in support of Kabila and would prove critical in ensuring that Kinshasa stayed in his power.

Of course, ulterior motives for these nations were all ever-present in their decisions to send troops: Angola most especially saw this as an opportunity to cut supply lines to the long-running rebellion in their own country from UNITA, who maintained bases across the border in DR Congo. Furthermore oil interests in Cabinda could be threatened with Rwanda and Uganda partitioning the DR Congo's vast resources amongst themselves and operating outside the scope of international law – conflict along the Atlantic coast could cause all sorts of disruptions to the prosperous petroleum industry in the region. Namibia and Zimbabwe's ruling elite both had significant mining interests in the country and saw this as not only a mission to protect those assets but perhaps also to expand them – furthermore Robert Mugabe, Zimbabwe's long-running head of state, could only be concerned over rebellions sponsored by neighbouring states aimed at toppling unelected leaders. And finally Chad, sponsored by France and Gabon in a manner of guilt for the lack of initiative in halting the Rwandan genocide until far too late, sent 1,000 troops to support Kabila's regime.

With dozens of thousands of international troops within the DR Congo, and rebel factions backed by other nations scattered across the east, this war was fought wholly within the borders of the former Zaire and with complete disregard for the citizens of this nation. It was a war primarily fought by neighbours hoping to divide the vast resources amongst themselves, aimed at protecting their economic interests, and territorial expansion. Perhaps most critical was the fact that with all of these troops present within the country, very little army-to-army combat occurred – yet over four million people perished, most of them civilians.

Wholesale massacres of women, children and unarmed men occurred throughout the country. It is estimated that 70% of those killed did not perish due to violence but due to inhospitable terrain and disease as millions were displaced and forced to live in foul conditions throughout the DR Congo's vast jungles. While a massive war was being fought for the rights to the country's huge resource wealth, its people again suffered. As the 20th century had begun under Belgian rule, it ended in much the same manner.

The United Nations arrived in 1999, two years after fighting began, with the Lusaka Peace Accord. Signatories to the accord agreed to a withdrawal of their troops from the DR Congo territory, as well as a ceasefire. Compliance with the accord was slow in the case of nations backing Kabila, and only Chad's troops met their target date of departure. In the case of the Rwanda- and Uganda-backed rebels, they would persist in the east for many years to come.

While 1999 may have heralded the official end to the World War of Africa, it was far from the end of hostilities within the DR Congo. RCD continued for a much longer period in the east, with its various factions fighting amongst each other, the local population and the Kinshasa government. Furthermore, new rebel factions were emerging amongst the jungles of eastern Congo, especially Ituri Province. What was supposed to have finished in 1999 would continue well into the next decade, though with the arrival of another large presence of troops – this time under the UN, arriving again 40 years after its first mission in the former Congo Republic, and this time called MONUC.

THE UN IN CONGO: TAKE TWO The creation of MONUC or Mission de l' Organisation des Nations Unies en République démocratique du Congo followed a familiar tale: it would be the largest UN operation yet, comprising a multi-national force that would rotate periodically, and be spread out across the country. While the UN's previous duty included taking down well-organised armies of Katanga, its new mission would be far more grey and open-ended: what was occurring in the DR Congo at the turn of the millennium was not so clear-cut as before, as tribal warfare and fractured rebel groups attacked primarily civilians. However, originally the UN would not be present in the DR Congo for this purpose: it was set up simply to monitor the acitivities of foreign-government forces in the nation and make sure they departed and complied with the Lusaka Peace Accord. It would have major bases in seven towns across the DR Congo: Kinshasa, Mbandaka, Kisangani, Kananga, Kalemie, Kindu and Bunia. Its air network would be subcontracted and extensive, and create an infrastructure amidst the chaos that had never existed while the country was standing on its own two feet.

In 1999, only a few hundred UN observers were in the country, but the operation was expanding quickly. By 2001, observers would be accompanied by soldiers, so-called 'Blue Helmets', and begin establishing themselves outward from Kinshasa. They would begin arriving in the east at the end of 2000, primarily to protect their own observers: their mission would be hands-off for several years and endure some criticism for this policy. Their presence however was a stabilising force, and it is perhaps that as the DR Congo entered the new millennium, MONUC stopped it from slipping further down the precipice.

ENTER JOSEPH Laurent Kabila was not a vast improvement on the previous head of state, and in fact was on occasion labelled as a 'mini-Mobutu' by his detractors. He had appointed Etienne Tshisekedi as prime minister once again, though kicked him out of that position almost as fast as he arrived. His desire for power and lack of interest in genuine reforms were one thing; how he treated members of his inner circle were another.

Laurent Kabila was known to have trained child soldiers, and kept some young men as his closest bodyguards. Perhaps youth was a part of the cause behind one of his closest aides pulling the trigger, or it may have been external machinations as the entire event was labelled a coup attempt. His assassin was killed as well, chased down and shot. What exactly occurred on that day is still unclear, though there was no mistake that Laurent's death would end his aimless rule before it became too entrenched for change.

Laurent's ageing philosophies would be moved aside by youth, then, as his son moved in to take power. Joseph Kabila had in fact fought alongside his father during the Second Congo War and departed shortly after it for military training in China. Kabila also spoke English, providing a window away from the francophone world and perhaps a different direction for the DR Congo. He was just 29 when he assumed the presidency, and few believed that he would last as long as he has.

In 2002, the Pretoria Agreement came into effect which reconfirmed Joseph Kabila's right to the presidency for the interim between elections and gave MLC leader Jean-Pierre Bemba the position of prime minister. The Sun City Agreement, as it was also called, was intended as a final accord to end continued fighting between factions across the DR Congo. South African President Thabo Mbeki hosted the summit, along with figureheads from Zimbabwe, Zambia, Namibia and Botswana. It provided a date for multi-party elections to be held two to three years in the future, with one president and four vice-presidents. The national army would be reworked again, and rebel soldiers would be reintegrated into a new army and police force.

All of this sounded great in principle, though in practice its stipulations were mostly unenforceable. Joseph Kabila and Jean-Pierre Bemba set about instituting the policies of the Pretoria Agreement as MONUC expanded its mandate and doubled the number of Blue Helmets in the DR Congo by 2003. Rwanda's troops would spend several more years in the Kivu provinces. Rebellions continued across the east with factions of the RCD in Kivu and Kisangani at odds with each other – the Mayi-Mayi were continuously fighting against Interahamwe and anyone else they saw fit, and riots erupted occasionally in Kinshasa. All of this may have been par for the course in the DR Congo at the time, but the most insidious acts were taking place in a remote northeastern district that had rarely made the news before.

THE ITURI CONFLICT Tribal warfare came to the fore in Ituri, though as a sideshow to what was occurring across the DR Congo in the late 1990s; as the rest of the country stabilised, Ituri slid deeper into conflict. It originated out of the Hema and Lendu tribes at odds with each other, stretching back decades to a 1973 change in property laws that allowed others to purchase land and force the original owners off it. Animosity began to boil, and conflict would occur between the two groups sporadically for the next few decades. However, Ituri's difficulties would not hit fever pitch until the arrival of Uganda in the Second Congo War.

Uganda had occupied Ituri by 1998 and declared it a province by definition – though it had been a district under Congolese law, and it is unclear whether or not Uganda believed Ituri to be Ugandan or Congolese territory – more than likely it remained grey to keep international bodies guessing. With a change in occupying forces, extremist Lendus began killing the Hema and destroying entire villages. While massacre was not uncommon across the DR Congo, Ituri brought the nation's troubles to a new level by wiping whole villages off the map.

Uganda's army attempted to restore order and keep the two tribes away from each other, all the while extracting goods from Ituri's farms and mines to be siphoned back to their own nation. They would receive criticism of aiding the Hema in their war against the Lendu. Mass migrations occurred as killing continued, sending refugees into Ituri's thick rainforests and spawning large refugee camps. As the Lusaka Peace Accord was signed, Uganda armed both the Hema and Lendu as the majority of their forces departed from the region – giving both tribes the means to attack each other by leaving arms caches behind, and a general lack of authority to keep both sides apart.

As the Second Congo War waned, the Ugandan army kept a minimal presence in Ituri until the arrival of MONUC in the region in 2001. In 2003, they would set up a base in Bunia: it would have the largest refugee camps, and be a completely disarmed town and sealed off from the rest of the province. The European Union would approve Operation ARTEMIS, allowing a European force to secure the town in preparation for MONUC. French special forces would arrive first, and on their arrival the town would be nearly deserted as all business owners had either fled or been killed. MONUC would conduct an observatory role while trying to keep the two sides away from each other, at least initially – a change in their mandate in 2004 required them to protect civilians who were at risk of violence. This would be a noted adjustment to their role in the DR Congo as they would now be responsible for protecting innocent people against ethnic conflict, rather than simply acting as observers. It would make their role more relevant, but far more difficult.

While encountering little resistance to the presence of Blue Helmets across other parts of the DR Congo, they would encounter fierce resistance from Hema and Lendu tribes in Ituri. In the worst act against peacekeepers since Rwanda, nine of them were killed in February 2005 by extremist Lendus. UN soldiers finally responded with authority – a subsequent attack on a Lendu militia base killed 50. MONUC would begin mass arrests across the province. No longer existing simply as observers, they became incredibly active in moderating the Ituri conflict and separating its enemies from each other.

This chaos has also led to a continued unmonitored extraction of resources by unknown groups across the province – including its valuable gold mines, and several multi-national companies have been highlighted by human rights groups as assisting the conflict between the Hema and Lendu: amidst chaos, business can continue without so many prying eyes.

PROGRESS TOWARDS CHANGE MONUC continues its disarmament programme in Ituri and is making progress at removing the threat of militias. It has also expanded its forces once again, with 17,000 peacekeepers stationed across the DR Congo, far more than it had originally intended under the Lusaka Peace Accord. Katanga had become reasonably stable on its western front thanks to the death of UNITA leader Jonas Savimbi, which led to the dissolution of the rebel group in 2003. However, Katanga was experiencing renewed conflict in the east as Mayi-Mayi militias fought in the jungle against the Tutsis and Banyamulenge who were, in their opinion, intruding on their land. Yet there would be a bright spot with the surrender of a major Mayi-Mayi warlord, Gédéon, in eastern Katanga. Several hundred of his followers would surrender as well.

Interahamwe have continued to be a problem in the Kivu provinces, and while attempts at bringing them under control with UN peacekeepers has been somewhat successful, they are still a known threat in the area to all involved.

Rwandan President Paul Kagame had stated publicly at the beginning of 2006 that all of his troops were finally out of the Kivu provinces; yet reports confirm otherwise, and locals continue to complain of harassment by underpaid Rwandan soldiers as well as DR Congo soldiers.

Uganda's rebel group the Lord's Resistance Army has been on the run for several years as it loses power and, it seems, will eventually dissipate – but for the meantime they have escaped to rear points in both southern Sudan and Ituri

Province. Ugandan President Yoweri Museveni has threatened to send the UPDF back into Ituri to eliminate the LRA, which seems very familiar to their first excursion into Ituri in the late 1990s.

In February 2006, Joseph Kabila signed a new constitution for the DR Congo and confirmed the general election date of 1 July the same year. It allowed a president to be elected for a maximum of two five-year terms, and share power with an elected prime minister. South African President Thabo Mbeki and African Union President Denis Sassou Nguesso presided over the ceremony.

The constitution would also change the layout of the DR Congo again. The country's provinces would be expanded from 11 to 26, turning all former districts into provinces. A new flag would be introduced, retaining the star of King Léopold but adding three diagonal stripes across its centre.

THE THIRD REPUBLIC Another coup attempt was uncovered in late May 2006, this time with foreign mercenaries involved. Yet, coup attempts had become less of a major issue thanks to the incredibly large foreign presence on the ground. A new era of colonialism, perhaps, though under the auspices of international assistance, was keeping the DR Congo moving along the same path that it had originally been created to follow way back in the age of Congo Free State under King Léopold's AIA and AIC. Namely, an internationalist zone in the centre of the continent, where all nations could arrive to carry out their business. The concept would be similar in many ways, yet the execution would be much different.

With Operation ARTEMIS a success in 2003, the European Union approved another intervention titled Eusec R D Congo in May 2005. The directive would allow a European force of security experts to monitor and assist with the integration of the new Congolese army. With the aim of eliminating corruption and the rampant disregard for the law that the army in DR Congo had become famous for throughout its independence, Eusec R D Congo was considered a solid success. And yet, the United Nations and European Union would approve another directive in 2006, allowing for a larger force, called Eufor R D Congo to monitor elections scheduled for 1 July of that same year. The elections were delayed again to the end of the month, though, after riots erupted in several major cities, killing about a dozen people. The international community, however, would not see these elections fail – with over US$3 billion invested already, their arrival and passing would be a major turning point in the history of the DR Congo.

The electoral process was completed by the end of 2006 with Joseph Kabila winning the presidency. Jean-Pierre Bemba complained of an unfair vote, but ultimately accepted the result with only a few protests from his supporters in the capital. Just as Kabila was sworn in as president at the end of the year, a rebel general loyal to the RCD-Goma faction began to create problems in the hills near Rutshuru – further aggravating the delicate situation in North Kivu. Laurent Nkunda, from the RCD-Goma faction, was upset that the new government was not doing enough to oust Interahamwe militias from their last remaining strongholds in eastern Congo. Virunga National Park's gorilla mountains and Rwindi Plains were shut down for two months, and 6,000 of his soldiers were stationed on the outskirts of Goma. However, the problem was short-lived as MONUC put a lid on it quickly, threatening to engage him directly. He backed off, and a resolution was reached in January 2007 that saw his soldiers integrate with the national army and take up positions looking for Mayi-Mayi in Maiko National Park and the Rwindi Plains.

In March 2007, the Palais du Peuple, or national assembly, was opened for the first time in over a decade; the reopening of the national assembly was seen by many as a positive step that the 'Third Republic', as the newly elected government would be popularly called, was decidedly different from what had transpired in the

3

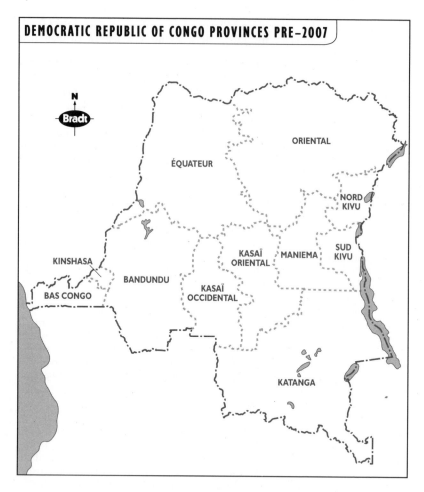

DEMOCRATIC REPUBLIC OF CONGO PROVINCES PRE-2007

N

ORIENTAL

ÉQUATEUR

NORD KIVU

KINSHASA

KASAÏ ORIENTAL

MANIEMA

SUD KIVU

BANDUNDU

BAS CONGO

KASAÏ OCCIDENTAL

KATANGA

past. However, a familiar pattern quickly emerged – in the middle of March an assassination attempt on Jean-Pierre Bemba resulted in open combat in Kinshasa, leaving hundreds dead. Factions loyal to Jean-Pierre Bemba were accused of agitating a difficult situation. Bemba fled to the embassy of South Africa with his family, urging his men to stand down. The Kinshasa government issued a warrant for Bemba's arrest, accusing him of high treason. Bemba was eventually given safe passage to Portugal for treatment at a hospital there. With their leader in Portugal, the MLC boycotted the country's parliament, citing their own safety concerns – accusations of Kabila's ruling party engaging in practices of intimidation and harassment of MLC senators emerged. The MLC ended their boycott of the parliament at the end of April, but as at the end of July, Bemba was still in Portugal. Kabila's government was continuing its reconstruction programme, and MONUC was tightening its grip on remaining pockets of instability in the east. Negotiations continue between Bemba and international monitors to ensure that if he does return to Kinshasa, he will be immune from prosecution - something that Kabila's government is not keen on seeing happening. Because of these continued struggles, international monitors have raised concerns that Congolese politics were falling back into old and familiar habits.

DEMOCRATIC REPUBLIC OF CONGO PROVINCES POST-2007

N

Bradt

SUD UBANGI
NORD UBANGI
BAS UELE
HAUT UELE
MONGALA
ÉQUATEUR
ITURI
TSHOPO
TSHUAPA
NORD KIVU
MAI-NDOMBE
SANKURU
MANIEMA
SUD KIVU
KWILU
KASAI
LULUA
LOMAMI
KONGO CENTRAL
KWANGO
TANGANYIKA
KASAÏ ORIENTAL
HAUT LOMAMI
LUALABA
HAUT KATANGA

Isolated conflict also persists as a rogue general by the name of Laurent Nkunda and soldiers loyal to him have staged further incursions on Interahamwe positions around Goma and in southern regions around Virunga park. Fighting not only MONUC but also Congo Army forces, thousands have been displaced as Nkunda attempts to wrest further control of the region west of Goma. General Nkunda has stated that he rejects the authority of the Kabila government, accusing them of corruption, and by some accounts, claims that his territory is a separate country entirely.

GOVERNMENT AND POLITICS

The DR Congo's political scene was finalised, more or less, by the end of 2006 – with a presidential run-off vote sealing the presidency for Joseph Kabila over Jean-Pierre Bemba. Kabila went on to appoint a familiar name in Congolese politics, Antoine Gisenga, as his prime minister.

The outcome of the elections of November 2006 that had begun in July the same year completed the first democratic vote that the nation had seen in over 40 years. Assisted by thousands of foreign staff and costing the international community over US$0.5 billion, it was heralded as a success, even while combat between factions erupted in Kinshasa and further afield.

They also voted in a new flag, the fourth in the nation's history, and a new set of provinces – changing the total from 11 to 26, promoting a far more decentralised nation than had been known in the past. Each province is headed by a governor, voted in by their own provincial legislature. A total of 40% of profits from resources are required to remain in each province, which should deter what happened in the era of Mobutu when every penny went into his personal bank account.

The DR Congo voted in a new constitution in December 2005, granting power to a single president, prime minister and four vice-presidents. The president and prime minister appoint the four vice-presidents, and the president himself will be decided by the majority party in the national assembly – the 2006 election results determined that this would be Kabila's Alliance pour la Majorité Présidentielle, or the Alliance for Presidential Majority. Bemba's party, the Union des Nationalists, is the official opposition – they emerged from the original rebel group MLC that Bemba had led during the war. However, due to Bemba's current exile, the opposition party currently has no leader inside the country - giving Kabila's party almost total control over the current political situation. The DR Congo has a bicameral legislature, with a national assembly and senate, comprising a total of 632 seats. The current election results will, in theory, keep this political scene in place for five years. In practice, however, the return or permanent exile of Mr Bemba could have dire consequences for the fledgling government.

ECONOMY

Vast resource wealth has made the DR Congo a place with great potential to do business, but this still has not really begun to improve the lives of locals – the average income is still only US$800 annually per capita, making it one of the poorest nations on earth.

Mobutu Sésé Seko enacted numerous massive projects in the former Zaire, including the Inga Dam at Inga Falls along the Congo River near Matadi. The dam's output has been at reduced capacity for years as instability persists, but recent plans have arisen to improve the structure, add another dam, and create larger output. The potential is massive – the DR Congo can potentially generate enough hydro-electric power to provide electricity to all of central Africa. The irony is, of course, that blackouts are still frequent across even major cities like Lubumbashi and Kinshasa. Power lines do not even exist to many towns, and they are supported only by diesel generators.

Kinshasa also has a history of nuclear power plants, though both quite old and mostly only for research programmes for the university. Given the DR Congo's additional vast uranium wealth, their potential for extra nuclear power is high. Its first reactor, the Trico I, was built by Belgium in 1958 but shut down in 1970. A second-generation model, the Trico II, operated from 1972 to 1988. There have been continuing concerns regarding the insecurity of uranium deposits in the DR Congo, as well as whether or not the old reactors are being monitored and sealed off in a manner consistent with international policy.

Katanga has the country's largest mineral wealth. Mines were opened up by the Belgians early in the 20th century, and the current national mining company accounts for most of the mining that occurs in the Katanga provinces (formerly one province, but as of 2006 split up into four). Gécamines, the national mining company, has allowed foreign mining investments to arrive in Katanga to set up mining outfits – however, they are still the all-seeing power behind what does and does not occur in terms of legal mining operations, and little gets done without their express permission. The famous Shinkolobwe Mine near Likasi was where the USA bought uranium for its two atomic bombs detonated in World War II; the Katanga provinces and many of the towns scattered across the landscape there would not exist if not for mining.

Further north in the Kasai provinces are major diamond-mining operations. The region was once known as the world's major producer of industrial diamonds, though now output has been, like everything else, severely reduced. Locals use ancient panning techniques to gather what they can from streams, and sell it to foreign companies. There is some foreign investment in the town as well; however, there have been continued accusations of exploitation from firms who arrive under the radar (bribing the right people) and extracting diamonds without anything going back into the country's economy.

On the Atlantic coast, Matadi remains a modestly successful town in the area, yet is by far the least useful of the region's major ports. However, thanks to MONUC and the arrival of large masses of cargo to support the operation there has been a heavy trade of goods on the shores of DR Congo. Some oil reserves exist in the coastal territory, but its output in this arena is far overshadowed by the larger reserves of its neighbours Angola, Congo-Brazzaville and Gabon.

In regards to actual employment for locals there are, however, some agricultural crops which are grown across the country. Palm oil, bananas, rubber, coffee and sugar are all cultivated and exported on a medium scale.

All of this comes down to potential – if the DR Congo could sort its problems out, and create a political system that was not so easily swayed by corruption and nepotism, its citizens would be some of the richest on the continent. Yet that is still only a dream – unemployment is high, education is low, movement of goods is either expensive or restricted. Highly educated Congolese have a hard time getting permission to leave, the government fearing that their brightest would never come back if given the chance to spend time abroad for conferences. Unfortunately, that may be the case until further notice.

PEOPLE AND CULTURE

With somewhere around 63 million inhabitants, the Democratic Republic of Congo is the most populous nation in central Africa. However, census reading can only hope to be vaguely accurate as little has been done to truly study the rate at which refugees have poured across the country's borders, and the full level of devastation from the nation's recent conflicts has not been fully measured. While huge numbers live in urban areas such as Kinshasa, Lubumbashi and Goma, the vast majority still live in small villages scattered throughout dense equatorial jungle.

Like the other Congo beside it, several hundred tribes make up the indigenous population, all of whom are descendants of Bantu lineage – with the exception of the pygmies, who live primarily in the deep rainforests of northern DR Congo. Small groups of European and African immigrants have settled in major towns, but not in large numbers – the country lacks the full-blown international diversity of its smaller neighbour across the river. Which is not to say it isn't a diverse place; it is inherently diverse from its hundreds of different Bantu tribes.

Most people who immigrated during the time of Zaire managed to leave as the situation deteriorated in the 1990s.

MUSIC The DR Congo's largest contribution to the cultural world at large would have to be its music. Widely listened to across central Africa, *musique Zaïroise*

Musical man of the hour in the DR Congo is Werrason, a grass-roots musician hugely popular in his own country as well as abroad. He's toured across the francophone world, performed in African music festivals in South Africa as well as closer to home. When I asked in Kinshasa who was the most popular of their contemporary musical acts, the answer was obvious. People always told me, 'C'est simple. Werrason'.

He was born in 1965 in the old Bandundu Province just east of Kinshasa, and moved to the capital as a teenager. He performed in several groups throughout his teens before organising several musical acts that performed in Kinshasa throughout the 1990s. It was his 1999 release 'Solola Bien' which brought him to the attentions of the French recording label Disque D'Or. He toured the record across the Western world, and became the second African to perform at the Palais Omnisports de Paris-Bercy, in front of 17,000 fans. In 2001, he followed up the success of 'Solola Bien' with the album Kibuisa Mpimpa, another great success and the beginning of a fully fledged solo career. He has joined the ranks of other francophone world music stars and continues to enjoy a large following in Europe, as well as Africa.

Werrason has also brought attention to the troubles of the DR Congo, and to the plight of child soldiers. Fondation Werrason is a camp where displaced kids can go for food and shelter, as well as training in a skill such as mechanics or farming. He was also given the title Ambassadeur Universel de la Paix by the United Nations for his assistance to his country.

You can hear samples of his music at the official website (www.werrason.org), in French.

regularily rings from bars and clubs as far away as Cameroon and Chad. Some Congolese musicians have also moved beyond the continent, building fan bases around the world, usually in francophone nations. Paris has, in fact, become something of a hotbed for Congolese music – and can be a better place to sample it than Kinshasa, where live performances are hard to find.

DR Congo's musical style originated in the 1940s with African jazz bands and then the 1950s as the Afro-Cuban musical style rumba really took off across the nation. Rumba became the basis for more experimentation as the DR Congo began to form a national musical style, with the soukous music style emerging in the 1960s. During the 1970s Kinshasa's suburbs became a hotbed for popular music, and during this period the most identifiable rhythms of Zairian music were established.

VISUAL ART Traditional wooden masks and fetish sculptures from the DR Congo are highly coveted and incredibly popular – the exaggerated facial features and body parts of indigenous African art are said to have originated in the DR Congo, and these sculptures are often sold as souvenirs in neighbouring countries. This visual style is said to have originated with the original Kongo Kingdom, as well as the Kuba and Luba peoples.

Kinshasa is home to the famous Académie des Beaux-Arts, a painting school where traditionalist African styles of two-dimensionalism and symbolism are promoted and are taught to new students. In the south, malachite sculptures and jewellery have emerged from traditional beliefs and are often sold to tourists. The Academie also helps students to move beyond these styles and build a true contemporary visual art scene in the DR Congo. Artists such as Chéri Cherin and Chéri Samba have used the 'art naïf' style with political overtones, twisting the

KONONO N° I

Call it a modern-day appropriation of the 'noble savage' if you will, or perhaps a more idealistic approach at bringing to light the exciting and raucous music of Kinshasa to the world at large beyond central Africa – Konono N°1 is a widely heralded group who have played relentlessly together in Kinshasa since the late 1970s to finally be 'discovered' by French producer Vincent Kenis, who has made it his mission to bring the electrified grooves of the Congo to the world at large.

Konono was founded by Mingiedi, who used the Likembé, a thumb piano, to great effect and incorporate the traditional rhythms of Bazombo trance music. Konono N°1 numbers about 20 people, give or take, and they all use a fascinating array of ad hoc electrified musical instruments, many of which are made from scrap car parts.

Using a wide variety of homemade instruments, many of them jury rigged with electronic wires to get distortion out of them, Konono N°1 has become something of a cult hit to Western audiences. Their album *Congotronics* was released in 2005 and the band even toured across Europe, North America and Asia to promote it. They have released two other albums, *Lubaku* in 2004, and an early recording was released on the compilation album *Zaire: Musiques Urbaines à Kinshasa* in 1987.

Kenis's label Crammed Discs is devoted to not only bringing out more acts like Konono N°1 to European audiences but also to re-releasing the old tunes of Zaire that have made the genre such a huge influence across central Africa.

For more information on their Congo releases visit their website (*www.crammed.be*).

traditional symbols used in African painting to study the current socio-political issues confronting the DR Congo. The sculptor Bodys Isek Kingelez takes a different approach altogether, constructing highly detailed maquettes of futuristic cities that bear no relation to any urban area in the nation. Artists working in new media from the DR Congo include Patrice Felix Tchicaya with his confrontational photographs and video installations. European art communities have been especially supportive of contemporary artists from the DR Congo, and artists have gained a prominent standing in group exhibitions featuring African artists.

4

Practical Information

TOUR OPERATORS

Go Congo Av Mboto 14/16, Kinkole, Kinshasa; e sales@gocongo.com; www.gocongo.com. Offers a wide variety of services both for tourists & business travellers arriving in the DR Congo.

Hakuna Matata Tours 11 Bunagana, Kisoro, Uganda; ☎ +250 0888 4822; e sales@hakunamatatatours.com; www.hakunamatatatours.com. Runs tours to Goma & throughout the DRC.

Jambo Safaris Kampala (Uganda), Kigali (Rwanda) & Goma (DR Congo); ☎ +250 083 1098 (Rwanda)/+254 722 747 434 (Kenya)/+243 099 774 5179 (Goma, DR Congo); e sjambos@yahoo.fr. Offers tours from Uganda & Rwanda to visit the city of Goma & Virunga National Park. Has a private lodge in the mountain gorilla reserve.

Undiscovered Destinations Saville Exchange, Howard St, North Shields, Tyne & Wear, NE30 1SE, UK; ☎ +44 191 296 2674; e info@undiscovered-destinations.com; www.undiscovered-destinations.com. Offers personalised tours to the DR Congo.

Volcanoes Safaris Linen Hall, Suite 447/448, 162–168 Regent St, London W1B 5TE; ☎ 0870 870 8480; e salesuk@volcanoessafaris.com; www.volcanoessafaris.com. Also offices in USA, Rwanda, Uganda. Established operators offering tailor-made gorilla (& other) trips. The only safari company signatory (2005) to the UN Kinshasa Declaration on Safeguarding the Great Apes.

World Primate Safaris 11 Crescent Pl, Kemp Town, Brighton BN2 1AS; ☎ 0870 850 9092; e sales@worldprimatesafaris.com; www.worldprimatesafaris.com. Offer specialist gorilla-tracking safaris in DRC, Central African Republic, Uganda, Rwanda & Gabon.

RED TAPE

PHOTOGRAPHY PERMITS The DR Congo still requires anyone photographing anything to have a photo permit; in practice, if you are snapping outside of a bus or taking discreet pictures, you will encounter little resistance. Avoid police and military officers and their structures if you choose to do this. Even when you have a permit I don't recommend photographing these things as it will give officials a reason to harass you, even if it is legal (and in general, it isn't). Permits usually cost around US$20, though permits sold in Kinshasa that are valid for the whole country can be as much as US$50.

You can also buy a photo permit in any provincial capital, but these are valid only for that province. The same goes for smaller towns.

Aside from military structures, the presidential palace and the Congo River in Kinshasa are areas where photography is banned. Keep in mind that whenever you're taking photos, even if it looks as though no-one's around, there is undoubtedly someone watching you. I failed to remember this on my first visit to Kinshasa and was promptly 'arrested' for taking photos near the palace – luckily, as with too many problems involving officials in the country, I paid a 'fine' and was on my way rather quickly!

PARK PERMITS Similar to photography permits, each park requires a permit to visit. They can be expensive – usually around US$100 for some outlying parks, and available only at provincial capitals. If you are going with a tour, they will undoubtedly organise this for you. Also consider that what may seem like a high price to visit a park on a tour is probably a result of the DR Congo's own bureaucracy getting in the way of affordability.

Each park also requires a separate permit, meaning that if you wanted to visit both parks near Lubumbashi you would have to purchase two permits. All of these parks have range officers who check these things, and given the continuing problems surrounding conservation in the DR Congo I recommend staying within the law. The more funds going into the park service, the more chance that the wildlife numbers across the country will rebound.

The positive side of buying a park permit is that a photo permit is not required – your park permit is acceptable for video and photography within the park for which that permit is issued. Outside the park, however, you may again have an uphill battle when photographing things in front of officials.

DRIVER'S LICENCES A licence to drive within the DR Congo is available for US$55 from any provincial capital. This should give you permission to drive anywhere in the country. International Driving Permits are accepted as well for people on tourist visas. If you are staying for a longer period of time, it is best to get a local licence.

Ⓔ EMBASSIES

The DR Congo has embassies in several Western countries, all of which issue tourist visas. The catch is that if you apply for a tourist visa overseas, they require more documentation regarding your stay – including a confirmed hotel reservation, confirmed round-trip tickets, references from your home country and possibly even a bank statement. Charges for the DR Congo visa can be high, but on the other hand, arriving at a border crossing in the DR Congo with a visa already in hand can save you a large amount of trouble. In my experience none of the documentation required for obtaining a visa in your home country is checked upon arrival in the DR Congo.

Visas are required by every nationality for entering the DR Congo. Some borders will issue visas, generally for much less than an embassy will issue them. When crossing from Brazzaville to Kinshasa, Bujumbura to Uvira, and Rwanda into the eastern DR Congo visas will be issued on arrival for a fee of around US$30. Visas are not available at any airport.

Belgium Rue Marie de Bourgogne 25, 1050 Brussels; ☏ +32 2 513 66 10
Canada 18 Range Rd, Ottawa, ON, KIN 8J3; ☏ +1 613 230 6391; f +1 613 230 9145; www.ambardcongocanada.ca
China 6 Dongwu Jie, Sanlitun, 100600, Beijing; ☏ +86 6532 1995; f +86 6532 2713
Czech Republic Soukenická 34, Prague 1, 110 00; ☏ +420 222 314 656/286 850 898; f +420 286 850 898; e ambrdcpaha@hotmail.com
France 32 cours Albert 1er, 75008 Paris; ☏ +33 1 06 07 64 85 37; f +33 1 64 61 02 76
Germany Botschaft der Demokratischen Republik Kongo, Im Meisengarten 133, 53179 Bonn; ☏ +9 34 92 37; f +9 35 22 17

Japan Harajuku Green Heights, Rm 701, 3-53-17, Sendagaya, Shibuya-ku, 151 Tokyo; ☏ +81 3423 3981; f +81 3423 3984
South Africa 791 Schoemann St, Arcadia 0083/PO Box 28795, Sunnyside, 0132; ☏ +27 12 343 2455; f +27 12 344 1510
Sweden Herserudsvägen 5A, 7et Box 1171 S-181 23 Lidingö; ☏ +46 8 765 8380/8591
United Kingdom 38 Holne Chase, London N2 0QQ; ☏ 020 8458 0254; f 020 8458 0254
United States 1800 New Hampshire Av NW, Washington, DC 20009; ☏ +1 202 234 7690; f +1 202 237 0748

✈ **BY AIR** Kinshasa is the major point of arrival in the region and well connected to the outside world: from Europe there are frequent flights from Paris and Brussels on **Air France** and **SN Brussels Airlines** respectively. Regionally there are flights to almost every nearby capital such as Luanda (with **TAAG Angolan Airlines**) Libreville (with **Air Gabon**), Douala (with **Cameroon Airways**), and **Hewa Bora Airways** does a short hop across the Congo River from Brazzaville. There are also reliable flights on major African airlines to Johannesburg, Addis Ababa and Nairobi with **South African Airways**, **Ethiopian Airlines** and **Kenya Airways**.

Lubumbashi is gaining ground as an international port of entry. There are frequent flights to Johannesburg and Nairobi, and a same-plane service to Paris via Kinshasa on Hewa Bora Air. Another Congo-based carrier, Bravo Air Congo, has recently begun offering services to and from Europe – Madrid, Paris and Brussels.

Arrival by air at Kinshasa's N'Djili Airport can be a harrowing experience, and arrival at Lubumbashi is not much better – if you have people to meet you it will be less of a hassle, but chaos, bribes and random searches of luggage (with things going missing afterwards) are all too common. Have your luggage locked and wrapped prior to checking in, and be prepared for a shock of the senses the moment you depart the aircraft. Have US dollars ready in small denominations, and allow an hour or two for some friendly arguing with officials.

🚢 **BY SEA** Passenger liners are a thing of the past to Boma, but cargo shipping is alive and well – though the usual historical problems have never really gone away, with the rail line from Boma to Kinshasa being a little unreliable at the best of times. Nonetheless shipping has become a critical industry from the coast and into Kinshasa.

🚗 **OVERLAND AND BORDER CROSSINGS** The DR Congo has numerous border crossings with its nine neighbours, and most of them will let foreigners cross.

To **Congo-Brazzaville**, you can either take the public ferry for very little money or arrange a ride on a *canôt rapide*, which costs around US$20 and includes a person who will handle your border formalities for you – which is a good thing in a country where doing it yourself can mean any number of extra 'fees'. The *canôt rapide* is quick and reliable with decent security. Few foreigners use the large overcrowded public ferry, and you will probably be singled out for using it if you decide to do so. There is also a boat that goes upriver from Kinshasa that stops at Impfondo, saving the long journey by road (though the boat journey is not exactly short either). Expect it to take a week.

To the **Central African Republic**, the three primary crossings from northern DR Congo into the CAR are from Bangui to Zongo, Mobaye and Bangassou. Relations with the CAR have effectively returned to normal, but crossing to either Mobaye or Bangassou should be assisted by local advice – even at the crossing near Zongo, this will not be a charge-free excursion. Keep in mind that to reach **Sudan** from the DR Congo you'll be crossing from war-ravaged Haut Uele Province into war-ravaged southern Sudan. With that said, one contact of mine could confirm a few things about crossing into southern Sudan: 'We met a couple of SPLA guys in Kampala, who were there 'incognito' so to speak. We had to submit permit requests to them, which take a day to process plus US$35.' These rules are similar for those wishing to travel from northeast DR Congo into southern Sudan to Yei – the border is indeed open, with some sort of transport heading into the region, but make absolutely sure you have the blessing of the SPLA to be there. Enquire in Faradje if you are serious about making this crossing.

There are several crossings to and from **Uganda**, which are well trafficked on both sides. The main crossing is in the southwestern corner at Kisoro and Bunagana, seeing frequent travellers heading into the DR Congo for organised gorilla-trekking tours. Ishasha is not a good place to enter as Interahamwe are still active in this area. Further north is Kasese, another decent option if you wish to visit Virunga National Park via Beni. In the northwest in Nile Province, the roads to Aru and Mahagi are open – though once inside the DR Congo at these points onward transport is non-existent and can be extremely dangerous due to the ongoing problems in Ituri.

For **Rwanda**, Gisenyi is right on the border with the DR Congo, and this is a good crossing place if you want to visit Goma, a large town right on the other side, and a good base for surrounding areas. However, readers have reported that as of Jan 2009 you need a letter of invitation from someone in Goma in order to be allowed across. Cyangugu is an easy entry point to Bukavu (though the roads are better on the Rwandan side to get between Goma and Bukavu) with little hassle. From **Burundi**, the DR Congo border is tantalisingly close to Bujumbura but also extremely volatile and prone to closures. Massacres of refugees by Interahamwe have been witnessed here by aid workers and if you do cross you'll still have a day-long journey north to reach Bukavu, or several days south to Kalemie on a nearly destroyed path. Nonetheless it's quite easy to get transport from Bujumbura to Uvira over the border, and visas are available at the frontier (for a short stay only, of about eight days). Numerous bus companies do the short trip throughout the day. It should be noted, though, that given the choice, people choose to travel north from Bujumbura to Bukavu via a far better road north into Rwanda and then cross into Bukavu via Cyangugu. Interestingly enough, travelling from town to town along the eastern DR Congolese border is best done via neighbouring countries.

There should be sporadic ferries from Kigoma in **Tanzania** across Lake Tanganyika to take you to Kalemie. There is a train service from Kalemie south to Likasi, recently rebuilt but at this point transports cargo only. In theory there should be a road north to Uvira, but the condition of this road and reliable transport to there are difficult at best.

From **Zambia**, the principal crossing is at Kasumbalesa to Chillilabombwe. Kasumbalesa is a vibrant town packed with trucks and plenty of low-budget restaurants and hotels for passing travellers. Foreigners are common here and officials are used to some level of efficiency. Transport onward to Lubumbashi, by private taxi or by minibus, is simple to arrange. There are numerous minor crossings available into DR Congo, though most are inadvisable due to transport problems and, of course, the sporadic conflict raging throughout the eastern part of Katanga Province. Of most interest would be from Ndola to Sakania, and to Mwenda from Mansa. For those with their own transport, there is a crossing at Kasenga and from there a dirt road southwest to Minga, as well as a turn-off west of Kolwezi to Ikelenge in Zambia. Keep in mind that these roads are incredibly rough.

And finally to **Angola**, the primary crossing is on the northern frontier at Matadi – it is open for business and sees traffic in both directions. Connections south to Luanda and north to Kinshasa are good, though a more direct route goes south through the border town of Kizenga. The border with Cabinda opens and closes intermittently, but given Cabinda's aspirations towards independence it should always be possible to pay a 'fee' to get in.

The crossing in Katanga Province at Dilolo is closed, covered with landmines, and obviously inadvisable. Even though eastern Angola's civil war is now in the past, this area is definitely off-limits until further notice. Eventually the rail link may reopen which could mean some sort of transport from Luanda to Kolwezi, but that is a distant dream at this point.

MEDIA AND COMMUNICATIONS

PRINT Kinshasa has an English-language newspaper called the ***Kinshasa Times*** (*www.kinshasatimes.com*) that is probably the best source of information for those living and working in the capital. The website aggregates English-language news stories from other sources, with some original content of their own.

TELEVISION On television, French news tends to be most common, as well as Radio Okapi. Newspapers generally have plenty of press freedom but a startling development in 2007 saw many local journalists specifically targeted and killed for their articles. Whether this will have a detrimental effect on a fledgling free press has yet to be seen.

INTERNET The internet has taken off in a big way across the DR Congo, and it's surprising to see how many businesses have websites and email contacts.Internet plans can be expensive, though. If you absolutely need the internet at your location and cannot use a café, expect to pay dearly for the privilege. Connections can be patchy to non-existent, with frequent cut-outs, even in Kinshasa. Furthermore, broadband internet outside Kinshasa is virtually non-existent – any internet plan still uses dial-up technology, and can therefore be quite slow.

RADIO Kinshasa is overrun with media and radio, and throughout the last elections they were put to the test. By far the largest (and most reliable) radio station is **Radio Okapi** at 103.5FM; funded by MONUC, it is an excellent source of news across the DR Congo. They also have streaming audio from their website (*www.radiookapi.net*). **Radio France International** is also available at 93.2FM, or from streaming audio on their website (*www.rfi.fr*). The **BBC** has its own local radio at 92.7FM, the only English-language radio broadcasting available in either Congo.

POST For snail mail, use **DHL**; it also doubles as a Western Union outlet. As a courier company, they will also arrange pickups from your location. It is difficult to discern if an actual government-operated postal service still exists, and if it does, whether someone would actually want to use it.

TELEPHONE The phone system is a confusing mess – mostly because of parallel developments of mobile-phone networks, various land networks that may or may not work, satellite phone networks used by international organisations in country, and a general lack of regulation for putting together a service. The capital has, by far, the most cohesive network of phones and internet connections, but can still see periodic shutdowns.

Mobile-phone use tends to be cheap and effective, hence phones are abundant, and getting your own should be a priority if you plan on living here. Naturally in the DR Congo, it is not as simple as that. There are two major mobile networks, **Vodacom** and **Celtel**, and calling between them is not as simple as it should be – many Congolese have two mobiles, one for each network. Within major cities coverage is fine, but in rural areas one, the other, or neither may work. Normally phone time is bought through ubiquitous prepaid phonecards, and these two companies are doing their best to reduce unemployment across the country – if you walk three blocks without seeing someone selling these things, consider yourself lucky. Buying a mobile phone is a simple task: in every town there are countless small kiosks where one can make a call on a mobile phone, and there are numerous shops at the capital's major hotels or in Kinshasa city centre where phones and phone credit are sold.

4

The international telephone code for the DR Congo is 243, and the internet designation is .cd. When dialling in country, add a zero to the number. Outside the country, remove the zero. The vast majority of phones in the DR Congo are mobiles that begin with the double-digits 99, 97,88, or 81 (099, 097, 088, or 081 if you're calling in country).

5

Kinshasa

04°18' S, 15°18' E

Rising out of the jungle unlike any other sight in central Africa are Kinshasa's towers, its lights, its chaos, its squalor. After spending weeks or months inside the far reaches of the Congos and arriving onto the paved yet pot-holed streets of the capital, one can easily be overwhelmed – quiet evenings of darkness are overtaken by raucous clubs, cluttered evening markets, throngs of touts and beggars. Truly maddening traffic unseen anywhere else in the Congos clogs the streets – from barely operating minibuses to convoys of tinted cars, thousands of people on the move in every direction, unknown faces of unknown people lurking in the corners of abandoned buildings, all living side by side in Kinshasa.

It is a cultural Mecca, a calling place for the dreams and fortunes of all Congolese from either country of the same name. Inundated with an influx of refugees as war raged in the east, as well as exploding with an expatriate population arriving to bring stability to the nation, its numbers have swelled beyond any previous notions of size. It is said that now, Kinshasa is the world's most populous francophone city: surpassing Paris and Montreal, and almost exceeding both of them combined. It is still a city of deep divisions between rich and poor, of garish excess and poverty living as neighbours, with the protected enclaves of a few international hotels, embassies and golf courses keeping the huddled masses at bay. It is as diverse and intimidating as any of Africa's largest cities. It is definitely not a place to miss – and indeed, it is hard to be in the west of DR Congo without passing through.

HISTORY

The place where Kinshasa now sits had always been a meeting point. Henry Morton Stanley opted to found the capital of the proposed Congo Free State on the eastern shores of Malebo Pool, in between two well-known villages called Nshasa and Ntampo, in 1881. Stanley would name the new town Léopoldville, after his monarchic Belgian employer, yet the locals would continue to call the town Nshasa – and as the Lingala language began to dominate they referred to the town as Kinshasa, even though Belgian and European maps called it Léopoldville without exception. It would be the stopping point for all expeditions further inland, as well as outward to the sea, with a railway completed to Matadi in 1898 to circumvent the Inga Falls that blocked the navigation of ships further upriver from the Atlantic. As the Congo rubber disaster unfolded, more of the disenfranchised were either forced to come to Léopoldville, or flee to its outskirts; it would grow rapidly from local migrants, the European population which arrived to man the government infrastructure, the missionaries who would found the oldest Catholic church in the Congos there, and the businessmen who needed a stopping point before heading up the Congo River on their steamboats. Its upmarket establishments would grow, with large mansions dotting the riverside, quiet tree-lined boulevards, and quaint restaurants catering to the European diaspora.

Meanwhile Kinshasa's local neighbourhoods continued to balloon, and in those neighbourhoods the first utterings of independence appeared when Joseph Kasa-Vubu and his ABAKO party were voted in as leaders of a suburb. His speeches incited riots, and those riots would pave the way for early independence from Belgium.

Throughout the 1960s, more riots were markers across a turbulent decade as the Congo changed its name as often as its government. Uprisings in the east threatened the nation in its entirety, the secessions in Kasai and Katanga brought UN soldiers to their first major mission, and Belgian interests began to pack up and leave the city they had created. Joseph Désiré Mobutu's ascendancy would settle the issue for a few decades as he officially renamed Léopoldville to Kinshasa, the nation to Zaire, and began building a stronger infrastructure for the capital. With government-sponsored housing projects, unprecedented levels of public transport, and rapid expansion into the jungle, Kinshasa began to grow at an exponential rate throughout the 1970s. The tree-lined boulevards still persisted, though, catering to the upper crust of Europeans doing business in Zaire, the new friends of Mobutu, and the emerging political elite of Africa. The high-class lifestyle was easy to find, yet out of reach for most of Kinshasa's population.

In the city's lower-class outskirts though, its culture would make its mark in music; the first rumblings and beats of *musique Zaïroise* would take the city by storm, then central Africa, then the greater francophone world. As gatherings were permitted, and public music systems became more available, so did the dancers and singers of Zaire who came to Kinshasa to find their fortunes. Nights became busy with music and dancing across the capital.

Local families prospered along with the economy in Kinshasa throughout Mobutu's reign, though the city was still highly dependent on jobs from the public service. Once it was announced that multi-party elections were to occur, the capital took a step back in history and descended again into rioting. Many were killed as the Forces Armées Zaïroise put down the dissent harshly. Corruption emerged as a serious threat to peace across the city. Soon Mobutu's government would crumble, and the rebel army from the east would arrive, sending around another bout of looting, and open combat between soldiers loyal to the old Zaire and those loyal to Laurent Kabila. The last vestiges of the Zairian Empire would evaporate quickly. Soon enough, rattled by a half-decade of upheaval, the capital would remain modestly quiet until the outbreak of the Second Congo War.

As 1998 rolled around and Kabila's grip on power was in trouble, the capital would be surrounded by his soldiers. Combat erupted on multiple fronts, with Rwandan and Ugandan troops marching from the east; Kinshasa was a genuinely dangerous place. Angolan, Namibian and Zimbabwean soldiers fought openly with the Rwandan and Ugandan armies; Chad would send troops as well to reinforce the capital. Evacuations of Europeans in the city, as well as a few Congolese lucky enough to tag along, were common during this period of fighting. Without the intervention of outside forces, the capital would have been lost entirely to the whims of Rwanda's and Uganda's governments.

With the Lusaka Peace Accord in place, in theory at least, by 1999, armies slowly began withdrawing from around Kinshasa. Continued fighting had sent even more displaced people into the city searching for food and medicine; more than ever, it had become a refuge for the downtrodden, a place of sparkling towers on the river where those who had lost all they had to a conflict in the jungle might be able to begin a new life.

Yet it would continue to be turbulent. Laurent Kabila would be assassinated in Kinshasa in 2001, sending more shockwaves throughout the city. More UN staff would be arriving, though, thereby making any reaction subdued. There would continue to be riots, though minor compared WITH the open chaos of the 1990s.

MONUC and other aid staff would continue to arrive in droves, transforming the city and injecting a large amount of much-needed cash and infrastructure back into the capital. Other businesses would arrive as well, as the transitional government signalled it would be fair to foreign investors. Supermarkets, nightclubs and restaurants all began to make new appearances in the districts across the capital.

Security across the city is quickly improving. Streets were deserted after dark only a few years ago, and taxis would charge triple if one wanted to get around after 21.00. Now, a normalisation is taking place: with a renewed sense of safety the capital is beginning to revisit its roots after nearly two decades of difficulties. The outskirts have swelled to enormous sizes, however; the economy is devastated worse than any period in the past; and a new era of trade and investment to give everyone some sort of employment in the city has yet to materialise. Yet it can sometimes feel like one step forward and two steps backward: shoot-outs between forces loyal to Jean-Pierre Bemba and the Kabila government left over 100 dead in the first few months of 2007.

Therefore Kinshasa, now, is mostly on its way up. Yet it is still in a dangerous middlepoint in its recovery, requiring a visitor to be careful, especially in the evenings. Nonetheless, for those who are willing to take precautions, there is no other city like it in central Africa.

ORIENTATION

Three districts dominate Kinshasa: **La Ville** is the city proper, with a few tall towers dominating the skyline amidst a clutter of older buildings that are slowly being renovated in this new era. It is the business and economic centrepoint of the city – crowded by day and nearly deserted at night. Southwest along the river and right beside La Ville is **Gombe**, an affluent area that houses the majority of Kinshasa's elite. It is also the city's main embassy district, and is home to the **Presidential Palace**, the **Grand Hôtel**, and the **Golf Club**. Beside it is the even more exclusive neighbourhood of **Ngaliema**, with the city's ethnographic museum, the old presidential compound of Mobutu, and some of the finest hotels away from the city. Directly south of La Ville is the **Rond-Point Victoire**, sometimes called **La Cité**, a crowded roundabout that is the true African centre of Kinshasa – the city's legendary music scene emanates from here. In between La Cité and La Ville is the **sports stadium**; northeast is **Le Marché**, Kinshasa's crowded market area. Further northeast is **N'dolo Airport**, where most domestic flights depart from. Continue along the river and one reaches **N'djili Airport**.

The city has two main thoroughfares: **Boulevard du 30 Juin** runs parallel to the Congo River, and is the largest street in the city. Some dare call it the Champs-Elysées of Africa. It extends from the **'Beach'**, where boats and ferries pick up and drop off passengers to Brazzaville, as well as the railway station when trains are available. It extends throughout the upmarket Gombe District. Perpendicular to its middlepoint is **Av Joseph Kasa-Vubu**, which can be considered a better gauge of the mass of unknown suburban expansion that has enveloped the old Kinshasa town.

Formally, the city is divided into several communes: Gombe is the city's main commune, encompassing both the embassy districts as well as La Ville. La Cité is in the commune of Kasa-Vubu, and the Grand Marché is in commune de

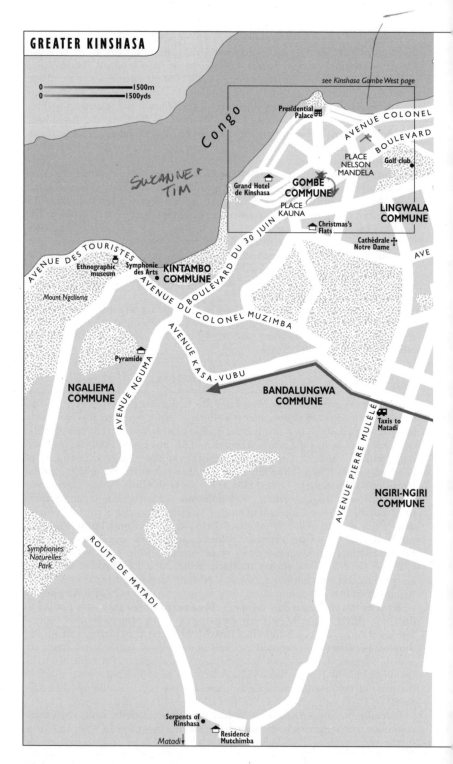

GREATER KINSHASA

see Kinshasa Gombe West page

Congo

Suzanne & Tim

Presidential Palace

AVENUE COLONEL

BOULEVARD

PLACE NELSON MANDELA

Golf club

GOMBE COMMUNE

Grand Hotel de Kinshasa

PLACE KAUNA

LINGWALA COMMUNE

Christmas's Flats

Cathédrale Notre Dame

AVE

AVENUE DES TOURISTES

Ethnographic museum

Symphonie des Arts

KINTAMBO COMMUNE

BOULEVARD DU 30 JUIN

Mount Ngaliema

AVENUE DU COLONEL MUZIMBA

Pyramide

AVENUE KASA-VUBU

NGALIEMA COMMUNE

AVENUE NGUMA

BANDALUNGWA COMMUNE

AVENUE PIERRE MULÉLÉ

Taxis to Matadi

NGIRI-NGIRI COMMUNE

Symphonies Naturelles Park

ROUTE DE MATADI

Serpents of Kinshasa

Residence Mutchimba

Matadi

0 ___ 1500m
0 ___ 1500yds

BOB × CHANTAL

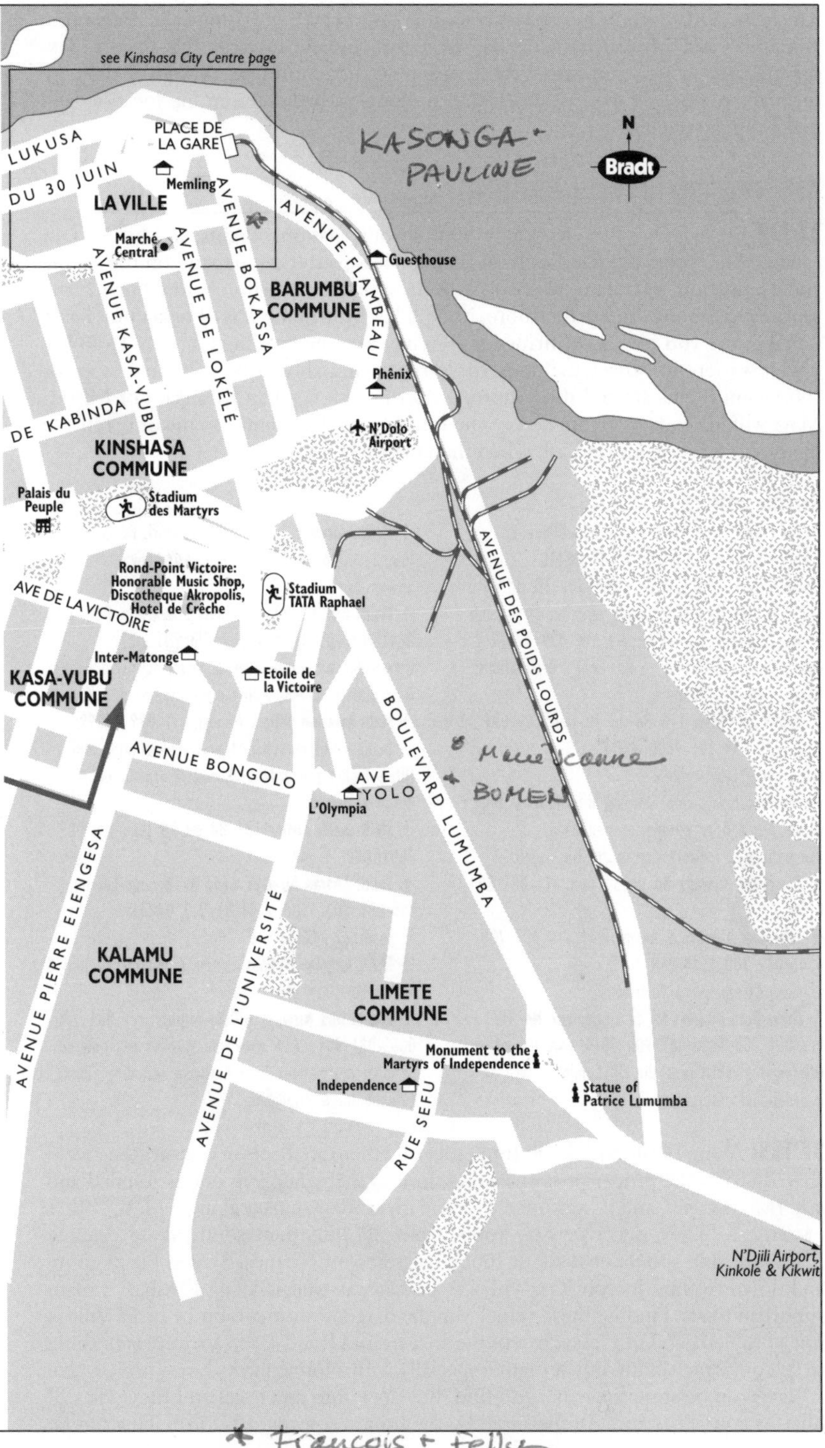

see Kinshasa City Centre page

KASONGA + PAULINE

N

LUKUSA

DU 30 JUIN

PLACE DE LA GARE

LA VILLE

Memling

Marché Central

AVENUE BOKASSA

AVENUE FLAMBEAU

BARUMBU COMMUNE

Guesthouse

AVENUE DE LOKÉLÉ

AVENUE KASA-VUBU

DE KABINDA

KINSHASA COMMUNE

Phênix

N'Dolo Airport

Palais du Peuple

Stadium des Martyrs

Rond-Point Victoire:
Honorable Music Shop,
Discotheque Akropolis,
Hotel de Crèche

Stadium TATA Raphael

AVE DE LA VICTOIRE

KASA-VUBU COMMUNE

Inter-Matonge

Etoile de la Victoire

AVENUE DES POIDS LOURDS

AVENUE BONGOLO

AVE YOLO

L'Olympia

Marie Jeanne
BOMEN

BOULEVARD LUMUMBA

AVENUE PIERRE ELENGESA

AVENUE DE L'UNIVERSITÉ

KALAMU COMMUNE

LIMETE COMMUNE

Monument to the
Martyrs of Independence

Independence

RUE SEFU

Statue of
Patrice Lumumba

N'Djili Airport,
Kinkole & Kikwit

Kinshasa ORIENTATION

5

Bodeke
MASINA

* Francois + Felly
LEMBA

93

Kinshasa. Other communes close to the city centre are Lingwala, Barumbu, Kintambo and Ngaliema to the far west, and Limete towards the airport. Taxi drivers may or may not know the location of the commune, though if they are unclear on where a road is, describing it along with the commune location will make things much easier.

GETTING THERE AND AROUND

BY AIR Kinshasa has two airports: N'Djili for international flights, and N'Dolo, in town, which generally handles local flights. However, it can depend on the airline and destination, so be sure to check with the airline in question before braving the journey to the airport. Furthermore, N'Djili has little in the way of ticket purchases – make sure you have a confirmed seat in hand before heading there. N'Dolo has a wide variety of offices for domestic carriers, and should be your first stop for short-haul flights around the country – anything closer than Kisangani or Mbuji-Mayi will likely depart from here. Schedules change frequently, so the only reliable method is to show up and ask when the next flight is leaving.

Airline offices

✈ **Air France** Hôtel Memling, Av République du Tchad; m 081 884 5548; f 088 08430

✈ **Air Gabon** Immeuble du Centenaire 30, Bd du 30 Juin; m 098 204 676; e fih_airgabon@yahoo.fr

✈ **Air Tropiques** N'Dolo Airport; m 099 37572. Offers short-haul flights to Bas-Congo destinations: Matadi, Boma, & Moanda.

✈ **Bravo Air Congo** 118 Bd du 30 Juin; m 099 930 1730/099 601 2000; e callcenter@bravoairlines.com; www.bravoaircongo.com. Offering international flights within Africa & to Europe, as well as a comprehensive network across the DR Congo.

✈ **Cameroon Airways** Bd du 30 Juin; m 081 884 0258

✈ **Ethiopian Airways** 9 Av du Port; m 081 700 6585/081 700 6588/088 4000; e fiham@ethiopianairlines.com

✈ **Hewa Bora Airways** Av de L'Equateur No 85; m 081 700 5000/081 700 5014; www.hba.cd. Offering flights all over the DR Congo as well as international destinations.

✈ **Kenya Airways** Immeuble Ruwenzori, Bd du 30 Juin; m 088 11239; e Kinshasa@kenya-airways.com

✈ **Malila Airlift** 2789 Av Colonel Ebeya; m 088 46438/088 05841; e malila.airlift@ic.cd; www.malift.isuisse.com. Flies to larger towns in western & central DR Congo, with mostly Antonov aircraft.

✈ **Malu Aviation** N'Dolo Airport; m 099 14999; e malu.avia@micronet.cd; www.maluaviation.com. Offers flights primarily to Kikwit & around on Antonov aircraft.

✈ **SN Brussels Airlines** 33 Bd du 30 Juin; m 089 75010/088 43544

✈ **South African Airways** 6147 Av Ngongo-Lutete; m 081 700 5908; f 44 87 013 07481; e saadrc@jobantech.cd

✈ **TAAG Angolan Airlines** Corner of Bd du 30 Juin & Av du Port; m 088 06146

✈ **Wimbi Dira Airways** N'Dolo Airport; m 081 700 0065/081 301 6634; www.wda.cd. Flies to numerous national destinations from Kinshasa, including Goma, Lubumbashi & Kisangani.

BY TAXI Along Boulevard du 30 Juin especially there are fleets of old cars that act as shared taxis – the proper protocol is to lean into the window as one is stopped and ask *'Bon Marché?'*, and if beckoned to come in, crowd yourself along with the other passengers. They ply a general route from 30 Juin then south along Avenue Flambeau, and should cost about 100Fc regardless of distance. Shared buses go up and down Avenue Joseph Kasa-Vubu to La Cité, as well as along Kinshasa's main suburban roads. Finding these vehicles in the daytime around Gombe or La Ville is not a problem, and to a lesser extent the area around Rond-Point Victoire is nothing to be concerned about, but at night, especially with a foreign face, hire a private taxi.

Taxis can be sometimes hard to find, but duck into any hotel and they will call one for you. They can also be hired by the hour, for around US$10. This can be handy, though you may have to pitch in initially for petrol – I've been in more than one Kinshasa taxi that sputtered to a halt with the driver asking me meekly for an 'advance' to get the thing going again.

CAR RENTAL Private rentals do exist, with or without a driver. Major rental companies operate in Kinshasa; an International Driving Permit is required in addition to a foreign driver's licence. Note that the rental companies listed may include a driver with the price of the car.

🚗 **Avis Auto Rental** Bldg Mayumbe, Bd du 30 Juin; m 099 36306; Grand Hôtel, Gombe; m 081 810 111

🚗 **Europcar** N'Djili Airport (chauffeur service); m 099 15400; f 2 706 2496; Gombe (chauffeur service): Av de L'Equateur 87; m 099 15400; f 2 706 2496

🚗 **Hertz** Gombe (chauffeur service), Av Lt Colonel Lukusa 6/8; m 081 700 5690/081 700 5693; f 088 44779; e afrimakin@afrima.cd

🚗 **Renka** Av du Tchad (inside Memling Hôtel); m 081 502 1957/081 501 9230; e renkakin@yahoofr. Touts itself as Kinshasa's 'discount rent a car' service.

BY TRAIN The main train station is at the very edge of Boulevard du 30 Juin, and sees regular arrivals from Matadi. Buy tickets directly at the station, though they will more than likely not sell them until the train has, in fact, arrived.

BY BUS, TRUCK AND BOAT Trucks and buses leave intermittently from around Kinshasa, usually from Marché de la Liberté for Kikwit or in Ngaliema commune for Matadi. Towards Mbandaka and Kisangani, at the very end of Avenue du Port, are various barges, boats, and steamers heading upriver. Schedules and prices change continuously, and one can only arrive and ask to find out what is feasible at any given time.

LOCAL TOUR OPERATORS

The DR Congo has an official tourist office, the **Office National du Tourisme**, or ONT, where one can gather information on the various formalities in reaching any of the country's attractions. They can be a decent starting point for local brochures and suggestions on how to get there, but in the end it will come down to who you pay, and how much you pay. They can also offer a substandard locally published guidebook to Kinshasa called *Voici Kin La Belle*, all in French obviously, and not worth spending money on if you're reading this.

Office National du Tourisme (ONT) 68 Bd du 30 Juin; ☏ 097 869 473/081 355 9679; m 089 57927; e ontrdc@netcourrier.com
Go Congo Mukonga 14, Kinkole; m 081 183 7010; f 32 3 789 1749; e sales@gocongo.com;

www.gocongo.com. Offers a wide variety of tours within Kinshasa as well as across the country.
Jeffery's Travels Bldg Mayumbe, Bd du 30 Juin; m 081 887 777; e jeffery@ic.cd, jt@ic.cd. Offering day trips & tours in & around Kinshasa.

 WHERE TO STAY

Kinshasa isn't the place to save money on accommodation – there isn't anything excessively dirt cheap in the city worth recommending, and even the lower-end places tend to be lacking in certain things that the same money would get a traveller in neighbouring countries. Most hotels do have a restaurant of some sort, however, and a private washroom of some sort is the norm – though usually with cold or intermittent water.

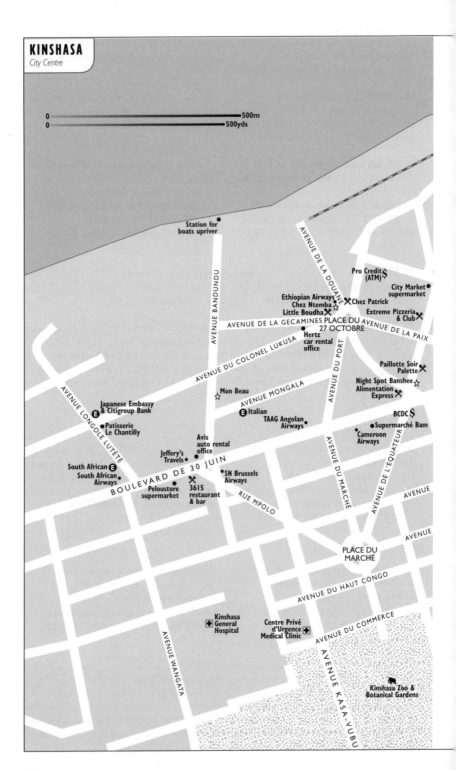

KINSHASA
City Centre

0 ————— 500m
0 ————— 500yds

Station for boats upriver

AVENUE DE LA DOUANE

Pro Credit (ATM) $

City Market supermarket

AVENUE BANDUNDU

Ethiopian Airways
Chez Ntemba
Little Boudha

Chez Patrick

Extreme Pizzeria & Club

AVENUE DE LA GECAMINES   PLACE DU   AVENUE DE LA PAIX
27 OCTOBRE

Hertz car rental office

AVENUE DU COLONEL LUKUSA

AVENUE DU PORT

Paillotte Soir Palette

Night Spot Banshee
Alimentation Express

Mon Beau

AVENUE MONGALA

Japanese Embassy & Citigroup Bank

Italian

TAAG Angolan Airways

BCDC $

Supermarché Bam

AVENUE LONGOLE LUTÉTÉ

Patisserie Le Chantilly

Avis auto rental office

Cameroon Airways

AVENUE DE L'EQUATEUR

Jeffery's Travels

South African
South African Airways

Peloustore supermarket

BOULEVARD DE 30 JUIN

3615 restaurant & bar

SN Brussels Airways

RUE MPOLO

AVENUE DU MARCHÉ

AVENUE

AVENUE

PLACE DU MARCHÉ

AVENUE DU HAUT CONGO

AVENUE WANGATA

Kinshasa General Hospital

Centre Privé d'Urgence Medical Clinic

AVENUE DU COMMERCE

AVENUE KASA-VUBU

Kinshasa Zoo & Botanical Gardens

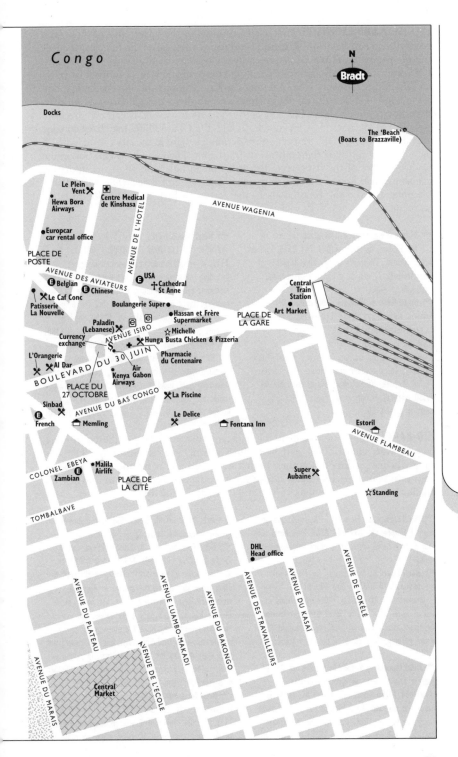

Congo

N

Bradt

Docks

The 'Beach'
(Boats to Brazzaville)

Le Plein Vent
Hewa Bora Airways
Centre Medical de Kinshasa
AVENUE WAGENIA
Europcar car rental office
PLACE DE POSTE
AVENUE DES AVIATEURS
USA
Belgian
Chinese
Cathedral St Anne
Le Caf Conc
Patisserie La Nouvelle
Boulangerie Super
Hassan et Frère Supermarket
PLACE DE LA GARE
Central Train Station
Art Market
Paladin (Lebanese)
AVENUE ISIRO
Michelle
Currency exchange
Hunga Busta Chicken & Pizzeria
L'Orangerie
Al Dar
BOULEVARD DU 30 JUIN
Pharmacie du Centenaire
Air Kenya Gabon Airways
PLACE DU 27 OCTOBRE
AVENUE DU BAS CONGO
La Piscine
Sinbad
French
Memling
Le Delice
Fontana Inn
Estoril
AVENUE FLAMBEAU
COLONEL EBEYA
Malila Airlift
Zambian
PLACE DE LA CITÉ
Super Aubaine
Standing
TOMBALBAVE
DHL Head office
AVENUE DU PLATEAU
AVENUE LUAMBO-MAKADI
AVENUE DE L'ÉCOLE
AVENUE DU BAKONGO
AVENUE DES TRAVAILLEURS
AVENUE DU KASAÏ
AVENUE DE LOKÉLÉ
AVENUE DU MARAIS
Central Market

EXCLUSIVE AND EXPENSIVE Two hotels compete for the upper crust of those who need to be in Kinshasa – the **Grand Hôtel** (sometimes called the Intercontinental) and the **Memling Hôtel**. Both are easily the best experience available in the city, and both have small shopping areas selling European goods in a country that rarely sees anything of the sort. The Memling also has the local office for Air France, and is the hotel of choice for the flight crews of both them and SN Brussels Airlines. Both hotels offer a direct bus service to the airport as well as express check-in. Needless to say, security is top-notch, though the Grand Hôtel may have an edge over the Memling in this respect – the Memling is right in the city centre, with all the activity of Kinshasa right outside its front door. The Grand Hôtel is out on the further reaches of the river, secluded in the green hills with all of the upmarket mansions that house the majority of Kinshasa's embassies. The Grand and Memling are also the only hotels in the country which accept credit cards for payment.

⌂ **African Dream Motel & Restaurant** (12 rooms) 121 Bd 30 Juin, Gombe; m 081 244 8570. Spotless rooms with AC, TV, secure car parking & plenty of other luxuries, as well as a highly recommended restaurant. $$$$

⌂ **Grand Hôtel de Kinshasa** (300 rooms) Av Batetela, Gombe; m 09 19 110 003; f 088 41500; e grandhotelkinshasa@ic.cd, grandhotelkinshasa@yahoo.fr; www.grandhotelkinshasa.com. Kinshasa's premier state-run hotel. Large outdoor pool, fitness room, satellite TV, full shopping area. Airport shuttle available for US$30 one-way. Accepts credit cards. $$$$$ (starting at US$160)

⌂ **Hôtel Memling** (180 rooms) 5 Av du Tchad; m 081 700 1111/099 700 2000; f 081 301 3333; e info@memling.net; www.memling.net. Including executive suite, AC, hot water, satellite TV, electronic safe & 5 meeting rooms available for booking. Has a pool, fitness centre, full shopping area. Airport shuttle available for US$50 one-way. Accepts credit cards. $$$$$ (starting at US$180)

⌂ **Hôtel Pyramide** (14 rooms) Av Nguma, Ngaliema; m 081 508 9552/081 508 9556. High-end boutique hotel in a very quiet neighbourhood. Has swimming pool, small but excellent restaurant. Large · rooms are complete with fridge, satellite TV, AC. Accepts credit cards. $$$$$ (starting at US$150)

MID-RANGE Value varies wildly in the mid-range bracket. Many of these places are popular with international staff based in Kinshasa, and can fill up quickly – or simply be persistently full as their rooms are rented into perpetuity. Call ahead of your arrival, or expect to spend some time hopping between places to find a room on short notice. For payment, cash is still the order of the day.

⌂ **Hôtel Christmas's Flats** 13 Av Nyembo, Quartier Socimat, Gombe; m 099 993 8567. New hotel with pool & higher-end rooms in a quiet neighbourhood. $$$

⌂ **Hôtel Estoril** 85 Av Kabasélé (ex Flambeau); m 089 122 1070/80; f 089 139 8115; e hotelestorilrdc@yahoo.fr. Motel-style rooms as well as usual hotel rooms. Small patio overlooking the street attached to an excellent restaurant ($$). Secure parking, Quite close to the train station. Sgl $$$

⌂ **Hôtel Etoile de la Victoire** Av Victoire No 25–27, Quartier Kauka, Commune Kalamu; m 089 63302/084 70780. Clean rooms with AC, TV, & hot water near the Rond-Point Victoire but still far away enough to be away from the usual chaos. Excellent security as well as a restaurant ($$) & 2 balconies

to watch the street life below. Will offer discounts for groups or extended stays. Sgl $$$, suite $$$$

⌂ **Hôtel Fontana Inn** 3 Av Colonel Ebeya, corner of Av du Kasai; m 081 685 2499/098 041 983; e hotelfontanainn@yahoo.fr. Popular with UN staff & other internationals on the ground in Kinshasa, rooms are large with refrigerators, hot water, AC & TV. Also has a heated pool & restaurant with its own pizza oven. They have a problem with telephones – no land lines exist, but the owners will offer their mobiles for short calls, making calling in & out a bit of a chore. Occupancy based on number of persons per room. Sgl $$$

⌂ **Hôtel Inter-Matonge** Av Bonga AIBI, Grand Place Victoire; m 081 369 5473/099 858 2146/099 893 7379. Recently renovated & just off the Rond-Point Victoire, with continuous AC, clean rooms, & cable TV.

Restaurant (**$$**) is small but offers basic dishes. Sgl **$$$**

🏠 **Résidence Mutchimba** Intersection of Avs Kananga & Lubumbashi, Quartier Pigeon, Ngaliema; m 099 788 8068; e resmutchimba@yahoo.fr. Far out in the suburbs but good value for a high-quality hotel. Rooms have balconies, bathrooms with hot water, secure car parking. Sgl **$$$**, suite **$$$$**

BUDGET Getting out of the central city area can save you money, but transportation may be difficult as shuttling back and forth between La Ville and your hotel can be time consuming at best, impossible at worst. Nonetheless for long stays on a budget, there are a few options.

🏠 **Guesthouse Hôtel** Av Flambeau. Very basic rooms in a large walled semi-residential block. The cheapest place in Kinshasa worth recommending for a long stay. No hot water or AC. Rooms often rented out to long-term residents, so availability can be patchy. Sgl **$$**

🏠 **Hôtel de Crêche** Rond-Point Victoire; m 099 993 3003. Little more than a place to lay your head & leave your bag, don't expect to get any sleep in these small rooms surrounded by noisy clubs. Drown out the din on the highly acclaimed rooftop terrace. Sgl **$**

🏠 **Hôtel Phênix** Av Flambeau; m 099 816 7777. A large hotel quite far from anything in central Kinshasa, but with good prices & a decent restaurant (**$$**). Some rooms have no AC, but do have fans.

Overall quality of the rooms is low, but it's one of the cheapest beds in town, though they are often full as the rooms are rented out to long-term residents. B/kfast inc. Sgl **$$**, suite **$$$**

🏠 **Independence Hôtel** Rue Sefu, Quartier Mombele, Commune Limete; m 099 909 0937. Basic beds in a secure 2-storey building, but far from anything in Kinshasa. Decent value for the quality of rooms, but Limete has a reputation for being a bad neighbourhood. Sgl **$$**

🏠 **L'Olympia Hôtel** (4 rooms) Rue Bongolo, Quartier Mombele, Commune Limete; m 099 782 3434/081 050 7860. Small hotel with an outdoor bar & decent security, deep in the suburbs of Kinshasa. Shared bathroom. **$$**

✖ WHERE TO EAT

EXPENSIVE The upper crust is well taken care of in Kinshasa, but keep in mind that the prices can be outrageous – expect to pay a minimum of US$50 at some of these places for two people. Mercifully, menus can be observed before entering. If you're on a budget, you'll definitely want to look elsewhere.

✖ **African Dream** 121 Bd du 30 Juin, Gombe; m 081 244 8570; ⏰ from 18.00 daily. High-end French cuisine with extensive selection of wines. Behind the motel. **$$$**

✖ **Asian Little Boudha** Av du Port 173 (Forescom Bldg), Gombe; m 099 990 9888; ⏰ from 17.00 daily, bar open after 22.00. A smaller Chinese restaurant in the city centre. **$$$$**

✖ **Grand Hôtel de Kinshasa** Av Batetela, Gombe; e grandhotelkinshasa@ic.cd; ⏰ from 06.00 daily. The Grand Hôtel has 6 restaurants, all catering to a certain vein of the travelling elite: L'Atrium, La Brasserie, La Paillote, La Pizzeria, La Terrasse & Le Pub. Prices vary a bit, but it all is in the high-end range

✖ **La Piscine** Av Bokassa, near Bd du 30 Juin; m 081 504 8520; ⏰ from 16.00 daily. Open-air restaurant dominated by a pool in the middle. Large variety of European dishes. **$$$**

✖ **La Villa** 169 Bd du 30 Juin, Gombe; m 081 508 4933/081 272 8282; e afrirest@ic.cd; ⏰ from 18.00 daily. Specialising in French cuisine, but also offering a variety of Congolese dishes. Has 4 private AC dining rooms & open-air BBQs on some evenings. **$$$**

✖ **Le Caf Conc** 13 Av de la Nation; m 089 891 0592; e cafconc@jobantech.cd; ⏰ from 07.00 daily. A restaurant of true fine dining specialising in French cuisine. Also has pastries & foie gras. **$$$**

✖ **Le Cercle Gourmand** Cercle de Kinshasa (Golf club), Gombe; m 081 715 5252; e cerclegourmand@gbs.cd; ⏰ from 18.30 daily. Excessively posh restaurant at Kinshasa's golf club catering to the city's elite. Interior decorated by the woman who runs the Symphonie des Arts. **$$$$**

✖ **Le Delice** Av Colonel Ebeya; m 088 841 682; ⏰ from 18.00 daily. Outdoor restaurant with a wide selection of European dishes, pizzas & wines. **$$**

✖ **Pizzeria Chez Nicola** Av Petit Pont, Gombe; m 081 502 2050; ⊕ from 16.00 daily. Serves Italian dishes as well as pizza, out in the diplomatic neighbourhoods. $$$

✖ **Restaurant Chez Nawab** 74 Av Katanga, corner of Bd du 30 Juin; m 099 823 1818; ⊕ from 17.00 daily. Indian & Pakistani fare with a nightly buffet. $$

✖ **Restaurant Chez Patrick** Av du Port 173 (Forescom Bldg), Gombe; m 081 990 9888; ⊕ from 18.00 daily. Offering grilled game meats & imported wines. $$$$

✖ **Restaurant La Perle** Bd du 30 Juin, near Pl de Nelson Mandela; m 084 48038. Upmarket Chinese restaurant with secure parking area, & a full upper level of private dining rooms. Buffet available on Mon & Wed. $$

✖ **Restaurant Mandarin** Bd du 30 Juin, INSS Bldg 7th level; m 088 41716/099 31358; ⊕ from 18.00 daily. Chinese restaurant occupying the top level of the Goverment Social Security Building, with secure parking, an extensive wine list & several set menus. $$$$

✖ **Restaurant Papageno, Memling Hôtel** 5 Av du Tchad; m 081 700 1111; ⊕ from 07.00 daily. Dishes served à la carte & in an AC environment. Offers b/fasts for those staying at the hotel. Immaculate service & quality, but you do pay for it. $$$$

✖ **Super Aubaine Restaurant** 6081 Av Lokele, Gombe; m 088 48368; ⊕ from 18.00 daily. Specialises in high-quality Congolese cuisine; large guarded parking area. $$$$

MID-RANGE AND TAKE-AWAY Every hotel of a decent size has some sort of restaurant, and they tend to offer food of similar quality to the rooms – and they aren't a bad option if you are feeling less than adventurous and don't want to negotiate a taxi ride across town. Many of these places also double as bars once it gets late enough.

✖ **3615** Bd du 30 Juin; m 099 995 1576. Better known as a nightspot, but offers excellent pizzas & burgers. Avoid it after 21.00 if you're not interested in carrying on conversations with local prostitutes. $$$

✖ **Extreme Pizzeria & Club** 278 Av de L'Equateur; m 088 01863/099 25126; ⊕ from 18.00 daily. Serving up Italian dishes, especially pizzas, & open late for drinks. In the city centre. $$

✖ **Le Chantilly** 707 Av Colonel Lukusa, Gombe; m 081 993 0300; e lechantilly@yahoo.com; ⊕ 09.00–20.00 daily. Pastry & ice-cream shop. Makes cakes on order, has parking area along with AC seating room.

✖ **Le Plein Vent** 7ème étage Résidence des Flamboyants, Gombe; m 081 993 0300; e lechantilly@yahoo.com; ⊕ from 19.00 daily. Specialises in European fondues, run by the same folks as Le Chantilly Restaurant. $$$

✖ **L'Orangerie** 585 Bd du 30 Juin; m 089 10344/081 493 7844/098 273 997. Offers a higher-end buffet on w/ends, & has a cheaper menu for snacks & drinks. In the city centre. Outdoor terrace & indoor AC dining room with an eye on quality. $$$

✖ **Paladin Lebanese Restaurant** Av de la Nation; m 099 822 0820/099 909 9199; ⊕ 11.00–21.00 daily. Lebanese eatery in the city centre, with take-away option available. Serves burgers as well as authentic Lebanese cuisine. $$

✖ **Patisserie La Nouvelle** Av de L'Equateur; m 081 998 9000; ⊕ 07.00–18.00 daily. High-quality European pastry shop in the city's centre with excellent b/fasts, fresh-baked bread, & a wide variety of products imported from Europe. $$

BUDGET

✖ **Al Dar** Bd du 30 Juin, Immeuble Travhydro; m 088 04134/099 49555; ⊕ 11.00– 22.00 daily. Popular budget Lebanese restaurant in the city centre along the main boulevard with burgers, juice, & the usual trappings of Middle Eastern eateries in the Congos. $$

✖ **Hunga Busta Chicken & Pizzeria** Bd du 30 Juin, Galerie du Centenaire; m 099 823 9796/081 514 1400; ⊕ from 10.00–21.00 daily. 2 separate

restaurants right next to each other, each specialising in some fast food – the chicken restaurant has burgers & fried chicken in a decidedly Western fast-food atmosphere, while the pizzeria churns out decent pizzas from its own pizza oven. Prices are not exceedingly cheap, but are on the lower end of Kinshasa's choices for eating out. $$

ENTERTAINMENT AND NIGHTLIFE

A few expatriate enclaves have popped up in recent years thanks to the influx of international staff. Most of them are incredibly expensive – expect to pay around US$9 for a cocktail and US$70 for a bottle of cheap liquor. They're geared towards those with expense accounts, and if you are on one, you'll have a great time. If you're not, make sure you look at the prices before ordering. Furthermore any place geared towards expats will encounter the ages-old practice of women (and sometimes men) for hire plying their trade – as a foreign male (or even lone female), you're fair game, so don't expect too much privacy in these places. All of these venues open around 21.00, get quite crowded by 23.00 and stay open all night. Most are closed on Sundays.

♀ **3615** Bd du 30 Juin; m 099 995 1576. Pronounced 'Trente-Six Quinze', it offers decent-priced drinks & good-quality Western food, open late with an open-air terrace.

☆ **Chez Ntemba** US$5 cover charge. The place to be if you're an upwardly mobile Congolese. Crowded dancefloor any evening of the week with plasma TVs blasting only the most popular of Congolese pop music.

☆ **Discotheque Akropolis** A trendy new nightclub right in front of Rond-point Victoire geared towards Congolese w/enders.

☆ **Hôtel de Crèche** A venerable institution of Kinshasa's on a rooftop terrace; live music is offered nightly. Plastic chairs, Primus beer, & an all-Congolese crowd with no pretences.

☆ **Michelle** Bd du 30 Juin. No cover, but it's made up by the high price of drinks. Western popular music & a small dancefloor packed with prostitutes.

☆ **Mon Beau** Av Bandundu. US$10 cover charge, the trendiest & most expensive club of its type in Kinshasa. Plenty of Western pop music & nary a Congolese tune in sight.

♀ **Night Spot Banshee** Av de L'Equateur; m 099 994 9329. Drinking spot in the city centre with pool tables, blue neon lights, a thatch roof, & plenty of plastic furniture. Also offers cheap food.

☆ **Standing** Av des Syndicats 315, Gombe; m 081 888 8880. Another expatriate enclave further away from the main boulevard, with much the same characteristics as Michelle & Mon Beau.

SHOPPING

There is one bona fide department store in Kinshasa, recently opened, called **Hassan et Frère** on the corner of Avenue de la Paix and Avenue des Aviateurs. They have a wide selection of imported furniture, stationery, imported foodstuffs, and other things for those who live long term in Kinshasa.

Several large supermarkets for the expatriate population have emerged along Kinshasa's Boulevard du 30 Juin. They stock a wide selection of imported wines and liquors, local fresh vegetables, as well as imported dairy and other products. Their selections are excellent and easily the best place to do any grocery shopping in the entire DR Congo – **Peloustore**, **Alimentation Express** and **Supermarché Bam** (all ⊕ 08.00–18.00 Mon–Fri; reduced hrs on Sat, Sun & holidays) are all of comparable quality with a large selection of European products. Some vegetable sellers hang out in front of Alimentation Express if you want some local produce.

For souvenirs, there is a large **Artisans' Market** just in front of the train station where plenty of decent deals can be had for the popular souvenirs of Congo – wooden masks, local weapons, fabrics – they're all available. Be prepared for a little bargaining. Probably the best place for high-end contemporary Congolese artwork is at the **Symphonie des Arts** out in the Kintambo commune (15 Av de L'Avenir; m 081 990 1000; e symphoniedesarts@ic.cd; ⊕ 09.00–18.00 daily). The souvenir shop has numerous excellent examples of recently created crafts, as well as an excellent selection of contemporary painting. The difference between here and the market by the train station is, of course, that you know these things will be of the highest quality available as they have been selected by a curator.

If you want to explore the latest in Congolese music, I recommend **Honorable Music Shop** (m *085 87187*) at Rond-point Victoire – it's a medium-sized shop with a large selection of compact discs and cassette tapes of local musicians, including up-and-coming acts who can afford to get a tape recorded. They also have a wide selection of music from around west and central Africa.

And finally, if you need some sort of European goods, both the **Grand** and the **Memling** hotels' shopping arcades have a variety of things hard to get anywhere else in the country.

PRACTICALITIES

MEDICAL CLINICS In the event of a problem, the **Centre Medical de Kinshasa (CMK)** remains the most common for a visit (*Av Wagenia;* m *12 20875;* m *088 05011*). In addition, the **Centre Privé D'Urgence** (*Av du Commerce;* m *089 50305*) is used to handling foreign travellers in an emergency. For anything exceedingly serious, however, medical evacuation to Europe or South Africa should be your first option.

Pharmacies are quite simple to find in the city centre. One of the most comprehensive (though a little expensive) is **Pharmacie du Centenaire** (*Galerie Centenaire;* m *098 22 2221;* ⊕ *24hrs*). Both the Memling and Grand hotels have pharmacies in their shopping areas.

BANKS The biggest of Kinshasa's banks is **BCDC** almost right in the city centre, and it has a very private, clean and personalised wing on the second floor where foreigners can open an account and receive cash advances by credit cards. The rest of the bank is an ancient mess, but BCDC accumulates most of the DR Congo's foreign funds because of their welcoming attitude in this little stretch of offices. **ProCredit Bank Congo** opened an ATM at the end of 2006, though as of yet it is not connected with international networks.

For money transfers, any number of places will do – and there are several different companies operating. **Western Union** is naturally the largest, but **Moneygram** and **BIAC** are two other options. Bank headquarters in Kinshasa can send and receive transactions to whomever they are affiliated with.

$ **BCDC** Bd du 30 Juin; m 089 24152/081 518 1768; f 088 04690; e dir@bcdc.cd; www.bcdc.cd; ⊕ 08.00–16.00 Mon–Fri, 08.00–12.00 Sat
$ **Citigroup** Corner of Avs Colonel Lukusa & Ngongo Lutete; m 081 700 7000; ⊕ 08.00–16.00 Mon–Fri, 08.00–12.00 Sat. While a subsidiary of the international banking corporation Citibank, they do not offer cash advances or money transfers on the spot. However, one can get access to their Citibank account from abroad, with some prodding.
$ **ProCredit Bank Congo** Av des Aviateurs 4b, Gombe; m 089 96600; f 49 69 255 77042; e info@procreditbank.cd; ⊕ 08.00–16.00 Mon–Fri

POST
✉ **DHL** 180 Av de Marché m 12 21526; ⊕ 08.00–17.30 Mon–Fri, 08.30–14.30 Sat. Should be your first port of call.

INTERNET Two internet cafés I have used often are just behind the Galerie du Centenaire, and charge a few dollars an hour. Speed and connectivity tends to be good, but not infallible.

FOREIGN EMBASSIES

ⓔ Angola Bd du 30 Juin, NR 44/13, Gombe; ☏ 12 32415; f 12 27890

ⓔ Belgium Bldg du Cinquantenaire, Pl du 27 Octobre; ☏ 20 109; f 12 21058

ⓔ Benin 3990 Av des Cliniques, Gombe; ☏ 12 28822

ⓔ Cameroon 171 Bd du 30 Juin, Gombe; m 099 16822

ⓔ Canada 17 Pumbu Av, Gombe; m 0895 0310/0895 0311/0895 0312; f 099 75 403/081 301 6515; e kinshasa@international.gc.ca

ⓔ Central African Republic Av Mont Des Arts, Gombe

ⓔ China 447 Av des Aviateurs, Gombe; m 081 333 0263; f 008 737 6366 7861; e chinaemb_cd@mfa.gov.cn; www.cg.chineseembassy.org

ⓔ Congo 176 Bd du 30 Juin, Gombe; m 099 71453

ⓔ Cuba Av Katanga No 87, Gombe; m 081 730 2489

ⓔ France 97 Av du Tchad, (near the Memling Hôtel); ☏ 12 21403

ⓔ Germany 82 Av Roi-Baudouin, Gombe; m 089 48201/089 48202/089 48203; f 813 46 44 61

ⓔ Greece Av des Trois Z, Gombe; m 081 880 5031

ⓔ Iran 78 Bd du 30 Juin, Gombe; m 081 907 2915

ⓔ Italy Av de la Mongala 8, Gombe; m 081 555 3651; f 081 555 3654; e ambitalykin@ic.cd; www.ambkinshasa.esteri.it

ⓔ Japan Bldg Citibank 2eme etage, Av Colonel Lukusa, Gombe; m 081 880 5912

ⓔ Kenya 4002 Av de Louganda, Gombe; m 099 31936

ⓔ Nigeria 141 Bd du 30 Juin, Gombe; m 081 700 5143

ⓔ Poland 63 Av de la Justice, Gombe; m 081 700 6327

ⓔ Russia 80 Av de la Justice, Gombe; m 098 43 1890; e ambrus@ic.cd

ⓔ South Africa Av Ngongo Lutete, Gombe; m 081 700 5800; f 088 03717

ⓔ Sweden 89–93 Av Roi-Baudouin, Gombe; m 098 586 735; e ambassaden.kinshasa@foreign.ministry.se

ⓔ Tanzania 142 Bd du 30 Juin, Gombe; m 081 407 0077

ⓔ Turkey 18 Av Pumbu, Gombe; m 081 1700 7371; e tckinsbe@raga.net

ⓔ United Kingdom 83 Av Roi-Baudouin (ex Av Lemera), Gombe; m 098 16 9111; e ambrit@ic.cd

ⓔ United States 310 Av des Aviateurs; m 081 884 4623

ⓔ Zambia 5458 Av de L'Ecole; m 099 99437

WHAT TO SEE AND DO

Describing what 'to do' in Kinshasa is difficult; this is a city low on sights, but high on atmosphere. It eludes the average tourist because it is generally bereft of historical monuments or formal cultural institutions, yet it is in many ways the real heart of central Africa, an immense social force in its own right. It is a city to be experienced; a city to hang out in; a city to speak to the locals; a city to have a drink; a city to get harassed by prostitutes and pestered by street kids. Take some taxis around, witness the vast night markets, blown speakers blasting Kinshasa's latest beats, and see where it all begins and ends in the Congo. Trying to 'do' Kinshasa is a fruitless effort, as it often defies description: while academics, journalists and politicians describe it as a dead city, it is very much alive – in a different way. It is like a refugee camp with an infrastructure, an ever-shifting mass of people without an absolute centrepoint of purpose. Kinshasa is not dead by any means: it is the quintessential African city, created out of happenstance by Europeans and overrun by circumstances of conflict. It is a large disorderly mass; witnessing it, and being a part of it, is what Kinshasa is all about.

Try not to be the outsider, the tourist, the observer: it can be your city as much as it has been that of anyone else. It is a city to construct your own experiences, to take away your own memories. It is never the same place twice, and while certain areas sort of keep up appearances in spite of it all, it was never meant to be anything more than a meeting point, a transit spot along Malebo Pool, rather than a permanent fixture. This could change in the future, but for now Kinshasa is more of a place to feel the rhythm of life than a place to tick off sights.

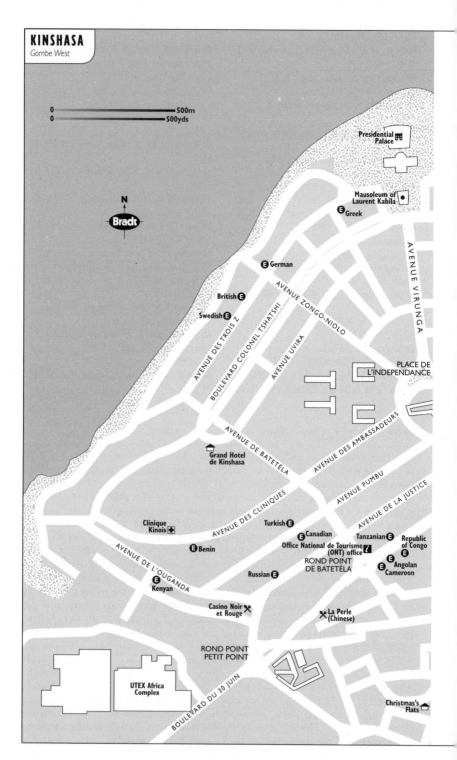

KINSHASA
Gombe West

0 ——————— 500m
0 ——————— 500yds

Presidential
Palace

Mausoleum of
Laurent Kabila

E Greek

E German

British **E**

Swedish **E**

AVENUE DES TROIS Z

BOULEVARD COLONEL TSHATSHI

AVENUE ZONGO-NIOLO

AVENUE UVIRA

AVENUE VIRUNGA

PLACE DE
L'INDEPENDANCE

AVENUE DE BATETÉLA

Grand Hotel
de Kinshasa

AVENUE DES AMBASSADEURS

AVENUE PUMBU

AVENUE DE LA JUSTICE

AVENUE DES CLINIQUES

Clinique
Kinois

Turkish **E**

E Canadian

Tanzanian **E**

Republic
of Congo **E**

E Benin

Office National de Tourisme
(ONT) office

E
Angolan
Cameroon

ROND POINT
DE BATETÉLA

Russian **E**

AVENUE DE L'OUGANDA

E
Kenyan

Casino Noir
et Rouge

La Perle
(Chinese)

ROND POINT
PETIT POINT

UTEX Africa
Complex

BOULEVARD DU 30 JUIN

Christmas's
Flats

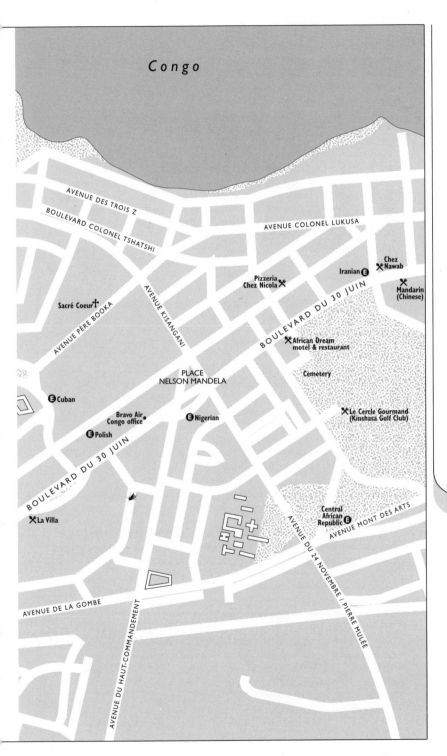

Congo

AVENUE DES TROIS Z

BOULEVARD COLONEL TSHATSHI

AVENUE COLONEL LUKUSA

Chez
Nawab ✗

Iranian 🄴

Pizzeria
Chez Nicola ✗

Mandarin
(Chinese) ✗

BOULEVARD DU 30 JUIN

Sacré Coeur ✝

AVENUE PÈRE BOOKA

AVENUE KISANGANI

African Dream ✗
motel & restaurant

PLACE
NELSON MANDELA

Cemetery

🄴 Cuban

Bravo Air
Congo office

🄴 Nigerian

Le Cercle Gourmand ✗
(Kinshasa Golf Club)

🄴 Polish

BOULEVARD DU 30 JUIN

✗ La Villa

Central
African 🄴
Republic

AVENUE MONT DES ARTS

AVENUE DU 24 NOVEMBRE | PIERRE MULELE

AVENUE DE LA GOMBE

AVENUE DU HAUT-COMMANDEMENT

Some 14 years after independence, and under the glowering presence of Mobutu Sésé Seko, Zaire was seeking to revitalise its image – and tell the world that it was a new nation, filled with riches, a stable government, magnificent cities, and destined to be a prominent player on the international stage. As is always the case in the Congo, nothing is ever done in half measures, and Mobutu found an opportunity to promote his nation with some familiar and famous American sports celebrities: Don King, George Foreman and Muhammad Ali.

Don King himself was newly released from jail and itching to get Ali fighting Foreman. Storms of sports writers had been speculating on Foreman, the new boxing champion, and whether Ali could even last a few minutes in the ring with him. Yet to fight Foreman, Ali's camp wanted a significant sum of money – US$3 million. Don King agreed to get him the money, but warned that the fight would have to be held outside the USA in that case. Ali's handlers agreed – and Don King found his funding in Zaire's coffers.

Mobutu had agreed to pay US$10 million for the fight, split between Ali and Foreman. Their arrival in Kinshasa was a massive public relations coup for Zaire, and in the weeks of preparation leading up to the fight the nation was in the world's media spotlight.

The boxers would reside at the presidential village outside Kinshasa in N'sele, while journalists stayed in the city. The capital itself was under the microscope by Mobutu and the FAZ – one notorious evening, the president rounded up 1,000 of the city's highest crime leaders and brought them to the stadium. At random, he picked 100, and had his soldiers execute them on the spot – he warned the remainder that if so much as a pocket was picked while Ali and Foreman were in the country, everyone else would suffer the same fate. Some say that while the Rumble in the Jungle was being staged, Kinshasa was the safest city on earth.

Muhammad Ali took advantage of this safety – he was seen continuously reaching out to the Zairians, talking to people on the street, gaining the favour of everyone in the nation. George Foreman, on the other hand, remained reclusive; by the time of the fight, Ali had all of Zaire rooting for him, and the trademark slogan 'Ali boma Ye', Lingala for 'Ali Kill Him', could be heard throughout Kinshasa.

The fight was originally scheduled for 25 September 1974, but Foreman was cut during a sparring match. Foreman's handlers asked that the fight be cancelled; Ali was furious. He begged Don King to fly in Joe Frazier, another prominent boxer, so the fight could go on in Kinshasa. Mobutu was not keen on having the fight cancelled either, and hinted to both of them that any attempt to leave Zaire before fighting was very unwelcome.

It was then delayed by five more weeks until 30 October. Foreman was seen as unbeatable, but over eight rounds Muhammad Ali wore him down in Kinshasa's intense humidity and won the fight. Both athletes went away with millions of dollars, in the largest purse ever to have been awarded to boxers in history.

Mobutu's Zaire came off better, having proven to the world that the African country, ridden by conflict for so long, could stage a major international sporting event. It has remained the largest event of its kind ever held on the continent until South Africa hosts the football World Cup in 2010. It also changed the sport of boxing for ever – elevating the prizes and audiences to levels never known before.

To learn more about the Rumble in the Jungle read Norman Mailer's book *The Fight*, penned just after he left Kinshasa in 1974 and watch the 1996 documentary *When We Were Kings*, that centres entirely on this moment in sports history.

There are a few conspicuous diversions, including the **Golf Club**, which charges US$30 for a round with equipment during the weekdays and US$50 on weekends. A walk along the **Congo River** can be interesting, and there is a viewpoint near the rapids at the western end of the city – if you are taking photos, be careful of the **Presidential Palace**, which is an area overrun with soldiers and officials. Tourists are more than welcome to pass by without a camera, however. Right in front of the palace is the **Mausoleum of Laurent Kabila**, and while historians may tell you one story about Father Kabila's exploits in the DR Congo, his popularity never really waned. And if the democratic part of the Democratic Republic of Congo really gets going again, the **Palais du Peuple** will be the national assembly building. Closed for several years, it was guarded by UN soldiers during the elections. Right beside it is the **Stadium des Martyrs**, where some football matches are played on a regular basis – however, very rarely does the DR Congo team play an international match here, as the fear of rioting is too great. For that, head down to any drinking spot and catch it on television. And both the **Marché Central** and the **Rond-point Victoire** are excellent places to catch the feel of Kinshasa, even during the daytime. At night, however, be on your toes in these areas.

Out in Ngaliema the **Ethnographic Museum** (⊕ *10.00–16.30 Tue–Sat; US$10 admission*) is a unique site that has many historical artefacts from the days of the Belgian Congo – 45,000 according to their director, and plans are under way to clean up and expand their showrooms. Pity that many of these artefacts have not been maintained properly: the original boat that Henry Morton Stanley used to traverse the rapids lies in the museum's courtyard, a rusting hulk these days. In its heyday it could be dismantled quickly and transported by land over great distances. There is also a pioneers' cemetery in the complex, and a small movie theatre that Mobutu built in 1970 to use for propaganda films. The museum is set on a hill overlooking the Congo River, with excellent views over to Brazzaville, and was the original spot that Stanley rested at when he arrived on the shores of Malebo Pool. However, being a hill in an otherwise flat area, the site is considered 'militarily significant' and is guarded by soldiers; this means that they may hit you up for a bribe to get through the gates, and that you shouldn't be taking any pictures.

Near to the museum is the highly recommended **Symphonie des Arts** (m *099 990 1000;* e *symphoniedesarts@ic.cd*), a great escape from Kinshasa in the Kintambo commune. It's a large mansion surrounded by a wonderful botanical garden, complete with various birdlife, and at the back is a stage where performances are held on occasion. If you're living here and need something to keep your children occupied, they offer dance classes throughout the year. As mentioned the souvenir shop and selection of paintings are excellent, and those with a large budget for souvenirs should definitely make a visit.

Along the road to Matadi is the large park **Symphonies Naturelles**, dubbed a decent escape from the urban sprawl of Kinshasa. It has a bar and restaurant, as well as several walking trails amongst the forest. Various varieties of plantlife dot the site.

Further south near the Résidence Mutchimba Hôtel are the **Serpents du Congo** (*Av Kananga 14, Quartier Pigeon, Ngaliema;* m *081 991 8530, 099 18530;* e *sdc@lesserpentsducongo.org;* ⊕ *10.00–12.00 & 16.00–18.00 Thu–Sun; US$10 admission, US$5 for children*), an excellent collection of snakes from around central Africa. At present there are 35 species on display, often nocturnal, though they're coaxed out of their hiding holes for visitors.

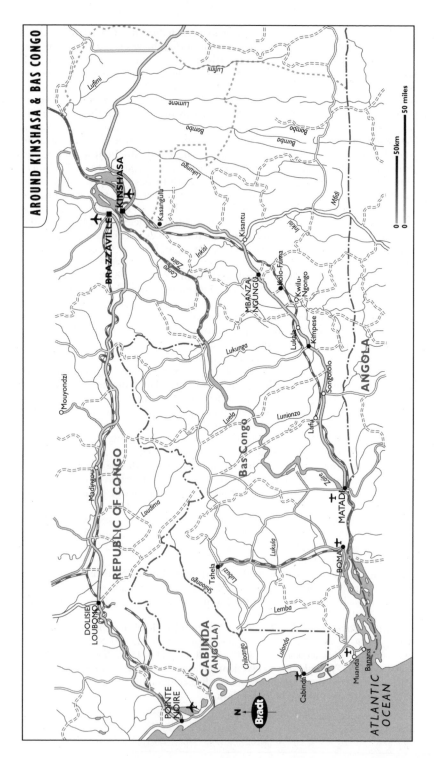

AROUND KINSHASA & BAS CONGO

6

Around Kinshasa and Bas-Congo

Head outside Kinshasa and you'll see some intriguing sights right near the big city – though, just like points deeper in the country, a 4x4 vehicle is necessary. The urban sprawl of the capital is enveloping even more of the eastern bank of the Congo River, as the population continues to multiply. With prosperity comes urbanisation, and families who have managed to save up a few hundred dollars buy small plots of land on the fringes of the city. They create modest-sized brick houses, do their best to grow small crops, and nurture them with the water from nearby rivers. What may have once been a wilderness is quickly becoming a central African suburbia of sorts.

Move southwest along the highway towards the coast and you arrive in Bas-Congo, an easier place to be than the raucous capital. Most of the war never really got this far, making the population less skittish and the infrastructure a little more enviable. On the other hand, it has always found its own way to go about things and has never been the preferred region for any head of state. Mobutu Sésé Seko was often snubbed in Bas-Congo, and Kabila's loyalties lay in the east. Yet the people of the province don't seem to mind too much as they have the nation's only port, an extremely important bargaining chip, and are right next door to Angola for their other amenities. They have mines, beaches, bridges, and the country's largest hydro-electric dam. Next to Katanga, they have managed their wealth better than any other region of the DR Congo.

Bas-Congo's sights are well worth visiting, and after the Kivus, this is most likely the only other region that truly understands what tourism can do for their own regional development. Matadi, Boma and Muanda all have plenty of natural sights as well as some of the best historical monuments in the nation. The police and military are a little more familiar with foreigners running around taking pictures of things. The damage of conflict has not displaced people into huge areas of wilderness. It's not only the gateway to the nation, but also a great starting point for people who don't want to battle with the difficulties of going too far inland in the DR Congo.

AROUND KINSHASA

KINKOLE (⊕ 04°19.35 S, 15°30.46 E) Kinkole is Kinshasa's Miami Beach, if you will: it is a party town for weekenders, a place to show off your fancy new car while cruising along the strip, filled with street-side food sellers and bars. A few years back the place was empty, as partying was something far from anyone's mind, but development has turned the area around. What it lacks, though, is a decent beach: don't come here expecting to find one.

It has a few other sights of note, however. Kinshasa's primary **Fish Market** is here, a winding and smelly place where the city gets most of its seafood. It's really far too small a market for the size of the capital, which could explain why fish seems expensive at times. The local speciality is *maboke*, a fish cut into pieces, covered in spices, wrapped in a palm leaf and smoked over charcoal. It's sold on the main thoroughfare from the highway to the river.

Local music can be heard on Sunday nights, starting at dusk and ending around 21.00. Things usually wind down around 23.00, as most people need to walk back to their homes – sometimes all the way back to the city. To get here, shared taxis go from the Marché de la Liberté to the suburbs in Kinshasa Province along the road to Kikwit. It will cost around 300Fc for a space in the shared taxi.

 Where to stay There are a few hotels in the town to stay at, the best of which is **Hôtel Grassius** (*10 rooms; $$*), with a rather murky-looking pool and a bar on the upper level where you can watch the street below. The rooms have fans but no air conditioning.

LOLA YA BONOBO SANCTUARY (⊕ *04°29.07.78 S, 15°16.02.40 E*) The curious bonobo, the last of the primate subspecies to be discovered, is a unique creature that is sure to entertain even those not really interested in animals. The best place to see them is near Kinshasa, at the **Lola Ya Bonobo Sanctuary** (⊕ *09.00–16.00 Tue–Sun; free admission Mon–Fri, US$10 Sat/Sun*).

Most of these bonobos were rescued from local markets, doomed to be sold for bushmeat, and then raised by dedicated Congolese women. Therefore, they have some decidedly human characteristics to their behaviour: they are innately playful, throwing sand at local visitors, and will steal your camera if you get too close. They are usually given water bottles, which they studiously use to collect water from their reservoir. They enjoy playing games with visitors, even harassing them to an extent. A visit to the sanctuary is easily one of the more rewarding things to do in the vicinity of Kinshasa.

The sanctuary was founded in 1994, but was not formally opened to the public until 29 September 2002. There are a few steep slopes, and a walking trail of several kilometres around an electrified fence which keeps the bonobos in and humans out. There is also a large information centre, and numerous placards which explain the behaviour and habitat of the creature. Usually the bonobos are most active in the morning, washing in the lake, and often retreat into the forest during the afternoon. Some visitors have lamented that the bonobos were not visible at all for the entire day. Nonetheless, a morning visit increases your chances of a sighting.

For more information on the qualities of the bonobo, consult the animal guide in *Appendix 1*, page 289. Note also that because these bonobos have been raised by humans, they are not a good indicator of how bonobos in the wild behave. For that, you'll have to get out to the new Yoko Kala Reserve east of Basankusu, the Salonga Parks, or Lac Tumba south of Mbandaka. There are future plans to release some of these bonobos into the wild in a reserve near the village of Kikongo, south of Bandundu.

Getting there and away The Lola Ya Bonobo Sanctuary is, sadly, not the easiest place to visit – it's along a muddy track southwest of Kinshasa, along the Lukuya River and situated right beside the **Lukuya Falls** – hardly worth recommending on their own as they drop about only 2m, the falls mark the entrance to the sanctuary, which requires a 4x4 vehicle to get around. At weekends there is a resident researcher who is willing to answer questions and provide an information session on the bonobo. Also be sure to visit their website for more information (*www.friendsofbonobos.org*).

One arrives in Bas-Congo upon the first checkpoint out of Kinshasa, a 'Péage' route, where a dollar or two needs to be paid for the privilege of driving on a paved road. The first town in Bas-Congo is **Kasangulu**, a rather nondescript place where you might notice that they actually put speed bumps on the highway. This is usually where the police sit, and stand in front of random vehicles – have about 200Fc ready in a handshake-friendly manner and you'll get to where you're going much faster.

ZONGO FALLS (⊕ *04°46.42.90 S, 14°54.27.96 E*) Truly an impressive sight on the Inkisi River, Zongo is worth a stop. The winding waterway crashes down about 60m in spectacular fashion, creating a cauldron of steam and mist between two sheer cliffsides covered in foliage. The water eventually finds its way to the Congo River. A hydro-electric dam is further downstream and provides some power for the region.

There is a hotel here which has eight bungalows (\$\$) and a bar/restaurant terrace on the river's edge (**\$\$\$**). They also offer campsites (\$) to visitors with their own equipment. The caretakers generally ask for 1,000Fc from anyone who visits, to help maintain the site.

Getting there and away To reach Zongo, turn off at Suna Bata (⊕ *04°54.02.51 S, 15°10.01.18 E*) and follow the winding maze of dirt roads from there. Parts of this track are simply mudholes, so anything less than a 4x4 will spell disaster. Furthermore, there are several turn-offs on the way so ask for some directions from local villagers. Some signs provide assistance, but not enough. With your own vehicle, plan on a one-way journey of about two hours from the turn-off.

Some large trucks can be seen plying this road, which means that in theory at least, one could get public transport to somewhere near the falls. Ask in Kasangulu or Sunabata if you are determined to do this.

KISANTU BOTANICAL GARDENS (⊕ *05° 07.55 S, 15° 06.07 E*) Near the small town of Kisantu is a highlight of Kinshasa's outskirts, the **Kisantu Botanical Gardens** (⊕ *until 17.00 daily; US$10 admission pp*), which are now being maintained (to an extent) by the DR Congo government. The gardens were originally founded in 1893 by Brother Gillet, who cultivated every kind of flower that could survive in the region's climate. Roughly 3,000 species existed here at the height of the gardens' popularity, but as usual, the war took its toll: most of the flowers were taken and sold by rampaging soldiers from various armies on their marches towards Kinshasa. Orchids especially were prized by collectors and all were removed. The only things remaining from the old times are things that couldn't be taken easily: the trees. Various species from all over Africa and South America remain at Kisantu. The flowers are being reintroduced, slowly, and this is being done primarily with tourism in mind; if you're passing through, it would be good to give them some encouragement by showing up.

Just south of Kisantu on the road towards Kizenga are several more small waterfalls: **Luguya**, **M'fidi** and **Mosi**. They're situated slightly away from the road, so that it'll take a bit of asking around amongst the locals to locate them.

MBANZA-NGUNGU (⊕ *05°15.06 S, 14°52.07 E*) One thing that strikes visitors to Mbanza-Ngungu is the pleasant climate: the humid, acrid air of Kinshasa or the humid overbearing sea breeze of Matadi is non-existent here. It's high up in the hills and exudes a pleasant mountain-town quality, with crisp weather in the daytime and almost chilly at night. It was once called Thysville and was a popular weekend resort town due to the pleasant climate. These are the hills that kept so many explorers from going too far inland during their early visits to central Africa, and the surrounding scenery is quite striking.

Getting there and away Mbanza-Ngungu is halfway between Matadi and Kinshasa, taking two hours to reach from either city. It isn't much of a hub for transport as most vehicles going to either place don't stop here, therefore shared taxis to closer destinations tend to be the only way to move on. Showing up at the taxi stand and stating your final destination will inevitably get enough advice to find transport.

For the caves (see below), a 4x4 is absolutely necessary – though even with that you may find yourself walking part of the way as the road withers away into a grass trail after a few kilometres. For either cave you must get permission from the local village chief at **Ntoto** (✪ *05°16.55.57 S, 14°52.06.26 E*) who will generally ask US$20 per person for a guided tour. The village is only accessible by foot. He has several lanterns available, but I'd recommend bringing at least one torch and an extra set of batteries. The caves are muddy even at the best of times, and slippery; bring decent boots and roll your pants up.

 Where to stay For lodging try **Hôtel Les Cascades** (*18 rooms;* $$) which has its own restaurant and terrace bar, with secure parking and breakfast included. A cheaper option, with shared bathrooms, is **Hôtel Kuma** (*10 rooms;* $).

What to see The best reason to visit Mbanza-Ngungu, however is for the famous caves in the nearby hills. There are two **caves**, Ndombolo Zipizuola (commonly known as Ngovo Cave) and Lukatu Poisson Aveugle (also sometimes called Dimba). Ngovo is the larger of the two, and the only one accessible in the wet season. Its navigable portion is several kilometres long, though in practice has never been fully explored. The last expedition was by an American group in 1973 who spent three months mapping the caves but never reached the end of them. The theory is that the system emerges somewhere near Zongo Falls. Therefore, don't get lost.

Lukatu Caves are under water for half of the year, and are most famous for their blind, colourless fish (their scientific name is *Coccobarbus geertsi*). These creatures have no eyes, and translucent skin. This is the only region in the world where the fish are known to exist, as attempts to breed them outside the cave have repeatedly failed.

MATADI ✪ 05°49.54 S, 13°27.56 E

Matadi is scenic and mountainous and historic and humid, the capital of Bas-Congo and primary port city of the DR Congo, a terminus for the nation's very first railway and the furthest point upstream one can travel by boat until reaching the rapids that stymied many an explorer. In its early days it was a small clutter of buildings right on the hill, buried amongst the mountains and cliffs of the shore, but in recent decades has enveloped the region entirely – with even Angola building its own port town right on the border. Business is booming, to an extent, with massive ships keeping the crane towers busy in the heavy humid air. As is often the case, many products exist in Matadi that never reach the hinterlands of the DR Congo, and it's a great place to stock up on supplies before going elsewhere. If you're waiting for a vehicle to get shipped in, drowning your sorrows at one of the country's most famous hotels, the Metropole, is a time-honoured tradition.

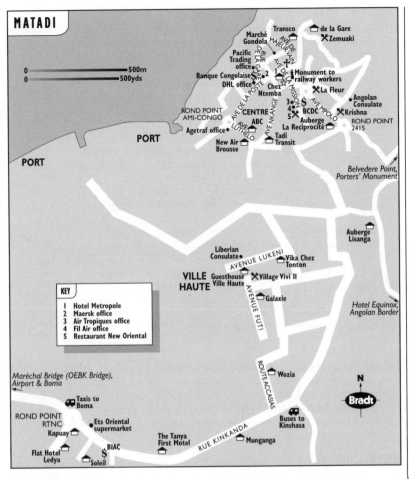

MATADI

KEY
1 Hotel Metropole
2 Maersk office
3 Air Tropiques office
4 Fil Air office
5 Restaurant New Oriental

6

HISTORY Diego Cão first arrived on the shores of Matadi during his maiden voyage up the Congo River in 1485, eventually navigating the Mpozo River and leaving a mark at the furthest point he explored. The Portuguese would found the village of Noqui some kilometres from where Matadi would be founded. Noqui would eventually be overrun and destroyed by the mid 19th century. Decades later, Henry Morton Stanley arrived on the same shores as Noqui during his voyage downstream from the east. He would found the fort of Matadi, just past the rapids, in 1879 upon his first trip commissioned by King Léopold.

Matadi's existence was critical to opening up the Congo. The first railway of central Africa was completed in 1898, but during its construction a well-beaten trail of Congolese porters moved goods through the rough landscape northeast to Malebo Pool. Thousands died in these years, hauling tonnes of items through the hills.

In general the wars that afflicted the rest of the DR Congo did not get to Matadi, with the exception of one rear-end invasion at the airport by Rwandan troops in 1998 who staged a bold landing and marched to Kinshasa from the west. Otherwise, the province remained mostly unscathed.

In January 2007, there were violent protests over the election of a new governor for Bas-Congo, as a local religious group accused of them being rigged. The figure

The seminal book *Heart of Darkness* grew from Joseph Conrad's own experiences in the Congo, and some versions include his *Congo Diary*: a brief, yet illuminating account of his few months in the country.

What he experienced was based on his sojourn there as a labourer, working for an unscrupulous employer (referred to as Delcommune), and his long trek from the docks of Matadi northeast to the bustling capital of Léopoldville (which he refers to as 'Kinschassa') while the railway to Stanley Pool was still under construction. In Matadi he would meet Roger Casement, the activist, and Conrad would undoubtedly be shaped by Casement's views on what was happening in the colony. He served on the ship *Roi des Belges*, experiencing further hardship along the way, and made one trip with the vessel upriver to Stanley Falls. He would return to Léopoldville three months later on 24 September 1890, and Matadi on 4 December. In all he spent less than five months in the Congo.

His time was not a pleasant one. The majority of Europeans he met, and the horrible conditions that Africans lived in, foretold his most important literary work. As a simple deckhand without any known ideologies, little would be hidden from him. Perhaps most intriguing is the lack of detail in his diaries regarding the worst excesses he may have seen in Congo Free State; those were saved for his work of fiction.

The accounts of his time in the Congo are found in the *Congo Diary and other Uncollected Pieces*, published in 1978. Several editions of *Heart of Darkness* have at least partial excerpts from the *Congo Diary*.

elected was a supporter of Joseph Kabila and not Jean-Pierre Bemba, who was extremely popular in the west. Over 100 were killed; yet, the city seemed to rebound quickly, with few repercussions afterwards. Jean-Pierre Bemba demanded the following day that a '*ville morte*' be observed, urging no-one to go to work or go outside. However life continued on, attesting to his waning influence across the region.

ORIENTATION One crosses the **Mpozo River** when arriving from Kinshasa, then winds along through the hills until finally arriving at the mouth of the Congo River, and the primary ports of the nation. To reach points west in Bas-Congo one crosses the **OEBK Bridge** (which stands for Organisation Équipage Banana-Kinshasa, also known as Pont Maréchal), a looming feat of engineering that dominates the Matadi skyline. The city runs on a roughly north–south axis with most new businesses operating in the hills around Matadi while the old town centre becomes more and more cluttered. To the east of the city are high peaks from where the surrounding landscape can be surveyed. The city is split into communes, the most notable of which for visitors being the **Commune de Matadi** which, as the name suggests, is the town centre. Head southwards and up in altitude and you arrive in **Ville Haute**, something of a nicer neighbourhood and sometimes called **Ciné Palace** due to the large conference area of the same name that dominates. On the road towards the OEBK Bridge and Boma is the **Commune de Kinkanda**.

GETTING THERE AND AROUND The city is well served by buses to Kinshasa, as well as aircraft at its airport on the north bank of the Congo River. Several flights depart daily for the capital, and a few each week westward to Boma and Muanda. **Air Tropiques** (m *099 832 1476*) and **Fil Air** (m *099 800 1486*) have offices beside each other in the town square. Sample fares include one-way to Kinshasa for US$125, Boma for US$75 and Muanda for US$85. A bus to Kinshasa costs around US$15 and will take six–eight hours. Boma is accessible by cramped shared taxis for US$6 with a two-hour travel time.

⌂ WHERE TO STAY

Expensive and mid-range Matadi's most famous old hotel is **Hôtel Metropole**, a little aged these days but a sight in itself – the central courtyard is a classic centrepiece of 1930s architecture and designed in such a way that it always remains cool, which is a prime attraction in this always hot and humid region of the DR Congo. The other hotels on the high end of things include **Guest House Ville Haute** in the surrounding hills and **Flat-Hôtel Ledya**, out near Rond Point RTNC and the most prestigious address in Matadi.

⌂ **Flat-Hôtel Ledya** (44 rooms) Av Sita, Kikanda; m 099 851 0208. Large secure parking area, high-end restaurant, pool & bar. All rooms have satellite TV, hot running water, AC. 23 sgls $$$, 10 dbls $$$, 2 suites $$$$, 7 apts $$$$, 2 presidential suites $$$$$

⌂ **Guest House Ville Haute** (5 rooms) Av Lukeni, Ville Haute; m 099 852 1181/829 3701. Set in a large private home in a quiet neighbourhood. High-quality rooms with AC, TV, hot running water. Family run. $$

⌂ **Hôtel Metropole** (63 rooms) Town centre, Matadi; m 085 513 7800. Large courtyard with bar & restaurant. All rooms have AC, cold running water, with hot water on request, & TV. B/fast inc. 55 sgls $$$, 8 apts $$$$

⌂ **Hôtel Vika Chez Tonton** (26 rooms) Av Lukeni, Ville Haute; m 099 877 9105/099 914 3333. Large hotel in Ville Haute with restaurant, disco, & parking out front. All rooms have AC & TV. 19 sgls/dbls $$, 7 apts $$$

Budget The city has plenty of low-priced hotels, but they can often get quite full – as Kinshasa's residents arrive here to pick up vehicles and process the paperwork for doing so.

⌂ **ABC Hôtel** Av Luthelo, Matadi; m 099 844 7618. Most rooms have AC, except for a few (often full) which have fans. Spacious courtyard. B/fast inc, & other dishes can be cooked on request. Sgl without AC $, sgl with AC $$

⌂ **Auberge La Réciprocité** Near Rond Point 2415, Matadi; m 099 843 0193. Has bar & restaurant, all rooms include AC & intermittent running water. Sgl $, dbl $$

⌂ **Auberge Lisanga** Ville Haute, on the road south to Kinshasa; m 099 851 2240/852 0175. Large complex run by a local church. Has many long-term residents. With secure parking, restaurant & conference room. B/fast inc. Communal rooms $, apt US$5 more.

⌂ **Hôtel de la Gare** Av de la Gare, Matadi; m 081 385 6626/099 863 8586. Rooms have AC & full bathtubs. Parking outside but not secured. Sgl $

⌂ **Hôtel Equinox** On the road south out of Kinshasa, on a hilltop overlooking the city; m 099 851 2382. Great views of the surrounding countryside, but you'll have to ask for some directions to get here (it's at ⊕ 05°50.37.78 S,

13°27.40.80 E). Has a restaurant & is set in a quiet neighbourhood. All rooms include AC, occasional running water, & TV. Sgl $/dbl $$

⌂ **Hôtel Galaxie** Av Futi No 14, Ville Haute; m 099 756 5597/099 852 3757. Basic rooms with fan only & intermittent running water. No restaurant. Sgl/dbl $

⌂ **Hôtel Kapuay** Near Rond Point RTNC; m 099 851 3917. Rather rundown place but has some parking out front & a terrace with a restaurant. Sgl without AC $, with AC $$, apt $$

⌂ **Hôtel Munganga** Rue Kinkanda. Has a restaurant & basic rooms. Sgl with fan only $, with AC $$

⌂ **Hôtel Soleil** Off Rue Kinkanda; m 099 851 0207. Large secure parking area & bar/restaurant within its walls. Decent rooms with TVs & AC in some of them. Sgl $$, with an extra US$5 for AC

⌂ **Hôtel Tadi Transit** Av Nkange, Matadi; m 099 871 3183/099 905 1237. A decent alternative if the New Air Brousse across the street is full. Basic rooms with AC but no running water. B/fast inc, other food available on request. Sgl $

🛏 **Hôtel Transco** Av Vivi 5381; m 098 51 2592. Rooms have AC. Hotel has a permanent restaurant & bar. Half-decent view of the river. Sgl $

🛏 **Hôtel Wozia** (26 rooms) Route Accasias, off Rue Kinkanda; m 099 851 2551/099 811 3443; e thiarsum@yahoofr. Set in a quiet neighbourhood halfway down a very bad dirt road. Has some internet services & a restaurant. All rooms have AC. Sgl $🛏 **New Air Brousse Hôtel** (15 rooms) Av

Luthelo No1, Matadi; m 085 511 8470; e airbrousse@yahoo.fr. Small but clean rooms have AC, TV, intermittent running water, & balconies with good views of the river & bridge. Has restaurant & bar, secure parking. B/fast inc. Sgl $$

🛏 **The Tanya First Motel** Rue Kinkanda No 30; m 099 035 1284. Has a secure parking area & a large terraced bar/restaurant out front. AC rooms with satellite TV. B/fast inc. $$

✕ WHERE TO EAT

✕ **Krishna Restaurant** m 085 180 9637; ⏱ 17.00–23.00 daily. Ethnic restaurant popular with recent immigrants. It serves up good Indian food on the second level overlooking Av Mpolo & has a well-stocked bar & AC dining area. $$$

✕ **Village Vivi II** m 099 851 0575/099 992 0440; ⏱ 17.30–23.00 daily. The best restaurant in Ville Haute, the Vivi is just up the road from Hôtel Galaxie. They have numerous Congolese dishes including locally caught antelope & fish, & plenty of manioc on the side. It has a parking area & is often filled with the upper crust of Matadi & those who wish to be near them. Some of the eating tables are outside which can get wet during the rainy season. $$$

✕ **Restaurant New Oriental** m 099 834 1405; ⏱ 11.00–22.00 daily. Is less expensive & offers shrimp, chicken & beef dishes as well as an evening BBQ on some days. $$

✕ **Zemuaki Restaurant** m 099 840 7577; ⏱ 16.00–21.00 daily. A cheaper option for Congolese fare in the town centre. It serves up some basic fish dishes local style. The atmosphere is a decidedly African-diner style, but can get quite busy in the evenings. $$

✕ **Restaurant La Fleur** ⏱ 12.00–20.00 daily. Serves inexpensive but quality Congolese food in a modest-sized house with a terraced dining area. $

ENTERTAINMENT AND NIGHTLIFE There are very few nightspots in the city, the most prominent of which is **Chez Ntemba Nightclub** right beside the Metropole. **Vika Chez Tonton** also has a large bar that blasts music deep into the night.

SHOPPING The **Marché Gondola** just behind the church is a small walkway filled with craft kiosks, old postcards and other knick-knacks and good for a quick gift stop. Near **Rond Point 2415** are several decent small shops to stock up on food and supplies before heading out of the city.

PRACTICALITIES

Banks and shipping Two banks in central Matadi can handle Western Union: **BCDC** (m *081 500 1016;* e *mtd@bcdc.cd;* ⏱ *08.00–16.00 Mon–Fri, 08.00–12.00 Sat*) and **Banque Congolaises** (*Av Majeur Vangu;* m *081 700 8489;* ⏱ *08.00–16.00 Mon–Fri, 08.00–12.00 Sat*). Out in Kinkanda there is the **BIAC** (*Rue Kinkanda;* m *081 700 4000;* ⏱ *08.00–16.30 Mon–Sat*).

If you're in Matadi waiting for a vehicle to arrive, there are a few places to check up on its delivery. At Rond Point Ami Congo on the southwest side is a multi-storey building and on the top level is the **Agetraf Office**. They are also responsible for Delmas and Grimaldi containers that arrive in Matadi. For **Maersk** (m *099 993 9444;* ⏱ *08.00–16.30 Mon–Fri*), head up Avenue de la Poste a little and their office is on the second level. **DHL** (m *099 851 3817/788 8818;* ⏱ *08.00–17.30 Mon–Fri, 08.00–12.00 Sat*) have an office right across the street, and finally **Pacific Trading** (m *085 180 8811;* e *albertnimy@yahoo.fr;* ⏱ *09.00–16.30 Mon–Fri*) is up the street on Rue de la Gare.

Consulates Matadi has an **Angolan Consulate** (⏱ *08.00–12.00 Mon–Fri*) near the general market, as well as, curiously enough, a **Liberian Consulate** (m *099 851*

1026; ☺ *daily, as the ambassador lives there*). Both will provide visas for onward travel to their respective countries.

WHAT TO SEE A great place to begin one's visit to Matadi is the top of **Point Belvedere** to the west of the town centre – it's a small drinking area and the highest spot in the city, with wonderful views of the OEBK Bridge to the west and the mountains to the northeast. There is a bronze map of the region which points out the peaks and the original roads and footpaths used in the late 19th century. From there **Peak Cambien** can be seen, a rocky outcropping that is the highest peak along the riverside and was used for initial surveying of the rail route northeast to Kinshasa. Follow the Mpozo River northwards from Peak Cambien and you'll run into the original **rail bridge** for the region, as well as the **Monument to the Porters** who perished during the decades before the railway was built. The monument is definitely off the beaten path, buried at the end of a grass trail near the river – you'll have to cross the rail bridge and then wind around to ☺ 05°49.37.06 S, 13°29.44.39 E. From the roadside it should take about half an hour. And of course the **OEBK Bridge** is one of the (only) feats of Congolese engineering, a landmark in its own right – spanning the mouth of the Congo River, it is also considered a strategic site – which means any foreign 'tourist' is assumed to be a CIA operative and needs to register (and explain themselves) to cross it. Needless to say, keep your camera tucked away when nearby; get your photos from somewhere further away, like Point Belvedere.

AROUND MATADI

Hiring a motorboat is an excellent way to see two points of interest down the Mpozo River just east of the town. The **Rock of Diego Cão** has several inscriptions of his on it, marking the furthest point of the Portuguese explorer during the maiden voyage of Europeans to the Congo River in 1485. Nearby are some **Fishermen's Caves** with excellent pastoral views of the river. At 12km east of Matadi is the village of **Pala Bala** (☺ 05°49.49 S, 13°33.14 E), where the first Protestant church of the region was built. The village was also where one of Henry Morton Stanley's closest friends during his expeditions, Léon Johnen, perished in 1887 from disease. West from Matadi along the river is the town of **Noqui** (☺ 05°50.44 S, 13°26.05 E), also spelled Noki or Nokki (not to be confused with the burgeoning port of the same name on the Angolan side of the river), which was the original Portuguese trading post in the area. Over the centuries it has seen the faces of many would-be explorers, including Sir Richard Francis Burton. It was also inhabited at the time of Henry Morton Stanley's arrival at the mouth of the river.

Follow Matadi's road north and you will arrive at several sets of rapids, first the **Yelala Rapids** roughly 15km outside the town. It requires a walk of several hours from the road, making it a full day's trip. Further north is the site of the **Inga Dam**, actually two dams, though together they run at a far reduced capacity. This area sports the largest drop of the Congo River as it heads towards the ocean, as well as decent road access, though the dams are well guarded. The possibility of a third modern dam is currently being discussed, and the potential is huge – enough hydro-electricity could be generated to power the entire nation, if not all of central Africa. Note that the dam is considered a strategic site, which means you can't simply show up and expect access; you'll need a permit to visit from the Minister of Hydro-electricity in either Kinshasa or Matadi, which isn't cheap, and runs to around US$200. Also be sure to get yourself a photo permit in addition to this from either city. You'll most likely also need your own private car to get there.

Following the same road further north are the final major rapids of **Isangila**, which was also the point in the river which finally did for the expedition of James Kingston Tuckey almost two centuries ago – had he managed to continue, he would have discovered the navigable regions of the river, and history may have been distinctly different.

BOMA ✤ 05°50.11 S, 13°03.33 E

Boma's history is rich, and it was an indispensable cornerstone of administration for the Belgian Congo through many decades. Capital of the entire colony from its inception in 1886 until 1920 or so, it remained the centrepoint of contact for Belgian officials until the administration moved completely to Léopoldville by 1929. Founded by the Portuguese centuries before the Belgians arrived, it was the primary stopping-off point for ships who wished to trade with the ancient African kingdoms. Later, James Kingston Tuckey and Sir Richard Francis Burton both stopped here for supplies, and established a base of communications for their expeditions upriver. It was the landing point of Henry Morton Stanley when he completed his momentous journey from the Indian Ocean to the Atlantic. It was the site of a small formal ceremony in 1959 when Belgium officially handed over power of the colony to the people of the Congo.

GETTING THERE AND AROUND Like everywhere else in the DR Congo, roads are rough and slow. You can catch a shared taxi from Rond Point Boma on the north end of the city to Matadi or Tshela, and sometimes large trucks go this way to Muanda, though usually you would get a boat down by the port Muanda. There are regular air connections at the airport on the usual suspects, **Air Tropiques** and **Fil Air**.

⌂ WHERE TO STAY

⌂ **Hôtel Maranatha** m 081 906 3983. On a hill overlooking town, with bar/restaurant ($$$), secure parking & AC. Sgl/dbl $$$, apt $$$$

⌂ **Hôtel Auberge du Vieux Port** (42 rooms) m 099 844 6318. The best option is this new & spacious hotel with a wonderful restaurant built out over the Congo River, where you can sit & watch huge ships crawl past on their way to Matadi, then go for a dip in the hotel's swimming pool. The hotel has secure parking, restaurant/bar ($$$) & a pool. All rooms have AC, TV, running water & riverside views. B/fast inc. 38 dbls/4 sgls $$

⌂ **Hôtel Excelsior** (30 rooms) m 081 954 7821. Something a little less expensive in the city centre

is this hotel, where all rooms have AC & running water. A little old-looking these days, but also has an excellent restaurant ($$) downstairs. 26 sgl/dbls $$, 4 apts $$$

⌂ **Hôtel Mabuilu** Route de Commerce; m 099 885 2352. Also at the upper end in price, this hotel has an immaculate & expensive restaurant ($$$), AC throughout, running water & TV. Sgl/dbl $$, 4 apts $$$

⌂ **Hôtel Premier Bassin** m 081 900 5845. Further out of town, with basic rooms with AC, TV & running water. B/fast inc. Sgl/dbl $$, apt $$$

✕ WHERE TO EAT

✕ **Hôtel Auberge de Vieux Port** The best place for some quality food, decent drinks, & as mentioned, excellent views of the river.

✕ **Big Staff Restaurant** m 099 994 4023; ⊕ 14.00–22.00 daily. Serves up good fish dishes in an AC dining room. $$

✕ **Restaurant Top Delice** m 099 859 5894; ⊕ 12.30–20.00 daily. Head here for large plates of locally caught fish. $$

✕ **Cherie 'B' Restaurant** m 099 753 8772; ⊕ 15.00–22.00 daily. Less expensive with a terraced area right beside the entrance to the port. It usually serves up a single plate during opening hours. $

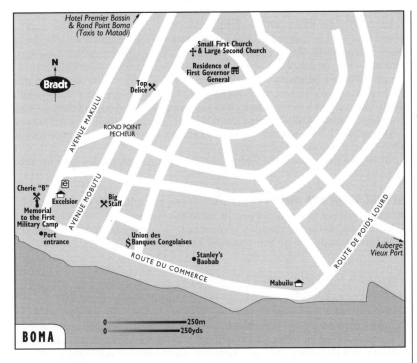

Map labels:
Hotel Premier Bassin & Rond Point Boma (Taxis to Matadi)

Small First Church & Large Second Church

Residence of First Governor General

N

Bradt

Top Delice

ROND POINT PECHEUR

AVENUE MAKULU

AVENUE MOBUTU

Cherie "B"

Excelsior

Big Staff

Memorial to the First Military Camp

Port entrance

Union des Banques Congolaises

ROUTE DU COMMERCE

Stanley's Baobab

ROUTE DE POIDS LOURD

Auberge Vieux Port

Mabuilu

0 — 250m
0 — 250yds

BOMA

OTHER PRACTICALITIES For **Western Union**, there's one bank on the Route du Commerce, at the **Union des Banques Congolaises** (m *098 204 965;* ⏱ *07.30–16.00 Mon–Fri*).

WHAT TO SEE Boma sits on a mountainside overlooking the mouth of the Congo River. There are a few points of interest: a small **metal church** was Congo Free State's first church and built in 1890, from metal parts imported from Europe. Beside it is a much larger **cathedral** for modern worshipping, and they are both situated on a hilltop with good views of the town and river below. Further down the hill is the **Residence of the First Governor-General** in the Congo Free State, a decent-sized mansion for the region. A 700-year-old **baobab tree** sits in town where Henry Morton Stanley was said to have spent his first night after traversing the Congo River in 1875 – it's a large hollowed-out tree with enough room for a snooze, though you'd be hard pressed to do so these days. Behind it is a small museum with some paintings, and in front is a bar. They normally ask for a US$5 admission fee.

The town is also awash with old administrative buildings of the first Belgian administration – including the first barracks used by the Force Publique, and several stopping points for traders and missionaries, as well as an ancient **cemetery** filled with graves of the first Europeans to set foot on these shores. Near the Auberge de Vieux Port are the **first cars** to have appeared in the Belgian Congo around 1905, but don't pay any money to see them – anything that could be removed from them, has been. They are little more than rusted hulks at this point: carcasses with tyres. Out in front of the port entrance is a small **Memorial to the First Military Camp** in the Congo, completed from 1886 to 1887. It's in the middle of a small market area and plenty of kids swarm around and pester visitors here.

TSHELA ⊕ 05° 00.29 S, 12°57.34 E

If you have a fair amount of patience, going north from Boma to the town of Tshela has several rewards. Tshela is at the terminus of a small railway, unused these days, and was once an important centre for agricultural interests. Near Tshela is the small village of **Maduda** (⊕ *04°55.21 S, 13°05.43 E*), where several highly decorated graves of ancient chiefs are located. North of the village are the **Nyambi Falls**, and southeast of the village (after following the dirt road, and then walking for some way) are **Lukula Falls**. All of these areas require some walking to visit, which implies having not only a guide or two, but someone to watch your vehicle while you're out on the forest paths.

Tshela is also notable as the birthplace of Joseph Kasa-Vubu, first president of the independent Congo.

GETTING THERE AND AWAY Visiting Tshela is easy enough, being directly north of Boma. Hang out at the taxi stands at the north end of town, and there will be vehicles going in that direction a few times a day. It should take three to four hours. The rail line exists, but no trains have used it in decades.

MUANDA ⊕ 05°55.00 S, 12°22.31 E

The DR Congo's only true ocean town, Muanda has a distinctive colonial atmosphere with numerous old buildings built on the sandy shores of the southern Atlantic. It is a busy place these days, but still a long way from Kinshasa and Matadi.

Muanda has an excellent stretch of beaches along the southern Atlantic Ocean, and in better days when the roads were well maintained it was a popular weekend spot for Kinshasa's expatriates. Now, however, the vast majority of visitors take a plane out here, and only when necessary. Yet the beaches are still pristine, the most famous of which being **Tonde Plage** 8km north. Boats can be rented for fishing here.

Near Muanda is the small town of **Banana**, which was the first colonial outpost built in the Congo. It was occupied intermittently by Dutch and Portuguese interests before the arrival of the Belgians, and in 1873 even had a regular passenger-ship service to Rotterdam. A few ancient buildings remain, as well as old cannons and various derelict reminders of the slave trade that was once so important to Europeans arriving at the river's mouth. Northwest of Muanda is the small fishing village of **Nsiamfumu** and the other well-regarded beach in the area, **Kumbi Plage**.

GETTING THERE AND AWAY By road, Cabinda is only an hour or less – however, eastwards to Boma the road is difficult and can take over six hours for the 120km stretch. It's better to go by boat, and several leave each week in either direction. The airport is functional, and both **Air Tropiques** and **Fil Air** fly to Muanda from Matadi and Kinshasa.

WHERE TO STAY The **Hôtel New Cliff** ($$$) is on the road between Banana and Muanda and is the best place to get a room, as well as some information for the surrounding area.

MANGROVES NATIONAL PARK (MUANDA MARINE RESERVE)

Somewhere between Muanda, Banana and Boma is the DR Congo's only marine park – sometimes called the Mangrove Park, Parc Marine, Muanda Marine

Reserve, and a variety of other word combinations. It's a less-than-clear area somewhere in the vicinity of Banana designed to protect the mangrove forests that occupy the mouth of the Congo River, and more importantly, the endangered populations of manatee which reside in them. The manatee flock to this area because it is difficult for fishermen and boats to catch them in the thick foliage. Other creatures in the region are hippos, crocodile and several species of snake.

This is the country's smallest protected area, at only 768km^2. It was created in 1992, possibly the worst time to found a park in the DR Congo as it was then collapsing under the final days of Mobutu's dictatorship. Oil speculation and continued hunting of marine animals in the region means that the park has existed only in name since its inception. Nonetheless, as the country finds some stability it will begin to pay more attention to this park. For more information, try your luck in Muanda – though there will be little to see aside from the mangrove trees, which, if you've arrived by boat from Boma, you'll no doubt have already seen.

7

Central Democratic Republic of Congo

The middle of the DR Congo has the least infrastructure, the fewest foreigners and the fewest amenities of any region across either nation. This is the 'in-between area' that few will visit during their time in the Congos, as arriving even by air can be problematic due to wacky flight schedules and often ridiculous police permits. Yet if you do visit, you will be seeing some of the most untouched wilderness left on the continent. The Salonga Parks are famous for being difficult to visit, and for being the largest remaining undeveloped tract of rainforest in Africa. Further northeast is the country's newest park, a bonobo reserve, protecting their habitat and allowing visitors to see them in their natural state.

Politically, the centre is a place of complicated treaties and intense mineral wealth. In the region of Mbuji-Mayi are some of the largest open-pit diamond mines on the face of the earth, which brings out all of the impoverished villagers in search of a job and numerous foreign businessmen out to make a fast dollar. It is the crossroads of the country, the interchange between Katanga in the east and the Kinshasa region, despite sitting in relative isolation. However, because the roads are so battered, most will choose simply to fly over it. It was home to the country's first secessionist movement in 1960 out of west Kasai, and is the only place where Tshiluba is widely spoken. In its south is where the deep equatorial rainforest slowly gives over to rolling savanna. For those with plenty of time, patience, and their own vehicle, this is an intriguing region to visit – but one that requires a high level of commitment to really get the most out of it.

MBANDAKA ⊕ 00°03.14 N, 18°15.25 E

Mbandaka (pronounced 'Ban-da-ka') is a cluttered, humid city on the southeastern edge of the Congo River. It's the most important transit point between Kisangani and Kinshasa, a stopping area for aircraft at its airport and boats along the river. It's the equatorial town of the DR Congo and Henry Morton Stanley, on his original voyage down the river, stopped here briefly to mark the Equator. In fact upon its founding in 1883 the original name was 'Equator' but was later changed to Coquilhatville, after the first officer-in-charge of the town, one Mr Coquilhat.

Mbandaka's claim to historical fame comes from the Coquilhatville Conference, held in 1961, which saw Moise Tshombe come to the table to bargain with Joseph Kasa-Vubu about bringing Katanga back from secession. While the conference ended in disaster, for better or worse, it was the initial catalyst that kept the new nation of Congo-Léopoldville together. Mobutu Sésé Seko changed the name from Coquilhatville to Mbandaka during his 'Africanisation' campaign of the late 1960s, though the local Congolese had used this name for decades before – as well as the now-defunct name of Wangata.

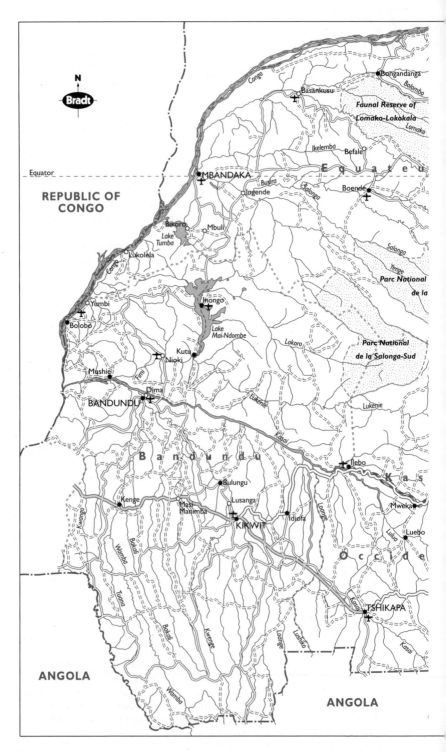

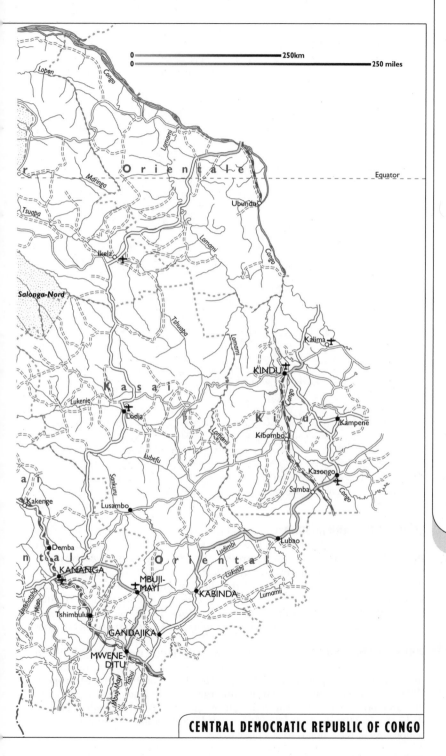

CENTRAL DEMOCRATIC REPUBLIC OF CONGO

The pygmies are the only indigenous tribes not descended from the general Bantu ethnic group and are widely recognised for their small stature and usually adhering to a traditionalist lifestyle. There are no famous pygmy towns, but only their villages – which are usually buried deep in the jungle and operating under their own rules. The word 'pygmy' itself is a racial slur of sorts, meaning someone of short stature.

Pygmies are hunter-gatherer societies, and males who hunt well are highly valued in their communities. Traps, spears, poison arrows and crossbows are all used to take down any manner of animal from small game and even up to antelopes and elephants on occasion. Elephant hunts by pygmies do occur, albeit rarely, and by an entire team of hunters. This does not occur as much as it once did since development across the countryside has reduced the number of available animals.

Foraging for foods and other vegetables is done by everyone in the village, and anything edible is taken for consumption – from fruits and vegetables to mushrooms, and even some insects.

Villages are traditional affairs, constructed with any available materials found across the jungle. Clothing is made from animal hide, baskets are woven from bushes, weapons and musical instruments are made from wood. Pygmies are not known to have a specific language but rather speak a slightly modified version of whatever tribal tongue is used in their surroundings. Some ethno-linguists have speculated that the few non-Bantuist words that pygmies use may hark back to an ancient tongue all their own, but this has not been extensively explored.

These villages have, in many respects, voluntarily cut themselves off from the larger Bantu infrastructure of the surrounding countryside. Their way of life, though, has naturally been threatened due to the conflicts across the region, especially in Ituri. Deforestation and refugees escaping conflict who run deep into the jungle have disrupted this traditionalist lifestyle.

The two most widely studied pygmy groups in central Africa are the Baka in northern Congo-Brazzaville, near Ouesso and the Cameroon border, and the Mbuti in Ituri Province of northeastern Congo-Kinshasa.

Two authors who have explored pygmy culture extensively are Colin Turnbull in *The Forest People* and Kevin Duffy with *Children of the Forest: Africa's Mbuti Pygmies*. *National Geographic* magazine as well has sent numerous photographers and authors to explore pygmy culture throughout history.

GETTING THERE AND AROUND The airport is a busy one for the region, with regular flights southwest to Kinshasa and northeast to Gemena and Gbadolite; contact **Bravo Air Congo** (*Av Clinique 01;* m *099 930 1701*), **Hewa Bora Airways** (m *081 730 1071*) or **Wimbi Dira Airways** (*Av Mudji 03;* m *098 312 232*) for current flight schedules as they fluctuate regularly. There are small aircraft which head east to Kisangani when the mood strikes them. For river transport, there are regular boats to Kinshasa and intermittent ones to Kisangani. To the Salonga Parks you'll have to get down to the docks and start bargaining; it takes at least a week one-way.

WHERE TO STAY AND EAT The city's top hotel is the **Hôtel Benghazi** ($$$) with fancy amenities like running water, air conditioning, and great views over to the river. For mid-range places try the **Afrique Hôtel** ($$) or the **Hôtel Metropole** ($$), in the town centre. The **Hôtel Auberge** ($$) is a better deal, however, in the same price bracket but situated right on the river. A decent budget place is **Auberge de Miel de Mondela** ($$), about US$10 cheaper than other low-end options. All of these hotels have a place to eat.

WHAT TO SEE Many people come to Mbandaka for the **pygmy villages**, though these are only accessible with guides. Pygmies throughout the DR Congo are justifiably skittish, having been hunted throughout the last conflict and even eaten on occasion in some of the worst acts of cannibalism from recent history. Thus, building relationships with them and explaining what tourists are, and promising they won't be eaten, has taken time. As of now your best option for visiting the pygmies is to contact **Go Congo** (*www.gocongo.com*) in Kinshasa to arrange a guide for when you arrive in Mbandaka, as they specialise in these tours (see *Chapter 4, Tour operators*, page 83).

By the river are the city's famous **Botanical Gardens**, once a very prominent sight and once the best in central Africa. The gardens were created in 1900 and occupy roughly 370ha, and at their height had over 2,000 different species of plants. Like everything else in the country conflict has taken its toll and the gardens are a little rough around the edges, so discovering what flower species remain has become somewhat difficult. It's still a good escape from town, however, about 6km away.

Also nearby is **Ires**, a small village with a garden, park and zoo. This could occupy a small amount of your time, but **Lake Tumba** 100km to the south is a much better option – with some guesthouses and a basic beach, the wilderness around the lake is also home to a group of local bonobos.

SALONGA PARKS

In fact two parks located in the heart of the DR Congo, Salonga North and Salonga South, the Salonga Park stands as one of the most untouched regions of the country. Its focus is the protection of the equatorial forests and wetlands that occupy the middle of the DR Congo, criss-crossed with far more rivers than roads. It is currently the largest rainforest park in Africa, occupying over 36,000km². It was designated as a natural reserve in 1933 and became a national park in November 1970 under Mobutu Sésé Seko. UNESCO added it to the World Heritage List in 1984. A 45km-wide corridor splits the two parks, allowing the local populations to navigate the region without disturbing the nature reserves. A road follows this corridor southeast from Boende, though like most roads in the DR Congo, it is barely functional. Fewer than 1,500 people live within the parks themselves.

Amongst the rivers are thick stretches of rainforest which are mostly impenetrable by foot, given the huge areas of swamp and marshy grasslands. The upside to this is that the wildlife within the park, while mostly unmonitored, has not seen the widespread poaching that other parks in the DR Congo have experienced.

The Salongas are home to some exceptionally rare creatures, including the bonobo, a species unique to the region. Also look for the slender-snouted crocodile, more forest elephants, giant pangolins, and some of the largest remaining hippo populations. Birdlife is vibrant, and the rare Congo peacock makes its home in the region. Other large mammals common to the DR Congo are in the Salongas as well – buffalo, bongo, leopard and duiker have all been recorded in the vicinity.

GETTING THERE AND AWAY Visiting the Salongas stands as perhaps one of the most difficult things to do in the DR Congo. You can either fly in via chartered aircraft to **Mongkoto** (✪ *01°44.36 S, 20°41.09 E*), or take a hired boat from Mbandaka to the town – the estimated travel time is around seven days, one-way. There are also irregular vehicles from Mbandaka southeast to **Boende** (✪ *00°17.16 S, 20°52.44 E*), where you can connect again to Mongkoto. Once in the area, there are no amenities available – aside from very basic accommodation in the towns of Mundja, Monkoto, and Anga where the park rangers reside; they may remember when the last tourists came to Salonga. An alternate route can be hacked through arriving in **Dekese** (✣ *03°29.09 S, 21°22.43 E*) and continuing to Ishenga or Oshwe; Dekese itself can be reached by trucks or a boat from Ilebo. Note that a permit will be required from the ICCN office in Kinshasa or Mbandaka to visit (this should be US$100 per person), and they can provide information on where to find a guide for the park.

FAUNAL RESERVE OF LOMAKO-YOKOKALA

This is the newest faunal reserve to exist in either Congo, having been approved in July 2006 after a 15-year battle by the African Wildlife Foundation in conjunction with the ICCN. It is designed to protect the habitat of bonobos east of Basankusu, as well as provide some science stations for researchers. Still very little is known about the life of the bonobo in its natural habitat, it being the last large primate to be discovered by Western scientists. The reserve is 3,625km^2 in size and occupies the relatively unpopulated area between the Lomako and Bolombo rivers.

Other animals make their home in the reserve's area, including the Congo peacock, African golden cat, giant pangolin and forest elephants. The primary focus, however, is the bonobo.

Tourism is also a primary concern for the reserve. With the income it generates and the positive pressure it can put on the government of the DR Congo to do more in protecting endangered animals, it will not turn away those who can manage to visit the reserve in its admittedly hard-to-reach location. Permit costs have not been decided yet, but should be similar to other parks across the country.

At the time of writing the primary concern was continuing to limit human activity in the park. Hunting and farming persist, and various land-use programmes are beginning to be implemented to assist local villagers in the area in their livelihoods while still protecting the reserve.

GETTING THERE AND AWAY Visiting this area takes time. There are weekly flights to **Basankusu** (✣ *01°13.26 N, 19°47.54 E*) from Kinshasa's N'Dolo Airport, and from there you must take a boat down the Lomako River to Andele – where a guesthouse is being built for tourists. There is no word yet on how much this will cost, but expect it to be similar to the gorilla trekking in the eastern provinces at a few hundred dollars per person. A science station currently exists at Limunda.

KIKWIT ✣ *05°02.40 S, 18°48.47 E*

Kikwit is the DR Congo's largest city east of Kinshasa, and it is still a troublesome destination to reach by road – over 500km from the capital, it will take at least a full day along this barely paved stretch of highway. Most choose to fly, and the regional airport is a busy one. Note that in the Kikwit region, specifically Bandundu Province, Kikongo is the local language – the same as that of Bas-Congo.

Kikwit is best known for the massive outbreak of Ebola in the surrounding villages around 1995, which effectively sealed off the town while health organisations attemped to contain the virus, which killed over 250.

WHERE TO STAY The top hotel in Kikwit is **Hôtel Kwilu** (*Bd Mobutu;* $$$), a throwback to the DR Congo's old colonial era, built for overlanding mining businessmen passing through when the roads were still well paved and commerce flowed a little more freely. On the low end check out **Hôtel Beech** ($) which has basic rooms for budget travellers.

WHAT TO SEE Aside from Kikwit being a stopping point for an overland journey, if you can arrange transport there are several falls near the Angolan border worth a visit: **Chutes Guillaume** (also called **Chutes Tembo**), and slightly upriver **Chutes Kasongo-Lunda**, south of Kasongo-Lunda. The roads to and from Kikwit have numerous bridges which pass over several picturesque waterfalls – both on the way to Kinshasa and past Tshikapa.

Heading south from Kikwit past the villages of Gungu is the **Lukwila Gorge**, a spectacular site with walls over 100m in height. The Lukwila carries sediment from the area downstream, making its water red. It was once a major attraction in the region, but reaching it these days takes a little bit of determination in addition to your own private vehicle.

ILEBO ✜ 04°19.51 S, 20°35.02 E

From Kinshasa, this is the first rail connection into the hinterlands of DR Congo – or, if you are travelling north from Lubumbashi, the last point on the train ride northwest before other transportation options take over. The town is an old one, originally known as Port Francqui, and plays its role well as a transit hub for the region. Its port is especially critical as it is relied upon to transport all cargo from the Kasai provinces downriver to Bandundu and Kinshasa.

The road improves from here to the DR Congo's capital, though the journey is still long – at over 700km, it takes a minimum of two days to reach Kinshasa. It is also easy to take a boat northwest along the Kasai River to Bandundu and then follow road connections from there to Kinshasa, or by simply purchasing an air ticket. However, Kananga and Bandundu see far more frequent flights than Ilebo, and if you've got this far you may as well make the overland journey all the way.

WHERE TO STAY The best choice for those staying in Ilebo is **Hôtel Palma** ($$), but it is still very basic. For those with the least amount of money to throw around, at the other end of the scale is **Hôtel Shashago** at US$5 per night.

WHAT TO SEE Going south from Ilebo on a bad road towards the village of Djokupunda are several notable natural sites, starting with the **Madimape Lakes** (also called the **Green Lakes**), once a popular spot for touring groups in the days of the Belgian Congo. Just south are some curious rock formations called **Baboon's Hole**, created by the irregular weather and drainage patterns in the region. The road exists, at least in theory, to the former colonial town of Charlesville, now Djokupunda, and just south of the town is a picturesque **waterfall** on the Kasai River. A road connects Djokupunda to Luebo which should allow you to get back on track.

KANANGA ✜ 05°53.43 S, 22°23.33 E

Kananga is primarily the stopping point for an overland journey from Lubumbashi to Kinshasa. Trains originating from Katanga terminate here, and you are forced to either secure road transport northwest to Kinshasa, or take another train further on to Ilebo. It is the second most important town in the Tshiluba-speaking region of the DR Congo, and like its nearby neighbour Mbuji-Mayi, enjoys a bustling economy surrounding the mining industry.

Formerly known as Luluabourg, the town was the capital of the secessionist Federal State of South Kasai, or the Mining State of South Kasai, in 1960 and 1961. The state in fact seceded prior to Belgian independence, a prelude to the chaos that would envelop the country as it was handed over to local powers. The leader of the day, Albert Kalonji, revived ancient Luba traditions and declared himself the *mulopwe*, or king, of the new state. However, retribution was swift and brutal – by the end of 1961 Kananga had been captured by soldiers from Léopoldville. Rebels persisted west of Luluabourg for several years in the Tshikapa region, until intervention by the UN in 1964 ended their rebellion for good.

GETTING THERE AND AWAY Aside from rail connections, Kananga has a busy airport with numerous connections to Kinshasa; aircraft often stop here *en route* to Mbuji-Mayi. Contact **Bravo Air Congo** (*Av Chabunda 131;* m *099 930 1681*) or **Wimbi Dira Airways** (*119 Av Kasa-Vubu;* m *081 518 1481;* e *kananga@wda.cd*). **Hewa Bora Airways** (m *081 604 0421*) and **CAA** also stop in Kananga. The road system is not nearly as enviable, but in classic DR Congo fashion large cargo trucks can be found moving out every few days.

WHERE TO STAY For accommodation there are several inexpensive places for those in transit, and nothing in the higher bracket. **Hôtel Amika** and **Hôtel Musumbe** both have rooms available for less than US$10.

WHAT TO SEE Kananga has a decent waterfall just south of it, the **Katende Falls**, accessible via a road off the main highway to Tshikapa west out of town. Downstream from the falls is an impressive **gorge** where the Kasai River passes through, though it takes a fair amount of walking from the nearest battered road – find someone to guide you to this.

MBUJI-MAYI ⊕ *06°07.48 S, 23°34.48 E*

Straddling the Bushimaie River, Mbuji-Mayi is the capital of Kasai Oriental Province, though this could be changing as new elections alter the face of the DR Congo's province maps. It was also the capital of the secessionist state of South Kasai in 1960, and has intense connections to the local population of Lubas. It is the largest urban centre where Tshiluba is spoken and is the political heartland of Etienne Tshisekedi and his UDPS party.

It is the most important mining town in the DR Congo; at over a million citizens, it has seen a rapid expansion of its population due to opportunities for employment in the surrounding mines. By far the most famous and important mineral available is diamonds, and both the legal and illegal trade of them exists across the area. The existence of diamonds has also made the city a somewhat suspect destination for any foreigner, or indeed anyone without a genuine reason for being there – permits may or may not be required (and if they are, they are the notorious mining permits from an ancient era of the DR Congo – and will set you back several hundred dollars). Check in either Lubumbashi or Kinshasa for the required permits to visit the city. It's on East Africa Standard Time (GMT+2). The town is a hotbed for journalists and businessmen interested in the diamond trade – and open-pit mines often photographed to show the dire working conditions in the DR Congo are abundant around the city.

GETTING THERE AND AWAY Mbuji-Mayi is well connected by air, with several major airlines flying in, including **Bravo Air Congo** (*Av Salongo;* m *099 930 1621*), **CAA**, **Hewa Bora Airways** (m *081 333 0064*) and **Wimbi Dira Airways**

(22 Av Salongo; m *081 525 6187;* e *mbujimayi@wda.cd).* The road network is still in very poor shape – even to nearby Kananga, it's preferable to find some sort of air transport.

WHERE TO STAY For lodging, rooms have shot up to astronomical levels in recent times as the mining boom has strained local infrastructure – if you don't have money, don't come to Mbuji-Mayi. The most popular hotel for visitors is **Hôtel Kumbi-Kumbi** *(Av Mama Yemo;* $$$$$). If they're full, try and find **Hôtel Tanko** *(Av de la Cathedrale;* $$$$$) or **Hôtel Kanka** *(Av du 24 Novembre;* $$$$$). The two best hotels in town are **Hôtel Ekinou** ($$$$$) and **Hôtel Kabe** ($$$$$), which will set you back at least US$200 a night. For something below US$100 try **Hôtel Kundu Kundu** ($$$) or **Hôtel Equinoxe** ($$$).

WHAT TO SEE If you've got your own transport and plenty of forms and permission, there are a few waterfalls in Mbuji-Mayi's vicinity, notably **Lubilashi Falls** to the northeast and **Kai Mutoyo Falls** to the southeast, which also has some impressive caves. These are off the main road, and I wouldn't go near them unless you can prove you're not out scoping for diamonds. Get a guide as the falls are buried deep in the jungle.

LODJA ✤ *03°31.30 S, 23°35.55 E*

Lodja is the official capital of nowhere in the DR Congo, which is saying quite a bit in a country filled with inaccessible jungle villages and towns constructed in colonial times that have since lost their purpose. Once upon a time the road from Kisangani to Kananga was well travelled, or at least sometimes travelled, and transportation brought cargo from the Congo River into the Kasai provinces. Lodja was the largest town and major trading centre along this route. Those days, however, have passed, and the route has been badly damaged. Naturally the impetus is there to repair the road and get infrastructure moving again between two of the country's major centres, and in the next few years the dirt track should be feasible instead of near impossible. Before this time, though, it is extremely unlikely anyone will arrive here without their own transport – and even then this will definitely be classified as a 'hard' route, meaning plenty of time, plenty of bribes, and possibly even some permits if you're particularly uncharismatic. The airport is functional, however, and you can occasionally find flights to Goma, Mbuji-Mayi and Lubumbashi. There is also river transport between neighbouring towns.

WHERE TO STAY For lodging try **Hôtel Fulangenge**, also sometimes called **Hôtel Intervale** (m *081 167 5966; sgl* $), for very basic rooms with only mosquito nets. Also in town are **Hôtel Mama Diessa** and **Hôtel Okadeve** which are of lesser quality. All have rooms for under US$8 per night.

KINDU ✤ *02°57.02 S, 25°55.11 E*

Kindu is the last point navigable by large boats on the Congo River after the rapids near Kisangani, and is also the capital of Maniema Province. It's a small town with few vehicles, terrible roads, and disconnected from everything in the general vicinity. And yet it's also the largest urban centre in the region, an important link between rail lines from the southeastern DR Congo. The city was originally called Port Empain in early colonial times, and was the largest slave-trading area in the whole of the eastern Congo in the days of Tippu Tip.

Rail lines were repaired in the past few years as conflict subsided, various rebel armies moved on, and international organisations began a strong push to rebuild the infrastructure. The railway to this region was, in fact, the most important thing to many non-governmental organisations as it allowed them to move large amounts of aid quickly. Compared with the roads in Maniema, an old train trundling along at 30km/h seems like a dream.

GETTING THERE AND AWAY Trains leave roughly once a month in the direction of Kalemie and Kamina. Air connections are excellent between Kindu and Kinshasa, Goma, and Kisangani – though again, formal schedules aren't all the rage here. It's still a place where the arrival of a plane will bring out everyone in town. Contact **Wimbi Dira Airways** (*Bd Lumumba;* m *081 700 7969;* e *kindu@wda.cd*) or **Bravo Air Congo** (*Bd Lumumba;* m *099 601 2000*) for flight schedules. Road crews are busy recreating the route from Bukavu to Kasongo, and hopefully within time the connection from Kasongo to Kindu will mean that a trip by truck to Bukavu will take only a week or so instead of a month.

WHERE TO STAY For lodging, **Hôtel Maniema** (*8 rooms;* $), with an enclosed garden, bar/restaurant and cold, running water, is the best address in town. If they happen to be full try **Hôtel Rail** ($$) or **Hôtel du Marché** ($).
Continuing on the road towards Bukavu you will arrive in the nondescript town of **Kalima** (⊕ 02°34.54 S, 26°43.21 E) which is a decent place to stop for the night as it has some cheap and secure hotels: **Hôtel Diplomate** (*sgl* $, *dbl* $$) and **Hôtel Tout Bouge** (*sgl US$5, dbl/apt* $).

WHAT TO SEE With so much going for it, perhaps it's not surprising that Kindu is a little low on sights. The **port** on the Congo River has some ships from points further north, and there is a small **beach** on the river as well. Most intriguing is the old **Slave's Market** which tells a story of days gone by in Kindu's history – that of the Arab slave traders who arrived here regularly in the 19th century to capture more locals for their business. The Arab influence is undeniable, as Kindu has one of the DR Congo's largest Islamic populations. To this extent the local tribes, the Barega and Basogora, are notably different from other cultures in the region.

8

Katanga

Independent for almost two years in the 1960s before being pulled back into the fold through military force, Katanga Province has always seen itself as different from the rest of the country; some in the region even refer to their province as the 'Other Congo'. Geographically it lends itself far more to the dry savanna of southern Africa than the equatorial jungle, and has seen extensive development throughout its time. This is entirely due to its mineral wealth: the highways seen in the region are privately funded by various international mining groups, slowly moving back into the province after years of conflict. Drivers are expected to pay a small toll along these roads, but given that overland travel is often extremely difficult or impossible in the rest of the DR Congo, this is a significant improvement. From the border town of Kasumbalesa north to the mining town of Likasi, a paved highway with only a modest number of pot-holes awaits those with a vehicle. Though after that, you return to the DR Congo's usual rutted dirt roads onward to Kolwezi and further points north.

The only operating rail lines in southern DR Congo originate in Katanga Province, to and from Lubumbashi – it is possible to travel here by train from Ilebo, a journey of four to five days. The rail link between Kalemie in the east and Lubumbashi has also recently been repaired, but seek local advice before using it. West to Angola, two European firms are currently repairing the rail line to Kolwezi and onward to Dilolo for a possible connection into Angola soon. The province also has two of the country's five national parks which include Africa's highest waterfall, large semi-flooded plains of papyrus and bamboo, numerous cave systems, and plateaux. The last major kingdom in central Africa, the M'Siri, originated in Katanga and their heritage endures in the town of Bunkeya.

Going around Katanga lends itself well to having your own vehicle, as there are huge transport gaps across the region – or, shall we say, more than usual for the Congo.

LUBUMBASHI ✪ *11°39.34 S, 27°28.50 E*

Lubumbashi is a unique city in the DR Congo: with clean, wide streets, its citizens have taken an active interest in the appearance of their town. The old colonial façades are recently painted, squalor is at least hidden away rather than in direct sight. It has two notable religious landmarks, a pleasant downtown centre, and a wide variety of amenities for an ever-increasing number of foreigners who pass through. It's a pleasant place to spend any amount of time, and indeed the attitudes towards those going about their business in Lubumbashi is seemingly more relaxed than that of cities further north.

The anglophone influence, as well, is undeniable here. Many people are prone to speak some English, with Zambia only a few hours' drive away. Most Katangese around Lubumbashi have at least visited their neighbour, and are more in touch

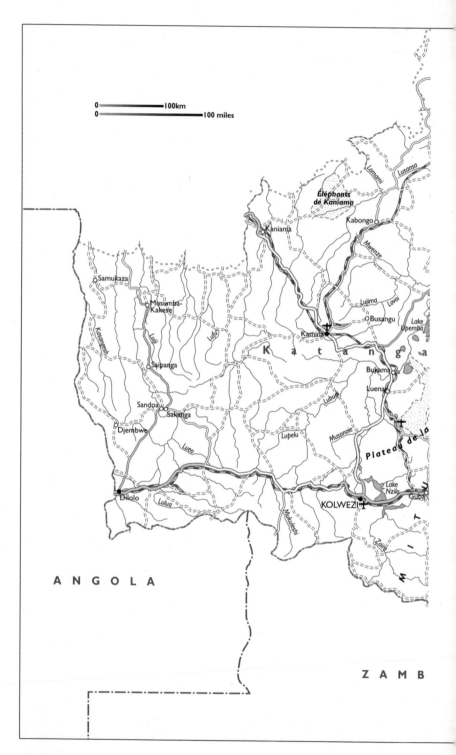

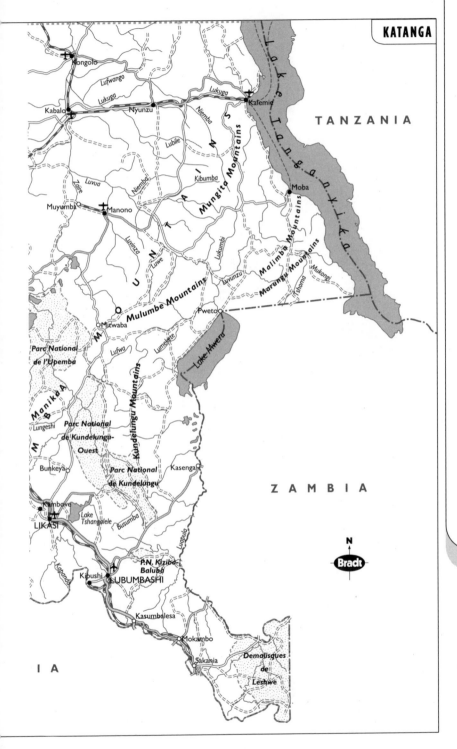

TANZANIA

Z A M B I A

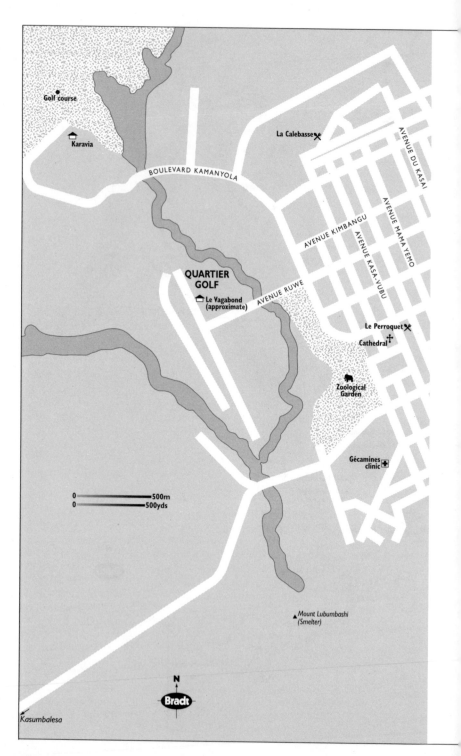

Golf course

Karavia

La Calebasse ✕

BOULEVARD KAMANYOLA

AVENUE DU KASAI

AVENUE KIMBANGU

AVENUE MAMA YEMO

AVENUE KASA-VUBU

QUARTIER
GOLF

Le Vagabond
(approximate)

AVENUE RUWE

Le Perroquet ✕

Cathedral ✝

Zoological
Garden

Gécamines
clinic ✛

0 ———— 500m
0 ———— 500yds

▲ Mount Lubumbashi
(Smelter)

N

Bradt

Kasumbalesa

LUBUMBASHI

Map labels:
Airport, Likasi, Planet Hollybum
Katanga Fried Chiken #2
Hotel du Lac
AVENUE PATRICE LUMUMBA
Cemetery
Sports Stadium
Orthodox
AVENUE DU 30 JUIN
La Brioche
Lubumbashi Museum
Hewa Bora Airways
CHAUSSEE LAURENT DESIRE KABILA
BIAC
Katanga Fried Chiken #1
Bravo
Air Congo
Oasis
Malachite sellers
Railway station
South African Airways/ Kenya Airways
Supermarket
Reka (Hotel & restaurant)
Beau Site
Park
Elephant's statue
Belle Vue/ Zottos Pharma
AVENUE MODRO
Trust Merchant
AVENUE LIKASI
Protestant Church

with the world of English Africa. This makes it easier for the anglophone to get around, though corruption is just as much a problem as anywhere else in the nation.

HISTORY The city was founded by Union Minière du Haut Katanga (UMHK) in 1910, strictly as a mining town – no African villages had ever existed in the area, as the surrounding terrain was unforgiving. Lacking arable land, and proximity to fresh water, it was a dry and empty scrubland before Belgian interest.

Lubumbashi's founding, then, was built out of necessity. The Belgians were losing influence in the region to British mining companies, and the anglophone labour that went along with it. A railway had been built all the way from South Africa into southern Belgian Congo, and the vast majority of non-Africans in the area were not Belgian at all. With such strong ties to the English colonies of Africa, UMHK and King Léopold sought to reassert their mandate over the Katanga region. The city was founded to keep these mining companies in check, to expand Belgian influence, and ensure that British rumours of aiming for annexation would remain simply rumours. While the directive was to found the city near an adequate water supply, its founders opted to build their new mining capital right next to a British smelter. With the railway already in place, supplies could be brought in quickly to transform an empty savanna into a bustling colonial town. In 1910, Elisabethville was born, with several hundred Belgian troops in tow, to demonstrate that they meant business in retaining control of Katanga.

The British would not disappear for long, though: as World War I raged in Europe, UMHK and Elisabethville found their Belgian funding inaccessible thanks to German interference. UMHK officials were eager to complete a railway line to Léopoldville, and invited further investment from British mining firms.

If the notion of a European power assisting in the secession of a province in central Africa, then assisting its government in hiring mercenaries to engage in combat against the UN, sounds intriguing to you, the secession of Katanga from 1960 to 1963 is indeed an intriguing story.

The entire engagement between foreign soldiers of fortune, usually referred to as mercenaries, against rebel forces loyal to Patrice Lumumba and UN 'Blue Helmets' is a curious footnote in the history of 20th-century Africa. Never mind the Belgian involvement, which was vast – their hopes of keeping the UMHK in a country friendly to Belgium, perhaps even allowing Katanga to exist as little more than a puppet state, speak volumes of European motivations for intervention across Africa to this very day.

The most troubling aspect of the secession, perhaps, is how forgotten it really is amongst world history. Congo itself has seen a resurgence in its role across history texts with Mobutu Sésé Seko's regime and the fallout from the Rwandan genocide that sparked the civil wars and internal strife that persist to contemporary times. Yet Katanga's brief years of independence are mostly buried, its history blurry and deep in the past, despite the modern-day parallels of the UN taking on greater roles to stabilise the very same country, and the increasing privatisation of conflicts in the Middle East and central Asia. These lessons have, at the very least, been pushed into a background largely ignored by pundits and analysts as the DR Congo struggles with all-too-familiar problems.

During the 1960s the Congo mercenaries were a big deal, celebrities of sorts, and many of them went on to write their memoirs of the Congo-Katanga affair. Robert Denard was the most famous, and went on to numerous other missions sponsored by the French government; however, he has never written his own personal accounts of his exploits.

Mike Hoare provides the largest base of first-person accounts available regarding Katanga. *The Road to Kalamata* is a short and simple read on the subject. Also by the same author is *Congo Mercenary*, which is a little hard to find, and *Congo Warriors*, which documents his time whilst working for the Léopoldville-based government and taking on rebels in the northeast. Jules Gerard-Libois's book *Katanga Secession* details the finer points of this moment in history from a political standpoint.

A compilation of articles on African guns for hire is available in *Mercenaries: An African Security Dilemma*. It discusses in detail the ramifications of Congo's use of foreign mercenaries in the 1960s, which set a precedent for numerous other conflicts across the continent.

A solid analysis of UN involvement against Katanga's forces can be found in Trevor Findlay's book *The Blue Helmets' First War? Use of Force by the UN in the Congo, 1960–64*. Controversy remains over UN involvement and if they did, in fact, overstep their boundaries when dealing with aggression from the secessionist province. Eric S Packham has a detailed account of the UN's involvement in post-independence Belgian Congo with *Success or Failure: The UN Intervention in the Congo after Independence*.

The British would maintain the infrastructure in Katanga throughout the war, and assist in completing the rail line.

Yet the British presence was not welcomed by Belgian officials in Katanga, and they would spend two years trying to reduce the number of anglophone workers at mines across the province. Working conditions were deliberately made bad for migrant workers, and Africans were increasingly being used for jobs that had normally gone to Europeans, paying them paltry wages. In 1920, a general strike ensued, and the British workers, eventually, received an increase in compensation; yet UMHK would go about sending British workers home once their contracts ran out, and the percentage of Belgian workers rose from 23% to 58% from 1917 to 1922. Anglophone influence waned after that, with solid Belgian domination of the mining sector by the early 1920s.

Increased pressure on African and European labour created distress for Elisabethville's citizens during and after the great depression. Forced labour for local Congolese was still permitted, and UMHK officials were determined to get more productivity from their workers as profit margins were squeezed. Belgian Congo had also created a secret police service, creating suspicion amongst locals as arrests without charge increased across the city. Life in Elisabethville was becoming less idyllic – Africans had their rations cut, and as World War II arrived, strife was rampant. A mass protest erupted in 1941, and was put down harshly by Belgian colonial forces – they killed 70 workers, and arrested numerous more Africans for conspiracy. Trade union reforms would begin throughout the war, but then lost ground after World War II ended and the colonial government sought to normalise the labour laws of their colony. Yet as African reform swept the continent in the late 1940s, Belgian attitudes were being forced to progress in regards to their treatment of indigenous workers, and conditions did slowly improve as 1950 arrived.

With independence, the Europeans in Elisabethville saw a chance to stem the tide of African independence and supported the secessionist government of Moise Tshombe. Belgium as well would lend Tshombe's rebel government unofficial support, as Katanga continued its mission of remaining separate from Congo-

AVIKAT

An infrastructure worthy of an independent nation was emerging in the secessionist state of Katanga as Moise Tshombe began his year-long war against the government in Léopoldville. With the majority of extractable resources in Katanga as well as a sizeable and competent mercenary force behind him, Tshombe began accumulating planes with the aim of having an air force.

Avikat was, originally, simply a cargo outfit based in Lubumbashi; yet as independence emerged Tshombe purchased nine CM170 Magisters, small jet-engined fighters. Tshombe's Katanga, therefore, had an air force ready to fight in July 1961 – with European planes and European mercenary pilots to fly them. Avikat grew its numbers in October with the addition of Dornier aircraft from West Germany. The main airbase for Avikat was in Luango, and while initially protecting their own interests as UN forces occupied other towns, they would begin all-out conflict against each other in September 1961.

Avikat was initially a highly successful air force. The first of only a handful of mercenary air forces in modern times, they hit ONUC positions with their Magister aircraft and enjoyed several victories. ONUC, though, would bounce back with the full support of its members and eventually seize Avikat cargo planes in Lubumbashi and destroy the majority of the Avikat fighter planes in Luango, while their own coalition air force of Ethiopian, Indian, Canadian and Swiss fighters would attack airfields used by Avikat. By the end of 1961 Avikat's fighter force was destroyed, its cargo planes seized, and the war pushed to the ground, where it would persist for over another year before Moise Tshombe officially ended the Katanga secession.

Very few books have been written on Avikat, though perhaps the most thorough is *Air Wars and Aircraft: A Detailed Record of Air Combat, 1945 to the Present*, by Victor Flintham. A detailed account of Avikat's operations can be found online at www.acig.org/artman/publish/article_182.shtml.

8

Léopoldville. The Belgians would secretly fund the mercenary army that gave ONUC a run for their money; the possibility of losing control of UMHK and the numerous lucrative mines scattered across the province was an unattractive option for European interests in Katanga. African support of the secession was sharply divided, and when UN forces invaded in 1961 the province would see more upheaval in the city.

As Mobutu arrived in 1965, his Africanisation programme saw the city's name change to Lubumbashi and the vast majority of European workers evicted from their positions across Katanga, which would be renamed Shaba Province. The workforce would be largely African, and he would nationalise UMHK, renaming it Gécamines. The city ballooned in size with Congolese from surrounding towns, as they arrived in Lubumbashi seeking work.

The year 1990 would be another critical time in Lubumbashi and for all of Zaire – Mobutu would suppress a student protest at the university with force, killing 11. Kinshasa was scheduled to host the francophone summit soon after, but international pressure against Mobutu's response to the protests had the summit moved at the last minute. This put further pressure on the dictator for change; during this time Shaba was renamed back to Katanga.

The city would encounter minimal fighting as Laurent Kabila and the AFDL moved westward from their bases near Rwanda, and fall to the rebel forces in April 1997. Several weeks after the invasion of Lubumbashi, Kabila declared himself the new President of the Democratic Republic of Congo; Mobutu Sésé Seko fled Kinshasa soon after, and Kabila's march to the capital continued.

Refugees would arrive from the hinterlands of northern Katanga as fighting ensued between the Mayi-Mayi and Interahamwe, and the mining operations would trundle slowly along in the midst of chaos under Gécamines; yet Lubumbashi would largely sit outside the open conflict of the late 1990s and early in the new century, allowing it to retain the same economic importance to the wider Congo as it has had since its creation.

ORIENTATION The city sits to the west of the rail line, which runs north–south through the entire town. If you follow the street west from the train station, you'll pass through an area where the roundabout near the **Park Hôtel** marks the real town centre. To the west, the **Lubumbashi River** marks the end of the town centre and on the other side are residential neighbourhoods, as well as the city's golf course – which sits on the shores of a small lake, beside the Hôtel Karavia. To the southwest, the copper smelter has a massive black hill beside it – affectionately called **Mount Lubumbashi** by some.

GETTING THERE AND AROUND Luano International Airport is north of the city. This is a half-decent air terminal for its size, and you can easily get flights to the rest of the DR Congo and also out of the country – currently it is the only other city in the country offering scheduled international flights.

A taxi around town should cost around US$2; to the golf club, expect to pay US$5 and to the airport no more than US$8.

Airline information

✈ **Bravo Air Congo** Av Mama Yeeno 534; m 099 930 1601; f 099 930 1600. Experimenting with several routes originating in Lubumbashi including Kolwezi & Kalemie. Schedules for these are erratic. Also regular flights to Kinshasa.

✈ **Hewa Bora Airways** Av Kasai; m 097 02 9777. With flights to Kinshasa.

✈ **Kenya Airways** Chaussée Laurent Désiré Kabila; m 099 991 8670/089 48 114; e kenyaairwaysgsa_fbm@yahoo.fr. Flies several times a week to Nairobi.

✈ **South African Airways** Chaussée Laurent Désiré Kabila; m 081 269 680/081 126 69681/081 266 9682. Flies to Johannesburg several times a week.

✈ **Wimbi Dira Airways** m 081 516 9022; e lubumbashi@wda.cd. Regular flights to Mbuji-Mayi & Kinshasa.

LOCAL TOUR OPERATORS For all of your permit needs, visit the **Park Hôtel** where visits can be arranged. Four wheel drives can be booked, money can be spent in spades, even aircraft can be chartered if you're in a hurry. They have a special deal with the Office National de Tourisme and ICCN to sell permits here.

🏠 **WHERE TO STAY** Lubumbashi's top address is the **Park Hôtel** which has a decidedly Old World atmosphere to it, a colonial throwback to be sure. Just around the corner is the equally character-filled **Hôtel Belle Vue** in an old but well-maintained building. Several newer hotels have appeared in recent years catering to the increasing number of foreigners arriving on business.

🏠 **Hôtel Karavia** Route du Golf; ☎ 224 515/243 225 011. Overlooking the golf club & a favourite for high-end businesses operating in Katanga with fully stocked rooms — private washrooms with running water, AC, TV. Has a pool, highly recommended restaurant & plenty of secure parking. Sgl $$$$, dbl $$$$$

🏠 **Planet Hollybum** (18 rooms) 975 Av Kilela Balanda; m 097 030 256/097 029 389; e planethotel@ic-lubum.cd. On the northern area of the city, with a high-end restaurant & terrace, loads of character & a selection of souvenirs. B/fast inc. Sgl/dbl $$$$

🏠 **Hôtel Beau Site** (43 rooms) 500 Av Lomami; m 081 970 2690; e hotelbeausite2004@yahoo.fr. High-end hotel in the town centre with private washrooms, views onto the busy street outside. B/fast inc. Sgl $$$, dbl $$$$

🏠 **Park Hôtel** (77 rooms) 50 Av Kasai; m 097 032 330/099 836 586; f 234 2793/234 2643; e cth_parkhotel@yahoo.fr. Lubumbashi's oldest hotel loaded with character, good views of the street below, & very central. Rooms have private washrooms, AC, TV. Has a courtyard in the middle of the hotel as well an excellent restaurant. Sgl/dbl $$$, suite $$$$

🏠 **Le Vagabond** Quartier Golf; ☎ 0997 024 126/0997 027 854; e levagabond@ic-lubum.cd. With pool, internet, & airport shuttle. Also has restaurant. Partners with a nearby guesthouse Dundee's (see next entry). Sgl/dbl $$$

🏠 **Oasis Hôtel** (20 rooms) Av Sendwe. No telephone. A good mid-range option in Lubumbashi with running water, AC, TV. Sgl/dbl $$$

🏠 **Hôtel Belle Vue** (17 rooms) Av Kasai; m 081 505 6409/081 815 1117; e eximint2@hotmail.com. Mostly B&B-style place again in the city centre with decent enough rooms — private washrooms, AC, TV, but no restaurant. Simple b/fast inc. Sgl $$, dbl $$$

🏠 **Hôtel Reka** (34 rooms) 696 Av Kapenda; m 097 045 132/081 871 5390. With a large high-end restaurant & decent rooms with AC & TV, probably the best value for your money in central Lubumbashi. Sgl $$, dbl $$$, suite $$$$

🏠 **Protestant Church** Av Likasi. Basic private rooms with sink & mosquito net. Shared washrooms. B/fast inc. Sgl/dbl $

✗ **WHERE TO EAT La Calebasse** (*78 Av Sendwe*; m *097 026 625*; ⊕ *from 18.00*; **$$$$**) is probably the city's top independent restaurant, and specialises in African dishes. Most of the larger hotels have some sort of restaurant, with **Planet Hollybum** (⊕ *from 18.00 daily*; **$$$**) and the Park Hôtel's **Safari Grill** (⊕ *from 18.00 daily*; **$$$**) coming highly recommended. For excellent European dining try the **La Casa Degli Italiani** on Boulevard Lumumba 2900 (m *099 702 5756 /0813331 157*; ⊕ *from 19.00 daily*; **$$$**), which has private parking as well as a VIP room.

For lunch or a quick dinner, **Katanga Fried Chiken** (yes, it's actually spelled that way) (⊕ *from 10.00 daily*; **$$$**) has two locations and is hugely popular amongst a young non-African diaspora. As the name suggests, it serves up some mean fried poultry in addition to staples of Lebanese cuisine, such as falafels, in spotless air-conditioned eating areas. For mid-range French, try **La Brioche** (*75 Chaussée Laurent Desiré Kabila*; m *097 021 780/097 021 781*; ⊕ *from 18.30 daily*; **$$**)

or **Le Perroquet** (*588 Av Kasavubu;* m *097 022 930/081 407 3635;* ⊕ *daily from 18.30; $$*). The majority of establishments close at 23.00 or midnight.

SHOPPING Right outside the Park Hôtel are several sellers of **Malachite**, who do a swift amount of business with foreigners passing through. Also recommended is taking a taxi out to the **Ruashi Market** for US$4, which has a great selection of local handicrafts. **Planet Hollybum** also has a good selection of local souvenirs.

PRACTICALITIES

Banks The only bank worth recommending in Lubumbashi is **Trust Merchant Bank** (*761 Av Moëro;* m *997 023 000;* f *0012 087 300 711;* e *tmb@ trustmerchantbank.com; www.trustmerchantbank.com*), as it can provide cash advances to credit card holders. Numerous foreign companies also operate local accounts from them. For Western Union money transfers, **BIAC** has the simplest access (*532 Chausse Laurent Désiré Kabila;* m *081 400 2000*).

Medical For anything serious, consider getting a medical evacuation to South Africa as air connections to Johannesburg are excellent. Several smaller pharmacies dot the town centre; a larger one is **Zottos Pharma** beside the Hôtel Belle Vue (m *997 021 532/081 815 1117;* e *eximint@ic-lubum.cd*). The best medical clinic in Lubumbashi is the **Gécamines** clinic (*Av Usines*), attached to the larger mining company's network, and will accept new patients who can pay for treatment.

WHAT TO SEE Lubumbashi is a little low on sights. Perhaps most intriguing is the only **Orthodox Synagogue** in the DR Congo, *en route* to the airport. It was completed in 1930 when European settlement was booming in the then Elisabethville, and the city held most of Belgian Congo's Jewish population. The structure has withstood the numerous incursions through the city's turbulent history. These days there are only a few hundred Jewish people left in Lubumbashi, and they continue to frequent the synagogue. Services are held irregularly, and they will most likely welcome a tourist.

Head to the town centre and see the **Elephant's Statue**, really only a modest sculpture, but this is the hub of Lubumbashi and a pleasant place to hang out. To the west is the **Cathedral of Saints Peter and Paul**, certainly not the daintiest of its kind, with high brick walls. Inside is equally spartan with a high brown dome and walls painted yellow. Function reigns over style. Lubumbashi's **Museum** (*Av Kasai;* ⊕ *10.00–15.00 Tue–Sat*) is a simple place with a few decent displays that document the region's history, and is good for a diversion.

Finally out at the Hôtel Karavia there is a **golf course** and you may wish to stay at the hotel if you're going to be on the greens often. Further south along the Lubumbashi River is the **Parc Zoologique**, really just an urban park these days.

If you have a vehicle a good day trip heads 100km east to the town of **Kiniama** (⊕ *11°28.05 S, 28°18′50 E*). After some walking you can see where the **Kafubu and Luapula rivers** merge. This creates some fancy whirlpools and the trip there has some decent scenery. Further along this road towards the Zambian border, about 1,000km from Lubumbashi, is the town of **Kasenga** (⊕ *10°23.29 S, 28°36.55 E*) where the **Lualuba Rapids,** also called **Johnston Falls**, create some incredible sights. They're the largest rapids in the DR Congo, bordering Zambia, and absolutely in the middle of nowhere. It should be possible to cross into Zambia from here, and it would make better sense to visit them *en route* to Lubumbashi than making a return trip. Oh yes – forget about public transport to here.

If you're arriving from Zambia, Kasumbalesa will be your first stop just across the border in the DR Congo. It's a crowded, tight, chaotic place where any number of trucks and people and cargo containers get stuck for days, weeks or months. Many sit in limbo waiting while their goods are inspected and reinspected, or while they weave through the byzantine bureaucratic procedures to discover who exactly needs to be paid off for their journey to continue. If you are bringing your own vehicle, check and recheck that all of your documentation is in order: these officials see a huge number of foreign vehicles and know their game inside and out.

Cheap accommodation and cheap food are easy to find. Note the posters warning of immigration controls on Zambia's side of the border: apparently tunnelling from the DR Congo into Zambia is a popular option for the most desperate. However, if you are travelling light, your stay here should be reasonably short, as Lubumbashi is less than two hours away on a well-paved highway. Minibuses ply this route frequently.

SAKANIA ✪ *12°44.48 S, 28°33.14 E*

Sakania is just over the border from Ndola, and may be a tempting option for getting into the DR Congo faster than heading to Chillilabombwe and then Kasumbalesa, but I would advise against it – road connections are much better on the Zambian side, as is the frequency of transport, making this route far preferable for reaching Lubumbashi. The rail line also continues here from Lubumbashi and to Ndola.

Sakania is the largest town amongst the animal reserves which make up the far southeastern corner of the DR Congo. These include the **Sakania Reserves** for elephants and hippos, and the **Damalisk Reserve** in the Leshwe region, the southeastern extreme of DR Congo.

Continue northeast from Sakania through the reserve on a horrible road, and then a 4x4 is necessary for the road along the Luapula River to the village of **Musolo** (✪ *12°22.25 S, 29°12.35 E*). On the river here are the **Giraud Falls**, extending over several hundred metres along the river – though not falling from any great height. They were named after a Belgian officer who discovered them while traversing the river in 1883. On this expedition he would be captured only a few dozen kilometres downstream by local villagers, and die in their custody.

LIKASI ✪ *10°59.09 S, 26°44.26 E*

The quintessential planned mining town of Katanga, Likasi has existed since day one as a living space for everyone employed by the Shinkolobwe Mine and smelter beside it. It's the largest town on the way to the L'Upemba Parks, a good place to rest and stock up on supplies if overlanding before moving onward. Yet the economic troubles of Likasi are unmistakeably present: the centre can be eerily quiet even in the day, as many former government buildings are locked up and seemingly abandoned. It was built around mines and refineries, and finally became a town in 1931 under the name Jadotville.

If you are the curious type, the old colonial neighbourhoods are an interesting sight: the planned mining suburbs just over the railway tracks, and the quiet tree-lined boulevards just off the town centre are rather pleasant. Keep in mind as well that a new arrival of foreigners will attract some attention, some good and some bad – the police especially will be interested in looking over your papers to see if they can extract a bribe. They are always out on the road leading into town in the afternoon with their rusted car parts, stringing them along the road so they have

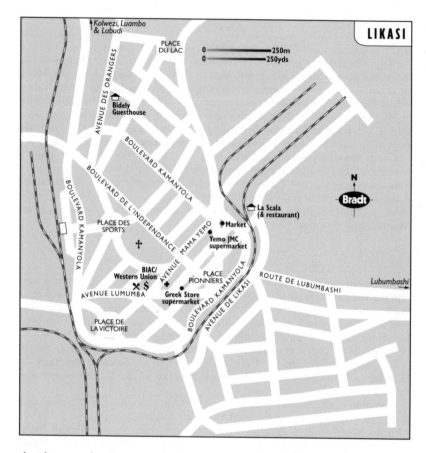

the chance to harass every vehicle passing by. A few hundred francs should get them out of your way.

GETTING THERE AND AROUND Likasi is roughly a two-hour drive north of Lubumbashi, on a decent paved road. There is little traffic, and roadworks do occur from time to time. It is, however, a 'Péage' route, meaning that a small fee of a few dollars is collected both at the beginning and end of the road. You'll pay more for a truck than a motorbike, and it might be worth convincing them that a Land Rover is a 'car' instead of a 'truck'. Some minibuses go north to Likasi intermittently, along with large trucks. Hitching can easily be arranged, for a fee. Stand at the turn-off on the way north out of Lubumbashi if you wish to hitch.

WHERE TO STAY AND EAT Likasi has two restaurants, neither of which is spectacular, and if you spend any real time in the town their selection will pale compared with anything home-cooked. A few hotels are scattered around town, none of which can be called inspiring. Best of the lot is the one with the restaurant, **La Scala** (*sgl/dbl* $), which has spartan lodging with at least private washrooms and occasional cold running water. A little more upscale is **Bidely Guest House** (*dbl* $$, *an extra US$10 if 2 males share the room*) which is in a decent residential area with running water and televisions, as well as secure parking. The other **restaurant** ($) is beside the BIAC office and has some basic dishes as well as a bar.

SHOPPING The best store in town is the **Greek Store** for groceries. Run by Greeks (funnily enough), a decent selection of imported foods is available – including imported sausages. Like anything else in the DR Congo, expect to pay a premium for it.

PRACTICALITIES

Banks No bank exists in Likasi, at least one that is open and communicating with the outside world. For any money dealings, head straight to the **BIAC office** (*Av Lumumba;* m *081 700 4000;* ☺ *08.00–16.30 Mon–Sat*) which allows Western Union money transfers.

AROUND LIKASI

There are plenty of great excursions in the Likasi area, aside from the national parks. Nearby is **Lake Tshangelele**, a very popular sight for migrating birds. The turn-off is 90km before arriving in Likasi; turn right, and follow the road to the north shore. Also in this area are the **Lufira Falls** near **Mwadingusha** (✪ *10°44.55 S, 27°14.41 E*), sending water from the Kundelungu Plateau rushing into the lake. Hydro-electric power was first established here for the DR Congo, and the dam was one of the country's most important before the creation of the Inga Dams near Matadi.

Southwest of Likasi are the **Kashinge Caves**, between two rivers, near the Moaishi and Kashinge streams. These caves were used as hiding spots during periods of inter-tribal war, and can be considered something of an archaeological site. They're not easy to find, so a guide is more necessary than usual.

L'UPEMBA NATIONAL PARK One of Africa's oldest parks, established in 1939, L'Upemba protects a large area consisting of the Bia Mountains east of the Lualaba River, wide open areas of savanna and numerous lakes – including Lake Upemba, the park's namesake. This was the ancestral homeland of the Luba people, and in

---

SHINKOLOBWE MINE

An unmistakeably large presence near Likasi, and indeed the sole reason for the town existing, is the ancient mine of Shinkolobwe. Even travelling northwest to the town from Lubumbashi, you will notice the massive 'tailings' of the copper and cobalt mines as the run-off has spilled into semi-solid pools of soil and cast-off minerals. These are the remnants of Shinkolobwe, an ancient and massive structure that is still active, if only barely.

While currently a central source for copper and cobalt, Shinkolobwe holds a large place in history by formerly producing uranium. Its largest customer was the USA, and by the dawn of World War II the Belgian company UMHK had sold over 1,000 tonnes of uranium to the Americans.

The bombs dropped on Hiroshima and Nagasaki in 1945 used uranium from Shinkolobwe. The mining company Gécamines continued to extract uranium throughout the rule of Mobutu Sésé Seko, but currently only has facilities for mining and refining copper and cobalt. Little has changed in the mine's standards and practices since they were left to the state in the 1960s. Conflict and a lack of able labour, along with delayed pay cheques which leave people without money for months on end, have led the mine to operate at only a fraction of its actual capacity. Nonetheless it is still the major employer in Likasi, with numerous geologists, scientists and businessmen working for Gécamines.

better times the entire region was subjected to numerous archaeological digs. UNESCO has lobbied to put L'Upemba on their list of World Heritage Sites, though this will most likely be a long time coming.

Most visitors to the park will be here for the wildlife and a few natural wonders. Typical species of the African savanna can be seen: antelope, hippo, leopard, lion, and most importantly herds of zebra – the zebra in their natural habitat is the main selling point for ICCN as it is the only place in Congo where they can be seen. They have an established infrastructure here for tourists.

The lakes are also a great place to witness birdlife, and are quite unique due to their huge regions of floating vegetation: giant forests of papyrus. The winds can rip entire acres of papyrus from these floating forests, creating temporary islands that drift out into the lake. The more wind that pushes them together, the denser these temporary islands become. This northern area was a common site of refuge for locals when Mayi-Mayi rebels began ravaging the region; villagers fled to open islands, stuck in the middle of these lakes, where they could not be attacked. Aside from Lake Upemba itself, the major lakes are Kabwe, Kabele, Mulenda, Nunda, Kalumbe, and Kabamba at the northern edge of the park. These wetlands make up the largest floodplain in the DR Congo and are a major source of water for the Congo River.

The park is also home to the **Tumba Caves** near the village of **Kabelwe** (✪ *08°41.09 S, 26°06.53 E*), between the Mwevu and Mungoy rivers, on the western coast of Lake Upemba. The caves are rumoured to be vast, but no real exploration has ever taken place. Reaching Kabelwe is a bit of a problem too, as it is far off the main access points to the park. Just south of the park are the **Kiantapo Caves**, which allegedly have some prehistoric markings in them. They were well studied half a century ago by the Tervuren Museum in Belgium, but are nothing of a tourist site these days; be sure to get local permission before going in.

There are also some major waterfalls here, coming down through cliffs and valleys in the Bia Mountains. The mountains create a semicircle, and all of the rivers flow down from it. Here can be found the **Dikolongo Falls** west of Lubudi, just north of Lake Dikolongo, falling 40m. The lake is home to a huge variety of fish species. Another waterfall to visit is **Kalule Falls**, falling almost 90m in a rocky valley covered in brush. These are easy visits in L'Upemba, both being near the park headquarters.

Practicalities L'Upemba follows a similar pattern for parks in the DR Congo: it's hard to reach and takes a private 4x4 vehicle to get there. From Likasi head northwest to the main town of **Lubudi** (✪ *09°57.04 S, 25°57.26 E*), the southern access point to the park, and then continue to the base camp at **Kayo** (✪ *09°52.00 S, 26°02.49 E*). There is also an airstrip here if you're inclined to charter a plane, though it's not really necessary to do so as the road is good enough – and should take around three days from Lubumbashi.

There is also a northern access point at **Lusinga** (✪ *08°55.55 S, 27°12.19 E*) along the painful route from Likasi north to Mitwaba. This might be a better entry point if you wish to visit the lakes. There is an airstrip here as well.

ICCN in Lubumbashi will sell you a permit for US$110, or you can buy it in Lubudi for the same price. It all depends on to whom you want to give the cash.

KUNDELUNGU NATIONAL PARKS Somewhere around 1970 the new Zairian regime thought that making a park out of the plains in the Kundelungu region would be a good idea. Prior to this it had been a popular hunting domain. The entire area is a 7,600km² plateau of savanna, lush grasslands that are popular with the big game in Katanga. The plateau circulates water to the major rivers in the area, including the Luapala to the east and Lufira as it cuts a deep valley through the region. Kundelungu is in fact two parks, with Kundelungu-Ouest being designated a protected spot slightly later. These two parks are connected to the L'Upemba Parks by a massive floodplain, the lowlands of the area and where the main route from Likasi to Mitwaba is located.

Kundelungu's **Lofoi Falls** is the first thing you should see in Katanga, and it's worth spending the time and effort to get out to the park if only for this purpose. Yes, I've included a few boatloads of other waterfalls in this guidebook to the Congos but this is the daddy of them all – Africa's highest at 347m – a huge river dumping its load off a sheer cliff into a steamy valley below. It's best to try and see it during the wet season as the water output is greater; at the height of the dry season, the river can only be a trickle, and water can evaporate before reaching the pool below.

Kundelungu is covered with lush vegetation, the likes of which have not been subjected to serious research. Some speculation exists regarding the potential for the plateaux in the area to contain unique species. The area is interspersed with Katanga's more typical savanna, and the usual wildlife suspects can be seen here if they have not all been sent into hiding from poaching.

Most importantly, the DR Congo's last remaining cheetahs exist in Kundelungu. Highly prized by poachers and hunters alike, their numbers have not fared well over the past decade. ICCN could send you on a wild goose chase throughout the park to see them, and indeed they may be there, but unless you have plenty of time on your hands it's unlikely they will show up in Kundelungu for a random tourist. Perhaps this is for the best at this time, as they have the opportunity to retreat into hiding and hopefully repopulate as the DR Congo becomes more peaceful.

Also worth visiting are the **Kiubo Falls** near **Musabira**, falling almost 70m over sandstone into a rocky pool. Numerous trails provide excellent viewpoints of the falls. Further north on the way to Mitwaba are the **Kiwakishi Caves**, northwest of the main road and the village of **Muvule** (⊕ 09°10.38 S, 07°12.30 E). These are a kind of sacred space for local villagers and were once used for refuge against Arab raiding parties in the 19th century; get permission, and a guide, before entering.

Practicalities Kundelungu isn't exceedingly difficult to visit, provided you have your own transport. Head northeast from Lubumbashi and take a left at the town of **Minga** (⊕ *11°04.48 S, 27°55.43 E*) and continue about 100km north to **Konko** (⊕ *10°12.00 S, 27°27.06 E*) which is inside the park proper. There is some basic accommodation here. The falls can be reached by a 4km-long hiking trail. Permits cost US$120 at the ICCN office in Lubumbashi. The main base camp in the park is at **Katwe** (⊕ *10°33.41 S, 27°51.15 E*) which is on a different road altogether from the falls past Minga – go a few kilometres north to **Katofio** (⊕ *11°03.14 S, 28°01.24 E*) then go left on a bad road that ascends the Kundelungu Plateau. This route is worth the views alone. Katwe should be your first stop to enquire about some safari-style drives – or more likely walking, as the rocky plateaux have few roads.

Pack all of your equipment for this trip; Katwe used to have a guesthouse, but it was pillaged. Konko may have some place to sleep, but camping with your own tent will be the most reliable option. A visit to the falls will likely require an overnight stay in Konko unless you start early enough. Permits should cost the same as Katanga's other parks, at US$110 and available in Lubumbashi.

BUNKEYA ⊕ *10°23.51 S, 26°58.10 E*

In many ways Bunkeya is the spiritual heartland of Katanga. The predecessor of the Belgian claim to the region was the Kingdom of M'Siri, at its height from 1856 to 1891, which stretched through most of central Katanga. Its king, Ngengelenwa Msiri, has been documented as either a crazed despot or an astute politician who sought to mitigate the incursions from the Europeans as they began their colonisation of the continent during the final decades of the 19th century. Both the Congolese and Katangans speak highly of him while European records consider him a twisted old man who brutalised his servants. These days he is highly regarded amongst Bunkeya's population as one of the few chiefs across central Africa who did not wish to bend to European colonialism.

HISTORY Msiri had established the capital of his kingdom in Bunkeya sometime around 1850 by consolidating tribes and driving away the Lubas, who commonly raided the region. The kingdom stretched from the west bank of the Lualaba River to the west of present-day Kolwezi, a vast area larger than Great Britain. The rich mineral deposits made his kingdom a trading centre, shipping ivory and gold west to Portuguese ports and slaves east to Arab holdings. He struck a deal with Tippu Tip, who was running his own state east of the Lualaba River, for protection from his attacks in exchange for a steady supply of slaves. Ngengelenwa Msiri was no fool, and managed to form an army of 3,000 to protect his kingdom; unlike other African leaders before colonial times, his astute trading practices had amassed a huge cache of rifles and ammunition. His army was as well armed as any European outfit in the region.

He was ardent at keeping out intruders, refusing permission from any explorers who may have arrived in the Garaganze, the original name for Katanga. It was not until 1886 that Msiri invited Protestant missionaries to establish themselves at Bunkeya. He also hired Arab advisors related to Tippu Tip, and sought advice on how to limit European expansion into his territory, surrounding himself with people from other cultures, to learn from them and better understand what their motives might be.

Msiri was eventually approached by explorers from both Britain and Belgium, who were seeking to expand their territorial mandates in the region. The British South Africa Company arrived in Bunkeya in 1890 and presented the king with a treaty, which he demanded to be translated before agreeing to it. He deemed the treaty unfavourable to his kingdom and rejected it outright, sending the company on their way. By this time the Berlin Conference had adjourned and his kingdom was within Congo Free State, though he was not made aware of this fact.

His downfall would come in 1891 when William Grant Stairs, a Canadian military commander who had travelled with Henry Morton Stanley on the Emin Pasha expedition (see box, page 172), arrived in the region. Military campaigns across the east were driving out anticipate the Arabs, and at Bunkeya they were equally relentless. Stairs was charged with ensuring the region was soundly under control of forces loyal to Congo Free State, and he sent a Belgian officer, Captain Omer Bodson, to arrest Msiri; on 20 December 1891, after an altercation, Bodson shot Msiri dead; Bodson was then killed by a nephew of Msiri.

Msiri's death did not precipitate the end of the kingdom, however, and the people appointed a new chief, Mukanda Bantu. He agreed to have the kingdom incorporated into Congo Free State, something Ngengelenwa Msiri was set against. Subsequent attacks occurred on members of Stairs's expedition by those who thought the entire deal was bad, yet the transition was relatively peaceful.

Moise Tshombe was descended directly from the Msiri kings, or so it is said, and this bolstered his leadership during the years of Katanga secession in the 1960s.

GETTING THERE AND AROUND Bunkeya is 75km north of Likasi on a brutal dirt road and should take the better part of a day by private transport. There are some minibuses that ply this route as well, near Likasi's market.

WHERE TO STAY There should be one or two basic hotels in town, and if not, try one of the various Christian missions to get a room. None should cost above US$10.

WHAT TO SEE The town itself is a modest affair with several Catholic and Protestant missions. The best thing worth seeing is the **Tomb of Msiri**, and every 20 December his death is commemorated in an elaborate ceremony. The town has held fast to its ancient traditions and you can see plenty of unique costumes, robes and furniture around. Whenever a new king is appointed there are more elaborate celebrations; the last was held in 1992. The nearby **Mount Mkulu** is an ancient burial site.

KOLWEZI ✪ *10°42.34 S, 25°29.39 E*

The road from Likasi to Kolwezi is impressively bad, making the 150km trip a full day's journey. The city was once an important mining centre for European interests, but many elements conspired to bring about its disrepair, not least of which was the invasion and occupation of the town by Angolan rebels.

THE OCCUPATION OF KOLWEZI

Catching the eye of the world in 1978 was yet another rebellion in Zaire; most rebellions in the country were local insurrections, put down harshly by Mobutu's FAZ and barely a whimper was made of such things to the outside world. Yet like most events in the Congo, once Europeans become embroiled the countries rise to global consciousness.

The prime example of this is the tragedy of Kolwezi. Katangese rebels, 4,000 strong, had received funding from Angola to begin their insurrection against Mobutu's rule as well as European domination of the resources there – they lived and worked in the Gécamines properties, enjoying comfortable lives in upper-class company-manufactured homes. Early on the morning of 13 May 1978, the rebels marched straight into Kolwezi and sealed the town off, fighting briefly with FAZ soldiers. This was definitely a good way to get the world to notice, as there were 3,000 Europeans in town during the invasion. The Katangese forces announced on 14 May that the second war of Shaba had begun, and announced their international assistants – Angola, Zambia and Cuba.

The rebels were ruthless inside Kolwezi – they killed with impunity and set fire to buildings without much thought for who or what may be inside them. Mobutu's FAZ tried an unsuccessful counterattack, and the dictator later begged for military assistance from the USA, France and Belgium to end the brutal uprising. Whole families were being executed by the rebels: a systematic extermination of the town's population was occurring. This included Europeans, and because of that, European soldiers would arrive shortly.

In the early hours of 18 May, French paratroopers arrived in Kolwezi in what was called Opération Bonite. They dropped by parachute and quickly took the airport. Katangese guerrillas retreated mostly into the forest where they staged counterattacks on the evenings of 19–20 May. Europeans began evacuating from Kolwezi. Belgian soldiers arrived, primarily with an interest in organising the evacuation. European forces were fast and organised, overwhelming the Katangese rebels quickly.

In total, some 250 rebels were killed before they fled on 21 May 1978. But the civilian toll was massive – as many as 700 Congolese and 170 Europeans lost their lives.

GETTING THERE AND AROUND A few minibuses attempt the route each day, and Hewa Bora Airways has recently begun flying here again from Lubumbashi. Furthermore, rumours persist of a 'permit' being required by foreigners travelling past Likasi on this road, which could mean a few more hassles for the unprepared overlander. The resurgence of interest in Katanga's immense mineral wealth will see this city changing soon, which should mean a variety of new hotels – especially if the border crossing to Angola, via Dilolo, manages to reopen.

WHERE TO STAY The top hotel in town is **Hôtel Lualaba** (m *099 768 1431; sgl* $$$*/dbl* $$$$) and is intended for the slowly returning numbers of mining investors coming to Kolwezi. A cheaper option is **Mampa Guest House** (m *099 424 4562; sgl* $$) with some basic rooms with, expectedly, basic amenities. The two best budget hotels are in the part of town called La Cité, one called **Modiem** (*sgl* $) and the other **Kolwezi Guest House** (m *099 710 8450; sgl* $). Be sure to brush up on your French or Swahili, as it is quite likely that none of these hotels will have anyone who speaks English.

WHAT TO SEE Kolwezi's **Komoto Mine** was one of Katanga's largest during its heyday and one of the locals will happily take a villager to its entrance; you might be able to walk inside if you pay a few people off, but there is little to see inside. **Lac Nzilo** is situated on the northeastern edge of town, and at its northwestern end is the **Nzilo Falls**, or rather a series of rapids, which drops over 30m through an impressive gorge. This is the source for one of the power stations that provided power to the mines. South of town are the **Lufunfu Caves** near the village of **Lufunfu** (⊕ *11°11.60 S, 25°37.00 E*) at the source of the river of the same name.

KAMINA TO KONGOLO ⊕ 08°44.15 S, 24°59.39 E & 05°21.54 S, 26°59.34 E

Kamina is an important but modest little town in the northern stretches of Katanga, where the railway from Lubumbashi splits. Trains either continue north to Kananga or northeast to Kabongo and Kabalo, eventually arriving in Kindu or Kalemie. A small dam was built here in ancient times, and during the 1960s a massive airbase was built in the region – probably the DR Congo's best airport, Kamina Air Base. It was built to help the ONUC as they fought the Katangese mercenaries, and was used as a forward base for aircraft during Operation Dragon Rouge as they arrived in the Congo from Ascension Island *en route* to Stanleyville. It was expanded during Mobutu's Zaire, and remains totally off-limits to visitors. Instead, occasional passenger flights need to nosedive onto a tiny dirt strip right beside town. Most people take the train, or brave the bad roads.

WHAT TO SEE Kamina is a good starting point for some natural wonders in the region, especially **Pitanshi Caves** (⊕ *07°55.60.00 S, 25°19.60.00 E*) which follow the Kilubi River. These caves were created by river erosion underground and are lit by sunlight through naturally created shafts. Generally they're only accessible during the dry season. A road heads to them northeast from **Kipukwe** (⊕ *08°06.11 S, 25°10.07 E*) and then doubles back onto the main road to Kabongo at **Samba** (⊕ *07°55.14 S, 25°13.13 E*). Continue on this road to **Kabongo** (⊕ *07°20.29 S, 25°34.57 E*) where **Lake Boya** is right beside it. The lake is popular with birdlife and surrounded by high reeds. Follow the road northwest along the railway for a few hundred kilometres and arrive at **Kaniama** (⊕ *07°30.43 S, 24°10.26 E*) which has a worse road going northeast towards the modestly impressive **Kaye Falls**. This is also the frontier of Katanga Province, with a border checkpoint a dozen kilometres ahead.

There is a brutal road north to here which eventually reaches the village of **Mani** (✦ *06°28.01 S, 25°20.58 E*), right on the border of Katanga and East Kasai. Mani has a few natural sights, not least the **Kabale Lakes** which can be good for birdwatching. The geography also begins to shift from Katanga's arid brush to moist forest foliage. The Lomami River is west of Mani, and if followed upstream for about 10km it will bring you to the **Lubangule Falls** in a shallow valley. The river merges here with the Lubangule River. Keep going along the road from Mani to **Kabinda** (✦ *06°08.10 S, 24°28.50 E*) and the road should link up with Mbuji-Mayi after grinding away for several days.

Northeast from Kabongo, the rail line arrives in Kabalo. The road also gets here via Lomani, a slightly different route, after around 500km – how long this might actually take is anyone's guess. Kabalo is the official split of the railway, either north to Kindu or east to Kalemie. If you're here by land, going north to **Kongolo** might be worth a try: this is Katanga's main border town with Maniema Province where the **Hinde Rapids** are an impressive sight at the point where the Lualaba River squeezes between two valleys and ends the navigable portion of the river. The rail bridge here that crosses the Lualaba is also impressive, spanning over 500m. Of course, the problem is that there is no direct road link between Kabalo and Kongolo: you must go east from Kabalo to **Nyunzu** (✦ *05°57.17 S, 28°00.59 E*) and then double back to the northeast to reach Kongolo. The good news of sorts here is that there is a northward link on a battered road to **Kasongo** (✦ *04°25.34 S, 26°40.06 E*) in Maniema Province, but ensure you stock up on petrol, because there will most likely be no stations between Kamina and Kindu.

MANONO AND AROUND ✦ 07°18.07 S, 27°23.46 E

Once the toast of the mining community for its wonderfully planned streets and incredible breadth of amenities for both Europeans and Congolese alike, Manono drifted far from its original purpose as subsequent wars brought infrastructure to a halt and shut down the surrounding industries – or at least slowed them to a shadow of their former selves. Manono is the largest city on the main road from Lubumbashi to Kalemie, a hideously long stretch of dirt that will take the most determined at least a couple of weeks.

Yet Manono gained another purpose in 2003 as Mayi-Mayi rebels moved south and began to terrorise settled populations in north central Katanga, creating havoc and disarray and driving thousands to flee into L'Upemba National Park. MONUC designated Manono as the base of operations for this humanitarian disaster, and numerous NGOs have done the same, thanks to the city's airport. If you're here, it's quite likely because you have to be.

This also means you should have access to some private transport, and there are a few sights in the vicinity to keep someone occupied for a few days – not including travel time. On the road southwards to **Mitwaba** (✦ *08°37.58 S, 27°20.38 E*) are the **Kalumengongo Falls** and **Manda Falls**, on the Kalumengongo River. They are situated east in a valley and take a little bit of hiking from the main road to reach. You can also follow a road westward to **Bukena** (✦ *07°42.03 S, 27°09.58 E*) where there are sulphur springs that emerge from the earth, creating noxious fumes.

You can also follow a turn-off east from Mitwaba to **Lake Mweru**, rarely visited from the Congolese side as it takes at least three or four days from Manono. The primary Congolese town on the lake is **Pweto** (✦ *08°28.15 S, 28°53.47 E*), on the northeast corner where the Luvua River drains into the lake. There is also a border crossing here to Zambia. The mountain north of town has excellent views of the lake, and rumour has it that there are ruins of an old Arab fort that was used when slave traders defended themselves against Belgian attacks in the late 19th century. Southwest along the lakeshore is the village of **Loanza** (⊕ *08°40.37 S, 28°41.58 E*) which continues to be an important outpost for missionaries in the region and has a unique collection of mud huts. If you're taking the time to reach Pweto, it's probably worth a stop.

KALEMIE ⊕ *05°55.46 S, 29°10.52 E*

This city of a quarter of a million, formerly named Albertville, has a lengthy colonial history – dating back to Arab traders who set up camps on the western shores of Lake Tanganyika, engaging in the trade of slaves and ivory before the arrival of the Belgians in 1890. The Belgian motivation for arrival was primarily from anti-slavery groups, led by a cardinal of the Catholic Church, who lobbied the government to send in their own troops and enforce some semblance of law in this remote corner of Congo Free State. A legion of volunteers from religious organisations, as well as a volunteer military force, arrived on the west coast of the lake and drove out the Arabs. On 30 December 1891, Fort Albertville was formally established by a colonel. It was not until 1916 that surrounding camps were combined into the larger administrative region of Albertville, and the town became the focal point for a rail terminus and port. It would be a busy connection to Tanzania and the Indian Ocean for several decades, until the upheavals across eastern Congo in the 1960s.

Mobutu's regime saw the city's name changed to Kalemie, and reinforced its status as the southeastern transportation hub for Zaire. Yet during the 1990s Kalemie's remoteness compounded its problems as revolution spread across the DR Congo, and the city became a transit point for soldiers and supplies coming from Tanzania. In the countryside surrounding Kalemie the Mayi-Mayi rebels were increasingly active at the turn of the 21st century, and this has brought a large number of refugees into the area, as well as NGOs and UN staff to try and resolve the conflict. Matters were not helped when the town was struck by an earthquake in December 2005, measuring 6.8 on the Richter scale, collapsing houses and buildings across the region.

Power cuts and water shortages are common as infrastructure has deteriorated. The town has no fixed telephone land lines and relies entirely on mobile networks.

ORIENTATION Kalemie's geography is unique: it sits on the west coast of Lake Tanganyika, with the Lukuga River creating its northern boundary. **Avenue Lumumba** runs north–south along the lake, the main boulevard and original layout of the Belgian town. The city centre's infrastructure dates almost entirely from the time of Belgian Congo, giving the town a unique look over so many other cities across the country – this also means it looks far more ragged than some other cities. The airport is near the north end of town.

GETTING THERE AND AWAY For flying, **Bravo Air Congo** (*Av Lumumba;* m *099 930 1691;* f *099 930 1690*) and **Wimbi Dira Airways** fly into the city once a week from Lubumbashi, but this schedule can change frequently – Kalemie is a sort of 'experimental' destination for these airlines, meaning that if it isn't turning the profits they expect, it may be dropped altogether. The road is OK west to Manono, but has been obliterated heading north to Uvira – bridges have been torn down and various stretches are simply mud, yet I've been assured that with a 4x4 or motorbike it should take only three days. Makeshift rafts bring vehicles and other cargo across the rivers.

There are also rickety boats that cross to Tanzania, irregular sea transport north to Uvira, and south to Mpulungu in Zambia. The rail line is being repaired, and

Zongo Falls, Bas Congo, DRC (SR) page 111

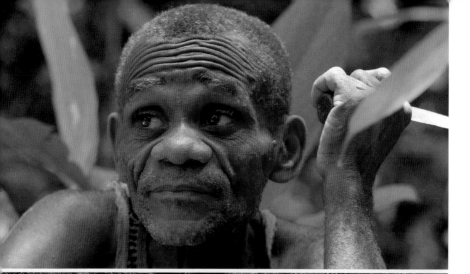

top **Mbuti pygmy in the Ituri rainforest** (KR) page 126

centre **Mbuti pygmy forest camp** (KR)

left **Mbuti women carry the staple food manioc back to their forest camp** (KR)

top Traditional dancing during the Nkumbi celebrations, Ituri rainforest (RK) page 211

centre Nightime party, Ituri rainforest (RK)

right Traditional face painting among the Mbuti pygmies (RK)

top **Village in the Ituri rainforest**
(RK) page 211

centre **Downtown Dolisie, Congo-Brazzaville**
(SR) page 270

left **Cathedral Saints Peter and Paul, Lubumbashi**
(SR) page 142

above **Rwenzori peaks, DRC** (RK) page 194

below **Lake among the Rwenzori range** (RK) page 196

Eastern lowland silverback male gorilla with two
infants, Kahuzi-Biega National Park (SR) page 209

CHE GUEVARA AND LAURENT KABILA

Che Guevara's time in eastern Congo was punctuated by a notable lack of grass roots leadership from the rebel force's highest commander, Laurent Kabila. Che had, in fact, sent numerous letters to Laurent and kept in regular contact for a period of years both before and during his arrival in eastern Congo. The two historical figures, though, would only meet twice.

The first time was in Dar es Salaam, in 1964 – Laurent Kabila was travelling across Africa petitioning governments friendly to his cause for support, key amongst them President Julius Kambarage Nyerere's in Tanzania. It was In Dar es Salaam, in a meeting with Laurent Kabila's Simbas, their commanders, and a Cuban delegation led by Che Guevara, that they would meet. Che spoke fondly of Kabila, and while his words were harsh for the other rebel leaders of Africa who were only seeking to feather their own nests and lead a revolution from the posh hotel rooms of capital cities, he was impressed by Kabila's presentation, presence and eloquence. Guevara agreed to provide support for the Simbas as soon as possible, and departed for Cuba.

The second meeting was nearly a year later. Guevara had been in the Simba training camps for several months in the mountainous regions northwest of Kalemie. He did not want to engage the enemy directly without the presence of Kabila. He would do so, though, in a botched attack on the town of Bendera. After another cordial but urgent request for Kabila to make his presence known in the Simba rebel enclave, Kabila repeated his mantra of 'arriving soon'. Finally, three months after Guevara's arrival in Congo, Kabila arrived in the Simba stronghold. Guevara remarked in his journals of how Laurent Kabila could impress the local population with his energy and natural charm, telling people what they wanted to hear while still maintaining an air of authority. Guevara continuously requested that Kabila assist him in organising a force to carry out attacks as soon as possible; Kabila, though, was evasive on this subject and always changed the topic of conversation when it started to revolve around his involvement in military action.

They spent five days together touring the rebel enclave, and very little progress was made for a definitive plan of action for the Simbas. On 11 July 1965, Laurent Kabila told Guevara he needed to cross Lake Tanganyika to Kigoma for a meeting with some rebel leaders and would return in two days. Kabila never returned, and the two of them never met again.

you would need to take a monthly train from Lubumbashi to Kabalo before finding the onward train to Kalemie. The entire journey should take around two weeks.

WHERE TO STAY The town has three principal hotels, with **Hôtel du Lac** (*20 rooms*; *Av Lumumba; sgl/dbl* $$) gaining most favour from private visitors. The others are **Hôtel Kavera** ($) and **Hôtel du Midi** ($).

WHAT TO SEE In the city centre is a **Catholic church** built around the turn of the 20th century, and very similar to the one built on the other end of the country in Matadi.

An old residential neighbourhood sits on a hilltop that overlooks the town and the lake. An old pastime for visitors was plying the walking trails dotted around this neighbourhood, providing excellent views of the surrounding countryside in eastern Katanga as well as across the lake to Tanzania. There are also several ancient pieces of **artillery** from World War I scattered about the hilltops, where the Belgian army clashed with German soldiers from Tanzania.

Obviously **Lake Tanganyika** is another main sight, the largest in the Albertine Rift, and second largest in Africa after Lake Victoria. It is also extremely deep and has a wide variety of unique sealife amongst clear blue water – it is common for scientific and commercial divers to work in the lake. Fishermen from Kalemie still practise a traditional method for their catch, heading out at dusk to fish by lantern. In the evening lake waters near the town are dotted with the light from hundreds of oil lamps. Most of the town's economy, in fact, is still based on fishing.

Follow a rough road 25km southwest from Kalemie on the road to Muhila and you will reach **Koki Falls**, flowing out of the Muhila Mountains east of the lake. The falls are unique in that they spew hot water, flowing out from an underground spring. The road south has some excellent scenery, passing through lush bamboo forests along a winding road that follows the plateau.

Along the coast south of Kalemie is the smaller lakeside town of **Moba** (✪ *07°02.53 S, 09°46.36 E*), established under similar circumstances in the 19th century. It in fact pre-dates the founding of Kalemie by about a year. In town there is a small chapel, and a monument to its founders. Frequent boats go here from Kalemie.

9

Kisangani, Maiko and the North

The wild north of the DR Congo is a place of sparse population, little development and a few famous parks. In its most general sense, one could say the north of the country is anything north of the Congo River, and west of the Beni–Bunia corridor. It comprises the least-visited parts of Equateur Province north of the river, most of Orientale Province, and is generally administered from the city of Kisangani – a historic outpost on the Congo River located at its last navigable portion. From Kisangani you can continue southeast to Maiko Park, which at the time of writing was the worst off of all the DR Congo's major wilderness spaces.

On the other hand, the north has the country's most enigmatic park, Garamba, as well as the equally intriguing Okapi Reserve. It's home to the old playground of Mobutu, Gbadolite, a smattering of hunting reserves bordering the Central African Republic, and curious towns such as Isiro, Buta and Gemena. If you're looking to move onward to the Central African Republic or Sudan, you'll end up here, and you'll be one of the few who gets this far. Yet the chance to see the progress of Garamba as its rangers and park staff work incessantly to protect its wildlife, and to see the curious okapi in its original habitat, make at least a short visit easily worthwhile.

KISANGANI ✪ 00°31.03 N, 25°11.41 E

A mid-sized city of old concrete buildings and towers looms against a vast network of jungle and rivers where mud huts are the norm – it is a true contrast of the region and a curiosity to see all of this infrastructure, dilapidated as it is, so far away from anything similar. Kisangani has always been the centrepoint for the northeastern end of the DR Congo, by many accounts the country's second city, as its founding anticipated the entire existence of the former Belgian Congo. Motorbikes zip along deteriorating roads, the sun seems to burn even through thick cloud, and crowds of people wash their clothes along the shores of the Congo River. Without the river, there would be no Kisangani – as it is the furthest point one can travel from Kinshasa without encountering rapids, and throughout its history has become the major transit point for the region. It has seen renewed life from MONUC staff arriving in spades, recent road-construction teams, and finally from foreign entrepreneurs seeking to capitalise on the discovery of diamonds amongst nearby hills and waterways. Kisangani is well poised to make the most out of the 21st century, perhaps, and as infrastructure improves across the entire nation it will again become the major river port that it once was.

Kisangani has seen many transformations, as its history narrates. Even now it is changing again, into something of a diamond centre – any visitor cannot help but notice the numerous gem dealers, buying minerals from any Congolese who find them in their travels around the region. For a visitor to do this, though, is a very bad idea – the police are busy tailing foreigners, sometimes demanding to see photo permits and even mining permits for being in the city. Officially, none is

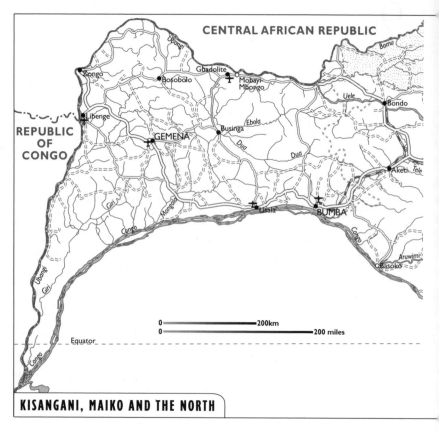

needed. Informally, if you are going to be doing anything too obvious in sensitive areas, make sure the police are on your side. Congolese jails aren't fun, nor is paying to get out of them.

HISTORY The history of Stanleyville/Kisangani is sprawling, complicated and bloody – it has changed hands countless times, and has seen more combat in its streets than any other European settlement across the Congos. Its chronology can be confusing at the best of times, tedious at the worst of times; perhaps it was doomed to this fate as the geographical centrepoint of Africa, as well as being the oldest and most remote outpost of the wild and undeveloped Congo Free State. Therefore, bear with me: there is a fair amount of ground to cover.

European and Arab arrival Henry Morton Stanley arrived on the spot where Kisangani would be founded in 1875; Arab traders, dominated more or less by Tippu Tip, were already active in the area and helped Stanley coalesce the local population into a trading centre that would suit both of their needs – the Arab ivory and slave trade, and Stanley's interest in an outpost that would serve as the furthest terminus of the navigable area of the Congo River. The region was already an important trading centre for local tribes who traded fish and handicrafts on the river's shores, near the Wagenia Falls. It was also a communications centre, the meeting point for various river tributaries in every direction – along the Congo River west, along the Uele north, the Ituri east, and the Opala south.

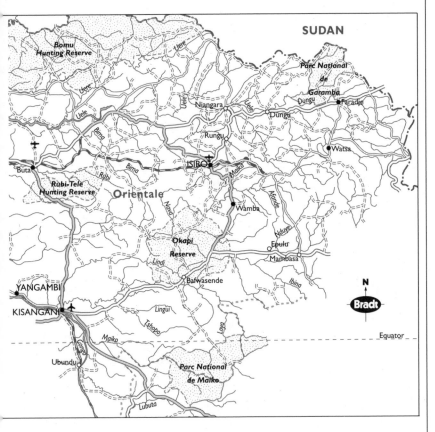

Tippu Tip, his sons, and other Arabs loyal to the Zanzibari sultans ruled Stanleyville from its founding in 1875 until 1893. King Léopold sent the first Belgian officials there in 1883, though Arab traders protested strongly until finally setting fire to the fledgling outpost, and burning it down in 1886. This act prompted negotiation with the Arabs, with Tip and his men retaining control of the outpost, but local trade began to shift towards Belgian interests after this.

Tip departed in 1890, and there was intense dispute over the increasing shipment of ivory to Belgian interests west rather than Arab ports east. As well, anti-slaving groups were clashing with Arab slave traders in the region; it is said that Tippu Tip saw how the tide was turning, and left before he could become embroiled in the situation. Major clashes erupted in 1892, pitting Arab traders against Belgian soldiers. The Arabs were defeated, and were driven out of Stanleyville entirely. Tippu Tip's state, ruled from Stanleyville, more or less dissolved into Léopold's territory.

The Belgian system of compensating locals, or rather not doing so, was a step backward from the Arab system of trade that had worked somewhat with Congolese for some decades – the forced labour, kidnapping, and total lack of interest in any kind of trading system with local populations decimated the fledgling commercial economy, broke emerging ties between the colonisers and the colonised, and almost entirely erased the status of Stanleyville as a trading hub – it was merely a shipping port then, a relationship of exploitation that saw goods flow only one way. The town existed solely as an administrative centre,

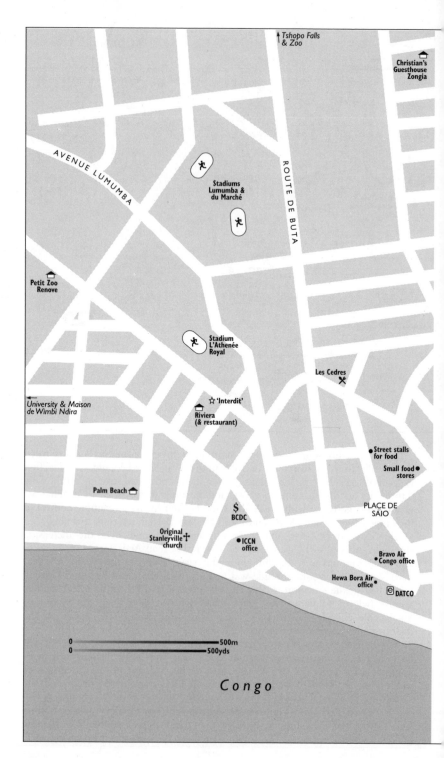

Tshopo Falls
& Zoo

Christian's
Guesthouse
Zongia

AVENUE LUMUMBA

ROUTE DE BUTA

Stadiums
Lumumba &
du Marché

Petit Zoo
Renove

Stadium
L'Athenée
Royal

Les Cedres

University & Maison
de Wimbi Ndira

'Interdit'

Riviera
(& restaurant)

Street stalls
for food

Small food
stores

Palm Beach

PLACE DE
SAIO

BCDC

Original
Stanleyville
church

ICCN
office

Bravo Air
Congo office

Hewa Bora Air
office

DATCO

0 ———— 500m
0 ———— 500yds

Congo

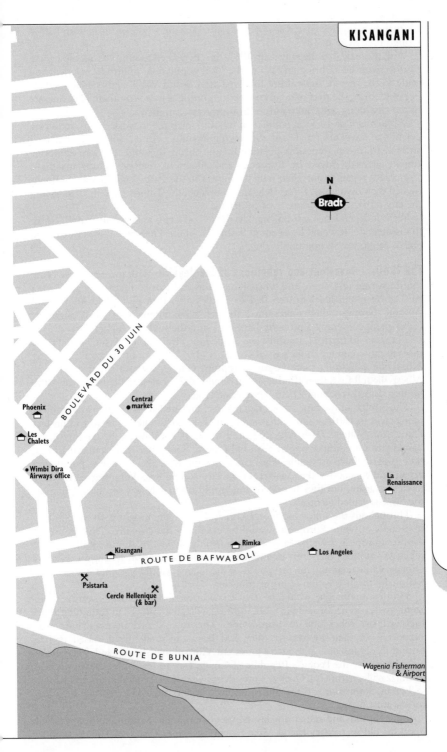

ultimately being designated as regional capital for the whole of the eastern half of Congo Free State in 1897.

With the arrival of the railway in 1912, the city gained ground – Congolese were paid to work on it, bringing cash to the local population, reintroducing fledgling trade to the region. Agriculture followed after World War I, and weekly markets began to form; the river and rail connections brought more commercial businesses to the city, along with thousands of Europeans to run them.

While much of the local population was still relegated to work camps, requiring permits to travel too far abroad, the town grew into a city as World War II arrived and passed. It experienced population booms during this time, as more economic activity arrived, driven by European and American interest in war materials. Congolese began to start their own businesses in the 1950s, and the more affluent owned their own houses. The Belgians completed the Tshopo Dam in 1956, giving the city its own reliable source of electricity.

Yet as independence arrived, Stanleyville fell off a cliff as the country itself began to disintegrate. It would be a central flashpoint in the 1960s as the structure of the entire nation was in question.

The 1960s – invasions and rebellions of Stanleyville With independence came the fracturing of Congo, and when Kasa-Vubu had Patrice Lumumba arrested, a rival government loyal to him fled to Stanleyville. Run by Cyrille Adoula and Antoine Gizenga, they represented the left-wing interests of the Congolese. Subsequent conferences brought them back into the fold of Léopoldville.

The death of Patrice Lumumba had created the ideal conditions for a leftist rebel movement to emerge in the east of Congo, and in 1964 out of the rural areas near Albertville a fighting force began to capture villages without much resistance. Albertville fell first, then Kindu; and in Kindu, they coalesced behind a name, the Simbas, and also behind a man – Nicolas Olenga.

The Simbas of the time were a ragtag force, but used spiritual charms to protect themselves in battle – rituals that indoctrinated each soldier were said to protect them from bullets. Their ferocity scared the ANC, and often the national army would flee into disarray rather than fight them. Soon after they captured Kindu, they moved north to Stanleyville, and evacuations of the European population began as they stood at the outskirts of the city. Joseph Kasa-Vubu begged the UN to step in again, but they hesitated, and would ultimately stay on the sidelines as the Simbas gained territory.

Throughout the following months, as ANC soldiers fought with the Simbas, thousands of white Europeans would be caught in the crossfire. This prompted various European governments to act, but only slowly. In the meantime a new rebel government had been assembled and was operating in Kisangani. Nicolas Olenga, while retaining the real power of the regime, would appoint Gaston Émile Soumialot to the position of prime minister.

Soumialot, though, would be the catalyst for a new leftist government in Stanleyville – as he formed the CNL in Brazzaville, then moved to Bujumbura and followed the rebel tide to Stanleyville. The town's African population was supportive of their motives, as they had begun to deify the deceased Patrice Lumumba. Soumialot appointed a president, Christophe Gbenye, and declared the Simba territory the People's Republic of Congo (not to be confused with the one in Brazzaville, naturally). Gbenye's presidency was short-lived, though, and he was sacked by Soumialot and the Simba military leaders later once the tide began to turn against them.

Indeed it did, and rather quickly. Moise Tshombe, now prime minister, called upon his old mercenary friend Mike Hoare for some assistance. The decision to use mercenaries was unpopular with both the Léopoldville government and their main international supporters, namely the US and Belgium, yet they allowed it anyway, rather than see the Congo partitioned and embroiled in a rebellion that they perceived as communist in nature.

Kindu was finally liberated on 5 November 1965, by a mercenary army – with some assistance from anti-Castro Cubans flying US aircraft; only much later would they realise that their communist compatriots were also involved in this conflict, supporting the Simbas. Hoare's mercenaries moved slowly across rugged roads, anticipating ambushes at every corner as their poorly equipped trucks became stuck in muddy tracks. Yet they were ruthless to the Simbas, and even though heavily outnumbered, would suffer few casualties.

A few weeks later Operation Dragon Rouge was initiated – which involved aircraft dropping Belgian paratroopers over Stanleyville, to rescue the 1,600 Europeans still trapped and held hostage in the city. When the Simbas had been reluctant to massacre Europeans, rumours persisted that they were killing them as the desire arose. A prominent American missionary and doctor, Paul Carlson, had been executed by the Simbas in spite of his selfless work in the region. The urgency of the mission was apparent to the government of Belgium – aircraft and troops were assembled on Ascension Island, and the small outpost in the Atlantic was essentially cut off from the outside world as the secretive operation was being organised.

The invasion was madness, as paratroopers, mercenaries, Simbas, Europeans, and the average Congolese fought in general disarray – the Simbas had promised to kill all Europeans if a rescue operation was staged. Paratroopers shot anyone who was African. Mercenaries looted stores and banks. No prisoners were taken – yet Stanleyville was 'liberated', and the Simbas lost their most important stronghold.

Operation Dragon Noir followed – a clean-up operation, as well as another rescue operation for Europeans who had been held hostage in smaller Simba territories and towns across Ituri. While some Europeans were saved, others were not – as the Simbas massacred missionaries and nuns while the rescue effort continued in other parts of the northeast.

Olenga, Gbenye and Soumialot fled, and tried to start another resistance movement in Cairo – but failed after much quarrelling. The remaining Simbas across the northeast were still receiving arms from Algeria and Egypt through Sudan, but Mike Hoare's mercenaries eventually shut down their supply routes.

The occupation and decimation of Stanleyville's population erased its economy entirely – Europeans had all but fled, and the vast majority of working African men were either murdered or hiding in the jungle. Yet their problems would not be over as the ANC's authority was minimal, and the city was mostly controlled by mercenaries.

The mercenary rebellions Some of Mike Hoare's mercenaries, veterans of the Katangan conflict, used their position as occupiers of Stanleyville to their advantage – they seized the radio station and airport, then demanded safe passage back to Katanga, where negotiations on its independence were to occur. Other mercenaries, led by Robert Denard, would remain in Stanleyville as well and play a wait-and-see game with Léopoldville's government. As Mobutu, already in control of the military, gained power, he supported Denard financially to run the Katangese mercenaries out of Stanleyville in July 1967. Moise Tshombe had recently fled Congo with the rise of Mobutu, but his interest in its politics was still far from over – and Stanleyville would remain its centrepoint for a while longer.

Yet Denard, after having run the first Katangese rebels out of Stanleyville after being paid by Mobutu, quickly received word from Tshombe that he wished to

9

The revolution that took place across the eastern half of the DR Congo in 1964 brought old enemies together, created new ones, and once again threatened to tear the country apart. Just as the UN had departed, declaring its ONUC mission a success, vast peasant revolts began to occur throughout the eastern provinces. At the rebellion's height it encompassed almost half of the DR Congo. Moise Tshombe had been brought in as prime minister, and he would use the same tactics against these rebels as he used against the central government to which he was now aligned.

The politicians loyal to Patrice Lumumba had lost their voice in Léopoldville with the dissolution of parliament in 1963, sending the MNC east to Stanleyville. Lumumbists formed the Conseil National de Libération, or CNL, and began to plan a method of revolution. With the UN out of the picture and the ANC still lacking real authority, the CNL could make great headway in their uprising. Pierre Mulule, a Lumumbist loyal to the CNL, had travelled to China for guerrilla-warfare training. He returned to the town of Kwilu, where he organised a small rebel group. They attacked government outposts and company buildings, eventually killing several European missionaries.

Meanwhile Burundi had sent its own support to a rebellion in Uvira, and with the government's assistance the rebels took the valley of Fizi-Baraka, between Uvira and Albertville, under their control. It was here that the Simbas rose up, led by Laurent Kabila, and they would eventually receive assistance from the Cubans.

Further uprisings occurred across the Kivu provinces and northern Katanga; the lack of UN troops or ANC troops created a vast area of territory without any real authority, and peasants aligned themselves with the CNL in Stanleyville. By August 1964, these three fronts created a massive stretch of territory, yet it was not cohesive – while all facets of the rebellion were fighting for the same cause, they could not gel into a singular force, or indeed one with a clearly defined structure of leadership.

Moise Tshombe acted quickly. He called upon Katangese soldiers exiled in Angola to come to his aid. He also called on some old mercenary friends, namely Bob Denard and Mike Hoare, to lead foreign soldiers of fortune to military operations across eastern DR Congo. Mike Hoare would lead the mercenary army; victories would be decisive and swift. The CIA also supplied air support, using foreign nationals stationed in the US as pilots – namely Cuban exiles – as it would be a far more covert method of operating than sending US personnel, and exploited a loophole in American laws that normally prohibited them to do so.

Stanleyville fell on 24 November 1964. Continued air raids and small fast-moving groups of mercenaries and Katangese gendarmes put down most of the rebellion almost as fast, and usually with brutal results. The CNL's central figures fled to Egypt, and the Simbas in the Fizi–Baraka corridor were quickly losing ground. Cuban assistance fled the region, and left the Simbas to defeat.

Moise Tshombe's handling of this rebellion created a rift between him and Joseph Kasa-Vubu; their internal bickering would allow a military leader, Mobutu Sésé Seko, to depose them both and take leadership of the Congo.

engineer a coup to overthrow the future dictator. He put Bob Denard and another old mercenary hand – Jean Schramme, who had backed him in Katanga – in charge of this operation. Schramme controlled a huge swathe of territory in eastern Congo, from Kindu to Bukavu, and Denard, still in control of mercenaries in Stanleyville, had been in contact with Tshombe. Tshombe himself was in Spain, and agitating for a coup against Mobutu and seeking to create an environment where he could return to Congo; but he would be captured, hijacked in a jet by Mobutu's operatives near Algerian airspace. Schramme and Denard did not know this until later; Schramme's forces attacked Kisangani, expecting assistance from Denard's men stationed there, but Denard had failed to organise his men for the attack. The ANC responded, summarily executing some of Denard's men and fighting off both groups of mercenaries.

Mobutu begged the US for help, but they were reluctant to aid the country once again – they eventually capitulated by supporting the ANC with four cargo aircraft. So, mostly on their own, the ANC drove the mercenaries southeast to Bukavu where they became surrounded. Mobutu arranged a safe passage agreement for most of them, airlifting them out of the country on Red Cross aircraft, on the promise that they would never return to Africa.

The Katangese mercenaries were the final straw, solidifying the authority of the ANC across all of Congo; from then on the nation would be a veritable dictatorship under Mobutu. As he began his Africanisation of the country's names, it would be a different city entirely – one called Kisangani, relegating Stanleyville entirely to history.

From Mobutu to chaos, again Under Mobutu's rule, businesses began to arrive back in the city, creating a new generation of factories, breweries, and industries surrounding textiles and paint. An airport was completed in 1977 for international aircraft, but Kinshasa halted all international flights due to a scandal over ivory smuggling less than a year later.

In 1986, the discovery of diamonds in the regions around Kisangani proved to be a major setback – the infamous corruption of Zaire's officials, and the slow disintegration of Mobutu's government, led to numerous internal conflicts between officials, departments and foreign companies – both legal and illegal – all fighting for a share of the diamond trade. It is no coincidence that as Kabila's army moved west in 1997 Kisangani was occupied quickly by both Ugandan and Rwandan troops under the banner of the RCD; yet once again driven by greed, they would fight against each other in 1998 and split their occupied territory of eastern Congo in two – with Kisangani under the Rwandan control of things. RCD fractured into two groups: RCD-ML based in Kisangani, led by well-known politician and theorist Ernest Wamba Dia Wamba, and the splinter group RCD-Goma, unsurprisingly based in Goma. As RCD-ML were driven out of Kisangani, their retreat into the forests of Ituri anticipated a future conflict there.

After Africa's World War, Kisangani was particularly devastated – all of the major local businesses were either shut down or operating at a minuscule capacity, the river port had been all but destroyed, terminating river transport, and no public transport existed. Wave upon wave of soldiers looted the city subsequently as it changed hands again and again. People made their way around on foot, or on bicycles. All progress that had been made between the rebellions of the early 1960s and the latest chaos of the late 1990s had evaporated. Kisangani entered the new millennium in the worst condition of all the DR Congo's cities.

In May 2002, an attempted mutiny of Rwandan soldiers sent ripples throughout Kisangani's streets, and rebels against RCD-Goma briefly occupied the radio station before being put down by Rwandan troops. RCD-Goma blamed the Kinshasa government, but as these things go, the list of possible culprits is long and has not been fully investigated. Rwanda would not mince words or actions, though: they flew in their top generals to Kisangani, and proceeded to execute *en masse* any soldiers who might have possibly participated. Human rights bodies estimate over 80 men were killed. Over 500 MONUC soldiers were in the city at the time, but did nothing to halt the killings. It is said that events like this prompted the UN Security Council to increase MONUC's mandate.

With the transitional government finally in place by 2003, and MONUC's long arms and blue helmets finally arriving to the east to solidify some sort of order and a lack of partitioning, Kisangani could begin to heal its deep wounds. Joseph Kabila visited the city for the first time in 2004, and crowds greeted him – while local police and soldiers were disarmed for his visit, and his own security forces took control of the city.

The rebuilding is slow, but signs of the city emerging again do exist – formal river traffic has restarted, and a Somali firm built a mobile-phone network for the region in 2002. The heavy UN presence has brought a huge infusion of foreigners to the city, increasing cash flow. The airport is a major hub for regional domestic air traffic. Somewhere in Kisangani's future there may be a light.

ORIENTATION The city lies between the **Tshopo River** to the north and the **Congo River** to its south, on an east–west axis. In the city centre are various town squares, and to the west is the old **Simi-Simi Airport** currently used only by the UN. Many buildings still stand abandoned, locked up while their owners wait for better stability. You can continue north to the town of Buta over the Tshopo River, or east out of town to either Maiko National Park and Bukavu or Nia Nia and Epulu in the Okapi Reserve. Road repairs have become a priority in the region which means that these should be reasonably well-groomed dirt roads by the time you read this. Southwards across the river is the suburb of **Lubunga**, with a battered route southwards to Lodja and Kananga, but it will be years before this road is repaired.

GETTING THERE AND AROUND Kisangani's **Bangoka International Airport** (though not currently offering any international flights) is a curious throwback to decades past, barely changed since the 1970s. It's a large empty structure divided into two parts these days – the MONUC section and the regular passenger section. It has a small café, two 'VIP' rooms which cost US$10 per person to use, and several airline check-in counters where flight schedules are still written on chalkboards. It's situated 30km east of the city, usually requiring a US$20 taxi ride to and from the centre – plus a dollar or five for soldiers guarding the roadblock at the entrance. Plan ahead if you are taking a flight: vehicles are hard to come by around the city, and getting a proper car requires calling a day or so ahead. Motorbikes are ubiquitous, however, making short trips with no luggage easy to manage. A ride across town should cost no more than 500Fc.

There is no central truck station, as usual, for the region. Ask around for vehicles heading to Buta or Isiro. The road to Bunia should be repaired and minibus companies have promised a link between there and Kisangani; if this is the case, it will make the entire region far more accessible.

✈ **Bravo Air Congo** 14 Bd Mobutu, Makiso; m 099 930 1651. Regular flights each week to Kinshasa & Goma.

✈ **Hewa Bora Airways** 17 Bd Mobutu, Makiso; m 099 853 9090. Regular flights to Kinshasa, Goma & Isiro.

✈ **Wimbi Dira Airways** Rond Point du Canon, Makiso; m 081 707 963/098 624 038; e kisangani@wda.cd. Regular flights to Isiro, Kindu & Kinshasa.

Also in town are **CAA** and **Cetraca** with less reliable flight schedules to Beni, Mbandaka and Kinshasa.

WHERE TO STAY Little exists at the higher end of things with **Les Chalets Hôtel** being the best-quality place to stay at the moment, though it can often be busy as a popular haunt with people working in the region. The second option after them would be **Le Palm Beach**, though they do not have nearly as much attention to detail. Everything else in Kisangani is acceptable enough by Third World standards, with modest prices for what you'd normally pay in the DR Congo. For most of them, though, running water continues to be a problem.

Les Chalets Hôtel 4 Rue de L'Industrie, Makiso; m 099 850 8407/099 849 9745/099 822 4316; e safimonique@hotmail.com. Well-maintained modest-sized rooms with satellite TV, AC, hot running water, secure parking. Has a bar, pool, private restaurant. Discounts offered for those with residency in the DR Congo or working for MONUC. Sgl $$$, apt $$$$

Christian's Guesthouse Zongia North of the city centre towards the Tshopo River; m 099 850 8478. Set in a pleasant residential neighbourhood with secure parking. Prices include all meals — b/fast, lunch & dinner. Primarily intended for those visiting Kisangani for religious (Christian) purposes & geared towards the missionaries of the region. Sgl $$, dbl/apt $$$

Hôtel La Renaissance Route de Bafwaboli, on the road to Irumu; m 099 400 0995. Large complex which was once the main residence for MONUC staff in Kisangani. Can still get quite full, & is geared towards those staying for extended periods of time. Apts are all inclusive with TV & AC. Secure parking & restaurant available. Sgl $, dbl $$, apt $$$.

Hôtel Kisangani (28 rooms) Route de Bafwaboli, Makiso; m 099 709 5728. Rather rundown hotel with a curious bar/stage arrangement in the front. In the back is a pleasant enough gardened area & restaurant. Rooms are showing their age with peeling paint, but do include AC & intermittent running water. Discounts for long stays. Sgl $$

Hôtel Petit Zoo Renove (14 rooms) 1km northwest of the Stadium L'Athenee Royal; m 099 709 8901. Pleasant enough place in a residential neighbourhood with large & simple rooms. Small bar, secure parking. Sgl $$

Hôtel Phoenix (18 rooms) 3 Rue de L'Industrie, Makiso (across from Les Chalets Hôtel); m 099 882 4225. Average rooms with non-satellite TV, AC, running water & secure parking. Has a small restaurant. Sgl $$

Hôtel Riviera (28 rooms) Near the Stadium L'Athenee Royal; m 099 406 0690. Close to town with a large parking area, highly recommended roadside restaurant as well as a private restaurant inside the hotel. All rooms include AC, TV, & running water. Sgl $$ (with shared bathroom), dbl $$$, apt $$$$

La Maison de Wimbi Ndira (8 rooms) On the road past the University of Kisangani; m 081 212 6902. Situated in a residential neighbourhood along the river a few kilometres west of the city centre, near the old airport. Has a friendly staff in a well secured compound, large dining area, & food can be made on request. Rooms are large with AC, though no TV. Running water is intermittent. Sgl $$

Palm Beach Hôtel Av Colonel Tshatshi No 6, Makiso; m 099 853 9280/099 876 4020; e palmbeach@yahoo.fr. Has a large secure car park, bar, pool, & spotless high-end restaurant. Rooms include AC, TV, & running water. Sgl $$, dbl $$$, apt $$$$

Hôtel Los Angeles Route de Bafwaboli, Makiso; ⊾ 212 883. Generally filled with long-term residents & a sleepy receptionist who you might need an air horn to wake up. Probably good for long-term stays, but amenities are basic — no AC, fans only. Sgl $

Hôtel Rimka Route de Bafwaboli, Makiso; m 081 264 9583. Simple rooms with no running water or AC. Some parking at the back, but no walls or gates to make it secure. Small restaurant out front. Sgl $

WHERE TO EAT, ENTERTAINMENT AND NIGHTLIFE Kisangani has something of a food problem, given that barge and rail transport to the city still isn't regular, therefore a great number of dishes that might be found in areas with better transport, like Goma or Kinshasa, are quite expensive in the city. The cheapest option is to buy bananas and peanuts from roadside vendors, or head to the **Central Market** to pick up some fresh local vegetables; or, if funds are tight, for a bargain they will sell you a huge stack of those always dreadful glucose biscuits. It's slightly better than starving, anyway.

For a proper meal the best eating in town is at **Restaurant Psistaria** (*Route de Bafwaboli, Makiso;* m *081 354 3454;* ⊕ *from 15.00 daily;* **$$$**) with an enclosed dining terrace as well as an air-conditioned interior dining room. They have a wide variety of dishes, as well as a pizza oven. A step down, but still of decent quality, is **Cercle Hellenique Restaurant and Bar**, nearby on a road towards the river (⊕ *from 10.00 daily;* **$$$**) and usually packed with people working in the region. They offer a Kinshasa-priced buffet as well as several other dishes in a quiet dining area with plenty of parking out front. Also **Hôtel Riviera**'s restaurant on the roadside is widely popular day and night (⊕ *from 12.00 daily;* **$$$**) for pizzas, burgers and fish dishes. Finally, **Restaurant Les Cedres** is a classic Lebanese-style standby with all of the trappings that their restaurants in the region possess: burgers and *shawarma* (a Middle Eastern-style sandwich) for an average price (⊕ *from 11.00 daily;* **$$**). Most establishments close at 23.00.

During the evening there are **street stalls** which make up some decent chicken (**$**) as well as fried plantains and whatever else happens to be circulating in the area that day. Nearby are some small **food stores** which can be good for some proper processed foodstuffs, including actual fruit juices, liquor and bottled water.

For nightlife, there are plenty of small streetside bars with plastic chairs in Kisangani's town centre offering up the usual suspects in a bottle. For something a little more high end, only one place seems to fit the bill, that being **Night Club Interdit** near the Restaurant Riviera. Dress well, and bring money.

PRACTICALITIES For Western Union seek out the big **BCDC Bank** (m *081 200 6010;* e *ksg@bcdc.cd;* ⊕ *08.00–16.00 Mon–Fri, 08.00–12.00 Sat*) in the city centre. They tend to have the best hours and most reliable service in the city.

WHAT TO SEE On your list of things not to miss in the DR Congo should be the **Wagenia Fishermen**, doing their business just in front of the **Wagenia Falls**. These villagers have been using an interesting tactic of catching fish along the river with large conical baskets suspended from wooden frames across the river. It's a unique sight and well worth visiting. The fishermen have taken it upon themselves to provide guiding tours to anyone who shows up, and charge US$20 for the privilege. There is a village on a small island in the middle of the river, and they may convince you to take a *pirogue* across and meet the chief; if that's your interest it should run to an extra US$10.

On the road north out of town is the **Tshopo Bridge**, which crosses the Tshopo River and provides a good view of the hydro-electric dam that keeps Kisangani's power running while it tends to cut out in neighbouring cities. Follow this road a bit further and you'll find the turn-off to the **Zoo**, a sorry place with about three animals right now and a caretaker who asks for US$5 to see them. Most of the animals were killed in the numerous insurgencies that have plagued Kisangani over the past ten years. The zoo's director has assured me that getting more animals for this space is not the problem, as the jungles surrounding Kisangani are filled with plenty of unique species; the problem is fixing all of the cages, torn to pieces by soldiers and anyone else who needed some extra chain-link fence. There is a hotel beside the zoo on the hilltop, currently closed, but it may eventually reopen.

Just down from the zoo is the pleasant **Linoko Beach** where you can pay about 500Fc to sit and have a beer, and get a decent view of **Tshopo Falls**. The place can get a bit raucous on Saturday nights, but is quiet enough in the daytime.

And finally, most obviously, the **Congo River** is a sight in itself. You can hire a *pirogue* to visit surrounding villages, and on certain mornings the floating river markets begin from here – there are entire villages that exist solely as rafts on the river, drifting between shores, and they trade their goods along the way.

Congolese in the vicinity of Kisangani are proud of the time that Hollywood came to town, even though it was over half a century ago. The blockbuster film *The African Queen* starred Humphrey Bogart and Katharine Hepburn as a Canadian boat captain and English missionary out to attack a German ship during World War I, on Lake Tanganyika. Despite not being set in the Congo at all, most of it was filmed near Ubundu (then called Ponthierville), just upstream from Kisangani.

Filming in central Africa was a unique challenge in itself and the stars were not immune to the elements. Ms Hepburn notoriously fell ill with dysentery from drinking too much local water. Bogart, a heavy drinker, managed to avoid any serious illness. Hepburn recounts her time in the Congo in her memoirs *The Making of The African Queen: Or, How I Went to Africa With Bogart, Bacall and Huston and Almost Lost My Mind,* published almost 40 years after the movie's release.

The movie itself is a good chance to see the Congo River and some of its local wildlife during the era of Belgian Congo. It also earned Bogart his only Academy Award, for best actor. The film was nominated for four other awards, including Ms Hepburn for best actress.

For production an entire village would become their set, west of Ponthierville, at Biondo, along the Ruiki River. Bogart, Hepburn and the large production staff would rough it out in the middle of the Congolese jungle for several months shooting the movie, learning Swahili, washing with buckets, avoiding mosquitoes, etc – Hepburn described her conditions as 'luxury primitive'. Scenes in the water were shot back in England, as concerns over the actors performing in Congolese rivers had come to light.

Unfortunately the movie credits do not honour the country, with the final credits indicating only that it was 'Filmed in Africa'.

MAIKO NATIONAL PARK

Maiko has fared the worst of all the DR Congo's parks during the decade of conflict since the fall of Mobutu. Much of my research surrounding this park focused on whether it even existed, if so was it open and if there was anything left. ICCN has assured me that yes, animals are still plentiful, but the average visitor is unlikely to see them.

The park has populations of eastern lowland gorillas, okapi and even forest elephants but some of the last remaining Mayi-Mayi rebels live in the middle of the park and hunt these animals for food; subsistence hunting, I was reminded, as opposed to commercial hunting, which would decimate populations even further. And yet, according to wildlife reports, elephants have been hunted within the park for their ivory and illegal mining continues to operate with impunity. Also, the Simba rebels, a throwback to the 1960s, still have a minor but benign presence in the south of the park. Finally, as mentioned, the road to the park's entrance at Mahulu is nothing short of a disaster – little more than a dirt trail at this point. And this is considered the 'good road' to get to Maiko.

Many of Laurent Nkunda's soldiers were reassigned to this area once they reached an agreement with Kabila's government for integration in January 2007. Maiko, and the surrounding areas, is a highly undeveloped region with very little civilisation. Rumours persist of some villages in the area where people still do not wear clothes, having never been pressured by anyone to do so. If they haven't heard about clothes, you can bet that they haven't heard about wildlife conservation.

The park was created in 1970 by Mobutu Sésé Seko, and occupies roughly a million hectares (10,000km²) between the Lubero and Maiko rivers. It has no airstrips, no lodges, and no amenities to speak of – even 4x4 trails don't exist, aside from a southeasterly road from Bafwasende down to village populations living in the park. Nonetheless if you happen to be a primatologist or wildlife conservationist, eastern lowland gorillas have been confirmed in the southern regions of Maiko. Other animals with confirmed sightings in the past few years include chimpanzee, duiker, okapi, forest buffalo and Congo peacock. Elephant traces have been found but there have been no confirmed sightings.

PRACTICALITIES Don't even think about visiting Maiko unless you have your own vehicle and several weeks to spare. These are the 4x4 routes that hard-core overlanders dream of tackling. If that's your bag, go for it – but also be aware that rebels may be still kicking around and will seize an opportunity when it arises. Be friendly, bring plenty of small banknotes, cigarettes, and perhaps a few cases of beer. It would be wise to hire a guide or two, and the largest town where people familiar with Maiko hang out would be **Lubutu** (✪ *00°44.53.10 S, 26°34.54.46 E*). There are two options for visiting the park – one involves heading northwest from Bukavu or southeast from Kisangani to the town of **Mahulu** (✪ *01°01.42.94 S, 27°16.15.78 E*) and slowly working your way in from there – more than likely by foot. The other option is through **Bafwasende** (✪ *01°00.00.03 N, 27°09.21.91 E*) where a road winds southeast to **Angumu** (✪ *00°06.58.75 S, 27°42.06.73 E*) and then to **Matshitshi** (✪ *00°13.29.57 S, 27°45.57.40 E*) where you can begin excursions into the northern part of the park. In theory, this road trail winds along to Kanyabayonga near Virunga National Park, and if you manage it, ask someone to give you an award.

Also remember that in spite of its remoteness, a permit is still required – generally purchased from the **ICCN** in Kisangani (m *099 770 02895;* e *dpiccnprov.iroentale@yahoo.fr*) for around US$100 per person. They can assist in finding you a guide as well.

ISIRO ✪ *02°46.15 N, 27°37.12 E*

Isiro is the largest town in the northeast of the DR Congo, a hub of sorts for what little transportation exists in the region. It sees regular flights to Kisangani, once had a critical rail connection to the Congo River, and several roads continue into Sudan and Uganda. It's also the closest major town to Garamba National Park, and unless you charter your own aircraft, you will end up here on the way to the area.

Isiro was called Paulis back in the colonial days of Belgian Congo, and was the hub for transportation, mining and farming in the province during the first half of the 20th century. It was named after Colonel Paulis, a prominent local businessman affiliated with the Congo railway system of the era. A university was opened in 1998, making it the third city in the DR Congo with a higher-education facility, after Kinshasa and Lubumbashi. The town is also the home of the first beatified female Congolese, Marie-Clémentine Anuarite Nengapeta, who was killed by Simba rebels in 1964. Pope John Paul II travelled to Kinshasa in 1985 to complete the beatification ceremony. Her body was buried in Isiro at the Catholic church.

If you're heading northeast to Garamba a decent stop is in the town of **Niangara** (✪ *03°41.31.81 N, 27°53.51.88 E*) which was once a historic point in the region. It should have several small monuments in the area, as well as a pioneer's cemetery. The local tribes were once renowned for their decorated courthouses, and if you ask around, some of them still may be remaining.

GETTING THERE AND AROUND Isiro is well served by the DR Congo's major airlines, with **Bravo Air Congo**, **Hewa Bora Air**, **Wimbi Dira Airways** and **CAA** all flying a few times a week into the airport – three times a week direct from

Kinshasa, almost daily from Kisangani, and three times a week again from Goma. The road north from Nia Nia eventually reaches Isiro, though it's currently 4x4 only. This route is a priority for the government's road reconstruction project, and this could change quickly to a dirt road reasonable enough for cars and minibuses.

Huge trucks move through the town in every direction intermittently, and you can catch a ride on them for a price – it will undoubtedly be higher for a foreigner, since the risk is higher; as well, expect to pay bribes along the way for every checkpoint encountered.

WHERE TO STAY A few hotels are scattered around town; best of the lot is **Hôtel Bomukambi** (m *099 718 3510/081 188 0775; sgl $$*) with private baths in each room as well as a basic restaurant. Another half-decent option is **Hôtel Carte Blanche** (m *099 993 8700; sgl/dbl $*) and your cheapest bet would have to be **Hôtel Anto** (*sgl US$5, dbl US$10*). Camping is also possible if you have your own equipment, and the consent of a local landowner.

PRACTICALITIES

Banks All of the DR Congo's major banks have branches in Isiro, though none of them can give out cash advances; your best option is **Western Union** on Boulevard President Mobutu (m *098 20 4965;* ✆ *07.30–16.00 Mon–Fri, 07.30–13.00 Sat*) for a quick infusion of money.

GARAMBA NATIONAL PARK

Garamba has a sprawling history, some of it good, a great deal of it bad. It's seen rebel groups run through its territory more times than any other park in the nation, beginning with the incursions of the 1960s and continuing through the 1970s and 1980s with the Sudanese People's Liberation Movement (SPLM) setting up camps in the region to avoid government attacks at the height of their own conflict. The SPLM's own incursions pushed refugees from Sudan into the park for some time. It continued with more disasters throughout the fall of Mobutu's Zaire, and finally ended with the Lord's Resistance Army fleeing from the Ugandan military, invading sometime around 2004 or 2005. They still have a hideout somewhere in the deeper regions of the park, but Garamba trundles on. The park was founded in 1938, the second national park created in Africa, after Virunga. UNESCO declared it a World Heritage Site in 1980 and put it on their list of 'sites in danger' in 1996, after three rangers were shot dead protecting the rhino population.

Needless to say such a bloody history has taken its toll on the park. Furthermore, being so close to rather lawless regions of both Sudan and the Central African Republic has made its own animal populations more susceptible to poaching than usual for the Congo. This is unfortunate, as Garamba stands as one of the most important regions for African elephant on the planet – by some accounts, the largest populations of elephant remaining spend at least part of their time in the park.

Garamba, however, is most famous for being the last natural habitat of the white rhino. I have been assured by various ICCN officials that they still do exist in the park; the ICCN promises that they are alive and well, but various conservation groups put their numbers at critical levels – roughly around ten in total. The positive side, if there is one, is that they are concentrated on the southern end of the park – the area most likely to be visited by tourists, which means that if you spend some time at Garamba you have a decent chance of seeing one. Provided, of course, that poaching and the bushmeat trade do not eliminate them entirely over the next few years. There may be hope that these two activities

9

can be curbed as a foreign conservationist group, the African Parks Foundation (*www.africanparks-conservation.com*), has assumed control of the park. Their annual budget, at over US$1 million, is massive compared with that of the other parks in the DR Congo.

Garamba stands as a forgotten corner of the Democratic Republic of Congo, having never really been a tourist sight to begin with. In its original days it was off-limits to tourism entirely, an animal reserve of sorts, where elephants were captured for domestication. This is an important fact as well – and indeed another highlight of the park is the domestication programme, which proved that the African elephant could be turned into a work animal. Throughout the late 19th century the elephant of the continent proved to be an impossible animal to work with, and was never used as a beast of burden; however Garamba proved the rest of the colonialists wrong, and a successful domestication programme was established around 1927. Elephant domestication in the region dates back to the time of Congo Free State in 1902, and involved selecting a young elephant from a herd, capturing it, and then having it endure rigorous training at their camp. With captive breeding programmes well developed before independence, the domesticated elephants were rented out as labour for several decades, but the breeding programme halted throughout the park when the Congo began reinventing itself as Zaire. The programme was restarted during the 1970s and 1980s, but fell into disarray again as the country disintegrated in the 1990s. At present, there remain only a few domesticated elephants.

Other animal populations in the park include hippo, giraffe, buffalo, waterbuck, antelope, baboon and chimpanzee. All have seen significant population decreases since the 1970s.

The park occupies almost half a million hectares (about 5,000km²) and is bordered by the Central African Republic and Sudan. Most of the poaching originates in Sudan, with armed men on horseback riding into the park. They use 'donkey trains' to get valuable tusks and rhino horns out of the thick wilderness; the use of pack animals is a critical indication, according to reports, of external investors supplying sophisticated equipment to poachers for their trade. These are more than mere villagers trying to make a fast buck, but an organised force. The sad fact is that soon they may have nothing to poach.

PRACTICALITIES Garamba's centre of operations is in a town called **Nagero** (✹ *03°44.58.30 N, 29°31.05.50 E*) on the southeastern corner of the park. It has an airstrip, a campsite, and some basic lodging. The other point of entry for the park is at **Gangala Na Bodio** (✹ *29°31.05.50 N, 29°08.17.10 E*) which also has an airstrip and lodging, and was the original point where elephants were trained. Some domesticated elephants remain, and the capture programme has apparently been restarted. They are aiming this programme not at turning the elephants into beasts of burden, but rather for offering riding safaris to tourists.

Note that I mention airstrips, because Garamba is generally only accessible as such: from Goma or Kisangani, via chartered aircraft. Check with ICCN in either city for advice on who can offer a flight up that way. The chances are, if you are nice enough and have plenty of time, you can wait for the next supply flight and get a ride with them – for a price. Although no airline companies have offices in Isiro, you can still fish around in the town for a chartered aircraft to Garamba, and provided a plane is there for a few days this should be the cheapest option (but still not that cheap) at around US$2,000 one-way. As usual, none of this exempts you from purchasing a permit – and since so few tourists have in fact reached Garamba in recent years, no-one could really confirm what price they should sell them at. A chartered aircraft from Goma will run to about US$6,000.

Should the road ever improve, it will be via Isiro to the town of **Faradje** (✪ *03°44.03.26 N, 29°42.31.52 E*) and then a 30km 4x4 road to Nagero. For Gangala Na Bodio, make your way from Isiro to the small town of **Dungu** (✪ *03°36.56.87 N, 28°33.52.24 E*) and then to Gangala Na Bodio, about 75km along the road leading to Faradje.

OKAPI RESERVE

Occupying a huge area in the northeast of the DR Congo, the Okapi Reserve straddles a not-quite-national-park status in the region; not that it would have mattered in the ensuing conflict of the 1990s and 2000s, but it nevertheless may have upped the budget and protected the animal populations a little bit more. It exists primarily for protecting the creatures after which it is named and their habitat – as there is almost no infrastructure within the park, it is not conducive to touring around. The reserve has expanded in recent years, on paper at least, to encompass over 1.3 million hectares (13,700km²) of the last undeveloped rainforests in Orientale and Ituri provinces.

The reserve protects the most important habitat for the okapi on the planet, and is also home to one of the largest remaining elephant populations in Africa. Furthermore, numerous species of duiker can be found within the park, and several hundred different bird species. It is also home to a large number of pygmy villages, and on the road between Kisangani and Komanda you can see their stout populations trading various foodstuffs for tobacco products. Towards Isiro the lush rainforest transforms into granite inselbergs, large stone outcroppings which loom over the normally flat plain of foliage. Various species have adapted to living in this region specifically.

The Okapi Reserve, nonetheless, can be easily visited thanks to a **Capture Station** at **Epulu** (✪ *01°24.07.82 N, 28°34.20.53 E*) founded in 1952 to supply the animal to zoos worldwide. They also engage in captive breeding, meaning that the okapi, unlike so many other animals in the Congo, is not threatened with extinction. They charge US$20 for a foreigner to visit, and at last count had 20 of the animals within the zoo. An estimated 5,000 live within the reserve's boundaries. The actual entrance to the park is at **Nia Nia** (✪ *01°24.20.08 N, 27°36.26.88 E*) where an ICCN office will sell you a permit (around US$100) for visiting the park – a network of roads (as usual, navigable only with a 4x4) goes around the park where you can view the local wildlife.

PRACTICALITIES Epulu is best visited from Beni, in the east, again with your own private vehicle – it takes roughly a day to get to **Komanda** (✪ *01°21.57.50 N, 29°45.47.27 E*) and then **Mambasa** (✪ *01°21.37.50 N, 29°03.28.77 E*), and finally along the road you can get to Epulu. This is possible by public transport as well, mostly by hiring motorbikes from Beni; but it will take at least US$75 each way, and for that price, you're better off finding someone with a vehicle to hire. If minibus connections between Kisangani and Bunia start it will make this route quite simple – but will still take about a day to arrive at the reserve from either destination.

From Kisangani the road has been repaired up to Epulu, and the story is much the same – a day's journey by private vehicle, and a complicated set of negotiations with motorbikes over a day or two otherwise. The good news is that if you've come as far as Nia Nia, the road onward to Isiro is right there, and you're almost at the top of the country and its least-visited park – Garamba.

Also keep in mind that rainy season runs roughly between August and November; all bets are off for 4x4 touring during these months.

In 1886, an uprising of Sudanese Muslims in Équateur Province had left the British Consul Emin Pasha isolated; the British, in their urge to extract Pasha from the area, sought out Henry Morton Stanley for the expedition.

Naturally, there were ulterior motives – Stanley hoped to expand the territory and influence of Congo Free State for Belgian King Léopold II, and accepted the mission. He contacted his old friend Tippu Tip, who spent much of his time in Zanzibar, and asked for his assistance. Tip agreed, and would join Stanley`s expedition when it arrived there.

Yet, they would not begin their journey west to Équateur Province from Zanzibar. Rather, they began a tortuous voyage south by ship, around the Cape and then north to the mouth of the Congo River, to gather more supplies. There was also concern over the local populations of east Africa, who were assumed to be hostile to their expedition. Stanley's choice to use the Congo River, navigable to the nearest point just outside the Ituri rainforest where they expected to meet Pasha, was a gross miscalculation. It would not be his last on the expedition.

Tippu Tip joined him for the long journey from Zanzibar to Matadi; the seas were rough, and the boat was ill equipped to handle him, his numerous wives and handlers, and all of Stanley's crew. It was a terrible month at sea. Time was ticking, but Stanley's expedition forged ahead.

After months they finally traversed the Congo River and arrived in Fort Bordo, also called Bangala. The expedition split from there, and so did their ideologies – Stanley's crew would continue onward to find Pasha while his second in command, Edmund Barttelot, would accompany Tippu Tip to Stanley Falls. Tippu Tip was less inclined to assist Stanley as he began to break certain clauses of their contract – he offered to supply porters to Stanley's expedition, but only on the condition that they be supplied with ammunition. Stanley did not, in fact, bring much ammunition with him for this purpose, and was reluctant to live up to this condition.

Tip, a hard businessman, considered this a breach of their agreement. He dragged his heels on supplying porters, and when he did, they were not the kind that the expedition needed – Manyuema people arrived, instead of the promised Zanzibaris, and Tip forced

BUTA ✦ 02°48.35 N, 24°44.21 E

At 300km north of Kisangani or roughly three days' drive by private 4x4, this was once a stopping point for the important rail link between Bumba on the Congo River and Isiro in the northwest of the DR Congo. Those days, of course, are gone, and Buta is an incredibly isolated place on a stretch of bad road. It is also the largest town of any kind in this region and a staging ground for the sights along the border with the Central African Republic. There are huge hunting reserves here – **Bomu** and **Bili-Uere** together occupy over 36,000km² along the border, quite likely the largest hunting domains on the planet. Just south of Buta is the hunting reserve of **Rubi-Tele**, and you will pass through this area by road from Kisangani. What animal populations remain in these areas, however, has been difficult for wildlife management organisations to gauge and I would not expect ICCN to provide accurate information – they are trying to sell you a permit, after all. Contact one of the tour operators listed earlier in this guide (see page 83) for the best advice on arranging a visit for sport hunting in the area.

Head northwest from Buta and you will arrive in the town of **Bondo** (✦ 03°48.49 N, 23°41.00 E) which was once a strategic mining town and sports the remnants of a rail line here. Arab influences can also be seen – the region was ruled by Sultan Djabir in the late 19th century and when Belgian interests arrived, they the expedition to treat them a certain way – no forced marches, no violence against them, etc. They would rest when they wanted, and even choosing their direction through the Ituri forest proved to be a challenge for Barttelot, as he set out to meet up with Stanley.

Stanley had gone out ahead, and was anxiously waiting for this assistance from his 'rear column'. Barttelot was leading the column to Stanley's position at a sluggish pace, constantly backtracking through the thick rainforest. Finally after excessive squabbles between the Englishmen and the Manyuema, Barttelot was shot and killed one night in a mutiny. Disaster struck, the column dispersed, and Stanley was stuck with Pasha on the shores of Lake Albert.

Stanley and Pasha went searching for the remaining rear column leaders, with whom they met up in Fort Bodo some weeks later. Both parties were exhausted and starving. Stanley's reunited expedition departed for Zanzibar soon after.

He would not be done with Tippu Tip, though – a lawsuit against him was filed in Zanzibar: through a prominent Arab banker he seized money owed for ivory sales, citing that it was required to compensate the Emin Pasha Relief Committee. Tip was furious, and under pressure from Belgium and England, Stanley eventually dropped the suit.

Tippu Tip would remain in Zanzibar and enlist one of his sons to run his territory in eastern Congo, under Léopold until he too was supplanted around 1891. Stanley's own writings would pinpoint the expedition's failures largely on the swindlings of Tippu Tip and the incompetence of his rear column.

Several books are available which describe Stanley's last voyage through the Congo, most recommended of which is *The Last Expedition: Stanley's Mad Journey through the Congo*, by Daniel Liebowitz and Charles Pearson.

A wealth of illustrations on the expedition is available in *In Stanley's Footsteps: Across Africa from West to East*, by John and Julie Batchelor.

For the record from the man himself, his writings of his last disastrous journey into the Congo can be found in *In Darkest Africa: Or the Quest, Rescue and Retreat of Emin Governor of Equatoria*, volumes 1 and 2.

clashed with the Arab business of gathering slaves and ivory. You can continue on a rough dirt road north to the village of **Gangu-Bili** (✪ *04°14.11.45 N, 23°36.40.22 E*) and hire a canoe to visit **Gangu Falls** a few hours' upstream. Northwest of Bondo on the road to the Central African Republic town of Bangassou is **Monga** (✪ *04°12.02.09 N, 22°48.44.25 E*) situated on the north bank of the Bili River. On the road here from Bondo there is a waterfall.

GEMENA ✪ 03°15.16 N, 19°46.38 E

Despite appearing as only a small place of dirt roads and shacks buried in the jungle, Gemena is the largest town in far northwestern DR Congo. The people of this region are exceptionally poor, as the rich resource wealth of the nation lies elsewhere. On the road to Zongo and into the CAR at Bangui are two different falls, though local guiding and your own transportation are essential: **Mole Falls** is east of the main road towards Zongo on the Mole River, and **Kotobongo Falls** on the Lua River, near the village of Bokada.

Gemena warrants a mention as it is the hub in the northwest and a usual stopping point for those moving onward to the Central African Republic. Or, if you are coming from Bangui, this may very well be your first evening stop and encounter with civilisation in the DR Congo. The **Catholic Mission** can rent out

9

Way up in the nether regions of the DR Congo, and far closer to any semblance of civilisation in the Central African Republic, is Gbadolite – a small town that rocketed to fame for being the home town of Mobutu Sésé Seko, and later his extravagant palace nearby that dwarfed the village in its entirety.

When it was completed, it was a sight to see in its own right – Gbadolite's airport had its runway refitted to handle jumbo jets and Concorde, which he chartered often to visit his properties in Switzerland and Belgium. Dignitaries from around the world were invited to dine at his lavish mansion far removed from the daily bustle of Kinshasa – or any daily bustle for that matter, being so deep in the jungle. The stories were unbelievable – massive doors over 3m tall, huge statues, a gigantic pool and huge arching hallways. It was said that the mansion itself was far too big for any human, and indeed most of Mobutu's entourage who would spend large amounts of time there living in its numerous guesthouses. He imported wedding cakes made the same day in Paris for his children, and even dairy cows – all of it was delivered by Concorde, or huge cargo planes. The money that went into Gbadolite, and then evaporated, was enormous.

It was incredibly isolated. About an hour-and-a-half northeast of the capital by jet, it was a place that Mobutu frequently escaped to – especially in his later years as Zaire began to crumble from under him. Family maintained Mobutu's mansion for some time, but as the revolution ensued, widespread looting essentially destroyed the building.

It was briefly the headquarters for the MLC, until being abandoned again and left to nature. There is very little left worth seeing, unless the ruins of a once-great mansion intrigue you. There are still regular flights from Kinshasa to this far northern city, confirmation that its airport is still in use. A land route to the city is difficult, to say the least – the simplest way would be to arrive from the Central African Republic. On the DR Congo side, the closest town of any size is Gemena, over 200km southwest.

Near the town are the **Kotakoli Rocks**, curious black stone formations that were said to once have been buried under an ancient sea in central Africa from prehistory.

rooms for a few dollars. Expect a three-day journey to the border from here, or at least two weeks to Kisangani via road, when there is transport through Buta and the nondescript river port towns of **Lisala** (✪ *02°09.11 N, 21°30.51 E*) and **Bumba** (✪ *02°11.10 N, 22°28.04 E*) – there are also riverboats from Kisangani to either of these towns, and you can catch a truck onward from there. Alternatively, you can also wait at the river and find some barges heading towards Kinshasa. The airport sees regular flights to the capital, as well as onward to Gbadolite, on **Wimbi Dira Airways** (m *081 516 0108;* e *gemena@wda.cd*). **Hewa Bora Airways** (m *081 313 3499*) and **Bravo Air Congo** (*Av Moboto 147*) also provides occasional flights to Kinshasa, via Mbandaka.

10

The East

The eastern frontier of the DR Congo is a unique landscape and what tourists come to see – towering mountains, active volcanoes, rare gorilla species, and other populations of rare wildlife. This area is a geographical wonder of Africa, and it is no surprise that it sits along the border as many of these landmarks make natural frontiers – Mount Stanley, second-highest peak on the continent; the volcano ranges that sit between the DR Congo, Rwanda and Uganda; and the numerous great lakes that have evolved here in Africa's Rift Valley.

The villages and lifestyle here are unique and varied. Visit the mountain towns of Kanyabayonga and Lubero, and you feel like you're in a different country altogether. Farmland creeps up the mountain slopes, round huts of mud and thatch form scattered patches of population. The saturated green colours and conical craters have made many writers over the decades compare this region to Switzerland; perhaps a disorganised, conflicted, undeveloped Switzerland would be a better comparison. The altitude in the Rift Valley makes the climate far less oppressive than in other parts of the DR Congo. It is home to two of the country's largest cities, Bukavu and Goma, as well as the most shattered province in the country – Ituri. It is very easy to spend several weeks travelling a north–south route and see far more variety than during several months in other parts of Africa.

The Kivus were also some of the hardest-hit regions during recent conflicts, sending refugees one way during the 1994 Rwandan genocide and then the other way during the wars of the DR Congo. The latest troubles occurred when Laurent Nkunda, a man with a patchy history throughout the DR Congo's last decade, rallied several thousand troops to his cause of ousting Interahamwe militias from their entrenched positions near Ishasha. The conflict was ready to fly out of control, but MONUC's expanded mandate and a new government with popular support under Joseph Kabila kept a lid on things. An agreement was reached and his soldiers integrated with the national army, with a promise that more would be done to remove the Interahamwe from their last few strongholds in the Kivus. At the time of writing, perhaps surprisingly, that is exactly what was transpiring.

GOMA ⊕ 01°40.07 S, 29°13.23 E

Black volcanic rocks permeate Goma's landscape, lending it a unique look amongst the towns and cities of the DR Congo. They are everywhere – used to build walls, roads, crushed and reconstituted into bricks, the city is a mixture of diffused black and grey colours surrounded by the lush green hills which create some of the best farmland in Africa – and, on occasion, nearby volcanoes erupt and demolish the town in its entirety. Huge lava fields northwest of Goma attest to the precarious position that the city maintains.

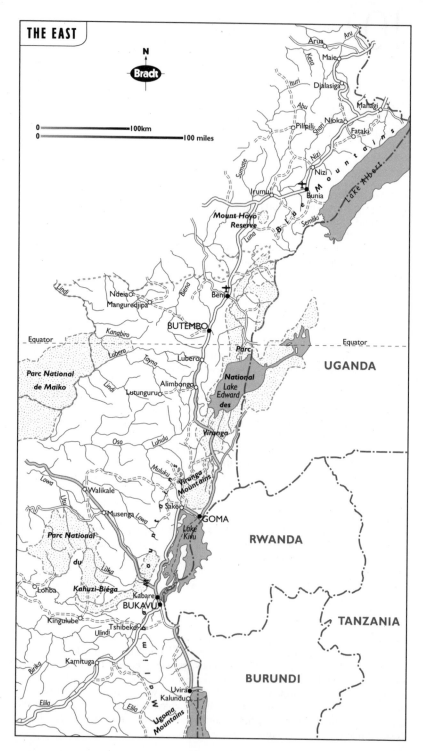

THE EAST

Bradt

N

0   100km
0   100 miles

Arua

Aru

Maie

Kasa

Ituri

Dialasiga

Abu

Mahagi

Pilipili

Shari

Nioka

Fataki

Nizi

Sumate

Nizi

Irumu

Bunia

Mount Hoyo
Reserve

Semliki

Luna

Lindi

Biena

Beni

Ndeia

Manguredjipa

BUTEMBO

Kanabiro

Equator   Equator

Lubero

Parc

Lubero

Tayna

UGANDA

Parc National
de Maiko

Lindi

Alimbongo

National
Lake
Edward
des

Lutunguru

Oso

Luhulu

Virunga

Muluku

Virunga
Mountains

Walikale

Lowa

Musenga

Sake

GOMA

Lowa

Lake
Kivu

RWANDA

Parc National

du

Luka

Kahuzi-Biéga

Kabare

Lohba

BUKAVU

Kingulube

Tshibeke

Ulindi

TANZANIA

Kamituga

Birika

Uvira

Kalundu

Elila

Elilo

Ugoma
Mountains

BURUNDI

Blue Mountains

Lake Albert

176

Goma's town centre was destroyed in 2002 by Mount Nyiragongo, the fourth time in a century that a major eruption had occurred in the region. It erased whatever may have existed of the area in decades past. In some older single-storey buildings, the attentive will notice that they are actually the top level of what were once two-storey buildings.

The city plods along, 2m higher than it was at the beginning of the millennium, with an increased focus on construction and development. It has been designated as tourist capital of the DR Congo, and will undoubtedly be the first port of entry for large numbers of visitors to the country. While unique in its own right as a town built on a lava flow, it is really the surrounding sights that make Goma so important – specifically Virunga Park and Lake Kivu.

HISTORY Belgians arrived in the area now known as Goma at the turn of the 20th century, encountering small settlements of Hutus and Tutsi, as well as other tribes including the Hunde and Twa. They created a permanent settlement in 1906 as a counterbalance to a German outpost built around the same time in Gisenyi. The site would be of strategic importance during World War I. Goma was chosen to become the administrative centre for North Kivu in 1948, and saw a major increase in population after this. Nearly 30 years later, in 1977, a major eruption by Nyiragongo would obliterate the town, killing 2,000, and setting its development back several decades.

Goma became an important post for NGO staff during the Rwandan genocide as thousands fled the civil war in their country. It then became a centre of conflict as Rwandan troops chased Interahamwe militias into Congolese territory, and armed Laurent Kabila, marching west with him all of the way to Kinshasa. Internal struggles resulted in Rwandan factions in the DR Congo: the Rassemblement pour la Démocratie Congolais (RCD) split into many groups, creating chaos in the town centre, but the city continued to grow as the base of operations for military in the region. The town changed hands several times between 1998 and 2003, primarily as a result of agitation from local rebel leader Laurent Nkunda.

Goma's fortunes were revived again when the UN decided to set up shop with MONUC at the end of the 20th century, and its airport is easily the busiest in the eastern part of the country. Aircraft rattle the window shutters constantly along the flight path, flying low over the entire town centre, interrupting conversations and on occasion causing people to duck if the pilots are a little late on take-off.

ORIENTATION Goma is right on Lake Kivu and squeezed by Gisenyi and the Rwandan border to its east, and Mount Nyiragongo looming to its north. It sprawls westward along the shore and northeast between the border and the airport, until eventually dissipating along the road north to Rutshuru district. In the middle is the **port** and a large hill overlooking the city. The true centre of town is **Rond Point de l'Indépéndance** which is surrounded by two banks and the **BDGL Building** (pronounced *Bay-Day-Jay-Elle*) which houses the office for Hewa Bora Airways and ICCN. **Boulevard Kanya Muhanga** is the main thoroughfare through town, once called Avenue Mobutu, and you'll notice that after the Rond Point de l'Indépéndance it gets a little rough – as the northern half was flooded by lava. **Avenue Katindo** is the main road west out of town and splits into two routes, **Katindo Gauche** (left) and **Katindo Droit** (right). Follow it left and you'll go along the pleasant lakeside road that winds through numerous old Belgian holiday residences and some of the city's nicest hotels. Follow it right and you'll get into the crowded suburbs, and eventually onward to Masisi. The road continues around Lake Kivu, and you can take it all the way to Bukavu.

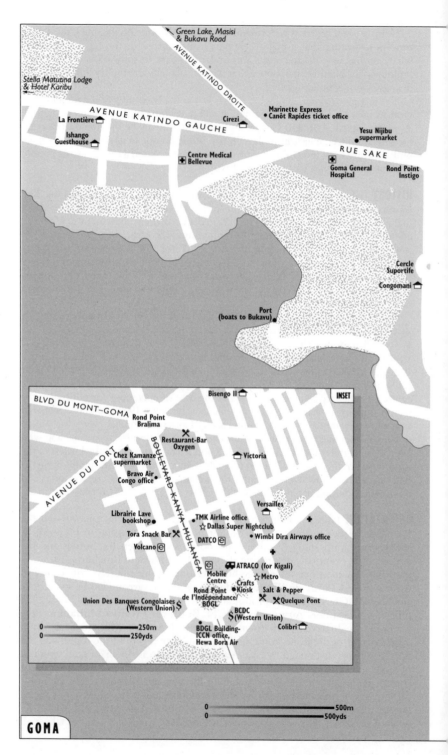

Green Lake, Masisi
& Bukavu Road

AVENUE KATINDO DROITE

Stella Matutina Lodge
& Hotel Karibu

AVENUE KATINDO GAUCHE

La Frontière   Cirezi

Marinette Express
Canôt Rapides ticket office

Ishango
Guesthouse

Yesu Nijibu
supermarket

RUE SAKE

Centre Medical
Bellevue

Goma General
Hospital

Rond Point
Instigo

Cercle
Suportife

Congomani

Port
(boats to Bukavu)

INSET

BLVD DU MONT–GOMA

Bisengo II

Rond Point
Bralima

Restaurant-Bar
Oxygen

Chez Kamanze
supermarket

Victoria

Bravo Air
Congo office

AVENUE DU PORT

BOULEVARD KANYA-MULANGA

Librairie Lave
bookshop

Versailles

TMK Airline office
Dallas Super Nightclub

Tora Snack Bar

DATCO

Wimbi Dira Airways office

Volcano

ATRACO (for Kigali)

Mobile
Centre   Metro

Crafts
Kiosk   Salt & Pepper

Rond Point
de l'Indépendance
BDGL

Quelque Pont

Union Des Banques Congolaises
(Western Union)

BCDC
(Western Union)

0   250m
0   250yds

BDGL Building-
ICCN office,
Hewa Bora Air

Colibri

0   500m
0   500yds

GOMA

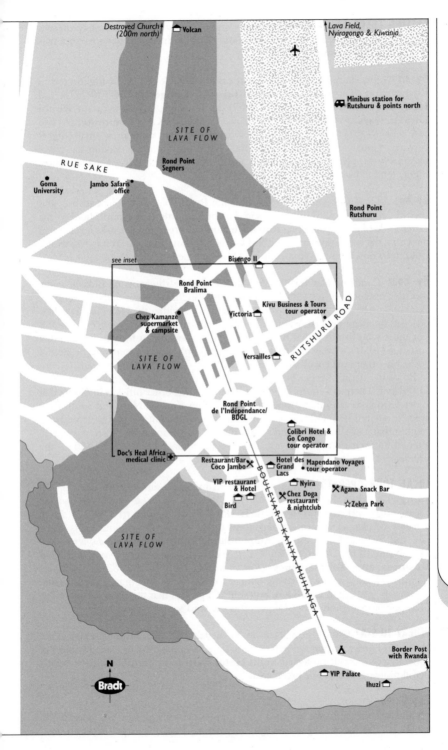

Destroyed Church
(200m north) | 🏠 Volcan

Lava Field,
Nyiragongo & Kiwanja

🚐 Minibus station for
Rutshuru & points north

SITE OF
LAVA FLOW

RUE SAKE

Rond Point
Segners

● Goma
University

Jambo Safaris ●
office

Rond Point
Rutshuru

see inset

🏠 Bisengo II

Rond Point
Bralima

Kivu Business & Tours
tour operator

Chez Kamanze ●
supermarket
& campsite

Victoria 🏠

RUTSHURU ROAD

SITE OF
LAVA FLOW

Versailles 🏠

Rond Point
de l'Indépendance/
BDGL

Colibri Hotel &
Go Congo
tour operator

Doc's Heal Africa 🏥
medical clinic

Restaurant/Bar ✕
Coco Jambo

VIP restaurant
& Hotel

Bird 🏠

Hotel des 🏠
Grand
Lacs

🏠 Nyira

✕ Chez Doga
restaurant
& nightclub

Mapendano Voyages
● tour operator

✕ Agana Snack Bar

☆ Zebra Park

SITE OF
LAVA FLOW

BOULEVARD KANYA-MUHANGA

N

Bradt

⛺

Border Post
with Rwanda

🏠 VIP Palace

Ihuzi 🏠

GETTING THERE AND AROUND Goma is one of the DR Congo's best-connected cities. Right near the border with Rwanda, Kigali with its international airport is only around three hours away by bus.

By air Goma's airport is the busiest in eastern DR Congo. Most flights stop in Kisangani on their way to Kinshasa; **Bravo Air Congo** (m *099 930 1631*) and **Hewa Bora Airways** (m *081 313 3499*) do this route, and on occasion **Wimbi Dira Airways** (m *081 700 7964;* e *goma@wda.cd*). **TMK Air Commuter** (m *080 856 0500/841 7710;* e *tmkgoma@kivu-online.com*) has numerous small flights between Goma and Bukavu, Butembo, Beni and Bunia – making air travel reasonably simple amongst the east's main urban centres. Prices for these short flights tend to hover around US$75 one-way.

By bus ATRACO buses leave from near the Rond Point de l'Indépéndance, and should cost around US$10 per person. For buses north to Rutshuru, head to the eastern side of the airport along **Rutshuru Road** where frequent trucks head in that direction; the cost is only around US$3 for the two-hour journey. West to Masisi and Bukavu by bus, follow Avenue Katindo Droit and the buses leave along this road.

By boat *Canôt rapides* leave from the port in the direction of Bukavu every morning except Sundays – it takes between two and three hours and costs US$40. Booking can be done right at the docks, or in town at either the Hôtel Ihusi or their office at the beginning of Avenue Katindo Droit (m *080 851 3736/099 413 4056*). For those who like to play it rough, there's a local overnight ferry to Bukavu that costs US$10. It's a lively and friendly boat, but don't expect a comfy night. Before going on either boat check the schedule at Ihusi – departure times do vary.

Be aware that it's likely a bribe/visa will be requested before getting on the boat to Bukavu. There is a mutual agreement among the border officials in Goma that short-term visas are only for single provinces; thus Kivu du Nord and South Kivu are separate entities. This can be a real hassle, and it's not the sort of tepid bribe request that you can laugh at and simply dismiss – they're serious. Plan to get there a few minutes early to hash it out, and be ready to drop US$10 or US$20 for the privilege of crossing the lake.

LOCAL TOUR OPERATORS Goma has two main offices for visiting tourists, **Go Congo** (*Colibri Hôtel, Colibri Rd;* m *099 773 4710;* e *sales@gocongo.com; www.gocongo.com*) and **Jambo Safaris** (*Rond Point Segners;* m *099 774 5179;* e *sjambos@yahoo.fr*) who can arrange tours to any of the surrounding sights in the city and Virunga Park. Also try **Mapendano Voyages** (*Av Jacaranda, across from Hôtel Nyira;* m *081 314 0727/086 77 250;* e *anmapendanosafari@yahoo.fr*) and **Kivu Business and Tour Agency** (*Rutshuru Rd;* m *081 812 8217; www.kbt-agency.populus.ch*), who will arrange similar tours. ICCN discourages tourists from visiting their office in the BDGL building and prefers that they buy permits from local operators instead, so visit these offices first to see if they can help.

WHERE TO STAY Goma's best hotels are by the lakeside, with **Hôtel Ihusi** near the Rwandan border getting top marks these days. A familiar luxury standby west of town in a quiet, well-protected area is **Hôtel Karibu**, of similar quality but many decades older, with a large green area.

Expensive

⌂ **Hôtel Ihusi** Near the Rwandan border post; m 081 312 9560. Ihusi is a large complex right on the lake with a few token birds (peacocks) wandering around. It has a pool, bar & restaurant, internet café, secure parking, & all rooms have excellent views of the lake. As you would expect for the town's best hotel, the rooms are well equipped with hot running water, satellite TV & refrigerators. They're busy building an extension for more rooms, though this may wreck the view for some lower-lying bedrooms; get a bed on the 2nd or 3rd level. Sgl/dbl $$$, suite $$$$

⌂ **Hôtel Karibu** (100 rooms) At the end of Av Katindo Gauche; m 081 313 6506/097 144 256; e hotel.karibu@caramail.com. Large well-groomed property on the lakeside west of town, Hôtel Karibu has an Old Zaire feel to it that's been cultivated & maintained even through the recent wars of the Congo. Boasts numerous bungalows in addition to its many rooms, a large pool, tennis courts & restaurant. Secure parking in addition to all of the usual amenities: AC, TV, hot running water. B/fast inc. Sgl/dbl $$$, suite $$$$

Mid-range

⌂ **Bird Hôtel** Off Bd Kanya Muhanga; m 099 772 0327. Pleasant place that offers a particularly good deal, including secure parking, a decent restaurant, & plenty of foliage with birds (hence the name) in a quiet neighbourhood. If you tire of the food there is always the popular VIP Restaurant next door. The staff are very attentive & the rooms have TV & intermittent running water. Sgl/dbl $$

⌂ **Hôtel Congomani** (25 rooms) Cercle Sportif. A new guesthouse with private rooms for w/enders in Goma. Well maintained with a terraced bar, satellite TV, hot running water, & secure parking. Sgl/dbl $$$

⌂ **Hôtel des Grands Lacs** (18 rooms) Bd Kanya Muhanga. Probably Goma's oldest hotel, a deteriorating colonial throwback with some beautiful interior gardens & large rooms with bathtubs & fixtures straight out of Old Belgium. Often full, & the fact that they have no telephone attests to their struggles to keep up appearances while dealing with an ageing building & little money to modernise it. Rooms vary in quality & cleanliness considerably. Has a parking area out front which should be secure enough, though no large gates to keep everyone out. The restaurant, Al Bacha, is half decent & specialises in Lebanese food. Sgl/dbl $$

⌂ **Hôtel La Frontière** Av Katindo Gauche; m 081 314 0690/081 567 1626. Nice terraced entrance with garden at the back, conference room, high-end restaurant & bar, secure parking. Rooms are large with refrigerator, TV & running water. Not quite on the lake, but rooms on the upper levels will have decent views of it. Sgl/dbl $$$, suite $$$$

⌂ **Hôtel VIP Palace** Near the Rwandan border post, at the very end of Rue Kanya Muhanga; m 081 318 0999/099 891 1034. Right beside Hôtel Ihusi & very similar in quality & style, though it doesn't have a lakeside bar & restaurant or as many rooms. With secure parking & internet café, rooms have all of the high-end trappings: running hot water, satellite TV, refrigerators. Divided into 3 classes: A, B & C. The only difference seems to be the size of the rooms, & slightly better views of the lake. Class A Sgl/dbl $$$, Class B US$15 more, Class C sgl/dbl $$$$

⌂ **Stella Matutina Lodge** Av Katindo Gauche; m 081 151 0760; e lodgestellamatutino@yahoo.fr. Well-groomed green space on the lakeside with a bar & high-end restaurant, secure parking, & a decidedly 'Old Europe' feel to its design. Popular with Congolese honeymooners, it seems. Internet available. Rooms have satellite TV & hot running water. B/fast inc. Sgl/dbl $$$, suite $$$$

⌂ **Ishango Guesthouse** South of Hôtel La Frontier; m 099 868 8626. Further into the suburbs west of Goma is a decent place with secure parking, restaurant & above-average rooms in a quiet neighbourhood. Has hot running water & TVs in every room. Sgl/dbl $$$, suite $$$$ – about US$5 less than Hôtel La Frontier.

⌂ **Nyira Hôtel** Off Bd Kanya Muhanga; m 099 801 1089; e nyirahotel@yahoo.fr. Beautiful old hotel with a large restaurant & BBQs on w/ends. Has a large gardened area for wandering about, large interior bar, several small dining areas. Rooms have TV & cold running water. Discounts for long stays. B/fast inc. Sgl/dbl $$$

⌂ **Versailles Hôtel** Off Rutshuru Rd; m 099 773 4710. Recently renovated though the rooms are still basic, with running water only. Has a restaurant, bar & secure parking. Sgl/dbl $$

⌂ **Victoria Hôtel** Av Touriste; m 081 054 6195. Multi-storeyed & recently renovated in the crowded residential eastern half of Goma's city centre. Rooms have private bathrooms with intermittent running water. Sgl/dbl $$

⌂ **VIP Hôtel & Restaurant** (8 rooms) Off Bd Kanya Muhanga, beside Bird Hôtel; m 081 146 3108. Better known for its restaurant, which garners plenty of popularity amongst local Congolese, VIP Hôtel & Restaurant has rooms of slightly lesser quality than those at the Bird Hôtel next door. They also have secure parking. Rooms include TV & intermittent running water. Sgl $$

Budget

🏠 **Colibri Hôtel** Av Colibri; m 099 773 4710(DR Congo)/250 088 848 22 (Rwanda); e kenrwnari@yahoo.com. New hotel aimed at the budget crowd with a spacious garden, room for camping, & basic amenities. Has the tour operator's office Go Congo inside. Sgl $, camping US$5 pp.

🏠 **Hôtel Bisengo II** m 099 416 6758. Buried in the central suburbs east of Rond Point Bralima & usually filled with long-term residents. Rooms are basic but reasonably secure. With private bathroom $, with shared bathroom less than US$10.

🏠 **Hôtel Cirezi** (11 rooms) Av Katindo Gauche; m 099 861 1755; e hotelcirezi@yahoo.fr. On a main road west out of Goma which can make it a bit loud at times, though on the other hand they have a secure parking area & small restaurant, along with high walls to drown out the noise. Rooms are basic affairs without TVs & they have intermittent running water. Sgl $

🏠 **Hôtel Volcan** (12 rooms) Bd Kanya Muhanga, north of Rond Point Segners; m 081 231 5597. Budget hotel that has been built in the lower level of a new building right in the lava flow. Has a small snack bar; rooms are naturally cool due to the dense volcanic ash. Sgl $

🏕 **Campsite** At the corner of Bd Kanya Muhanga, towards the Rwandan border post. Large grassy area for camping & plenty of room for overlanders' parking. At the back is a bar/restaurant & toilets/showers. US$7 pp.

🏕 **Chez Kamanze Supermarket & Campsite** Near Rond Point Bralima. The supermarket has recently completed a campsite behind their building with plenty of room for parking, shared bathrooms & a bar/restaurant. US$7 pp.

✖ **WHERE TO EAT** Goma's culinary scene is one of the best in the region.

✖ **Al Bacha Restaurant** At the Hôtel Des Grands Lacs; ⏱ 11.00 daily. Has Lebanese fare – including *shawarma*. **$$$**

✖ **Chez Doga** South along Bd Kanya Muhanga; m 080 831 3112; ⏱ 19.00–midnight daily. This is another highly regarded nightspot & also a decent place to get some food. It has a stage with live music at weekends, an internet connection, & small supermarket in the same complex. **$$$**

✖ **Coco Jambo** Bd du Kanya-Muhanga; ⏱ 18.30–23.30 daily. Is one of the more popular standbys for expatriates, & rightfully so, offering excellent dishes in a decidedly touristic setting of thatched huts & Western dance music. It's also a popular nightspot. **$$$**

✖ **Salt and Pepper Restaurant** Near Rond-Point BDGL; m 084 93 108; ⏱ 18.30–22.30 daily. Offers cheap & excellent Indian & Chinese dishes in addition to a few Congolese standbys. The dining area is a little bit small, so the later you arrive the less chance there is of a seat being available. **$$**

✖ **Tora Snack Bar** Just north of Rond Point de l'Indépendance; ⏱ 10.00–18.30 daily. Has recently been completed & boasts a cafeteria in addition to a supermarket area, along with a pavement terrace useful for people-watching. **$$**

✖ **VIP Restaurant** Across the street from Chez Doga; m 081 146 3108; ⏱ 18.30–22.30 daily. It's popular with local Congolese & serves a wide variety of national dishes in an unpretentious atmosphere. **$$**

✖ **Quelque Pont** Next door to Salt and Pepper; ⏱ 19.00–23.00 daily. This market eating area has a pool table & plenty of plastic chairs. It's a great place to grab an evening drink. They usually cook large skewers of meat (called *brochettes* in French) along with chicken & occasionally fish at very low prices. **$**

✖ **Restaurant Bar Oxygen** Near Rond Point Bralima; ⏱ 12.00–16.00 daily. Has some decent cheap Congolese food but nothing special – rice, manioc, the meat of the day – a good place for an afternoon snack. **$**

Finally, the city's top hotels will not disappoint for a high-end meal – **Hôtel Ihusi** (**$$$**), **Hôtel Karibu** (**$$$**), **Stella Matutina Lodge** (**$$$**) and **Hôtel La Frontier** (**$$$**) have the best restaurants of the lot.

ENTERTAINMENT AND NIGHTLIFE In the city centre there are two nightclubs: **Metro Nightclub**, which leans heavily on music from India, and **Dallas Super Nightclub**, geared more towards working-class Congolese. Near the border is

Agana Snack Bar (🕐 *20.00–midnight daily;* $) in the southeastern suburbs with plenty of beer and music in the evening and some cheap snacks to go along with them, including fish. Just nearby is the popular nightspot **Zebra Park** with plenty of neon lights and pool tables, busy with well-to-do Congolese at weekends.

SHOPPING There is a small **crafts kiosk** on Rond Point de l'Indépéndance that is a good place to stock up on wooden statues and masks. Situated right near the buses back to Kigali it's popular with day trippers from Rwanda who come for a visit. If you're heading further north there is another kiosk at the **minibus station to Rutshuru** offering similar items. Naturally, bargaining is expected to an extent.

For supermarkets, both **Yesu Nijibu** on Avenue Katindo and **Chez Kamanze** near Rond Point Bralima stock a modest variety of things but comparatively little to what can be found in Rwanda. They seem heavy on the liquor and glucose biscuits while being light on anything fresh.

Also of interest is Goma's **central market**. Built on the lava, the stalls sell practical items alongside a good selection of fabrics. There's a lively atmosphere and it's a spot for food and entertainment – several theatres, bars and a pool hall are located in the vicinity.

PRACTICALITIES

Banks For Western Union, Rond Point de l'Indépéndance is the place to visit. Both **BCDC** (m *081 312 6063;* e *gma@bcdc.cd;* 🕐 *08.00–16.00 Mon–Fri, 08.00–12.00 Sat*) and **Union Des Banques Congolaises** (m *098 204 965;* 🕐 *07.30–16.00 Mon–Fri*) have branches here that can assist with sending and receiving cash.

Medical Goma's **General Hospital** (*Rue Sake;* m *080 851 9634*) can treat emergencies and assist with illnesses, but for things less pressing it's better to visit **Centre Medical Belle Vue** off Avenue Katindo Gauche, which has a few doctors to prescribe medicine. If you need to visit a doctor, both will charge around US$5. **Doc's Heal Africa** (*Av Rond Point;* m *099 404 2513;* 🕐 *08.00–15.00 Mon–Fri, 08.00–12.00 Sat*) hosts European doctors on occasion and is the best clinic in the city.

There are several **pharmacies** along Rutshuru Road, stocked with some basic medications. Doing the circuit between the pharmacies looking for the one that has something you need is a time-honoured tradition in Goma for sick visitors.

Media and communications Goma has three internet cafés of note: **Mobile Centre** on Rond Point de l'Indépéndance, **DATCO** just behind it, and **Volcano Internet** a little to the west. All charge roughly US$1 per hour for a slow connection. Mobile Centre can also sell a local SIM chip if you need a mobile phone; these tend to be less than US$5.

There is one English-language bookshop: **Librairie Lave Littéraire** (m *099 413 3614*) in Avenue Béni. It opened in 2006 and moved to purpose-built premises in 2007. Under the same ownership as the Ikirezi Bookshop in Kigali (e *ikirezi@rwanda1.com; www.ikirezi.biz*), it stocks a selection of English-language publications as well as several Bradt guides for the region. If you lose this book, they should have a copy in stock (and if they don't, they can order it).

WHAT TO SEE Aside from **Lake Kivu** which makes Goma an attractive resort town of sorts (the city was, originally, a kind of beach destination for well-to-do Belgians) the city is most interesting because of the surrounding volcanoes. Check out the **destroyed church** at the northern end of Boulevard Kanya Muhanga, once a large cathedral that was flooded by lava. It's an open-air space covered in

Laurent Nkunda and his soldiers continue to make headlines in Western newspapers as prolonged conflict drives residents out of their homes, creating refugee camps closer to Goma, as well as across the border in Rwanda. All of this was supposed to be over and done with at the end of 2006, when the last round of fighting shut down parts of the region, but Nkunda has insisted on a renegotiation of sorts, accusing the government of providing support to Hutu militias.

In December 2007, rebels loyal to Nkunda took Rumangabo, a major market town along the road from Goma to Kiwanja. This means that, in effect, at the time of writing it was impossible to travel directly from Goma north to parts of Virunga aside from Nyiragongo. The Tongo Chimpanzee Sanctuary may or may not be accessible. Most importantly, if you plan on visiting mountain gorillas in the DR Congo, enter via Bunagana and not Goma.

Most of Nkunda's centre of power is several dozen kilometres east of Goma in the region surrounding Masisi. Green Lake is currently accessible, and all reports indicate that the road around Lake Kivu is still safe. However, these things can change at a moment's notice – it is imperative to check on local updates before setting out in the area, as territories shift while the Congolese army, MONUC, and Nkunda rebels jockey for position in the next round of negotiations. People in Goma will be well informed on the situation for exit points out of town. Goma is a critical centre of operations for MONUC and this will likely mean that rebels will not attack it directly – meaning that there should not be any concerns of the conflict spreading right into the city limits.

graffiti, a pyramid rising from the black earth. If you follow the lava flow north you'll eventually reach the city's edge and a large **lava field** which is unique in its own right – near the road north to Rutshuru is a large hill where the lava originally erupted, spouting from the ground several kilometres from the volcano. It was originally predicted to flow southeast into Gisenyi, but flowed almost directly south to envelop central Goma instead.

Follow the road west out of the city and you will eventually encounter a turn-off to **Green Lake**, a beautiful small body of water in a volcanic crater. Near the lake are several pits where volcanic ash is being mined and turned into bricks. Westward are the **Mokoto Lakes**, four quiet bodies of water surrounded by lush green volcanic mountains – to reach the lakes follow the turn-off north from Sake. Keep heading west and you will arrive in **Masisi**, a popular spot for viewing pygmy villages. There are also some beautiful villages filled with dairy farms, a curiosity to be sure in the DR Congo. This is also the heartland of Laurent Nkunda, and while he has given up his opposition to the Kabila government, going into this area with the intention of seeing pygmies should probably be done with a local tour operator – if only for the fact that you'll need a guide in any event. In this same area is **Jambo Village**, a campsite run by Jambo Safaris, and they offer boat trips to the small **Pig Island** (**Île de Cochon**) in Lake Kivu. Along the lakeshore are many old Belgian mansions.

A few kilometres north out of Goma are hillsides of lush volcanic farmland and hundreds of wooden cabins built after the eruption of the volcano. Their black exteriors and aluminium roofs make them a striking backdrop against the lush green of the area. As you gain altitude, some striking views of the city can be had – and it is in these hills that the original Rwandan army camped out and staged attacks on military positions in the city below during recent conflicts. This is also the beginning of **Virunga Park**, most notably the hiking trail leading to **Mount**

Nyiragongo (see *Virunga National Park* below for further details).

VIRUNGA NATIONAL PARK

If there is one park in all of Africa that you should visit, it is Virunga. This is more than mere hyperbole: it is easily the most varied region on the continent, if not one of *the* most varied on the planet. It is home to two of the world's most active volcanoes, the largest remaining population of mountain gorillas, and a mountain range that boasts the only glaciers in Africa. Also it's the only park in the world to have populations of three great ape species: the mountain gorilla, the lowland gorilla and the chimpanzee. These are only the highlights: there are also the Rwindi Plains, a great place for a classic east African wildlife excursion; and Lake Edward, still one of the best places to see large groups of hippos going about their daily activities. There is also Mount Tshiaberimu, with a small population of gorillas that was only habituated to human presence in 2001 and, according to research, could be a new subspecies, and there is also the Tongo Chimpanzee Reserve, the first place of its kind to protect the natural habitat of this creature.

The park was declared a World Heritage Site by UNESCO in 1979; and then in 1994 was added to the list of World Heritage Sites in danger, because of the influx of an estimated million or so Rwandan refugees after the Rwandan genocide.

Some may point out that poaching and a decade of strife have taken their toll on Virunga, and they would be right. Yet throughout the conflict there were numerous international groups who invested time and money to protect the most vulnerable aspects of Virunga, and even the local population rallied together to protect the mountain gorillas during the worst outbreaks of combat in North Kivu.

They realised what the animals meant to their region, and risked their

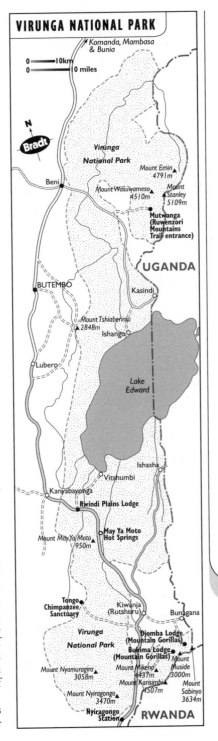

10

185

own lives in the hope that eventually the tourists would come back. The entire park was closed between 1997 and 2004; its reopening was a big deal to the people of this region. There are still some issues with poachers and Interahamwe in the area of Ishasha, but aside from that, the park is very much open for business – waiting for a new generation to discover why Virunga was talked about so highly, so often, in more peaceful times.

ORIENTATION Virunga can be a confusing park to get a hold of – in essence, it is a long north–south corridor that straddles the border of the DR Congo, covering most of the mountain range between Goma and ending just north of Beni. Beginning at the southern fringes of the active volcano **Mount Nyiragongo** it encompasses more volcanoes on the borders of Rwanda and Uganda near the stations of **Bukima** and **Djomba** – these are the world's primary remaining mountain gorilla habitats which are shared between the three countries. Head further north and there is the vast countryside of the **Rwindi Plains**, a savanna grassland and several villages on the shores of Lake Edward. East of Rwindi Plains is **Ishasha**, once known for vibrant hippo and bird populations, though rarely visited these days. Further north along the lakeshore and east of Butembo is **Mount Tshiaberimu**, another gorilla-trekking site. Follow Beni's road southeast towards Kasindi and you reach the towering **Ruwenzori Mountains** as well as **Ishango**, the main point of interaction on the north shore of Lake Edward.

PRACTICALITIES ICCN has offices in Goma and Beni to assist with travellers visiting their regions of the parks, but if you're planning on visiting Nyiragongo, don't go to the ICCN office in Beni. Most permits for visits are bought at the entrance to any of the park's various attractions, and this is usually simpler than arranging one in their faraway regional offices. The good thing about Virunga is that in comparison with other parks in the DR Congo, many of its sites can be reached by public transport. When that is not the case, most other points of entry are close enough that hiring a motorbike for the day (bargain for between US$20 and US$30) is practical enough.

WHAT TO SEE
Mount Nyiragongo (3,470m) Goma's residents know Nyiragongo all too well, and it is perhaps one of the more famous volcanoes in the world as it erupts and sends Africans fleeing in all directions every few decades. It is a near-perfect conical shape, the most active volcano in Africa, and indeed one of the most active in the world. Most importantly for tourists, lava activity in the crater is constant and makes for some spectacular light shows.

Nyiragongo was named after a native woman whose spirit is said to haunt the area; ancient belief was that the damned must atone for their sins at Nyiragongo, in the perpetual cauldron of lava. The entire geography of the region has been shaped by this region of volcanoes, with some speculation that lakes Edward and Kivu were once joined. Major eruptions have occurred in 1832, 1904, 1977, and of course 2002. The 1904 eruption killed thousands; 1977 saw its lava lake drain and spit out the volcano's side; 2002 wasn't a party either, as Goma's town centre was obliterated and several dozen people, returning too quickly after being evacuated, burned to death. You might think these sorts of things would deter people from settling in the area, but the rich farmland keeps them coming back; however, it takes years for this to happen, and in the meantime the resulting gases and ash have decimated agricultural production in recent years as well as caused respiratory problems for those who have resettled around the volcano.

Looming over Goma and across Lake Kivu is the ominous Mount Nyiragongo, which with its sister volcano Nyamulagira, has collectively caused 40% of all the volcanic eruptions in east Africa known to man. Nyiragongo last erupted in 2002, causing a bad situation in the east to become worse as lava flooded Goma, destroyed the airport, and killed 45 people. About 15% of Goma was destroyed in the eruption and 300,000 people were evacuated. Lava came straight down the main avenue, devastating the city; buildings were immersed in rivers of molten lava 2m high, power plants and fuel stations exploded as the heat came too near; rarely, if ever, has a major city experienced the destructive nature of a volcanic eruption as Goma did in 2002, and it was made worse by the presence of rival armies in the city who used the natural disaster to begin widespread looting, furthering the chaos and misery. The lava flows were finally halted when they encountered Lake Kivu, the ash and debris sending steam into the sky on meeting the water.

This was the first major eruption in a generation: in 1977 the mountain split and lava that had been pooling in Nyiragongo's crater flowed down its slopes, killing 70 and wiping out entire villages. Research revealed that the crater's structure had shifted thanks to the eruption of a nearby volcano, altering the undergound forces in the area that kept Nyiragongo as the usual place for lava to pool.

The existence of these active volcanoes in the Great Rift Valley of Africa is a double-edged sword, as anyone who travels through the region witnesses: volcanic soil is incredibly fertile and rich, creating ideal land for crops along the hillsides in Rwanda and the DR Congo.

Presently the volcano still sends plumes of smoke into the sky, and the lava in its crater begins to pool again. Nyiragongo, in fact, has the world's largest-known open lake of lava. Long lava flows that have since cooled and hardened can be seen from the hilltops around Goma. Villages have been rebuilt either on or near the lava, and just as people regrouped after 1977, they have done so again since 2002.

From the base camp in Kibati, the hike begins through about an hour of high forests; birdlife and small mammals have begun to return to this area after being scared away by the eruption. After an hour you arrive at the sight of the first eruptions in 2002, where lava began to emerge from the side of the volcano. The lava here is in scattered chunks, and unstable. From here to the main crater called Shaheru is about an hour-and-a-half of hiking up a steep slope. There are casts of trees here, buried by the lava, sticking out from the mountainside. Further up is the biggest lava flow, where most of the lava crashed down the mountainside. After this is the fissure which was created by volcanic activity back in 1977 and remained open until the 2002 eruption.

This is generally the halfway point of the hike, and a rest spot. Above here is the original vegetation of the region, or least that which has survived between eruptions. Huge heather trees up to 5m in height punctuate the side of the volcano from here. The heat begins to become noticeable, and many smaller plants have a burned look to them, covered in ash.

There are cabins at the foot of the volcano, 3,200m above sea level, and often used by the guides and porters as refuge. After these huts the trail goes up a steep slope of rock to reach the crater, at 3,425m. The crater is 1.2km in diameter, and 700m deep. Most visitors camp on the side of the crater, which allows for better viewing at night. Your guide will pick out a spot where gases are not going to be a problem.

Often the crater can be covered in cloud and steam, for hours or even days. When it does clear the undulating lava is a sight to behold, and the red light emanating from the crater can be seen for many kilometres in every direction.

Getting there and away Beginning a hike up Nyiragongo begins at **Kibati** (⊕ *01°34.10 S, 29°16.44 E*), 17km from Goma on the road north to Kiwanja. Permits are sold for US$100 per person, which allows for several days on the mountain. A guide is assigned to each hiking group, and he asks for US$6 per day – this is all he should be given. Porters are available, and they ask for the same price. The ascent takes around five hours. Most visitors spend the night and return to Kibati the following day.

The easiest way to reach here is by hiring a motorbike, which should cost less than US$5 one-way. The problem is that upon returning, there are no bikes waiting, and no mobile-phone reception to call someone in town to send one! Tour companies are hoping to hire a few motorbike drivers for this trip. Try arranging a return time with a driver if you can, a few days later, and tip him if he actually shows up. Another option is taking the frequent minibuses from Goma to Kiwanja and getting off here, which should cost less than US$2.

Also at the foot of the mountain is the Goma Volcano Observatory, a research centre that monitors Nyiragongo's activity. There is a small information centre here, and on occasion researchers are available to answer questions.

Mount Nyamulagira (3,058m) This volcano is possibly more active than Nyiragongo, though as it sits just behind its more famous and slightly taller neighbour these eruptions rarely evolve into critical situations which drive out huge numbers of residents in Goma. Nyamulagira once had a lake of lava like Nyiragongo, but it drained in 1938 after a massive eruption. It has erupted dozens of times since: in 2002, 2004, and most recently at the end of 2006. Lava flowed down the volcano but did not come near Goma. It may have damaged vegetation in the nearby Tongo Sanctuary, however.

DIAN FOSSEY

The eminently famous gorilla researcher Dian Fossey began her career in the Congo at probably the worst possible time to do so. During the incursions of white mercenaries into the east, the rise of Mobutu Sésé Seko, and persistent tribal conflict across the region, she set up a small camp at the foot of Mount Mikeno in Albert Park (now Virunga National Park). It was not long until she was detained, as Mobutu, having recently taken control of the army, began a crackdown on all foreigners inside the country assuming they were spies. Her camp was dismantled and she was taken down to Rumangabo, where she was held for two weeks. Reports of her treatment vary wildly, and so does the story of how she left Congo – by her accounts she was denied permission to leave and escaped through Bunagana, aided by a friendly priest; by other accounts she was formally kicked out. At any event she spent fewer than six weeks in the country as the security situation disintegrated further.

She would begin her research again on the Rwandan side of Mount Mikeno, which brought her the legendary status she now maintains. Yet her work and foundation have done much to assist in the protection of Congolese gorillas, making a positive impact on conservation efforts in both Virunga and Kahuzi-Biega parks.

Most biographies of Dian Fossey deal in some depth with her time in the Congo during the 1960s. Her autobiography, *Gorillas in the Mist,* also turned into a movie starring Sigourney Weaver, touches on her initial difficulties in the Congo. Also worth reading is the *Dark Romance of Dian Fossey*, which spends a dozen pages explaining the factors that led to her leaving the country. It's also worth visiting the website of her foundation, the Dian Fossey Gorilla Fund International (*www.gorillafund.org*).

The volcano used to be a popular hike with tourists, and had some guesthouses along the trail. Its ascent time is much the same as Nyiragongo, taking one day to the top and another day to descend, but the trail has been destroyed by lava, and ICCN could not confirm when it would reopen. Permits are sold in **Rumangabo** (✪ *01°20.39 S, 29°21.30 E*), a few dozen kilometres along the road north from the Kibati station for Nyiragongo.

There used to be a road heading to the foot of Nyamulagira, but any trace of it has been erased by numerous eruptions. Instead the mountain is only accessible by foot – a seven-hour hike.

Djomba and the mountain gorillas The volcanoes which make up the border between Uganda, Rwanda and the Democratic Republic of Congo are the last great place on the planet to see mountain gorillas. Their habitat has been eroded over many decades to the point of their near extinction, but concerted efforts from local populations to keep various groups from killing them have kept their numbers mostly intact.

Of course, the primate population is a shadow of its former self. Several decades ago there were literally thousands of mountain gorillas on the slopes of these volcanoes; now there are roughly 300.

Usually, you will only need to hike for a few hours to find a mountain gorilla group. It's the region's best-kept secret for this kind of trekking, as most tourists have still been turned off by constant warnings regarding the security situation in the country.

Tourists usually head out in a group of eight with trackers and guards. It is easily possible to stay in the volcanoes for several days at a time to view the gorillas, as lodging is available at two separate sites. If you're interested in mountain gorillas, visiting the DR Congo side of the volcanoes is certainly the best place to see them – and your presence will help anti-poaching efforts in the country.

The largest gorilla group in the Virunga volcanoes is the Kibirizi group, of around 32 individuals, and this group found recent fame as they were discovered entering and exiting a local cave. Gorillas normally do not dwell in subterranean enclaves, so this was big news in gorilla-research circles.

Getting there and away The DR Congo section of the volcanoes has two main sites, at **Djomba** and **Bukima**.

Bukima is accessible by a road just south of **Rumangabo** at the village of **Rugari** (✪ *01°24.44 S, 29°22.24 E*). The road winds eastward up into the mountains for 15km and is usually done in a private vehicle, but if you don't mind walking then it is quite simple to take the Goma-Rutshuru (Kiwanja) bus and ask them to let you off at Rugari. The trip should cost around US$2. For the Djomba Lodge head to **Bunagana** (✪ *01°17.57 S, 29°35.47 E*) where either a motorbike or private transport can take you south to the site. It's best to co-ordinate this with the Jambo Safaris office (see page 199) right on the border if you are freshly arrived from Uganda, as they will have the best advice on getting up to the lodge. Djomba used to be a hub for gorilla-trekking tours in Virunga and had several other accommodation options available, which means in the future there may be some cheaper alternatives at the site.

Practicalities Djomba is much more organised for tourists, with a lodge (*basic shared rooms, 4 people to each room, b/fast inc; sgl $$; it is also possible to rent out the entire room at $$$$*). There are also basic camping facilities being set up at Bukima (*US$5 with your own tent, US$10 with tent inc*). The site is basic but has a washroom, and food (Congolese dishes) will be available. Permits are generally sold in Goma

Sara Evans

Since 1996, over 100 Congo Rangers have lost their lives protecting wildlife in Virunga National Park. Many others have been kidnapped and mutilated. It's not just poachers who make life so dangerous for the rangers that work here, it's also the presence and activities of armed rebel groups who use the park as a hideout.

Although the civil war may have been officially over since 2003, renegade militia (both Congolese factions and rebel groups from neighbouring Rwanda and Uganda) continue to use the Virungas both as a battle and hunting ground. With its sweeping forests for camouflage and abundant wildlife for poaching, the Virungas offer obvious attractions to the rebels.

Hidden deep in the forests, rebels have easy access to all sorts of wildlife for both filling their own bellies and for selling on as bushmeat elsewhere; the fact that some of the animals they hunt are endangered species does not suppress their appetites.

Twenty years ago, the park's Lake Edward was once home to the world's most important hippo stocks. Then, there were almost 30,000 of them; now there are estimated to be just 300. The decimation of the hippo population has been largely attributed to prolonged rebel activity around the group.

One rebel group – the Mayi-Mayi – have planned the slaughter of the lake's hippos with almost military precision. During 2006, unchallenged and in broad daylight, Mayi-Mayi rebels aboard motorboats armed with AK47s moved from pod to pod shooting hippo until the waters of Lake Edward turned red with their blood. Meat and ivory (from the animal's long canine teeth) was then sold, with the profits used to purchase more arms. This was neither an unusual nor an isolated incident.

Such scenes might seem impossible to imagine happening in a national park elsewhere, but the Virunga National Park is far from typical. Against thousands of armed rebels, over 3,000 square miles of jungle, forest and savanna, and the wildlife within it, is protected by only 640 rangers.

Hugely outnumbered, with no military training or weapons and access to just one off-road vehicle, in the Virungas just defending patrol posts and staying alive is the biggest challenge facing the Congo Rangers. Little wonder that hippo, elephant and buffalo numbers in the park were able to fall so low.

Recognising the impossible odds stacked up against the rangers in their efforts to protect endangered wildlife, a collaborative initiative between the EU, the Frankfurt Zoological Society (FZS) and Wildlife Direct (formerly known as the African Conservation Fund) was set up to help relieve the situation in 2006.

or Bunagana at any of the tour operators, and cost US$300 for a day of guided trekking. This may change, however, with rumours of ICCN pushing the permit cost up to US$400. The price rise will coincide with whatever happens in Rwanda or Uganda, who have both indicated that they will be raising their own trekking permits into the US$500 stratosphere. The intention in the DR Congo is to keep permits around US$100 cheaper than their neighbours.

Pack warm clothing, as the volcanoes in Virunga are high – there is **Mount Mikeno** (4,437m) near Bukima, **Mount Muside** (3,000m), **Mount Sabinyo** (3,634m) and **Mount Karisimbe** (4,507m). The average elevation of a trek is at least 2,000m. These volcanoes can also be shrouded in cloud and moisture, making packing rain gear a good idea. Finally, and perhaps obviously, bring some solid hiking shoes. You may see the Congolese wandering around the mountainside in sandals, but I guarantee you won't want to do the same thing yourself.

Robert Muir, the DR Congo project leader with the FZS, explains: 'In their work protecting wildlife in the Virungas, the Congo Rangers haven't lacked commitment or bravery – they've lacked training and tools. Our mission has been to help fill the gaps in the rangers' resources and provide practical support in the provision of training and equipment.'

Support first materialised in the form of training by professional military officers from Britain and South Africa. During training, 52 rangers were selected for further intensive instruction. Of these, 49 got through the course and were divided into three troops. Equipped with their own uniforms, vehicles and rifles, these men are known as Advance Force Rangers.

These elite rangers are meant to be deployed in emergency situations only. In the Virungas this means they work non-stop. Although poaching by rebels has been reduced and many arrests have been made, the situation remains tenuous.

Left virtually to their own devices by the government, rebels still rule the Virungas. Gorillas have been killed and eaten and although the Mayi-Mayi did agree in January 2007 to leave the gorillas alone, threats are still made to wipe out the species in the park. Rangers are still killed and maimed.

In May 2007, the Burusi Patrol Post in the eastern section of the Virungas was raided by the Mayi-Mayi. One ranger was killed on the spot, the pregnant wife of another ranger died later from her injuries, three were seriously injured and 13 kidnapped. Weapons and communications equipment were also taken.

Better equipped and better trained, the Congo Rangers have more of a fighting chance than ever before. But they still face incredible risks. To fully protect the wildlife that inhabits the world's most dangerous national park, more men, more training and more equipment are still needed. Until the rebels are either assimilated into the regular army or leave the Virungas, the Advanced Forces of the Congo Rangers must continue to operate in full-time emergency mode.

The Congo Rangers need funds for vital and basic equipment including boots, uniforms, vehicles and communications equipment as well as for medical costs for injured rangers and their families. To find out more about donating as well as donating online, see www.wildlifedirect.org.

For background information on the various conservation projects in the Virunga National Park and to read blogs posted by members of the Congo Rangers, see www.wildlifedirect.org. To find out more about the work of the Frankfurt Zoological Society, see www.zgf.de.

Tongo Chimpanzee Reserve This is in fact a sanctuary for chimpanzees and sits just west of Virunga National Park, occupying roughly 200ha of land in thick bounding vegetation that covers the volcanic soil at the foot of Nyamulagira. Most of this growth is only a few centuries old, covering new lava flows as they descend down the mountainside. The chimpanzees here have been seen fashioning tools and have been studied by numerous primatologists. Luckily, they have not been heavily targeted by poachers as have the mountain gorillas. The entire area has significant populations of chimpanzee, as well as various species of monkey and baboon. Larger game sometimes migrates here from the Rwindi Plains, though it's unlikely a visitor will encounter it.

The sanctuary began in 1987 with the Frankfurt Zoological Society (*www.zgf.de*) as they identified a threatened group of chimpanzees in southern Virunga and began to monitor them. The practice of harvesting brush for charcoal production, common across Africa, was reducing their available habitat. The society worked with ICZN (Institut Zaïrois pour la Conservation de la Nature), predecessor of the ICCN to ensure that they would have a protected area. The intention was also to habituate these chimpanzees for tourism, creating a financial lifeline to keep the reserve in operation. A network of trails was created throughout the forest, trackers followed the chimpanzee groups, and eventually made them comfortable with a human presence. An experimental tourist project was opened at the end of 1989, and this was the first part of the world where tourists could see habituated groups of chimpanzees in the wild. The tourism industry helped supplant the charcoal industry, and with the co-operation of local villages the surrounding vegetation saw less destruction. Of course the situation worsened in the region, and by 1993 the tourist industry had evaporated and the sanctuary had been encroached upon; ICCN kept some rangers in the sanctuary, but much of the work done today is an attempt to get back to where the sanctuary was in 1992.

The chimpanzees are free to roam around the park as they see fit; this means that if tourists wish to see them, they must set out in the morning, much in the same spirit of gorilla trekking, and go searching. The trails have not been properly maintained, which means this is not a simple walk in the park; bring some decent shoes and a daypack.

Practicalities Tongo once had a great tourist infrastructure, but these days you're hard pressed to find somewhere to sleep in the area. The nearby village at the foot of the sanctuary may have a place to stay, otherwise the sanctuary is best done as a day trip from **Kiwanja** (Rutshuru). Generally a motortaxi ride there and back should be around US$20. The park asks for US$20 admission from each visitor, and they should have a guide who can help find the chimpanzees. The road to the park is halfway between Kiwanja and Rumangabo, and crosses west through Virunga across thick vegetation and the northern limits of Nyamulagira's lava plain. It is quite likely that you will see some monkeys, baboons and maybe even chimpanzees on the road along the way.

Rwindi Plains The plains are a beautiful savanna valley surrounded by towering mountains to their west and east, and Lake Edward to the north. It feels like a slice of Katanga dropped on the far eastern border, with rolling grasslands and long periods of sunlight. Winding streams amongst the plains create ideal refuges for hippo populations. Lion, leopard and elephant also thrive here.

Poaching and rebel activity have taken their toll on populations in Rwindi. Animal populations that used to be in the thousands now are often in the hundreds. This is true for big game that is often targeted by illegal hunting, and the elephant population is said to hover around only 400 at the moment. Hippos are at dangerously low levels, a shocking decline as in the past streams were literally clogged with them. When I passed through, the area had massive antelope populations and the road was often blocked by groups of baboons. There have been confirmed sightings of lions, but as they are nocturnal and the area is vast, seeing one is unlikely. Waterbuck, buffalo, jackal and warthog are also common in the area.

The plains occupy several hundred square kilometres and have dozens of vehicle trails criss-crossing the savanna. It is possible to head to **Vitshumbi** (⊕ *00°41.57 S, 09°22.26 E*) to view bird and hippo populations in addition to plains animals when the region is deemed safe. While hippo can sometime be seen along the river, Lake Edward is their usual haunt. Ishango tends to be a better option for viewing them, however.

On the road northwest towards Kanyabayonga the track winds up the mountains and provides an excellent panorama of the entire plains. There is a

plaque here that commemorates the building of the road, replacing an old trade route used by caravans. The road was completed in 1931, and 2007 may be the first time it has seen any maintenance.

Practicalities The **Rwindi Lodge** (✆ *00°47.20 S, 29°17.34 E*) is accessible by minibus from Kiwanja (Rutshuru), a half-day's journey at most. At the time of writing it was being renovated. It has about a dozen private thatch bungalows that date back to the days of Belgian Congo, and a main structure where meals are served, as well as a bar and pool. ICCN is also in the process of rebuilding the road network around the plains for wildlife viewing. The bungalows will likely be expensive, at around US$75 per night. This will be on top of the normal permit, which should be US$70 each day for guided vehicle tours. Camping is also available nearby for a mere US$5 per night. For further information, contact a tour operator in Goma or email ICCN's Rwindi base directly (✉ *larwindi@yahoo.fr*).

At the time of writing, Rwindi is still the most problematic area of all Virunga's regions to enjoy. The main north–south road from Kiwanja, to the lodge, then north to **Kanyabayonga** is lined with soldiers – the chances are your bus will slow down and someone will hand each soldier some money. They're protecting you against not only any wild animals that might cross the road, but also from both remaining rebel groups – who, unfortunately, have taken up residence in the northern parts of Rwindi. The plains are a minor staging ground on the road northeast of Kiwanja in the vicinity of **Ishasha** (✆ *00°44.26 S, 29°37.22 E*) near the Ugandan border, but this area is very insecure as it is one of the last strongholds for Interahamwe in eastern DR Congo. Rumours continue of Mayi-Mayi rebels in the vicinity of Vitshumbi, and park rangers have been battling with them as they stage raids on their buildings, seizing equipment and food. Stick to the western area around Rwindi Lodge until someone can advise you otherwise.

Mount Tshiaberimu (2,848m) Incorporated into Virunga National Park in 1938 and once called Kiavirumu or 'mountain of the spirit', this is a unique ecological zone in the Albertine Rift – and the most important area of flora in the hills west of Lake Edward. The lowland vegetation of bamboo forest gives way to deep coniferous foliage and patches of flowers at higher altitudes. This mountain southeast of Butembo, with views of Lake Edward, is a beautiful sight in its own right in the impressive eastern ranges along the border. However, most importantly it is the home of mountain gorillas, one group of which was habituated to human presence in 2001. At last count there were 22 gorillas and one was born in 2006 – he was called 'Musomboli', Swahili for 'Voter', as he was born in August that year when the Congolese were going to the polls.

As is often the case in the DR Congo, the gorilla population here has taken a nosedive in recent decades. The original survey of gorilla populations here in 1931 put their numbers at 20,000 – while widely considered to be an overestimation, the reduction in numbers is still drastic. A 1963 survey which counted 80 individuals seems more realistic. This major depopulation is more unfortunate than usual since the gorillas of this mountain boast unique features; research is ongoing as to whether they are lowland gorillas, proper mountain gorillas, or a unique subspecies. They have even been given their own scientific name, *Gorilla gorilla tshiaberimuensis*. The altitude of their habitat is above 2,800m; it is considered the smallest isolated gorilla population in the world.

Good news does exist in Tshiaberimu, however, as a decade's worth of conservation efforts have led to the local population, the gorilla's biggest threat, reducing their incursions into the remaining wilderness. The gorillas were originally identified as being at risk in 1995, when they numbered only 17.

Tourism has been established as a primary goal to drive home the value of these creatures to the economic well-being of the surrounding population in addition to retaining their natural heritage.

Practicalities Mount Tshiaberimu can be reached from a winding road southeast of Butembo. The central taxi stand is also a good place to hire out a car for the day, and should cost around US$50. The road is not good, however, and it will likely be easier with motorbikes – the distance is only a few dozen kilometres, so it shouldn't be too painful. First you need to reach the village of **Burusi**, then 12km later follow a connecting road to reach the base camp called **Kalibina** where there is some basic accommodation. There is also a winding road for 46km here along Lake Edward from Ishango, though this will take longer and transport is not as easy to find.

At the foot of the mountain there is an ICCN station were permits are sold, for US$250 a day. As usual this includes a guide and armed guards. They only accept six visitors each day, and prior bookings can be made in Beni or Ishango.

Ishango (✪ *00°08.14 S, 29°36.10 E*) Following the River Semuliki southward along a road from the Beni–Kasindi border into Virunga National Park, you arrive at the quiet northern shores of Lake Edward. This area has not been caught in nearly as much combat as the southern coast, though in recent years has still had problems with rebel activity. It is known as a prime spot for birdwatching, as several species migrate here at various times of the year. This is also a great place to get some photographs of hippos and elephants. Be careful about swimming, however, as hippos are incredibly aggressive and the prime killer of humans in the area.

The countryside around Ishango is home to many of the same animals as can be seen in Rwindi, including elephants, antelope and baboon. Some of the more common birds found in the region are eagles, herons, cormorants, storks and pelicans. When the skies are clear there are great views of the mountains that line the western shore of Lake Edward, as well as the Ruwenzoris to the north. Fishing tours are also popular here, or another option is to visit the village of **Kiavinyonge**, immediately west of Ishango (✪ *00°09.08 S, 29°33.17 E*) where the villagers go out every morning on their boats.

Practicalities Ishango is reached from **Kasindi** (✪ *00°02.33 N, 29°42.52 E*) on the Ugandan border, and is along a 30km road south from the main road to **Beni**. From Beni it is quite feasible to reach here as well, but via motorbike, unless walking the 30km from the main road sounds like fun – there should be a minibus service soon, direct to the border from Beni. The **Ishango Lodge** is run by ICCN and has about eight bungalows here; at the last check it was open for business. They charge US$50 per person for a visitor's permit, and the lodge is US$25 per night.

THE RUWENZORI MOUNTAINS

The Ruwenzori range is Africa's most mysterious. Generations of explorers passed them by without noticing, as they are often shrouded in cloud. It was not until 1888 that Henry Morton Stanley, at the foot of the mountains on a clear day, noted them in European records.

Unlike the volcanoes only a few hundred kilometres south, the Ruwenzoris are not volcanic in nature. They were created by the Albertine Rift, tectonic plates pushing up against each other in Africa's Great Lakes region. These are the only mountains in Africa with glaciers. The continent's other highest peaks, Kilimanjaro and Mount Kenya, see regular snowfall, but permanent icepacks elude them. In the Ruwenzoris you ascend above the cloud cover to a different world entirely – strange primeval vegetation grows to unreal sizes in the higher elevations. Often frozen lakes provide freshwater streams to villages below. Unique birdlife is in abundance across the mountainsides. And some of Africa's most difficult climbs are on Mount Stanley.

The range has been well developed for tourism, and is seeing a resurgence in interest due to its proximity to the Ugandan border and a well-marked trail to two peaks. The highest peak, Margherita, is still very much for experienced alpinists, however.

HISTORY The Ruwenzoris were the famous 'mountains of the moon' that traders from ancient times spoke of when arriving in Egypt from sub-Saharan Africa. Ptolemy included them in his map of Africa during the 2nd century; they were widely considered to be the source of the Nile River until the mid 20th century.

The range was first spotted by people in Henry Morton Stanley's company when he passed through the region in April 1888 during his expedition to rescue Emin Pasha. Two members of Stanley's expedition, Mounteney Jephson and Thomas Parke, saw the glaciers of the range in the distance after assuming them to be unusual clouds. They recorded the mountains and reported them to Stanley. Up until this time, the existence of the Ruwenzoris had been in doubt.

It was not until Stanley's company returned to the region with Emin Pasha that they attempted a summit. Emin Pasha and Stanley's military commander, William Grant Stairs, began the climb in June 1889. They began in Katuba, but lacked the proper equipment to reach the summit, and departed after arriving at the 3,200m mark.

In 1891, Emin Pasha returned with a Dr Franz Stuhlmann in tow to make another attempt on the mountains. It was on this ascent that they confirmed the mountains crossed the glaciers and ascended the peak they called Mount Stanley. They had a camp at the base of the mountains, in the valley of Butahu, which they nicknamed the 'Camp of Bottles', referred to in local languages as Kampi ya Chuba. It remains a visiting point to this day. They left a bottle here, and subsequent visitors added to the collection.

In 1906, the Duke of Abrizzi, an Italian, came well prepared with a team that made the first ascents of Margherita. The first attempt from the Belgian side of the mountains did not come until 1932, when a scientific team led by Count Xavier de Grünne arrived. It was on this expedition that the entire range was finally surveyed.

Tourism was big on the Zairian side of the border throughout the reign of Mobutu Sésé Seko, but Mayi-Mayi rebels moved in sometime in the late 1990s which essentially shut down the tourist business. As with most of Virunga, the Ruwenzori Trail reopened for business in 2004.

ORIENTATION The Ruwenzori Mountains run along a south–north axis which forms the border between Uganda and the DR Congo. The range consists of six major mountains, with Mount Stanley being the highest and most important for visitors from the Congolese side. Mount Stanley itself has several smaller ridges; from south to north: **Mugule** (4,450m), **Wasuwameso** (4,420m), and **Moraine** (4350m), which can be visited *en route* to the main peak, **Margherita** (5,109m), Mount Stanley's highest point. Other peaks on Mount Stanley are **Albert** (5,087m), **Alexandra** (5,091m), **Moebius** (4,916m), **Elena** (4,968m), **Savoia** (4,971m), **Elizabeth** (4,928m) and **Philip** (4,920m), from north to south. On a clear day, all are visible from Wasuwameso or Moraine.

The trail up to the peaks is well marked, and reasonably well maintained. It takes three days to reach the **Kiondo Hut**, where the trail splits, to continue to either Wasuwameso ridge for some spectacular views of Mount Stanley and its peaks, weather permitting, or to head east for a day to **Moraine Hut** (4,495m), which passes by some frozen lakes and, while about 100m lower than Wasuwameso, gets closer to Peak Margherita. This is also the staging ground for heading out to the glaciers.

THE TRAIL From the ICCN station at **Mutsora** (1,700m), the first day's walking is through dense scrub forest typical of the lowlands of the Albertine Rift. Huge trees covered in moss begin to envelop the trail as it winds along the valley of the Butahu River, crossing numerous streams as they flow into the river from their originating points along Mount Mugule. It takes roughly five hours to reach the first hut, **Kalonge** (2,138m). From the hut there are striking views of the valley to be had.

Continuing onward across another major stream, the Nwamwamba, the trail runs into numerous steep sections, covered in mud and roots and vines, the entire region teeming with thick moss of many colours. The lowland bamboo forests give way to massive heather trees, and the temperature begins to shift drastically as the trail finds its way into the cloud systems that continually blanket the mountains and where the humidity rises significantly. Unique birdlife begins to emerge, and the day ends when arriving at **Mahangu Hut** (3,310m). This is generally considered the hardest part of the trail, and should take around five hours. There is usually fresh water available here from the mountain streams.

From Mahangu the trail continues north into the cold alpine air, and the trail can often get blocked by snowfall. The trail is covered with huge roots of the heather trees and ascends sharply. It is along this stretch of trail that the heather trees shift to the strange, huge flowers that the Ruwenzori range is known for. It's a curious botanical wonderland of beautiful saturated colours, massive foliage of species that most people would assume could only grow as large as a palm and certainly not at these altitudes. This is also where the trail ascends above the near-permanent cloud cover, and the entire region becomes enrobed in a moist fog. Water can be heard flowing under the moss. After about four hours you come to the **Camp of Bottles** (4,030m), the historic staging ground for ascents in the region. Another hour's hiking onward reveals the next hut, **Kiondo** (4,200m), and the trail splits from here. The nights get mighty cold from here on and the hut is often blindsided by high winds. The hut has a beautiful view of **Lac Noir** (Black Lake: 3,757m) to the southeast, down the mountain. There are also great views of other peaks in the region: Alexandra, Moebius, Helena and Savoia.

From Kiondo it is most common to continue the ascent north to **Wasuwameso** (4,510m), only an hour or so along the trail, and take photos of Peak Margherita before descending back to Kiondo – or rushing back to Mahangu, as Kiondo can be an uncomfortable place to spend the night.

If you have a bit more time, from Kiondo you can continue northeast along the trail – crossing a glacier and following the trail along the often frozen lakes, **Lac Vert** (Green Lake: 4,157m) and **Lac Gris** (Grey Lake: 4,253m). This route requires some basic climbing gear – ice-axes, crampons and the like. Part of the trail is quite slippery and requires hanging onto a cable that's been installed. Some guides might not be experienced with this stuff: make sure yours is. The vegetation dissipates into dirt, a clear alpine trail, with the massive flowers seen only a few hundred metres below now disappearing to be replaced mostly by lichen. The hike should take around three hours to the final hut, **Moraine**, a small and beat-up old cabin that visitors dread staying in. There is also room for camping on the shores of Grey Lake, which could be a better option provided you have a tent to pitch.

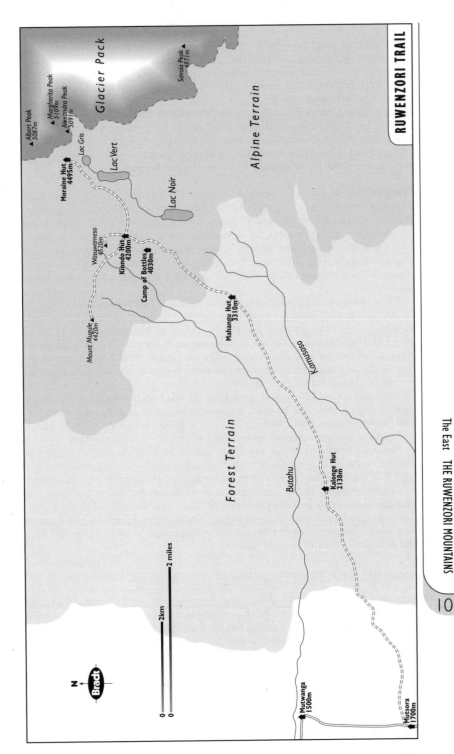

RUWENZORI TRAIL

Glacier Pack

Albert Peak
5087m ▲
Margherita Peak
5109m ▲
Alexandra Peak
5091m ▲
Savoia Peak
4971m ▲

Lac Gris
Lac Vert
Moraine Hut 4495m ♠
Lac Noir

Alpine Terrain

Wasuwameso
4520m ▲
Kiondo Hut
4200m ♠
Camp of Bottles
4030m ♠

Mount Mugule
4420m ▲

Mahangu Hut
3310m ♠

Kamusoso

Forest Terrain

Butahu

Kalonge Hut
2138m ♠

N

Bradt

2km
0

2 miles
0

Mutwanga
1500m ♠

Mutsora
1700m ♠

This can be done in a round trip for the day, finishing again at Kiondo, or if you're really quick about it, spending the night in Mahangu. The descent from Mahangu to Mutsora should take only a full day.

Beyond Moraine are the permanent glaciers, as well as the climbing routes to reach Peak Alexandra and Peak Margherita, and are definitely not intended for hikers. The permanent glacier begins at about 4,800m, an hour's hike from the Moraine Hut. Continue north along the base of Peak Alexandra, with Peak Albert coming into view. Between Alexandra and Albert is the Congolese route to Peak Margherita, by all accounts harder than the Ugandan route. It is also possible to continue east between the Alexandra and Moebius peaks to reach Margherita from the Ugandan side. From Moraine to the peak is another two days' hiking.

Practicalities For a tour operator, contact **IT Agency** (m *081 961 4254; www.itagency.com*) who can arrange trips up the Ruwenzori Mountains as well as rent out vehicles to visit Ishango. They also have an office in Kasindi. They charge US$660 for a six-day trip up the mountains, and this should include a hike to Moraine Hut. This includes porters, heaters, and transport to Mutsora. They can also rent out climbing equipment from either office: boots, crampons, harnesses, ropes, sleeping bags, and so on, from US$3 to US$10 for the hike, depending on the item.

From Beni or Kasindi you must get to the village of **Mutwanga** (✪ *00°20.27 N, 29°44.59 E*) at the foot of the mountains and then continue a few kilometres up a vanishing and rocky route to the ICCN station at **Mutsora** (✪ *00°19.03 N, 29°44.45 E*). Mutsora is seeing an infusion of money which includes major renovations to their once-dilapidated offices as well as several bungalows at the foot of the mountain. From here you can buy a permit at US$100 per person for the ascent. This should include a guide, though I have a hunch he'll want some tips later on, and it's unlikely he will speak English. The huts have fireplaces and bunk beds, though Kiondo and Moraine are in desperate need of some maintenance. If you can bring some plastic to hang over the windows, which are often broken, it will make your sleeping much easier. Bring a mummy-style sleeping bag.

Naturally if you are doing any hiking off the main trail, such as making an attempt on Peak Margherita, you'll need to pack in all of your equipment – as you may have guessed, there is no mountaineering store in either Mutwanga or Beni. If you are going to spend some serious time on the mountains I recommend picking up the book by Henry Osmaston, *Guide to the Rwenzori: Mountains of the Moon*. Also pick up a detailed elevation map with climbing routes, such as *Rwenzori Map and Guide*, published in 1989 but still very relevant. It can be purchased from the publisher's website (*www.ewpnet.com*).

KIWANJA (RUTSHURU) ✪ 01°11.36.54 S, 29°26.52.61 E

Rutshuru is in fact a district, comprising the space between the border of Uganda and Virunga National Park to the west. Most maps use Rutshuru as a marker point for the collection of villages that makes up the most densely populated region of the district. The largest village you pass through in the district is Kiwanja, and is the proper capital of Rutshuru district. It's a simple one-road town with large trucks parked on the roadside in the evenings, with sprawling suburbs of dirt trails and mud huts stretching into the jungle. It's also a good place to catch a minibus further north to Kanyabayonga, Lubero and Butembo, or east to Bunagana.

Near Kiwanja are the **Rutshuru Falls**, buried in the jungle on a turn-off from the main road to Goma, just past the road east to Bunagana. At 30km north on the road to the Rwindi Plains Lodge is the volcano of **May Ya Moto** (950m), whose underground geothermal activity has created some **hot springs** along the river to the right of the road. These are not the relaxing beach-type hot springs championed in other tourist guides, but rather the underground heat activity here creates boiling mud and extremely hot water. Wear your bathing suit somewhere else.

GETTING THERE AND AWAY See Virunga practicalities on page 186.

WHERE TO STAY AND EAT For lodging, the newest place in town is just past the park checkpoint and is called **Busanza Guesthouse** (*10 rooms;* m *081 056 5145;* e *busanzagh@yahoo.fr; sgl $, camping US$3*). These are easily the best rooms in town with private baths and running water. **Hôtel Grefamu** on the north end of town just off the main road is the oldest place in town and certainly looks like it. Rooms are basic but have mosquito nets and either shared bathrooms for a mere US$6 or private bathrooms, with running water, for US$16. Further down the quality scale is **Mulende Hôtel** on the main road where the rooms have no bathrooms or nets for US$3. Across the street is **Hôtel Kathatha** (22 rooms) for US$5, with no private bathrooms. They have three double rooms for US$10 and three apartments for US$15. There is also a restaurant here, and another one a short distance to the south, with fish dishes for US$2.

Finally the **Centre d'Accueil Protestant** has more simple rooms for US$7, and if you get there on a Saturday, there is usually a wedding going on – try to be the guest of honour and get a free drink.

BUNAGANA ✪ 01°17.57 S, 29°35.47 E

This small village at the foot of a volcano could be your first taste of the DR Congo, if you have arrived here for gorilla trekking. It's certainly nothing spectacular, little different from the frontier on the other side, criss-crossed with dirt roads and barely any vehicles compared with the relative affluence of Uganda. Hopefully you've stocked up on supplies on the other side of the border; the only things to buy in Bunagana are charge cards for a mobile phone, and fresh fruits.

Jambo Safaris (m *099 772 8103/080 888 8774/+256 782 433 277(Uganda);* e *kwafrica_safaris@yahoo.fr*) have an office right past the border, on the northern side of the road. They can arrange tours to their lodge in Djomba as well as Bukima, and also rent out a vehicle for the day if necessary. It generally isn't, if you are heading strictly to see mountain gorillas – hire a motortaxi instead. Other transportation can be had to Kiwanja, though the most reliable method tends to be hiring a motorbike.

WHERE TO STAY AND EAT **Chez Mama Kennedy** (*6 rooms;* m *099 773 4710;* e *congoguide@yahoo.com*) is right behind the Jambo Safaris office and has basic rooms for US$5, with a shared washroom. They can also cook up some simple meals, and arrange transport up to the trekking sites. A little further into town is a **new hotel** that has fancy trappings like private bathrooms, and they should have some parking available – at the time of writing it was still under construction. If you follow the road west towards Kiwanja the nearby Protestant church in the village of Tshengerero has purchased a **campsite** on the right-hand side of the road, easily noticed by its concrete signage out front. It's in the middle of rolling hills with basic washrooms and a restaurant, and should charge less than US$10 for an evening. While nearly completed, the church was prevaricating on when it may be finished when I visited – perhaps a few tourists passing along the road might give them some incentive to do so.

Butembo is a curious town of riches where there should really be none, a financial centre in a place where you wouldn't imagine it. New office blocks are going up along the wide dirt thoroughfare that cuts through town, and new construction is creating beautiful new mansions in the suburbs with green hills and even, on occasion, well-maintained lawns. Sometimes shining new vehicles dot the otherwise motorcycle-clogged streets of the town. Shops are filled to the brim with sandals and luggage, clothes and cheap electronics from Indonesia. Butembo is one of the DR Congo's most affluent towns, surrounded by almost nothing; an oasis of prosperity in the mountains of the east.

It's a curiosity to be sure, and whiling away your time wondering how all this fancy stuff gets here, after grinding along awful roads for so long, is the main pastime. Here's a hint – the city was the site of a large gold mine in the 1920s, and enjoys the profits from agricultural plantations in the region these days. Perhaps most importantly is that its isolation has helped its prosperity – far from the prying eyes of Kinshasa's often-ineffectual governments, and not on any major invasion routes for the neighbouring armies of Uganda and Rwanda, the hard-working tribes of the surrounding region have been left to their own devices – and have achieved much as a result. It's a lesson that the entire country could learn from.

GETTING THERE AND AWAY Butembo is well served by minibuses from Goma, which come here direct and take one full day. If the going is slow, or the bus gets a flat or three (the road is incredibly rough) they will usually overnight in **Lubero** a few dozen kilometres south. **TMK Air Commuter** (m *099 829 9348*) flies in and out of here on a regular basis to Beni, Bunia and Goma. **Cetraca** also comes into the airport on occasion, usually *en route* to Beni. There are plans to build an international airport with a 3km-long runway near Butembo, financed entirely by local businessmen, which could see regular flights from Uganda and Rwanda arriving here.

 WHERE TO STAY Butembo has a string of good hotels.

Expensive

⌂ **Auberge de Butembo** (13 rooms) m 081 305 2534/099 838 6655; e auberge.butembo@ laposte.net. Situated on a hilltop amongst well-preened lawns, with secure parking & an architectural style of an old central African lodge. Rooms are comfortable enough with cold running water & TV. There is also a good restaurant. If you have your own camping supplies, they will let you stay on their property for US$5 per night. $$

⌂ **Hôtel Butembo** Right in the city centre with plenty of secure parking & a large restaurant serving 3 meals a day. It's a new place & the rooms have plenty of shiny tiles & clean furniture. The rooms are in a courtyard that sits several metres in from the main road, making it more quiet than expected. $$

Mid-range

⌂ **Centre d'Accueil Joli Rêve** About 1km south; m 099 709 7006, All rooms have AC, private bathroom, & there is some parking at the back. There is also a small restaurant. $$

Budget

⌂ **Hôtel Oasis** On the south end of the main road, is similar to the Semuliki & has a small restaurant. Sgl $

⌂ **Hôtel Semuliki** (23 rooms) At the north end of the city; m 099 777 6361. An ageing yellow concrete structure with simple rooms & occasional running water. They also have a decent restaurant & some room for secure parking. Sgl $, dbl $$

PRACTICALITIES There are two places for **Western Union** on the main boulevard: **Union Des Banques Congolaises** (m *098 204 965;* ⊕ *07.00–16.00 Mon–Fri*) and **BCDC** (m *083 500 1083;* ⊕ *08.00–16.00 Mon–Fri, 08.00–12.00 Sat*).

BENI ⊕ *00°29.32 N, 29°28.16 E*

Situated in a lowland region of the Great Rift Valley which divides the DR Congo from its eastern neighbours, Beni's surrounding countryside shows hints of the deep Ituri rainforest which envelopes the region just a few dozen kilometres north. It's not as cold as Butembo or Lubero, with warm nights that can be spent in a few nightclubs around the city.

This is the northern capital of Virunga National Park, an administrative centre on the very fringes of North Kivu Province. It is perhaps one of the most tourist-friendly towns in the country, and in the past saw plenty of visitors plying the overland route around the park and onward into Uganda. Beni is an easy place to be, with a more laidback kind of atmosphere than the conflict-ridden regions of the country elsewhere. However, it remains a simple town with a single north–south road where visitors can find pretty much everything they may want.

GETTING THERE AND AWAY Beni's airport is a busy one, being the hub for **Cetraca**, from where you can get to Bunia and Kisangani on a regular basis. **TMK Air Commuter** (m *099 839 8575*) do their milk run into Beni at least once each day, giving you the chance to head south to Goma. There are also occasional flights to Kampala on charter aircraft.

Shared taxis head to Butembo every 15 minutes, taking two hours and costing around US$3. Heading north or east is far more problematic, and is generally done by hiring a motortaxi for a long-distance ride. This is your best option for reaching Kasindi, Mutwanga or Ishango. There are regular trucks from **Oicha** (⊕ *00°41.49.17 N, 29°31.04.27 E*), 25km north of Beni, to Bunia – but only twice a week, on market days. There are also regular minibuses to Bunia from Beni, though they leave incredibly early and still have not settled on a fixed schedule. Check out the shared taxi stand on the south end of town for information on when the next bus might be leaving in this direction.

WHERE TO STAY AND EAT The best place to stay in town is **Hôtel Beni** (m *099 770 5249; sgl/dbl* $$) which is the only hotel with regular electricity. It's been recently renovated and has a newly paved parking area out front and one of the city's better restaurants, in addition to a small garden. They also sell a few things that no-one else does in town such as mosquito repellent. A second choice would be **Hôtel Source Kasungulu** (m *099 432 7477; sgl/dbl* $) which has shared bathrooms with running water and electricity for a few hours each night. Their restaurant is also above average, though has some unreliable hours. Pretty much the same is **Centre d'Accueil Vanzwa** (m *081 305 1584; sgl/dbl* $) near the south side of the city.

For cheaper beds in town try **Hôtel Majestic** (*4 rooms; sgl* $), whose rooms are of questionable quality and is right behind a rowdy nightclub. You may find yourself spending all that saved money on booze to drown out the noise. Also in the lower range is **Hôtel Sinamakosa** (*sgl* $) on the road to Kasindi, and nearby is **Hôtel Au Bercail** (m *081 152 0351; sgl US$5, dbl US$10*) with no amenities to speak of aside from a door that locks.

Aside from the hotel's restaurants, near the main roundabout on the north end of the city are **Okapi** ($$) and **Majestic** ($$), which usually serve fish dishes in addition to being watering holes after dark. **Snack Wimpy Pizzeria** ($$) sits on a terrace beside these restaurants and serves up the same foods as well as pizza.

An interesting detail of the DR Congo's hinterlands, is the millions of cast-off pieces of clothing that have made their way to a final resting place of sorts deep in the jungle. Being something of a hotbed for inexpensive textiles labour (and all that entails), as well as a country that receives large shipments of aid from the world at large, the Congolese dress themselves in the gifts given to them – which more often than not are the pieces of clothing that no-one wants.

It becomes obvious that these people do not know, or even care, what may appear on their shirts and clothes. This is something interesting in a country where so many people pay close attention to their appearance; but the DR Congo's poorest cannot even indulge in that luxury.

In Beni some years ago I encountered a younger fellow wearing a Home Depot shirt, intended as a uniform for employees there; it had a patch stencilled onto it, proudly sporting the name 'Matt'. His name was, indeed, not Matt; and he had no idea what Home Depot was in the first place. It was simply a clean shirt, one he bought at the market, for a low price.

Numerous other relics of Western culture pop up on the backs of the Congolese: television shows from the 1980s (*Alf* anyone?), strange Christian jamboree festivals held halfway around the world, excess volunteer shirts for any number of random organisations; shirts from rock bands that have come and gone, shirts from businesses long bankrupt. Their meanings can become bizarre reminders of the global intervention that has always been a hallmark of Congo Free State, and sometimes they can be an inadvertent reminder of how impoverished so many millions of them are. At a refugee camp in Bunia I spotted a man wearing a Nine Inch Nails shirt that on the back read 'Now I'm Nothing'.

Poke around at local market stalls and you'll find cast-offs from parts of the world that one may have never put in the same room as the DR Congo. Ask the people where they got them, and they may simply shrug. It's clothing, and since most of them can't read English, the colours and patterns are far more important than whatever it may mean to a random foreign visitor passing through.

For Western Union visit **BCDC** (m *082 500 1082;* ◷ *08.00–16.00 Mon–Fri, 08.00–12.00 Sat*) on the south end of the main road towards Butembo.

PRACTICALITIES For a tour operator, contact **IT Agency** (m *081 961 4254; www.itagency.com*) who can arrange trips up the Ruwenzori Mountains as well as rent out vehicles to visit Ishango. They also have an office in Kasindi.

BUKAVU ✪ *02°30.05 S, 28°51.25 E*

Situated on a number of hills jutting out into Lake Kivu, Bukavu is easily the most scenic town in the whole of the DR Congo. Old colonial mansions dot the lakeside peninsulas, interrupted by winding dirt roads descending to the shore. Various remnants of Belgium's old colonial past sit overlooking Lake Kivu, known at that time as Costermansville. It was founded in 1901 and named in the honour of Paul Costermans, one of the original architects of the Congo Free State. It has seen some nasty combat during its time – in the late 1960s it was the site of battles between Moise Tshombe's Katangese soldiers, Mobutu Sésé Seko's regular army, and several hundred mercenaries led by Jean Schramme – this was the situation that Dian Fossey (see box, page 188), blissfully unaware of Congolese politics, found herself arriving in before departing the country. Bukavu was again caught up in battle during the late 1990s as the RCD ran through the city, and yet again in 2004 when Laurent Nkunda's troops staged minor attacks in the hills west of the centre. Yet in spite of all this it shows no real scars of combat or displacement on the surface. The town is hidden away in a small bay at the extreme south end of Lake Kivu, rarely having to deal with larger weather patterns that might dominate the open waters.

Increasingly, several high-end hotels have taken up property beside the old mansions as Bukavu aims to regain some status as a lakeside resort, an escape from the busier environment of Goma. Their business comes from those tourists who take the plunge and cross here from Rwanda, or from those who take the *canôt rapides* here. The lifestyle is a little more laidback than the regional capital, though Bukavu was once the main commercial centre for the Kivus. Infrastructure has left the city behind in a way, as the mountainous countryside and lack of road improvement has shifted economic interests in Rwanda and Burundi to the more immediate frontiers of Uvira and Goma. Nonetheless some estimates put Bukavu's population as larger than Goma's, at nearly a million versus 750,000. While an attraction in its own right, Bukavu is best visited as a staging ground for visiting Kahuzi-Biega National Park or Idjwi Island. Both are within a day's journey.

ORIENTATION Bukavu begins officially at the Rwandan border crossing of Ruzizi, near Cyangugu. To get there you need to cross a rickety wooden bridge and walk up a hill to arrive at the far busier Congolese side of the river. While situated on five peninsulas, the main thoroughfare of the island is on the westernmost piece of land jutting out into the lake: **Avenue Lumumba** houses the main seat of government for South Kivu Province as well as most of the city's amenities. Continue west along the lake and there are the boat stations for Idjwi Island and Goma. The **Central Market** area is the crossroads of the city, where all routes meet, and while not great for shopping, is a useful point of reference.

GETTING THERE AND AROUND Bukavu has no real transportation centre. Boats to Goma leave from the western side of the city, including the *canôt rapide* (m 099 413 4060/080 853 8163) service for US$40 one-way. They leave every day except Sundays. Further north are several slow boats to Goma, the cheapest of which costs US$10 and departs at 17.30, arriving the next morning at 07.00. **Bateau *Miss Rafique*** is a mid-class boat which leaves at 07.30 and arrives at 13.00, and has three classes: first class is US$20 for a private bunk; second and third cost US$8 and US$5 respectively.

The **Roundabout and Site of Future Bukavu Monument** before the ports is where you can generally find transportation by road north along the west coast of Lake Kivu. To get to Uvira, you will generally need to take a private taxi to points further south along the Ruzizi River. No minibuses exist – you need to hire a private jeep, or simply ask when (and where) the next truck is leaving. Bukavu has an **airport** quite far from the city, several dozen kilometres to the northwest along the road to Goma. Interestingly enough both **Bravo Air Congo** (*Av Lumumba;* m 099 930 1641) and **Hewa Bora Air** (*Av Lumumba;* m 081 317 6704/099 728 3823) have offices in Bukavu but sell tickets departing from Goma – the airport here is too small for large aircraft, and **TMK Air Commuter** (*Av Lumumba;* m 080 855 8772) is the only airline which offers regular flights from the city. They all stop in Goma, and it is therefore necessary to secure another flight from there for other destinations. **Service Air** (*Av Lumumba*) has an office right beside TMK and offers cargo flights to various

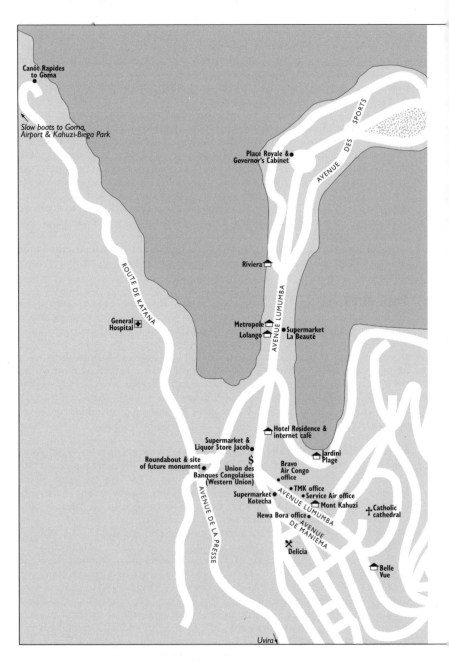

destinations, changing frequently. They can be a good option for some obscure routes such as from Bukavu to Kalemie or Kindu.

WARNING Bukavu receives few tourists, and is host to only a modest crew of Western aid workers. Consequently, there's not much to do. Security is an issue after dark – more so than in Goma. Bukavu has both a high rate of violent crime

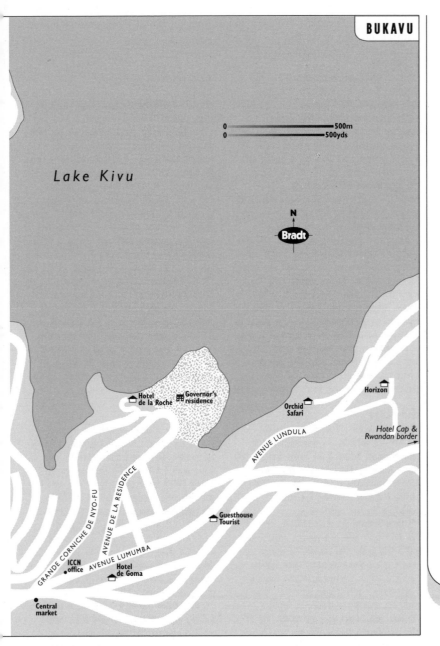

Lake Kivu

0 ————————— 500m
0 ————————— 500yds

N
Bradt

Hotel
de la Roche

Governor's
residence

Orchid
Safari

Horizon

AVENUE LUNDULA

Hotel Cap &
Rwandan border

GRANDE CORNICHE DE NYO-FU

AVENUE DE LA RÉSIDENCE

Guesthouse
Tourist

AVENUE LUMUMBA

ICCN
office

Hotel
de Goma

Central
market

and a loose network of police and presidential guards that go on the prowl for foreigners to shake down.

WHERE TO STAY Bukavu's best hotels are along the lakeside, with **Orchid Safari** getting top marks and **Hôtel de la Roche** not far behind. **Hôtel Résidence** is one of Bukavu's oldest hotels as well as one of its best, though it is right along the city's main thoroughfare. Also at the top end of things is **Hôtel Horizon** on a hilltop with a good view of the lake.

Expensive

🏠 **Hôtel de la Roche** On the lakeside near the Governor's Residence; m 081 069 6262. Large multi-storeyed building constructed right on the lake with a secure parking area & very popular restaurant that juts out into the water. Rooms are excellent with AC, hot running water & satellite TV. There is an open grass space that is popular with local wedding-makers. Sgl $\$\$$, dbl/suite $\$\$\$$

🏠 **Hôtel Horizon** (30 rooms) Av de Goma-Muhumba; m 099 440 6270; e hotelhorizonbkv@ yahoo.fr. Situated on a hilltop on the second easternmost peninsula in Bukavu & recently renovated for a new generation of visitors. It's in a quiet residential neighbourhood with a huge secure parking area. Rooms are sparkling with new shining bathrooms that spit out hot running water like it was a common thing in the Congos, AC, private stocked refrigerators, safety deposit boxes. There is a restaurant on the second level with large plasma TVs & a formal buffet dinner several nights of the week, in addition to a terrace with some great views of both the city & the lake. Suites have their own private balconies. There is also a conference room available, & a games room with pool tables is under

construction. B/fast inc. Sgl/dbl $\$\$\$$, suite $\$\$\$\$$

🏠 **Hôtel Orchid Safari** Av Kahuzi-Biega, at the end of the road; m 081 312 6467; e marcmoreau33@hotmail.com. Bukavu's best hotel these days, a luxury resort kind of place with excellent lakeside views & all-inclusive bungalow-style dbl rooms. They have hot running water, satellite TV, clean sheets & AC. Hugely popular with holidaying NGO & UN staff. The restaurant is one of the best in the city & is high on atmosphere with a definitive decoration reminiscent of an old hunting lodge. There is also a small souvenir shop, & secure parking. 2 classes of rooms. Class A sgl $\$\$\$\$$ & dbl $\$\$\$\$\$$; class B sgl/dbl $\$\$\$\$$

🏠 **Hôtel Résidence** (45 rooms) Av Lumumba; m 081 317 6280/081 317 6352. The second-oldest hotel still operating in Bukavu with numerous old photos & maps of Zaire on its walls. The foyer has the faded grandeur of a colonial past with marble floors, large brass pillars, & an old lift in front of the receptionist's desk. Just inside the hotel is an internet café that is the city's most reliable. Sgl/dbl $\$\$\$$, suite $\$\$\$\$$

Mid-range

🏠 **Hôtel Belle Vue** (19 rooms) Av Lumumba; m 099 778 4636. On the main winding road between central Bukavu & the market area, the Belle Vue is nondescript but good value. Rooms have TVs & occasional running water. The hotel has secure parking & a basic restaurant, & a veranda overlooking the lake. Sgl/dbl $\$\$$

🏠 **Hôtel De Goma** Behind Av Lumumba; m 099 776 7011. Quiet hotel in a pleasant neighbourhood with a lush garden that envelops the entranceway. There is a courtyard with sitting space near the garden as well as a restaurant. A good option for budget boutique-style lodging. Rooms are simple affairs but clean & well maintained. Sgl/dbl $\$\$$

🏠 **Hôtel Jardini Plage** Along the lakeside; m 099 430 3976. Another hillside hotel that can get lively in the evenings with its nightclub, it also has a basic restaurant. Complicated stairways criss-cross each other to several different parts of the building. Rooms are simple affairs with cold running water & mosquito nets. Sgl/dbl $\$\$$

🏠 **Hôtel Metropole** Av Lumumba. No telephone. An ageing throwback of a hotel that looks like it was

abandoned for a decade or so & then reopened without any intention of renovating. Rooms are large but rundown. They have full bathrooms, but the rusted pipes & bathtubs keep the water from flowing. Nonetheless it seems popular with some NGO staff who come through the city. Sgl/dbl $\$\$$

🏠 **Hôtel Mont Kahuzi** Av Lumumba; m 099 402 1806/081 075 0944. A new hotel with plenty of rooms & a good restaurant right in the middle of the airline office neighbourhood. They are quite clean at this point with plenty of new tiles & running water, along with satellite TV. There is some parking at the back. Sgl/dbl $\$\$\$$, apt $\$\$\$\$$

🏠 **Hôtel Riviera** Just off Av Lumumba on the north end of the peninsula; m 081 079 4077. Quiet & tired-looking these days, Bukavu's oldest-running hotel was once a happening place popular with tourists. These days it can best be described as average, with simple rooms that are showing their age. They are large, however, & come with mosquito nets & occasional hot running water. Most have views of the lake. There is a pool as well as a popular restaurant, & parking out front. Sgl/dbl $\$\$$

Budget

⌂ Guesthouse Tourist Av Lumumba; m 099 866 9315. Also called Hôtel Tourist, this is a classic ageing Congolese building with some parking in the back, a simple restaurant in the front, & spartan rooms – they have mosquito nets & intermittent running water. B/fast inc. Sgl $

⌂ Hôtel Cap On the road towards the Ruzizi border crossing; m 099 867 3780. Budget hotel built on a steep slope along the lake, with good views for sitting during the evening. Rooms are communal with space for 7 people, & are rather basic with no extras. Bathrooms have cold running water. Shared spaces $

⌂ Hôtel Lolango Av Lumumba, beside Hôtel Metropole; m 099 400 6826. Very simple accommodation on the main peninsula's thoroughfare with some parking available. Rooms have no running water or TV, & the receptionist's office at the end of an alleyway is missing a front wall. It has a desk, though – & this is the cheapest place to get a room in Bukavu. Sgl/dbl $

✗ WHERE TO EAT Bukavu's culinary scene does not have many independent operations, making hotel restaurants the primary point of interest for those seeking a well-prepared dinner. **Hôtel De La Roche** (⊕ *from 18.00 daily;* **$$$**) on the lakeside is especially popular and welcomes drop-in customers instead of those resident at the hotel. **Hôtel Orchid Safari** (⊕ *from 18.00 daily;* **$$$**) is in the same price bracket, and is the best place to try well-prepared local dishes. **Hôtel Riviera** (⊕ *from 07.00 daily;* **$$**) is slightly cheaper and remains busy in the evenings but serves up Western food only, as well as hideously expensive breakfasts. **Hôtel Mont Kahuzi** (⊕ *from 08.00 daily;* **$$**) is much the same but has a nicer restaurant with attentive staff. For a cheaper option with some lively nightlife, try **Hôtel Jardini Plage** (⊕ *from 18.00 daily;* **$$**). The only real independent restaurant in town is **La Delicia** (m *099 861 1536/080 852 3857;* **$$**) serving up basic Congolese and Western dishes in a spartan air-conditioned dining area. Most of the restaurants close at 23.00.

SHOPPING For groceries the **Supermarché La Beauté** (m *099 772 0075*) on Avenue Lumumba is a good spot to start with the only-in-Congo selection of unchilled juices, sausages, waffles and other imported foodstuffs that could get through the border without paying extortionate bribes. Another good supermarket is further up the hill at **Jacob**, which also has a fine selection of liquor to drown your sorrows if you end up in Bukavu too long with nothing to do. **Supermarket Kotecha** is another large clearing house of food and goods on Avenue Lumumba. For souvenirs, you are confined mostly to the selection at **Orchid's Safari Club**, though naturally the prices will not be the best. For all other practical items, the main stretch of Avenue Lumumba is the first place to go looking. The **market** for vegetables and fish is found along the road to the port, and is a far better option for buying vegetables than any of the supermarkets.

PRACTICALITIES

Medical and banks Bukavu's **General Hospital** is about the only clinic in town, and basic at that. A better option is to make a run for the border and see what can be had in Cyangugu if it's particularly serious. For Western Union, the solution is again on Avenue Lumumba at **Union Des Banques Congolaises** (m *098 204 965;* ⊕ *07.00–16.00 Mon–Fri, 07.00–12.00 Sat*).

Media and communications Satellite televisions blast out TV5 from France regularly which is great for learning about what's going on in the world outside the DR Congo, but not so great for learning about what might be going on a few kilometres outside town. Bukavu is well connected to mobile-phone networks, however, and is a good place to make some international calls to points in east Africa and beyond – I even managed to call Afghanistan on Celtel from here!

The East BUKAVU

10

207

The best **internet café** is at the Hôtel Residence, just to your left as you enter the foyer and they charge roughly US$2 per hour. Heavy rains can cut out connectivity, however, as they rely on some kind of wireless connection stuck to the building's rooftop. Back up early, back up often.

WHAT TO SEE Bukavu is a little low on proper sights, with the **Catholic cathedral** in the middle of town being the primary place of interest. It has a unique metallic green roof and large arches on all four sides which extend from ground level. Also nearby is the **Governor's Residence**, closed to the public but a decent green area with good views of the lake. If the monument ever gets built at the main roundabout on the western edge of town, it will be a good diversion.

Southeast of town on the Ruzizi River are the **Ruzizi Falls** on the border with Rwanda and Burundi. Be careful about photographing the falls as this is a border area and it's patrolled.

About 50km northwest of town, past the airport, is the village of **Kakondo** (✪ 02°15.00.62 S, 28°41.57.05 E). It has some hot springs in the vicinity. Also in this area is the village of **MBayo** (✪ 02°16.16.69 S, 28°45.51.07 E) which has a pleasant waterfall, as well as pygmy villages. Orchid's Safari Club runs a guesthouse here, as well as in **Irangi**, a small village off the road northwest towards Maiko National Park. Contact Orchid's Safari Club in Bukavu for information on arranging a visit (see *Where to stay* above).

Finally, a visit to Bukavu is really best done for the reason of going to **Kahuzi-Biega National Park**, just a few hours' drive away. Before you go, you may wish to contact the **ICCN office** on Avenue Lumumba (m *081 064 9729*) to finalise your arrangements.

IDJWI ISLAND

Idjwi is the largest island in Lake Kivu at 200km² in area, with a population of around 90,000. It's a rustic place, meaning even more rustic than usual for the DR Congo, with very few vehicles and numerous tiny villages along the shore. It is a thin, mountainous stretch of territory best known for its pineapple and papaya plantations. There are also a few caves on the island in addition to some birdlife.

GETTING THERE AND AWAY Idjwi is a good escape from the bigger world of the DR Congo, or as a good entry from Rwanda for those who want to get their feet wet with that country's much larger neighbour. There are regular boats from Goma to reach the north end of the island, but it is also possible to take a boat from the eastern shores of Rwanda to Idjwi Island, usually at Kibuye, and immigration officers on Idjwi should sell the same US$30 visa that other border points in the Kivus are offering. Note that if you cross from the north end of Idjwi to the south there is the same immigration process that you need to follow when crossing provincial boundaries – try not to pay anything, be friendly, and make sure they know you're a tourist. Thus Idjwi has several points of immigration – from Rwanda, from Bukavu or Goma, and from the north and south of the island.

PRACTICALITIES Congomani Village (m *081 265 6056*; e *mbakurabert@yahoo.fr*; *sgl/dbl* $$) is located at the southwestern end of the island, with 25 rooms and accessible from Bukavu. The owner is trying to get a speedboat for a reliable service direct to there; until then, you can take the slow boat from Bukavu's port to here. It takes about two hours and costs US$3.

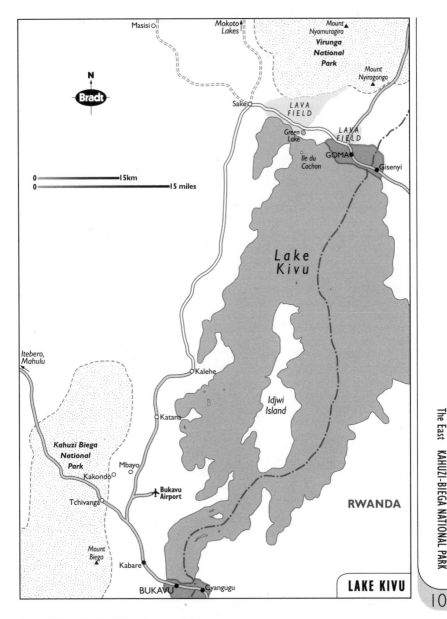

KAHUZI-BIEGA NATIONAL PARK

If you are something of a gorilla fan, Kahuzi-Biega is undoubtedly a place not to miss. It has soldiered on through the DR Congo's various wars and conflicts and emerged on the other side a wearier place than it was in days gone by, but still existing, and still going strong into the new millennium. Protection against poaching, in addition to UN patrols to limit incursions from the Mayi-Mayi and Interahamwe militias, has ensured that the world's last remaining natural habitat for eastern lowland gorillas is reasonably intact.

The Albertine Rift has been a boon for birdwatchers over the decades, and has the largest concentration of unique species in Africa. The Itombwe Mountains are in the southwestern hinterlands of Lake Kivu, comprising a huge green area in the region. West of the major north–south road corridor to Uvira, the undulating mountains are mostly uninhabited and covered by thick forests in highland areas (montane forest), along river streams, as well as bamboo forests.

Research here has revealed 83 unique montane forest species, half of the entire number found on the continent. A total of 563 different species have been found within the Itombwe Mountains, 43 of them endemic to this region. The Congo baw owl and Schouteden's swift are two birds that exist nowhere else outside Itombwe. Finding these species is unlikely for the casual visitor, however – they are only known from single samples collected over half a century ago. No surveys were done from 1960 until 1996, and even in 1996 the level of research completed was minor due to ongoing conflict.

Itombwe is not officially protected, and is not even within the environs of any national park. Birdwatchers would therefore do well to talk to ICCN in Bukavu about arranging a visit, though their expertise on birding is minimal. The closest village is **Kamituga** (✪ 03°03.18 S, 28°10.55 E) on the northwestern edge of the mountains. The most likely access point for visitors would be **Uvira** (✪ 03°24.27 S, 29°08.09 E) on the border with Burundi.

You can see the mountain gorillas of Rwanda or Virunga, or smaller western gorillas of Congo-Brazzaville, but the huge majestic eastern lowland silverback gorillas are only available here.

The park was founded in 1939, almost at the same time as Virunga's inception. Lowland gorillas were traditionally found between the Fizi Valley near Kalemie and Lubutu in the north, and the park protects their most central habitat. It was declared a World Heritage Site in 1980; and in 1997 was put on the list of World Heritage Sites in danger, as conflict and the presence of militias and illegal miners severely impacted on the park and its wildlife. Continued conservation efforts through the DR Congo's conflicts, as well as recently trained anti-poaching teams, have saved the lowland gorilla populations in the park from decimation, and there are currently three habituated families.

The park is a large sprawling area of lush hills dense with jungle foliage. In the rainy season heavy downpours can delay tours, though once one is under way there isn't any turning back.

Expect to walk for one or two hours through steep terrain to encounter your first gorilla family. Congolese guards and rangers accompany any group going through, and do their utmost to make sure any visitor gets an optimum view of these creatures when they are encountered. It is normal to be less than 3m away from a gorilla family in the dense wilderness; this can provide for some excellent photo opportunities, though it may have the unfortunate effect of habituating the gorillas too much to human presence. Visits are therefore limited to one hour.

While the gorillas are the primary attraction, some forest elephants are rumoured to exist in the dense western regions of the park, though arranging to visit them will be difficult at best. Other attractions are visiting the summits of Mount Bugulumiza (2,400m), accessible via road, or the summit of Mount Biega (2,790m), a two-hour hike from the main access road. Birdwatching in the park is also excellent, with a variety of small species making their homes in the dense foliage.

GETTING THERE AND AWAY You must purchase a permit from either the ICCN office in Bukavu (*Av Lumumba;* m *081 064 9729*) or at the base camp in Tchivanga – there is no difference in price, which is US$300 per person for a seven-day permit. There are no discounts on time spent at the park. Indeed this can seem outrageous to those unfamiliar with gorilla trekking, though do consider that you will be accompanied by a ranger or two, several armed guards, and most likely in a very small group. And as mentioned, this is the *only* location in the world to see lowland gorillas in the wild. If you're keen on these animals, the price is probably worth it.

Car hire from Bukavu should cost anywhere from US$40 for a taxi to US$100 for a 4x4 vehicle. Comfort is the only difference, as it will be necessary to walk in the jungle for a chance to see the gorillas, and the road to the park is possible by any means of transport. By extension, this trekking means that you should be reasonably fit and have a day pack with some basic provisions and first-aid equipment. Rangers will have these things as well, but I recommend packing your own – this is the DR Congo, after all.

Provided a gorilla family is within a reasonable walking distance, you can arrive back in Bukavu by late afternoon. There is also a campsite beside the park if you plan on spending several days visiting.

For off-the-beaten-track stuff, ICCN has a separate base camp at **Itebero** (01°42.37 S, 28°06.35 E) along the road to Maiko and Kisangani. They will likely have nothing to assist you here, but can give information on entering the mostly unvisited western region of the park. Mayi-Mayi have also been spotted in this area, so don't get too eager before receiving confirmation that it's safe to visit.

UVIRA 03°24.27 S, 29°.08.90 E

Located in the extreme southeast of South Kivu, you'll most likely be in Uvira as a result of arriving from or departing to Burundi. Certainly, fortune has not favoured Uvira over the past few years as it has played host to massive refugee camps from the waning conflict of Mayi-Mayi rebels further south in the DR Congo as well as refugees from conflict in Burundi. It also has a rather pleasant beach on Lake Tanganyika, though you'll probably be competing with the locals doing their laundry for your suntanning time. Nonetheless it's a central transport hub for this sparsely populated area, and sees boats from as far away as Kalemie arrive on its shores periodically. Buses and trucks are easy to find onward to Bukavu and Bujumbura.

WHERE TO STAY Uvira has a few hotels that cater to those who need to be here and a few more that can accommodate those passing through. Chief among them is **Hôtel de la Cote** (*sgl/dbl* $$$), which should have all of the usual Western amenities that are normally hard to find in this region. For a cheaper option try **Hôtel Mavan** (*sgl/dbl* $$) and on the bottom end both **Hôtel Kas** (*sgl* $) and **Hôtel Manunira** (*sgl* $) can provide a bed and a lockable door, if nothing else.

ITURI PROVINCE

The DR Congo's far northeastern corner, Ituri is a rolling region of lush rainforest barely penetrated by civilisation – intermixed with the dense jungles are some of the last remaining outposts of the pygmies in eastern central Africa, numerous small villages connected only by footpaths and, if they have survived, many large mammals resident in the thick foliage. Ituri conjures up dreams and myths of the deep African rainforest, and it lives up to these expectations in many ways. See the countryside from the air, and you'll notice how undeveloped it is compared with

'We have always lived in the forest. Like my father and grandfathers, I lived from hunting and collecting in this mountain. Then the Bahutu came. They cut the forest to cultivate the land. They carried on cutting and planting until they had encircled our forest with their fields. Today, they come right up to our huts. Instead of forest, now we are surrounded by Irish potatoes!' – Gahut Gahuliro, a Mutwa born 100 years earlier on the slopes of the Virungas, talking in 1999.

The Batwa (singular Mutwa) pygmies are the most ancient inhabitants of interlacustrine Africa, and easily distinguished from other inhabitants of the region by their unusually short stature and paler, more bronzed complexion. Semi-nomadic by inclination, small egalitarian communities of Batwa kin traditionally live in impermanent encampments of flimsy leaf huts, set in a forest clearing, which they will up and leave when food becomes scarce locally, upon the death of a community member, or when the whim takes them. In times past, the Batwa wore only a drape of animal hide or bark cloth, and had little desire to accumulate possessions – a few cooking pots, some hunting gear, and that's about it.

The traditional Batwa lifestyle is based around hunting, undertaken as a team effort by the male members of a community. In some areas, the favoured modus operandi involves part of the hunting party stringing a long net between a few trees, while the remainder advances noisily to herd small game into the net to be speared. In other areas, poisoned arrows are favoured: the hunting party will move silently along the forest floor looking for potential prey, which is shot from a distance, then they wait until it drops and if necessary deliver the final blow with a spear. Batwa men also gather wild honey, while the women gather edible plants to supplement the meat.

Today, the combined Batwa population of Rwanda, Burundi, Uganda and the eastern DRC is estimated at around 100,000 people. As recently as 2,000 years ago, however, east and southern Africa was populated almost solely by Batwa and related hunter-gatherers, whose lifestyle differed little from that of our earliest common human ancestors. Since then, agriculturist and pastoralist settlers, through persecution or assimilation, have marginalised the region's hunter-gatherers to a few small and today mostly degraded communities living in habitats unsuitable to agriculture or pasture, such as rainforest interiors and deserts.

The initial incursions into Batwa territory were made when the first Bantu-speaking farmers settled on the forested montane escarpment of the Albertine Rift, sometime before the 16th century, and set about clearing small tracts of forest for subsistence agriculture and pasture. This process of deforestation was greatly accelerated in the early 20th century. By the 1930s, the few substantial tracts of highland forest remaining in the region had all been gazetted as forest reserves by the colonial authorities. In one sense, this move to protect the forests was of direct benefit to the Batwa, since it ensured that what little remained of them would not be lost to agriculture. But the legal status of the Batwa was altered to their detriment – true, they were still permitted to hunt and forage within the reserves, but, where formerly these forests had been recognised as Batwa communal land, they were now government property.

Another 50 years would pass before the Batwa were faced with the full ramifications of having lost all legal entitlement to their ancestral lands in the colonial era. In the 1970s and 1980s, the Batwa communities resident in most of the region's conservation areas were evicted, a move backed by international donors who also insisted that hunting and other forest harvesting – the traditional subsistence activities of the Batwa – should be criminalised. Adding insult to injury, while compensation was awarded to non-Batwa farmers who had settled within protected areas after they were gazetted and illegally cleared forest to make way for cultivation, the evicted Batwa received compensation only if they had destroyed part of the forest reserve in a similar manner.

In the early 1990s, Rwanda's last forest-dwelling Batwa were evicted from the Gishwati Forest Reserve to make way for a World Bank project intended to protect the natural forest. The World Bank later concluded that the project had failed, with more than half of the original forest having been cleared for pasture prior to 1994, and it admitted that the treatment of indigenous peoples had been 'highly unsatisfactory'. Since 1998, returned refugees have been settled in the remaining forest, resulting in further destruction, but the former Batwa residents of Gishwati are mostly still landless.

Today, more than 40% of Batwa households in Rwanda are landless, and none has legal access to the forest on which their traditional livelihood depends. Indeed, most Batwa now eke out a marginal living from casual wage labour on other peoples' farms, porterage, simple craftwork (particularly pottery), and singing and dancing at festivals – many are in essence forced to live as beggars. Furthermore, with Batwa men no longer able to fulfil their traditional roles as hunters and providers, many have turned to alcohol and drug (or spousal) abuse, leading to the imminent collapse of Batwa cultural values.

Locally, the Batwa are viewed not with sympathy, but rather as objects of ridicule. The extent of local prejudice against them can be garnered from a set of interviews posted on the Ugandan website www.edrisa.org. The Batwa, report some of their Bakiga neighbours: 'smoke marijuana ... like alcohol ... drink too much ... make noise all night long ... eat too much food ... cannot grow their own food and crops ... depend on hunting and begging ... don't care about their children ... the man makes love to his wife while the children sleep on their side' – a collection of circumstantially induced half-truths and outright fallacies that make the Batwa come across as the debauched survivors of a dysfunctional hippie commune!

Prejudice against the Batwa is not confined to their immediate neighbours. The 1997 edition of Richard Nzita's otherwise commendable *People and Cultures of Uganda* contrives, in the space of two pages, to characterise the pygmoid peoples of Uganda as beggars, crop raiders and pottery thieves – even cannibals! Conservationists and the Western media, meanwhile, persistently stigmatise the Batwa as gorilla hunters and poachers – this despite the strong taboo against killing or eating gorillas that informs every known Batwa community. Almost certainly, any gorilla hunting that might be undertaken by the Batwa today will have been instigated by outsiders.

This much is incontestable: the Batwa and their hunter-gatherer ancestors have inhabited the forests of the Albertine Rift for countless millennia. Their traditional lifestyle places no rigorous demands on the forest and could be cited as a model of that professed holy grail of modern conservationists: the sustainable use of natural resources. The Batwa were not major participants in the deforestation of the region, but they have certainly been the main human victims of this loss. And Batwa and gorillas cohabited the same forests for many millennia prior to their futures both being imperilled by identical external causes in the 20th century. As Jerome Lewis writes: 'They and their way of life are entitled to as much consideration and respect as other ways of life. There was and is nothing to be condemned in forest nomadism ... The Batwa ... used the environment without destroying or seriously damaging it. It is only through their long-term custody of the area that later comers have good land to use.'

Quotes from Lewis and Gahuliro are sourced from Jerome Lewis's exemplary report *Batwa Pygmies of the Great Lakes Region*, published by the Minority Rights Group and downloadable as a pdf at www.minorityrights.org.

From *Rwanda: the Bradt Travel Guide* (3rd edition, 2006) by Philip Briggs & Janice Booth.

A grisly side effect of the brutal guerrilla wars in recent history has been that when food is scarce, people will kill and eat whatever they can to survive – including other humans. Cannibalism has, perhaps, been one of the most insidious things to emerge from the darkest equatorial jungles since the end of the Congo wars and the escalation of the Ituri conflict.

In a nation where the powers of sorcery and magic are still very much believed by the vast majority of the population, killing an adversary and eating a part of his flesh can be seen as inheriting the power of your enemy. Both Hema and Lendu tribal warriors have engaged in this practice, this ritualistic cannibalism – though it is unfortunately by no means the only explanation for this act.

The pygmies of Ituri, largely removed as participants in the conflict, have been targeted by both tribes. They make solid workers, but threats of coercion and death have over time not been enough motivation for a pygmy to obey his captors – especially when a pygmy's tribe has already been decimated. The notion of being killed and eaten can have serious spiritual implications, of one's soul being devoured by the enemy, and not having any access whatsoever to an afterlife.

Human Rights Watch has released several reports of cannibalism in eastern DR Congo, and interviewed numerous witnesses to cannibalistic acts. Field workers from Médecins Sans Frontières have also confirmed acts of cannibalism. In peacetime, cannibalism was largely unknown across the rainforest and therefore it seems to be more of a tactic to instil fear in the enemy or local population. As well, perhaps it empowers the same warriors who undoubtedly would live short and brutal lives within Ituri's harsh conflict.

other agrarian regions in Africa and the DR Congo. Winding along the battered dirt trails on a motorbike, surrounded by towering trees, is a thing of beauty for the adventurous traveller.

Yet Ituri is still the least resolved of Congo's conflicts. The Hema and Lendu have packed up and gone home, leaving their nasty tribal war behind in some respects, but these things have a way of lingering. Rumours persist of illegal mining operations in the deep forest canopy where no-one visits, some pointing the finger at Uganda for setting all of this up while pulling back to their own frontiers. Dozens of villages have been burned to the ground in recent years, and those who have survived this conflict are just returning to where they may have once had a home – building it with sticks and mud again, trying to get some crops growing.

BUNIA (⊕ 01°33.31 N, 30°14.59 E) Bunia became the main capital of Ituri district after the establishment of Irumu, the original Belgian settlement, a fort to guard trade routes from Stanleyville to British east African interests. Large mines built in the mountains made Irumu obsolete, giving Bunia most of the 20th century to develop a sound infrastructure. Somewhere during the Congo wars Ituri changed from a district to a province, and Ugandan soldiers came and went through Bunia on their way west. Yet this is not what turned Bunia inside out.

The provincial capital of Ituri saw its fortunes obliterated sometime between 2001 and 2002. Bunia was shut down and abandoned by its former residents as the Ituri conflict raged, changing into a textbook example of a medium-sized town without the resilience or the necessity for its residents to remain and continue its existence. It appeared briefly on the international stage in June 2003 when French paratroopers landed here. A large army of paparazzi followed them into the city, celebrating the arrival of military force to stop the bloodshed, then departed almost the same afternoon. However, this event was arguably the beginning of MONUC's expanded mandate to not just 'observe' the conflict in the DR Congo and report on treaty violations, but also to guarantee some semblance of safety to the citizens of the country against wanton violence. As a shell of its former self, it saw a resurgence of activity with UN and NGO staff coming and going on a regular basis. Roads to the city were closed, and soldiers and armoured personnel carriers roamed the streets, to ensure that the town remained disarmed – an edict put out by the UN to ensure that those who seek safety in Bunia would not be subject to violence.

With the town secured by the paratroopers, more foreign staff arrived. Bunia's airport became a stage of operations for the entire Ituri mandate. Even as the paratroopers left some months later, replaced by blue-helmeted UN peacekeepers, Bunia continued to swell in size – the refugee camps became larger, enveloping the surrounding hills. Thousands of tarpaulin huts grew from the grass, Toyota Land Cruisers filled with tired-looking European aid workers followed, and the deep scars that the Hema and Lendu had inflicted on each other began a very slow healing process. Yet the city centre was abandoned, a stretch of empty buildings and dirt roads. The daily activity amongst thousands of unemployed refugees was watching white armoured personnel carriers of the UN roll through town in a display of authority.

With increasing pressure from MONUC, and the completion of elections in the country at the end of 2006, Bunia's two conflicting tribes laid down their arms. The city reopened to the outside world, or the rest of the country at least, and many former residents returned to the city. Now it is a quiet town with a few dirt boulevards, many small shops, and one of the country's best airports. The refugee camps are gone. Bunia is quietly entering a new era.

Getting there and away Bunia's airport is excellent, repaved and frequently visited thanks to the large UN operation based here. **Cetraca** flies three times a week to Beni, and **TMK Air Commuter** finish their run from the Goma airport in Bunia. **Eagle Airlines** (m *099 402 1668/+256 4134 4292 (Uganda);* e *marketing@flyeagleuganda.com*) also operates a flight directly from Kampala twice a week.

Minibuses leave very early for Beni and Butembo at 06.00. You can also get shared taxis to Mahagi on the Ugandan border. There should also be regular minibus services to Kisangani very soon, as the road is being repaired.

Where to stay

⌂ **Hôtel Lusakivana** m 099 409 6874. The best place to stay in town & once the only place for intrepid journalists to come & arrange their time around the province. The hotel has a bar & restaurant, satellite TV, & running water. Sgl/dbl $$$

⌂ **Hôtel à Coté** With particularly nice rooms for the price range, & rooms all have a private bathroom. Sgl $, dbl/suite $$

⌂ **Hôtel Bunia** m 081 170 7508/898 1827. Much better value than the Ituri, the Bunia also has an ethnic restaurant serving Chinese & Indian food, & is good value for the price. Sgl/dbl $$

⌂ **Hôtel Ituri** Right in the city centre; m 081 292 1280. With simple rooms & a restaurant. Sgl $$

⌂ **Hôtel Maracana** Near the Tribunal de Grande Instance. A hotel of good quality but cheaper than the Lusakivana, its rooms sport private washrooms & TVs. They also have a small bar & restaurant. Sgl $$

⌂ **Hôtel Drudro** m 099 842 642. Situated in the Quartier Nyakasanza & is the cheapest bed worth recommending. They have a bar but no restaurant. Sgl US$8. Dbl/suite $

Practicalities Union Des Banques Congolaises (m *098 204 965;* ⊕ *08.00–16.00 Mon–Fri*) is the only bank in the city that handles Western Union.

For groceries try **Alimentation Source de la Vie** on Rond Point Sonas which sells plenty of goods imported from Uganda as well as local sausages.

MOUNT HOYO RESERVE (✣ *01°15.00 N, 30°00.00 E*) This was once the centrepoint of Ituri's tourist industry in the times of Zaire and Belgian Congo, a beautiful geographic masterpiece where the tall mountains of the Albertine Rift Valley collided with the majestic rainforests of the province. The pygmies who lived in the region of Mount Hoyo were said to be some of the least sullied by outside societies, remaining steadfast to their ancient traditions and lifestyle.

Rampant tourism in the 1980s to see the 'last of the pygmies' wrecked much of this, as the villages learned to capitalise more on foreign visitors than their own interest in remaining as a primeval culture. Further incursions from local traders who introduced tobacco and alcohol made these villages more interested in bartering for external substances than living in a traditional manner. Thus, it no longer remained the 'real' pygmy experience but a watered-down, sanitised version that tried hard to maintain a magazine-style veneer of what was expected of them by visitors paying a mint to get there and see what brochures promised them, rather than what may have once been a culture that existed solely for its own sake.

Yet those fortunes took a much different road once the nation known as Zaire dissolved and armies rolled across the region, as well as intense tribal conflict casting the entire existence of these pygmy villages in doubt. The territorial integrity of Mount Hoyo was thrown out the proverbial window, this mountain reserve losing any protected status it may once have had. News reports that documented a wholesale slaughter of the pygmy population emerged, as well as insidious reports that cannibalism was being practised against pygmies to drive them out of their villages and gain 'magic' powers that some said could only be attained by eating their flesh and organs.

Ituri's premier wildlife reserve is still a place that is not entirely secure. Some militias are said to remain in the area, and at the time of writing ICCN warned me of the security situation there. This is unfortunate, as while the pygmy populations of this area are far from a local attraction at this point, the reserve remains filled with natural wonders.

What remain in Mount Hoyo are its numerous **caves**, a dozen listed of note, buried amongst jungle vegetation and winding streams. These caves have special significance to the pygmies and were used frequently in the 19th century to elude Arab slave traders. The best ones to visit are **Maria Theresa** with two large stalagmites nicknamed Adam and Eve for their two white free-standing columns; **Matupi** has excellent rooms and some unique rock formations, as does **Yolohafiri**. The reserve is also known best for its waterfall called **Escaliers de Venus**, or Stairways of Venus, named so as the water comes down over rocks that appear to be steps. Finally the mountain itself can be ascended over two days, though a guide (and maybe some security) will be necessary as the trail has not been properly maintained and is probably impossible to find by an outsider.

Getting there and away Mount Hoyo Reserve is southeast of **Komanda** (✣ 01°21.56 N, 29°45.48 E), and you head east on a road just before the town. There was once a lodge at the entrance to the reserve offering some rooms and assistance to visit all of the sights, though continuing conflict has kept it closed. And naturally, being the DR Congo, insecurity and conflict do not exempt you from requiring a permit to visit – go to the ICCN office in Beni to get one, at US$50 per person.

Part Three

REPUBLIC OF CONGO

Name Republic of Congo

Location Central Africa – from the Atlantic coast eastward to the western bank of the Congo and Oubangui rivers

Size 341,500km^2

Climate Tropical, with rains from November to April

Population four million (2007 estimate)

Life expectancy 53 years

Capital Brazzaville: population around one million

Other major city Pointe Noire

Languages French (official), Kituba, Lingala

Religion Christianity, Islam, Matsouanism

Currency Central African franc (CFA; trades as XAF): £1=CFA877, €1=CFA656, US$1=CFA447 (July 2007)

Airlines Aéro Service, Trans Air Congo, Aéro Business

International airports Brazzaville Maya-Maya (BZV), Pointe Noire (PNR)

International telephone code 242

Time GMT+1

Electrical voltage 230V

Flag Green and red with a yellow stripe running diagonally through the middle

National sport Football (soccer)

Public holidays 1 January (New Year), 1 May (Labour Day), 10 June (National Sovereignty Day), 15 August (Independence Day), 1 November (All Saints' Day), 25 December (Christmas)

11

Background Information

HISTORY

The Republic of Congo, as it is now known, was always a product of French colonialism. But more than that, since its birth it has always maintained very close ties with the motherland. Its inception would mark the beginning of French colonies in central Africa, and its capital Brazzaville would remain a political centrepoint for the region during the first half of the 20th century.

A delicate game occurred in the 1870s between Belgium and France as King Léopold of Belgium worked his magic to obtain a colony for his country, whilst France, having created a port at Libreville in 1843, was considering departing the outpost altogether. The regions around the Congo River were vast and wild jungles where few bothered to tread – Africa was still very much only a port of call for ships, not a place for building infrastructure, and the only trade that occurred was with local tribes who brought whatever they found out of the bush. It would remain this way until a bright young man arrived in 1874, though he would not be French at all originally – but Italian.

PIERRE SAVORGNAN DE BRAZZA Born Pietro Paulo Francesco Camillo Savorgnan de Brazza to Count di Brazza Savorgnan in Via dell Umiltà, a suburb of Rome, and a descendant of Roman Emperor Alexander Severus, Pietro had a revelation early in childhood. A visit from a French admiral inspired him, exciting his senses for the seas and the French navy. Perhaps surprisingly, his father approved his joining the navy of a neighbouring nation and, using some contacts he had, Count di Brazza Savorgnan managed to get his son a placement at France's prestigious naval school. A slight man who was known as soft spoken and good looking, he always considered himself an outsider as an Italian amongst the Frenchmen in the navy.

He served on the warship *Jeanne d'Arc* to Algeria, where French forces were shooting down tribal insurgents with machine guns. He noted in his diaries, famously, shock and dismay at the way soldiers were dealing with the uprising. Later he would board the ship *Venus* and voyage south to Libreville, his first encounter with sub-Saharan Africa. His long journey southward had piqued his interest in European adventurers and their escapades across the continent, including Sir Richard Francis Burton. At Libreville he was surprised to discover the French were considering abandoning the port; he hatched a plan to not only keep the outpost in place but head deep into the interior, along the large Ogoué River, winning treaties in the name of France.

His proposal reached the attention of the Minister of Marine, Admiral Montaignac, who happened to be a friend of Count di Brazza Savorgnan. There was considerable enthusiasm for his project – the French could explore inland and claim this otherwise unknown territory as theirs, increasing their holdings in Africa. Pietro had only one request before he embarked, and that was to be granted naturalised citizenship – from August 1874 he would be French, and known as Pierre Savorgnan de Brazza.

He entertained notions of being the lone white explorer amongst his dark-skinned companions heading downriver, but was pressured into taking a scientist, Alfred Marche, and a doctor, Noël Ballay. He would stock up on trinkets and fireworks, giving rise to doubts regarding his sanity, as he would bring only a small amount of weapons and ammunition into undiscovered territory.

His philosophy towards expansion was unique, and a distinct departure from what explorers had managed in other regions – a concept of *association*, of bringing tribes together by treaty under the French flag. Meant more as a voluntary joining of communities, de Brazza thought this was a far better method of gaining territory than brutalising local people, but he would receive some criticism as his practices were considered simple trickery and bribery as he used the trinkets and fireworks he brought along to convince tribal leaders to sign these treaties. He would have only one major confrontation on this journey, killing several natives who had ambushed his party – but would later express respect for their fierce fighting skills.

In August 1877, he discovered the source of the Ogoué River and set out on foot. Local people had mentioned to him the presence of a large river in the area, which inspired him to press ahead. However, since his party was weak and low on supplies, he turned back and had returned to France by the end of the year.

DE BRAZZA'S CONGO Pierre de Brazza would return quickly to Libreville, and by late 1879 was readying a second expedition down the Ogoué in search of the source of this mighty river. This time he was far more focused, though did stop to found an outpost along the Ogoué that would later be called Franceville. He talked continuously with local chiefs, trying to discover where this new river was – and after months of running around in circles, encountering the incorrect waterways, late at night his party finally encountered a large open expanse dividing the wilderness.

Chief of the local tribe, the Makokos, mentioned to de Brazza how they had been hoping for a new ruler to arrive and assume power over all of the smaller factions. It had not been since the decline of the Kongo and Loango kingdoms that there was genuine authority, and more importantly good trade, between various populations interspersed amongst the jungle. He was happy, then, to draw up a treaty with de Brazza in Fafa, a small village along the Congo River. They would travel southward to the town of N'Tamo and sign the treaty on 28 August 1880. A trading post would be founded and called, simply enough, Brazzaville. De Brazza and the local tribes buried ammunition below a French flag, before proclaiming: 'May there never be war until this tree bears a crop of cartridges.'

Another explorer was quickly gaining ground in the region. Henry Morton Stanley, on his second voyage into the Congo, was establishing trading posts along the eastern edges of Malebo Pool in the name of King Léopold. Léopold had, in fact, sent various invites to de Brazza to join his cause of a colony for Belgium – but the explorer always refused him, for ever loyal to the French Empire.

Their approaches at colonisation were mirror images of each other: de Brazza with his notion of *association* was in direct conflict with Stanley's belligerent and ruthless attitude, with little respect for local cultures and no hesitation to use violence to get his way. Léopold liked this attitude however, as it was seeing far better progress than the soft French method being practised across the river.

The two, in fact, did meet in the waning months of 1880. De Brazza spoke a modest amount of English, Stanley a small amount of French, and Pierre crossed the river one night to speak to Henry and compare notes. Little came of the meeting as they used their broken languages carefully, and de Brazza failed to point out to Stanley that he had already signed a treaty with the Makoko tribe ceding the west bank to France. Stanley had signed no real treaties yet, but was rather simply invading whatever land he happened along. Stanley would also receive consternation from his Belgian employers after this meeting, who wrote to him later and asked why, as an American, he could not have simply shot him on sight!

CONGO FRANÇAIS In 1883, Pierre Savorgnan de Brazza and a compatriot, Albert Dolisie, began another trek west from their new town of Brazzaville in search of the coast. Some weeks later, following the general path of the Congo River, they arrived on the shores of the Atlantic at Loango – a relatively new native village bearing the name of the ancient kingdom. He would sign a treaty with the chief of Loango and set up another port, which would later become Pointe Noire.

The 1884 Berlin Conference drew formal borders across Africa, confirming the territories of Portugal, Belgium and France across the region; the eastern and southern bank of the Congo River became King Léopold's Congo Free State, with the west and northern banks belonging to France. This huge swathe of new territory would come under control as French Congo.

Much was made at the time of how the tribes in French Congo were treated compared with their neighbours in Congo Free State – more humanely, with more respect, and almost as equals. However, it was not all rosy, as the Tio people disputed their treaty agreement as simply being a trade agreement and alliance of forces – and not a carte blanche to total subjugation under the French Empire.

French Congo would stretch as far south as the northern and western banks of the Congo River and all the way north to France's Saharan holdings in Chad. Now with trading posts at Libreville and Brazzaville, France was forming a solid presence in central Africa just as it was on the verge of leaving the area altogether.

THE *CONCESSIONAIRES* AND THE RUBBER DISASTER Most of French Congo in the 1890s was a wild jungle, punctuated by ports and trading outposts, and little more than lines on the map of Africa which delineated France's colonial interests from that of other European nations in the area, namely Germany and Belgium. Belgium especially was working frantically across the river to satisfy the demand for rubber, using any means necessary, and stories were continuously emerging from Léopoldville of horrors that were occurring in the wilderness.

The French government at the time was instituting a different approach to capitalising on the jungles of Africa with land grants to concessionary companies, or *concessionaires*. Most of French Congo would be divided up into various territories and assigned to them, as they surveyed the region for rubber trees and other resources which could be exported to Europe. Notably these *concessionaires* had almost absolute title over the land to which they were designated, including its inhabitants. Regarding violence, it would not be a stretch with Congo Free State across the river doing it, for French capitalists to try the same thing.

De Brazza had originally opposed the notion of partitioning his colony amongst private companies so they could do what they wished with it. He protested, and was unceremoniously dismissed in 1898 as Governor-General of French Congo due to mounting pressure from concession companies. De Brazza's soft touch in dealing with African peoples was creating discontent amongst traders at the time, as they worked more fervently to match the rubber output of Congo Free State. From 1900, French Congo was divided amongst 42 concessionary companies, all searching for rubber trees mostly, and ready to use force against the locals to get it.

Concessionary companies complained that the locals did not understand their authority – or more than likely did not respect it. They petitioned the French government for clarification on their rights to convince local workers that they were *obligé à travailler* (obligated to work) under their agreements. Indeed, when put to a minister back in Paris it was stated publicly that 'coercion' was in the country's best interests; some subtle prodding to get the natives working in harmony with the concessionary companies could not be construed as a bad thing. Yet few, if any, wanted to know what this really meant: systematic torture and violence spread across French Congo in the early years of the 20th century as rubber was tapped from trees deep in the jungle and sent out to the ports of Libreville and Loango.

Just as had occurred across the river, there would be reports of atrocities emerging from French Congo. De Brazza, now living back in France, offered to investigate these reports – perhaps just to be in his beloved colony again, and more than likely sparked by genuine concern for the native tribes to which he had been so sympathetic. In 1905, he travelled back to Brazzaville, and prepared a damning report of what was going on in the concessionary territories – but the French government, fearing a disruption of trade and reputation, would suppress it for many years. *En route* back to Paris, de Brazza would die in suspicious circumstances in Dakar that same year.

Concessionary companies would continue to operate in the colony until the 1930s, though their powers would be curbed significantly after World War I. The French government had discovered that government revenues were far higher in a competitive marketplace, and the disaster across the river in Belgian Congo suggested that a more delicate approach to European subjugation of native tribes would be better received worldwide. The last of them would disappear just as the railway they had lobbied so hard for was finally completed.

FROM CONGO FRANÇAIS TO AFRIQUE ÉQUATORIALE FRANÇAISE

Far away but quite close in terms of the French Empire were the agitations of the Germans in Morocco. In 1906, Theodore Roosevelt mediated a summit in Spain, allowing France to control the territory while German investments were preserved.

In 1910, Congo Français was changing as well, having been renamed Afrique Équatoriale Française (AEF) and split up into four different areas: Gabon, Chad, Oubangui-Chari (now known as the Central African Republic) and Moyen Congo, or Middle Congo. Brazzaville would remain the capital of the AEF and seat of the Governor-General, but each separate colony would gain its own governor.

Germany would express their discontent by moving their warship into the port of Agadir in July 1911 in response to continued disagreements over which European power should hold Morocco, and eight days of negotiations led to a slight change in the AEF's makeup – its northwestern area would be ceded to the German Cameroons in exchange for France maintaining a territorial hold in Morocco. Locals would complain of the German invasion as it was, noting a significant difference between a laissez-faire French attitude towards their daily lives compared with a more stern German attitude. There would be a near split in the French Congo as German territory stretched all the way down to the Congo River. A small area would keep the two parts of the French colony somewhat cohesive, though, including a town that would become modern-day Impfondo.

Yet France would gain much of this Congo territory back as combat occurred throughout the region during World War I – indeed a minor front mostly unmentioned were battles that occurred in the north between German Cameroon and Middle Congo, and as favour shifted against Germany, France managed to acquire large chunks of territory. What was lost by France in their 1911 exchange was assigned back to the AEF in the Treaty of Versailles, and the remainder was governed as a separate protectorate.

THE CONGO OCEAN RAILWAY

Malebo Pool had always been a meeting point along the western banks of the Congo River, yet due to the rapids up ahead, the navigable portion did not extend straight to the ocean, thereby cutting off trade and transport directly upriver and deep into central Africa. Plans had existed since de Brazza's arrival for some sort of railway to cut through the jungle, opening up the interior to coastal trade, and several routes were surveyed from Brazzaville to the port of Loango. However, Stanley and Léopold would beat de Brazza handily by completing a railway from Léopoldville to Matadi in 1898, and the idea of a French line would be shelved by 1900. It was revived a decade later in 1910, as *concessionaires* had surveyed large metal deposits across the Congo landscape, and believed they could turn tidy profits if there was only some way to transport these metals to the coast in a method not nearly as difficult as by road.

The project would finally be awarded to Société de Construction des Batignolles, but work on the railway would not begin until 11 years later. France was undergoing numerous problems throughout the second decade of the 20th century with the advent of World War I, taxing the resources of all French companies and drawing attention away from any fledgling mining operations that may have been struggling in the region.

Finally, by 1921, all parties involved were ready to begin the promised rail line. The labour used was local – and in a situation not unfamiliar in the Belgian Congo, thousands of men died while working their way through difficult terrain. The path chosen was not a great one, and required numerous bridges and tunnels to be built. Mountains that divided Malebo Pool and the coast needed to be traversed, and there was outrage at both the lack of progress and the lack of respect for the local workers. Chinese workers were imported in 1932, nearing the end of the project, yet the global stock market crash of 1929 had devastated values for raw materials. By 1934, the railway was complete, though there was little interest from the companies that had lobbied so hard for its construction to actually use it.

THE RISE OF FREE FRANCE In 1940, half a world away, Germany's troops had marched on Paris and forced the surrender of the French Empire to Axis forces. General Charles de Gaulle would flee to England and make his famous appeal to French citizens from there, imploring active resistance.

Across the AEF there was immediate resistance among governors, most notably Félix Eboué, then Governor of Chad, though other governors sided with the Vichy regime of Phillipe Pétain. De Gaulle would begin to head south from England to Brazzaville, which had seen a bloodless coup weeks before as Vichy-opposed French deposed the governor by locking him in a trunk, and shipping him across the river to Léopoldville. Indeed in the weeks prior to the Free French deposing the Vichy governor in Brazzaville, Léopoldville had been providing sanctuary and funds to resisters of the Pétain regime.

De Gaulle appointed Edgar de Larminat as High Commissary of Free French Africa, and with the outspoken Eboué calling for resistance, his visits to Cameroon, Oubangui-Chari (Central African Republic) and Chad were mostly a quiet tour of capitals demanding the governors endorse the rebel government. De Gaulle would be involved in a botched naval attack on Dakar before reaching Middle Congo, arriving to cheering crowds in Brazzaville, and forming the Conseil de Défense de L'Empire on 23 June 1940. The Conseil would set out the conditions for a Free France government to be formed in Brazzaville. De Gaulle and Larminat would quickly set about formulating a plan to retake the rest of France's African colonies. While most of the former AEF colonies were supporting the Free France government, Gabon would remain loyal to Vichy. De Gaulle would rally troops, both Africans and Frenchmen in exile, and invade Gabon.

They would go out on foot, attacking on three fronts, marching deep inland. Very little human resistance was encountered – Gabonese regiments were

11

implored not to involve themselves in the matters of white men, and the largest difficulties encountered were harsh terrain, insects and animals, and malaria. Spirits were still high by the time Free French troops arrived on the outskirts of Libreville on 13 October 1940, where they would finally encounter resistance.

Three weeks of combat and siege followed, including British ships bombarding Libreville. Gabon fell to Free France and a governor loyal to de Gaulle was installed. De Gaulle would move on to Algeria, and Larminat would remain and act as a leader in advance of a government for Free France. Libreville's former governor, shamed, hanged himself while imprisoned on a ship.

Brazzaville would form a government for the AEF and its leader would be the first central African governor to oppose the Vichy regime, Félix Oboué. Born in French Guyana but educated in France, he would be the first black man to run any European colony in Africa. He worked hard at equalising rights for Africans, promoted traditional institutions, but ensured his government remained loyal to France. Brazzaville flourished under his authority, but his reign was cut short as he died of a heart attack on a trip to Cairo in 1944. As a result of his contributions in the war he was buried at the Panthéon in Paris – the first African to ever be interred there.

Charles de Gaulle would return to Middle Congo in 1944 for the Brazzaville Conference, which laid out new standards for Africans and reaffirmed the devotion towards a Free France; notably the citizens of French colonies should be considered equal to French citizens, including the right to vote in French parliamentary elections. Each colony would get its own legislative assembly, rather than simply a governor, and adjustments would be made to reduce exploitation between France and the colonies, giving more equality for trade and labour practices.

As World War II came to an end, Brazzaville would lose its importance on the world stage. There were changes afoot in France though, which would usher in a new era for Moyen Congo.

FROM THE MIDDLE CONGO TO THE REPUBLIC OF CONGO In the wake of World War II de Gaulle, with a new French parliament, enacted the Fourth French Republic and signed into law promises laid out at the Brazzaville Conference – this gave the members of AEF, now a loose federation rather than a sprawling colony, seats in the French parliament as well as positions in the newly devised French Union. France no longer had an empire, but something akin to the British Commonwealth, which was also forming at the end of the war. The notion of 'decolonisation' was being uttered in many high circles as the old European nations started to give their colonies more leverage in their own destiny, as well as more influence in the affairs of their former colonisers.

France in the Fourth Republic was having serious colonial insurgencies, most notably in Algeria and Vietnam. The AEF remained a mostly benign and quiet place during this time, yet with all of the AEF's members slowly drifting apart in their ideologies. Inside Congo-Brazzaville there was also change afoot on the political front with the emergence of political parties; refugees from Belgian Congo had also moved across the river, creating another rift between the locals and non-locals.

Belgium had been expelling individuals involved with the Kimbanguanist religious movement and many of them found their way to Brazzaville. This helped galvanise Moyen Congo's own religious sect, the Matsouanists, who worshipped a similar merging of Catholic faith with ancient beliefs in sorcery under the leadership of the priest André Matsoua. Both times the Matsouanists had managed to sway the electoral vote for whom should represent Moyen Congo back in

France, electing their deceased leader. By default, the second-place winner was sent instead – Félix Tchicaya, who enjoyed the trappings of a Parisian lifestyle more than his home country of Congo. Nonetheless he was leader of the PPC, or Parti Progressiste Congolais, the first political organisation in Congo.

Other parties quickly formed in the beginning of 1950: Jacques Opangault led the left-wing Mouvement Socialiste Africain, or MSA. Both parties relied heavily on tribal politics to win their popularity, with the MSA having a stronghold in northern Congo and the PPC having its power base around Pointe Noire. Tchicaya's time in office was uneventful, but from 1950 onward the capital of Moyen Congo was moved to Pointe Noire. Brazzaville remained the capital of the AEF, and the split caused urban intellectuals to disperse between the two towns.

Matsouanists would begin to regard another man as the successor to their deceased religious leader, Abbé Fulbert Youlou. Youlou, formerly a Catholic priest, galvanised the Matsouanists into supporting him and won an election for Mayor of Brazzaville in 1956 – he retained the *Abbé* portion of his name, a religious designation, even though he had officially left the priesthood. Tchicaya, having lost much support throughout the 1950s while residing solely in Paris, lost much of his popular base to Youlou's new political party the UDDIA, or Union Démocratique de la Défense des Intérêts Africains.

Times were changing across France's colonies in the 1950s – the policy of *Loi Cadre*, whereby colonies were permitted to vote in their own rulers, had arrived. France was *en route* to granting outright independence to all of its AEF colonies at the end of the decade, and Fulbert Youlou again ran for the presidency. The results were deadlocked between the MSA and UDDIA, but a single defection from the MSA gave Youlou the majority and thus the presidency. He would, then, become first president of a newly minted Republic of Congo. MSA leader Jacques Opangault would be designated as prime minister.

A MARXIST REVOLUTION, OF SORTS In Brazzaville, Congo had a large intellectual base that was unlike its other African neighbours. Having supported Free France in the 1940s and a refuge for French citizens during the Vichy regime, the level of education amongst its population was high. Congo had also managed to become a heavily industrialised society by 1960 – at least in its southern regions, where the vast majority of people lived. Trade unions were not uncommon, and the MSA was gaining ground within the unions for popularity. There was also a great deal of contact with France c1960, and Congo trade unions were in regular communication with left-wing forces amongst communist groups. Congolese who lived in France for periods of time before returning would bring the rise of socialist agendas amongst Congo's population. A large bureaucratic structure, with a significant percentage of citizens in the public service, would further socialist ideals in the new nation.

This ideology was in direct conflict with the Matsouanists, who opposed any kind of modernisation: they were against identity cards, any form of tax, and deliberately sabotaged census surveys. Youlou's main platform of support was beginning to erode in the early 1960s, as the popularity of socialist ideologies grew. Unemployment was also high, as a result of Pointe Noire's oil exports losing much of their value at the end of the previous decade. Youlou himself was beginning to institute one-party reforms, trying to consolidate his power and remove opposition, merging the MSA with the UDDIA in 1962.

Trade unions staged a general strike beginning on 13 August 1963, demanding Youlou step down. Riots ensued across Brazzaville for three days, and while much property was damaged, only three had died – they were referred to as *Les Trois Glorieuses*, the three martyrs who had died for the revolution. The army, a benign force until this point, allowed staunch socialist Alphonse Massamba-Débat to take power as prime minister. He would soon form the Conseil National de la Révolution (CNR), and promise Marxist–Leninist-style reforms. The Soviet Union and China, eager to assist a new recruit into the communist fold, sent aid and advisors to Brazzaville. Cuba had already been active in the region across the river in Congo-Léopoldville, and Brazzaville would become a base of regular contact for Patrice Lumumba's Cuban assistance as they were driven out by conflict in the east of Congo-Léopoldville.

The CNR would continue where Youlou left off, though on its own socialist track: consolidating power to one party, revising the government to reflect a communist-style structure with a politburo for party members loyal to Débat, replacing the prime minister position with the more socialist-sounding 'Premier' desk, and allowing long-time leftist intellectual Pascal Lissouba to ascend to his second in command. A year later he would form the sole permitted political party in Congo, the MNR, or Mouvement National de la Révolution. It would contain numerous wings to devour all branches of life: for women, trade unionists, cultural affairs, and most notably for youth, the JMNR. The JMNR would specifically receive aid from the Soviets, and act as the 'eyes and ears' of the political party. Like a Big Brother, they would root out opposition to the MNR and anyone who might be considered a threat to the stability of the regime.

The army at the time had begun to see the JMNR as a genuine threat to their own authority across Congo. With the JMNR taking over nominal security functions in every section of society, the authority of the national army could indeed be next. The army leader, Marien Ngouabi, openly protested the rising power of the JMNR in a conference to Débat. Débat and his prime minister of the time, Ambroise Noumazalay, reprimanded Ngouabi and demanded he accept a post in Pointe Noire. Ngouabi, though, had other plans.

FROM MARXIST REVOLUTION TO MILITARY DICTATORSHIP Marien Ngouabi successfully rallied all branches of the military to a coup in 1968. Leaders of the MNR, including Massamba-Débat and Ambroise Noumazalay, were arrested. Ngouabi was reinstated to his position as military chief, and Débat would remain the nominal head of state for Congo until further notice. The government and the MNR were significantly weakened in the wake of the coup; under the watchful eye of the military, Congo's politics rolled along slowly. The planned Marxist revolution was still very much stalled.

Noumazalay would be dismissed as premier three years later, creating a behind-the-scenes jockeying for an anticipated replacement to Débat as he was sure to fall soon after. There was a noted increase in anti-French sentiment, as the tentacles of the Soviet Union, Cuba and China worked their ways deeper into Congo's society. Nonetheless, France never suspended diplomatic relations with Brazzaville, nor suspended financial assistance to the former capital of Free France as it turned towards socialist ideals.

Ngouabi, though, was arrested in July 1968 for allegedly plotting another coup – surprising that this could happen given the military's control over the government, but he was quickly freed by his own soldiers and then successfully toppled the government soon after. Ngouabi quickly dissolved the politburo, erasing all party control within Brazzaville, and appointed himself president. Massamba-Débat fled for his home village, and the socialist revolution, again, was stalled.

Marien Ngouabi appointed a friend from nearby Cabinda, Alfred Raoul, as prime minister (changed back from premier, as socialist and francophone government systems collided), using an outsider without any tribal base as a neutral figure amongst the usual local rivalries inherent in Congo's repressed party politics. In this, perhaps, Ngouabi hoped to create an overseeing system that would not be sullied by factional rivalries as Congo's politics were in the 1950s; yet his military regime was, to say the least, unpopular. He quickly set about creating a formal government, promising again that this would be the establishment that would begin the transition to socialism. The government would be mostly ineffectual and constantly under threat. Ngouabi used continued excuses of right-wing plots against him to, familiarly, consolidate his power and purge anyone within the government and army who might oppose him. Nonetheless, the long-awaited socialist revolution was just around the corner, he promised, and on 3 January 1970, he renamed the nation to the People's Republic of Congo.

RISE OF THE PCT AND, PERHAPS 'SCIENTIFIC SOCIALISM' Around this time Marien Ngouabi approved the creation of a single new left-wing political party, the PCT, or Parti Congolais du Travail. They drew up a constitution very similar to that of the Soviet Union, and along with their aides from the USSR began to court assistance from China. Cuba was still active in Congo-Brazzaville along with Angola, altering inter-state politics between neighbouring nations. The influence of socialist dictatorships in the People's Republic of Congo allowed Mobutu Sésé Seko, avowed friend of Western governments, to get away with what he wished on the other side of the Congo River. Ngouabi began to complain of problems from the far left, groups wishing to depose him and his socialist ideologies for something that was more true to Marxism–Leninism than a single party propped up by the military. The pattern was the same: depose those closest to him, strip governmental bodies of their power and people of influence, then bring in people loyal to his ideas of a military-assisted single-party state. Prime Minister Noumazalay was sacked, Ngouabi's close Cabindan friend Alfred Raoul was imprisoned. He accused them of engineering student protests, and his army was unfortunately sent to dispatch the protesters, killing a few of them along the way.

In spite of this Ngouabi kept the proverbial carrot on the end of the stick, promising a Marxist–Leninist state sometime soon, once his regime regained stability and when it was not continuously fighting for its life. He appointed five men into his inner circle to manage the state as he deposed former government officials, among them Denis Sassou-Nguesso; these would be the 'special revolutionary staff' that would bring the long-promised socialist reforms to Congo. The PCT would be held in check by the army, counterbalancing each other perhaps, though Ngouabi would remain the undisputed leader as protests were dispersed and coup plots unearthed. Criticism from the trade unionists and PCT resulted in the latest incarnation of the politburo to be dissolved outright, eliminating a legislative branch of the fledgling socialist government.

On 18 March 1977, as a surprise to most involved, Marien Ngouabi was assassinated. The actual perpetrators remain unclear, though the list of suspects is almost as long as independence in Congo itself. The military, having lost their leader, followed in his footsteps admirably by purging any known opposition to Ngouabi and their establishment. Alphonse Massamba-Débat was arrested and sentenced to death, Pascal Lissouba was sentenced to life in prison. His life was spared by the machinations of Gabon's president, Omar Bongo. Lissouba would eventually be freed from jail and live for over a decade in exile.

Joachim Yhombi-Opango would ascend to the top of the army, with Denis Sassou-Nguesso appointed as defence minister. Tribal politics were in vogue again, and even though Sassou-Nguesso was a more popular individual for the post, Opango's tribal connections put him in the top spot – though like everyone else who had assumed this position, only briefly.

11

As the Cold War grew to envelop the Congos in the 1960s, the communist powers of Russia and China began to send their own representatives into both the new Congolese nations to shore up support for a socialist revolution. The nation most at the forefront during this decade was Cuba, and the Cubans fought not only against the capitalist influences of the West on Congo's soil, but also against themselves.

In 1964, with the help of the CIA, Joseph Kasa-Vubu's government had begun amassing an army of mercenaries based out of Katanga to fight against the insurgency in northeast Congo, which grew after the death of Patrice Lumumba. His left-wing ideals had inspired a generation to fight against the government of Léopoldville, and this new battle saw some old names arriving again – but on the opposing side. Bob Denard and Mike Hoare, mercenaries who fought in Katanga for Moise Tshombe in the early 1960s now found their hired guns putting down the rebellion in the northeast. In addition, the CIA had enlisted Cuban pilots and soldiers who were opposed to Fidel Castro's revolution on the island to attack the Lumumbists' training camps and strongholds around Stanleyville. Operation Dragon Rouge, as it was called, was conducted against Congolese soldiers who were being trained by Cuban socialists – the most famous of whom would be Ernesto 'Che' Guevara.

Guevara had disappeared from Cuba after taking part in the socialist revolution there; his whereabouts were unknown until many years later, and his time in the Congo was unaccounted for, a black hole in his popular life, until he had long departed the region. His resurfacing in Tanzania gave him time to write extensively on the subject, and there is thorough documentation on his time in eastern Congo thanks to his diaries.

Cuba had planned a two-pronged approach to spread 'revolution' throughout both Congos. Their presence in Congo-Brazzaville was the most assured: as Fulbert Youlou was ousted from government and Alphonse Massamba-Débat took his place. The revolutionary rhetoric of the new Brazzaville government was the perfect platform for another front in the Cold War as it was being played out across Africa. Initially, though, Cuba's interests in supporting Débat's regime were entirely because of Angola: Cuba had been training the MPLA, or Popular Movement for the Liberation of Angola. Their training camps near Brazzaville were critical in the broader guerrilla war against the Portuguese that was raging throughout the 1960s. Furthermore, with the America-friendly government of Kasa-Vubu and Tshombe across the river, the fall of Brazzaville to Western-friendly forces was a genuine threat. While the MPLA was the primary concern, Cubans arrived in their hundreds throughout Congo-Brazzaville as Massamba-Débat welcomed their presence.

Congo and Africa as a whole, though, were becoming more appealing to Cuban revolutionaries as their own forays into South America had been faltering in the 1960s. Che Guevara had toured several African countries for three months before arriving in Tanzania and meeting Laurent Kabila, to discuss aiding his Simba rebel group in eastern Congo against the forces of Léopoldville.

EASTERN CONGO Cuba's move into eastern Congo was a bold and brave move; it required a fair amount of resources, including several hundred highly trained Cuban soldiers moving discreetly from Havana to the shores of Lake Tanganyika. Many of them took different routes by aircraft and with fake documents, to throw off the CIA. Che Guevara and over 100 other Cuban revolutionaries arrived at Lake Tanganyika in 1965, and prepared to cross into the small rebel-held area of Fizi-Baraka – a valley between modern-day Uvira and Kalemie.

The Cubans training Kabila's rebels in this area did so under much frustration. There was not as much dedication, according to Guevara's diaries, to the revolutionist cause as shown by his own Cuban soldiers. He spent three months doing weapons training for the local rebels, as well as language training for his own countrymen. The goal of Cuba in eastern Congo was intended as long term, and Guevara was prepared to die for this cause.

Laurent Kabila, the leader of the Simbas, was still not present as Guevara made the decision to lead an attack on the edge of the Fizi-Baraka enclave – Kabila had promised his arrival soon, but would only arrive months after the Cubans had established themselves in eastern Congo. On 29 June 1965, Che Guevara, over 100 Cuban soldiers and 200 Simba rebels attacked the town of Bendera. The attack was a complete failure, resulting in the deaths of four Cubans and over 40 Simba rebels.

Guevara was not willing to give up, though, and told his men that much worse would have to be endured if the revolution was to be successful. Yet the Simbas did not trust him, and the authority of the Cubans over the Simbas was faltering. There was a lack of organisation in their ranks, even as they tried to plan further attacks.

The forces of Léopoldville, on the other hand, were increasingly successful against Lumumbist forces in eastern Congo. Starting with Stanleyville, they were routing rebel forces in the northeast with both the ground troops of the ANC and European and South African mercenaries led by Mike Hoare. They finally arrived at the frontlines with the Simbas, in Fizi-Baraka, in October 1965. Patrol boats funded by the CIA had also been dispatched into Lake Tanganyika, making communication and supply more difficult with Kigoma – the central point of contact with the rebel-friendly government in Tanzania. Not only squeezed by both sides, they were also attacked from the air – the CIA had enlisted Cuban exiles on American soil to fly combat sorties across the region to oust the rebels.

The CIA, though, was not entirely convinced that there were Cubans assisting the Simbas. The four dead Cubans in Bendera were found by Western intelligence operatives and assumed to be Soviet, or possibly employed by the Chinese. The usage of Cuban exiles against the rebels was more of a twist of fate than a determined attack of anti-communist Cubans against pro-communist Cubans; they were enlisted, originally, because the CIA did not have the authority to use American pilots in its Cold War forays across Africa. Therefore, with Cuban exiles as refugees on American soil, they fitted the bill perfectly.

The air sorties were devastating psychological attacks against the Simbas, and Guevara's Cuban soldiers were quickly losing ground. For all of their training to the local rebels and their own willingness to die for their cause, Guevara had detected a volition amongst the population that was less than absolute. While he was willing to fight until the end in eastern Congo, his communications with Fidel Castro had changed his mind. Castro had requested to Che that he 'avoid annihilation'; he would be more useful a revolutionary alive than dead.

By the end of November 1965, Che Guevara had fled by boat back to Kigoma. He would disappear and resurface in other points across the world, but the Cuban mission in eastern Congo had been eliminated entirely by the forces of Léopoldville. It was a decisive Cold War victory for the CIA, who assumed that they had thwarted a Soviet-funded insurgency. The fact that it was the Cubans who had engineered external support to the Simbas remained unknown for many years.

BRAZZAVILLE With the defeat in eastern Congo, Fidel Castro decided to reinforce the Cuban presence in Congo-Brazzaville by increasing the number of soldiers and intelligence officers in the country to 400. He was seeing the fledgling socialist government of Massamba-Débat as under threat from Léopoldville across the river, and

continued overleaf

their investment in the MPLA could not be risked. Yet there was a critical rift of ideologies emerging between Cuba and Congo – while Cubans assisted the Congo authorities in preparing their country for a full-fledged communist state, they could not help but notice that there was not nearly as much conviction as there should be for the communist lifestyle. And indeed this could only be true – Congo still had firm relations with France and West Germany, and while courting the favour of the communist bloc by allowing the Chinese and Soviets to train their military, the political ideology could be best described as confused. Castro, though, saw in Congo striking similarities with Cuba: small countries which could easily be used as pawns in the games of larger powers. This envisioning of Congo allowed their investment in the country to soldier on, if too optimistically, for several more years.

It was not until a ten-day popular uprising engineered by Marien Ngouabi in 1966 that the Cubans realised there could be little hope for a Cuban-style Congo. Débat had managed to stay in control of the country but Cuba saw the writing on the wall, along with the other communist officials in the country at the time. By the end of 1966 most of Cuba's presence in Brazzaville had disappeared, though they kept many of their own nationals in the country to continue their support of the MPLA. It was with the assistance of Cuban subterfuge that several hundred MPLA soldiers trained near Brazzaville would sneak into Congo-Léopoldville, then march southward to the border town of Sangololo to regroup. From there they marched further south into Angola.

When Marien Ngouabi finally took the presidency of Congo-Brazzavile in 1968, the last of Cuba's trainers and intelligence departed the country. Now the country was fully in the hands of a right-wing military regime, there would be no hope for the proposed revolution that Cuba had originally aspired to in Brazzaville.

THE 1970S Cuba also assisted MPLA soldiers who had taken Cabinda, and fought against Mobutu Sésé Seko's ANC and Mike Hoare's mercenaries for control of the enclave. The Cubans had arrived via Pointe Noire, and with a surprising level of efficiency repelled Mobutu's plans for the annexation of Cabinda.

Cuba also assisted Katangese rebels who invaded Kolwezi in 1978. Since the country was deeply involved in Angola's actions during this time, perhaps some involvement from Cuba could be expected. The Cubans had no actual presence on the ground, and to what extent they were truly involved is unknown; however, the rebels were famous for announcing upon their occupation of the town that Cuba was, somehow, assisting them.

EXIT THE PEOPLE'S REPUBLIC OF CONGO Yhombi-Opango arrived in 1979 with most of the same problems as those who came before him: coup plots, protests, and a large distrust of the people around him. He tried to limit the power of the trade unionists in Congo, and made provisions to the elite intellectuals living in Brazzaville and Pointe Noire. He also began to court the West again, after so many years of Congo trying to draw support from the Eastern Bloc. China had shown little interest in the latest juggling of Congo's various political figures and the Soviet Union, though still providing support, was not providing the nation with as much solid guidance as it perhaps required in the light of another turbulent decade on the road to socialism.

A massive protest in February 1979 sealed his fate: he agreed to a National Council meeting, the same kind that permitted the fall of Youlou and the rise of Massamba-Débat nearly two decades before. Criticism of his approach forced him to resign – though his ideology was perhaps the most stable Congo had available for a long time. Pointe Noire's oil exports were not providing nearly as much money into Congo as required for it to be self-sufficient; while not an OPEC country it could sell oil below market value, creating sales based on volume, and Opango opted for a regime of stability over what would surely have been a turbulent and chaotic move into the always-promised, but still not materialising, society of 'scientific socialism'. With Opango out of the picture, Denis Sassou-Nguesso quickly moved in to take his place and propel the PCT into power and checking the influence of the army to below that of the politburo – after a decade of continued chaos the military regime was effectively finished.

During the 1980s, Sassou-Nguesso perpetuated much of the same history that Congo had been plagued by since independence: riots, anti-government rallies, attempted coups, and regular sacking of anyone within his government who might be planning his downfall. Ironically he continued his predecessor's process of courting the West for aid, selling them oil, and creating a more bilateral system of foreign relations so he was not so dependent on the USSR and China. He was even appointed chairman of the Organisation of African Unity between 1986 and 1987, and despite his regular travel abroad within this period, which created the ideal climate for a coup, he managed to retain the presidency. He brought in reforms requested by the World Bank and International Monetary Fund. An important event moved his opinion away from the single-party socialist state, and that was an assassination attempt in May 1989. Cuban intelligence agents warned him that this was not the first time such a thing had been planned, nor would it be the last. He called together a National Council in 1990, aiming at reforming Congo's politics once again.

In 1991, he made a televised speech and apologised for the excesses of the regimes he had been involved in. He promised more transparency, and a move towards multi-party elections. His usual platform of support for the eventual radical socialist changes promised in Congo had essentially vanished with the USSR. With France's Western policies and politicians always looming over Congo, and without the endorsement of China, and with a close eye as to what was occurring elsewhere amongst the regimes of francophone Africa at the time, Denis Sassou-Nguesso agreed to multi-party elections to take place in the near future. From 1990 the name of the nation would be changed as well, from the People's Republic of Congo back to simply Republic of Congo.

Chaos ensued in Brazzaville as those who had been hoping for the long-promised full transformation to socialism found themselves cheated. Shoot-outs in the capital were common, as left-wing groups tried to regain control of the government and perhaps put the nation back on a road to Marxism. Such agitations did not succeed, though, and in 1992 Congo's first multi-party elections since independence were held. Denis Sassou-Nguesso was ousted in the first round, receiving less than 17% of the vote.

RISE OF THE NINJAS Pascal Lissouba had returned to much fanfare prior to the 1992 elections, and won them handily as leader of his new political party – the UPADS, or Union Panafricaine Pour la Démocratie. Tribal politics had once again come to the fore, with Lissouba's party gaining support from the area between Pointe Noire and Brazzaville. Denis Sassou-Nguesso's PCT still gained support from the north, and two other parties established their popularities in Pointe Noire and the Poule region near Brazzaville respectively. In the resulting cabinet shuffle as parties were given seats, Sassou-Nguesso resigned out of protest, pulling the PCT out of parliament. Lissouba's UPADS, then, would not have a significant majority of seats and would, by Congolese law, not be able to force another election. Meanwhile, combat had continued in Brazzaville and across the country.

REPUBLIC OF CONGO PROVINCES

Bétou

Souanké

Bomassa

Dongou

LIKOUALA

Sembé

Ouésso

Impfondo

SANGHA

Mbomo

Pikounda

CUVETTE
OUEST

Makoua

Owando   CUVETTE

Liranga

Ewo

Obouya   Loukoléla

Mossaka

Okoyo   Abala

Gamboma

PLATEAUX

Mayoko

Bambama

Djambala   Mpouya

NIARI   LEKOUMOU

Ngabé

Makabana

Vinza

Sibiti   POOL

Mouyondzi

Dolisie   BRAZZAVILLE

KOUILOU   BOUENZA

N

POINTE
NOIRE

Kinkala   KINSHASA

Bradt

Factions loyal to each political party had become mobilised with weapons, and anti-government demonstrations persisted across Congo as left-wing groups lobbied for their promised socialist reform. The army clashed with opposition militias in 1994, which officially began the period of civil war. Other reforms continued while conflict raged, including a decentralisation of local authorities in 1994, and liberated media and press in 1995.

It is important to note that while these clashes were divided along party lines, they were tribal in nature. Tribes voted for their specific parties, parties represented specific regions across the country, and what may have once held the veneer of a political war was a growing civil war based in tribal conflict. Over 2,000 had been killed between Pascal Lissouba's faction and the factions of rival parties, including the opposition group the Mouvement Congolais pour la Démocratie et le Développement Intégral (MCDDI), a staunch anti-Marxist force hoping to take power away from the multi-party parliament. Led by Bernard Kolélas, the party had formed their own militia, the Ninjas, who would fight against Sassou-Nguesso's militia called the Cobras and Lissouba's national army. Inspired by the socialist JMNR youth militias and undoubtedly too many Samurai movies, the 'Ninjas' are young men who dress all in black and prefer to attack by ambush.

CONTINUING INTERNAL CONFLICT Sassou-Nguesso had left the Congo and lived abroad from 1994 to 1997, and when he returned, his mansion, populated by his Cobra militia, was surrounded by Pascal Lissouba's forces. Omar Bongo, President of Gabon, had engineered a ceasefire between the two sides two years before but it did not hold once Sassou-Nguesso had left. With Lissouba ready to eliminate Sassou-Nguesso's forces, assistance from Angola pushed Lissouba's militia back. Sassou-Nguesso's force also boasted mercenaries from the Central African Republic and Rwanda, further bolstering their numbers. Mortar fire landing in Kinshasa about this time also led Laurent Kabila to send several hundred troops across the river to assist Sassou-Nguesso's forces. With so many sides against the militias of Lissouba and Kolélas, they were finally driven out of Brazzaville and into the Poule region. Sassou-Nguesso's militia had finally taken back Brazzaville from Lissouba and promptly began looting the capital in victory.

Lissouba's forces began clashing with the Ninjas in the Poule region west of Brazzaville, creating a party-oriented tribal conflict trying to win territory. The Ninjas persist to this day, though their power has been greatly reduced, and are kept out of conflict in Brazzaville as a result of foreign mercenaries maintaining a zone of control west of the capital.

Denis Sassou-Nguesso, reinstated as president on 25 October 1997, promised a three-year democratic transition from 1998 to 2001. However, constant combat between party militias enabled him to shelve these plans and postpone any challenges to his position a little longer. He also held a dubious presidential election in 2002 and won with an overwhelming majority; the opposition parties boycotted it fervently. That same year he passed a new constitution, extending his power until 2009 and engaging in some modest democratic reforms.

The civil war was declared officially over in 2003 despite continuing problems by the Ninjas loyal to Kolélas in the Poule region. Their presence has created a territorial divide and rendered the Congo Ocean Railway effectively useless for regular trade. In 2006, Denis Sassou-Nguesso was again elected chairman of the OAU, now called the African Union. There is an uneasy ceasefire persisting across Congo while all sides wait for the next elections. The Poule region remains unstable and the Ninjas have little opposition to their activities in the area.

GOVERNMENT AND POLITICS

Denis Sassou-Nguesso is the current President of Congo and will continue to be so until the next elections – scheduled for 2009 or so, but highly dependent on his decision and other internal factors. The newest constitution of the nation was ratified in 2002, after the previous one was suspended in 1992 as the first open fighting erupted in Brazzaville. Congo's original political structure was based heavily on what was found in France; however, it was modified after the 1997 civil war to accommodate the demands of the opposition. Sassou-Nguesso, and Prime Minister Isidore Mvouba are both members of the PCT, or Parti Congolais du Travail. Other major parties with parliamentary presence are the UPDS, or Union Panafricaine pour la Démocratie Sociale. Congo's parliament has two chambers: the National Assembly and the Senate.

Political affiliations are often designated by tribal affiliation, with much of Sassou-Nguesso's power derived from his popularity in Congo's rural regions. Opposition to the PCT is scattered and unfocused – they currently have no strong opponents for the forthcoming elections.

Congo maintains close ties with France, and less so with its former socialist partners Russia, China and Cuba, but all three of these nations still play an important part in Congo, as they share such similar histories throughout the 20th century. The nation also maintains a prominent standing in international bodies across the African continent – Denis Sassou-Nguesso has twice been appointed as head of the African Union.

Congo is divided into ten provinces, with Poule, Niari and Kouilou the most populous. Northern provinces such as Sangha and Likouala are sparse stretches. In practice, provinces do not have a great deal of autonomy, though this varies from region to region.

ECONOMY

Congo's economy has shifted west towards the city of Pointe Noire; given that the only genuine infrastructure of the country runs between its three main cities, the others being Dolisie and Brazzaville, and the Poule region still being a rather volatile region to do business, the north of Congo remains very much a wild and mostly untouched wilderness. Petroleum reserves off the Atlantic coast have been good to Congo, supporting its various Marxist revolutions for decades and bringing a large amount of infrastructure to Pointe Noire. Expatriates have also done much to help develop the city, and along with the oil reserves it remains an important port of call for vessels along the west coast of Africa.

Forestry also dominates. Massive logs in large Mercedes *camions* work their way southward from Congo's rainforests to waiting ships on the Atlantic; these are run mostly by Malaysian firms, and have opened up the far reaches of western Congo to business. It keeps a large number of local Congolese employed, and while the pay is not spectacular, foreign investment is slowly bringing the economy of Congo around. Malaysian companies also operate farms in the region, and there are locally produced agricultural products that are traded with neighbouring countries. The scale, though, is far smaller than that of the oil and logging businesses.

Brazzaville remains the administrative and political capital of the country, and still hosts the vast majority of bureaucrats and foreign expatriates in Congo, creating a large number of service-sector jobs. River trade used to come south and call at Brazzaville's port before goods were unloaded west to the ocean railway, especially from the former French city of Bangui; yet continued instability has meant that little of this occurs today. Even as conflict subsides, companies have been hesitant to use this slowly moving service in recent times. The Congo River can swell or shrink to such levels that barges cannot pass for many months, making the entire process unreliable for regular business.

PEOPLE AND CULTURE

With a population of roughly three million, Congo is not particularly dense, and only has two main urban centres – Brazzaville and Pointe Noire, with its third town, Dolisie, quite far behind in this respect. The vast majority of citizens are descendants of Bantuist tribes, with the exception of the pygmies, who are descended from a different ethnic lineage.

Numerous sub-cultures have sprung up across Congo, making it a diverse place – in every small town there are west African Muslims who seem to be responsible for basic day-to-day commerce. Africans from neighbouring countries also have their own areas of each city. Furthermore there are large populations of Asians, especially Chinese, who have lived in Brazzaville and Pointe Noire for decades. Russian and French communities can also be found in these two cities, and other scattered pockets of immigrants from around the world. While Congo may be in central Africa, newcomers have found it an easier place to integrate than other countries on the continent – and have made their own indelible mark on the culture and spirit of the country.

French influence abounds across Congo, and the cultural exchange between the nation and France has always been strong – numerous writers, artists and politicians of Congo have spent at least some time visiting or living in their former colonial leader. Their writers and artists have had some success throughout the francophone world. Inside Congo, the painting school in Brazzaville's Poto Poto neighbourhood is particularly revered: carved wooden masks, and to a lesser extent metal works are also popular traditional cultural artefacts.

The country has had a thriving literary scene for around 50 years, starting with the writer Jean Malonga and his novel *Coeur d'Aryenne* (Heart of Aryenne) in 1953. Congo continues to produce excellent francophone writers, including Sylvain Bemba and Guy Menga.

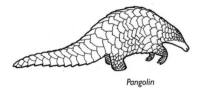

Pangolin

12

Practical Information

TOUR OPERATORS

Specific to the Republic of Congo, several European companies offer organised tours.

Mistral Voyages 73 Cours Pierre Puget, 13006 Marseille, France; ☏ +33 4 91 54 73 71; f +33 4 91 53 95 72; e info@mistralvoyages.com; www.ecotourisme-gabon.com. Offers tours to Ndoki-Nouabalé & Odzala parks via charter aircraft from Gabon.

Nomada Tour Calle del Mar 47, 46003 Valencia, Spain; ☏ +34 902 141 122/+34 963 515 220; f +34 963 516 319; e info@nomadatour.com; www.nomadatour.com. Offers 2-week trips visiting parks & reserves in northern Congo, starting in Brazzaville.

Oasis Overland The Marsh, Henstridge, Somerset BA8 0TF; ☏ 01963 363400; f 01963 363200; e info@oasisoverland.co.uk; www.oasisoverland.co.uk. Visits the Congo coast only on their longest trans-African trips. Overland from Gabon to Pointe Noire, then south into Cabinda.

Wild Frontiers PO Box 844, Halfway Hse 1685, South Africa; ☏ +27 11 702 2035; f +27 11 468 1655; e wildfront@icon.co.za; www.wildfrontiers.com. Does tours of Ndoki-Nouabalé National Park in small groups. Entry & exit via charter aircraft from Libreville. Also offers other tailor-made tours.

RED TAPE

PHOTOGRAPHY Unlike the draconian laws on photo permits across the river in the DR Congo, tourists can be tourists with their photographic equipment in Congo. The only exception is anything that looks remotely military, as well as any bridges, airports, harbours or other large government structures. Also consider cultural sensitivities when photographing in remote areas, and ask for permission before photographing people.

PERMITS No special arrangements are required to visit any park within Congo, but given how difficult it is in the first place to even reach any of them, informing some sort of official that you will be visiting should be on a list of things to do nonetheless. For reserves such as Lefini and Lac Télé, the situation is markedly different: the Ministry of Forestry and Environment needs to sign off on a permit for any visit. These are usually free, and take only a single business day to issue.

ⓔ EMBASSIES

Congo-Brazzaville has only a few embassies around the world. Their presence abroad is small – focused mainly on those nations who have supported them throughout a history filled with ideological upheaval. Representation can be found in the US, UK and France, and all three will issue visas for any Western passport. Visas can be obtained upon arrival for UK and French citizens – provided you have a hotel confirmation or invitation letter. The cost is CFA20,000. Visas are not available at any border crossing, though representation in neighbouring countries is good. Across the rest of Africa, though, their consulates can be difficult to find.

Angola 3 Av 4 de Fevereiro, Luanda; ✆ +244 2 32 59 73

Austria Graben 27, A-1010, Vienna; ✆ +43 1 532 49 09; f +43 1 533 70 87 80

Belgium 16, Av Franklin Roosevelt, 1050 Brussels; ✆ +32 2 648 38 56 f +32 2 648 42 13

Central African Republic Av Boganda, BP 1414, Bangui; ✆ +236 61 20 79

China 7 San Litun Duong Si Jie, Beijing; ✆ +86 10 6532 5259; f +86 10 6532 2915

Cuba Sta Av 1003, Miramar, Havana; ✆ +53 7 24 90 55

Czech Republic Dukelských hrdinů 34, European Business Centre, Praha 7, 170 00; ✆ +420 220 809 391; f +420 220 809 394

DR Congo 179 Bd du 30 Juin, Kinshasa; ✆ +243 12 34 028

Egypt Rue Tiba Mohandessin, Cairo; ✆ +20 2 350 18 26

France 37 bis, Rue Paul Valéry, 75016 Paris; ✆ +33 1 45 00 60 57; f +33 1 40 67 17 33

Gabon BP 269, Libreville; ✆ +241 73 29 06

Germany Botschaft der Republik Kongo, Grabbeallee 47, 13156 Berlin; ✆ +49 40 07 83; f +49 40 07 78; Rheinallee 45, Bonn, 53173; ✆ +49 228 35 83 55; f +49 228 369 86 13; e botschaft.kongobrz@t-online.de

Italy Via Ombrone 8/10, 100 Rome; ✆ +39 06 4140 0612; f +39 06 4140 0218

Japan Harajuku Green Heights, Rm 701, 3-53-17, Sendagaya, Shibuya-ku, 151 Tokyo; ✆ +81 3423 3981; f +81 3423 3984

Kenya Botschaft, 2nd Floor, City Hse, Corner Wabera St/Standard St, Nairobi; ✆ +254 2 24 73 65; f +254 2 33 17 92

Morocco Av Iman Malik, 7 Rue Sanhaja Souissi, Rabat; ✆ +212 3765 9966; f +212 3765 9959

Namibia 9 Korner St, PO Box 22970, Windhoek; ✆ +264 6125 7517

Nigeria Lobito Crescent 447, Abuja; ✆ +234 9 413 74 07; f +234 9 413 01 57

Russia Kroptkinsky 12/Pomerantsex 11, Moscow; ✆ +7 95 236 33 68

Senegal BP 5242, Dakar; ✆ +221 634 50 22; f +221 825 78 56

South Africa 960 Arcadia St, Arcadia 0083; ✆ +27 12 342 55 08; f +27 12 342 55 10

Switzerland (UN) Chemin François Lehmann, 241218 Grad Schonnex, Geneva; ✆ +41 22 731 88 21

United Kingdom The Arena, 24 Southwark Bridge Rd, London SE1 9HF; ✆ 020 7922 0695

United States 4891 Colorado Av NW, Washington, DC 20011; ✆ +1 202 726 5500; f +1 202 726 1860

United States (Permanent UN Mission) 14 E 65th St, New York, NY 10021; ✆ +1 212 744 7840; f +1 212 744 7975; e congo@un.int

GETTING THERE AND AWAY

✈ **BY AIR** To the Republic of Congo, your options are limited for flying. The only airline offering any real frequency to the country is **Air France** (*www.airfrance.com*), which flies a small aircraft three times weekly direct from Paris to Pointe Noire. They also fly a much larger plane four times weekly to Brazzaville. However, their prices reflect their monopoly on this route – flying direct from Paris to Congo will set a traveller back a small fortune, with no discounts for an advance purchase. You can also reach Brazzaville with **Ethiopian Airlines** (*www.flyethiopian.com*) via Addis Ababa, for about a third of the price, when the ticket is booked a few months ahead. There is a lesser-known twice-weekly flight from Johannesburg to Brazzaville with **Interair South Africa** (*www.interair.co.za*) – also known as Inter Aviation Servi. They also offer an irregular service from Cotonou (Benin) to Brazzaville, *en route* to Johannesburg.

Regionally, Pointe Noire and Brazzaville are well connected – **Air Gabon** flies to both cities from Libreville (when they do fly, as they have had continuing financial problems for several years), and **TAAG Angolan Airlines** flies from Luanda. **Cameroon Airways** flies from Douala to Brazzaville, sometimes via Libreville, but the status of the airline is patchy at best, with frequent reports of them being bankrupt. Hewa Bora Air does the incredibly short hop across the

Congo River from Kinshasa's N'Djili Airport to Brazzaville's Maya-Maya Airport, and continues onward to Pointe Noire. Several airlines operate a Cotonou–Brazzaville flight aside from Interair: **Aero Benin**, **Benin Golf Air** and **West African Airlines**. **Air Mauritanie** also flies from Bamako (Mali) to Cotonou, then Brazzaville – many of these flights are intermittent – here today and gone tomorrow. Your best bet is to visit an airline travel agent in west Africa if you need to get to either Brazzaville or Pointe Noire, and they should be able to find something – usually via Cotonou, often with a stopover in Libreville.

BY SEA If you need something heavy sent down, you can get it shipped to Pointe Noire quite easily. Pointe Noire is, in fact, the only deep-water port in Africa south of Dakar and therefore sees plenty of ships passing through.

BY LAND From the **DR Congo**, frequent ferries run between Kinshasa and Brazzaville both on fast motorboats called *canôt rapides*, and on the crowded public ferry. There are boats that head south from Cameroon into Ouesso and onward boat transport south to Brazzaville. **Cabinda**'s border with Congo at Pointe Noire is open, provided you are willing to pay for access: about US$100 will get you across, not including a fee for a vehicle.

From **Gabon** there are two options that bring you to Dolisie: the most common route is from N'Dende south, taking about three days. Less common is from Bakoumba to Mbinda, and then south via a once-weekly train connection – border officials on the Gabonese side are famously corrupt and transport is intermittent. It is also possible to cross from Franceville to Okoyo, though the road is bad and this area is known for outbreaks of the Ebola virus.

From **Cameroon** head towards the southeasternmost corner of the country, to a village called Bolozo, and then cross the river to the large town of Moloundou. Motorboats can also be hired for a journey along the river to Ouesso. There are also other roads southeast towards villages across the river from Ouesso, though transport to them is patchy at best.

There is also another difficult but navigable road from Impfondo to the **Central African Republic**, which while possible to use, will take any determined overlander a serious amount of time – with no services to speak of in between. It is slightly better to just take the regular barges upriver to Bangui.

GETTING AROUND

See page 43.

MEDIA AND COMMUNICATIONS

INTERNET High-speed internet is reasonably easy to find in Brazzaville and Pointe Noire, but outside these cities non-existent. Most people who spend serious time outside Congo's two urban centres bring satellite equipment to ensure connectivity.

NEWSPAPERS Several newspapers can be found throughout the city, in either French or Lingala. No English-language media specific to the country exist, and if you need it, the internet should be your first stop – I recommend the site www.allafrica.com, which compiles news reports on a country by country basis from a wide variety of sources.

RADIO For radio, options are quite wide – but again, only in French. **Radio France International** can be found at 93.2FM. Other stations include Radio Brazzaville,

12

Radio Congo and Radio Liberté. Brazzaville also receives almost every radio station from Kinshasa, making the choice here especially huge – but again, only in French and tribal languages.

Across central Africa, the **BBC** broadcasts on short wave from Ascension Island and South Africa; check availability on their frequency charts at www.bbc.co.uk/worldservice.

TELEPHONE Congo's mobile-phone network is reasonably comprehensive, and as with most places in Africa, the prepaid phonecard is king. Most prominent of the lot at the moment is MTN, and you can go to their office on Avenue Foch in Brazzaville for some guidance on getting onto the network.

Land lines in Congo are generally six-digit numbers, prefixed with the city code first. For mobile numbers, seven digits is the norm without a city code. Adding a zero at the beginning of a mobile number is not necessary.

TELEVISION French media outlets dominate Congo, and it is common to see **Le Monde** and **TV5** emanating from almost every television throughout the city. The unfortunate fact is that these channels rarely delve too much into local politics, but keep the Congolese up to date on what's happening in the outside world – and ironically it's often easier to find out what's going on in France than in other parts of Congo itself.

Lesser bushbaby

13

Brazzaville

⊕ *04°16.20 S, 15°17.21 E*

Comparisons with Brazzaville's larger neighbour are inevitable – across the river where the massive metropolis of Kinshasa sits, where activity can be intense and the evenings bustling; the capital of Congo is nearly a mirror image. At times quiet and quaint, it is often a sleepy and better-organised city. Its centre is walkable, and numerous cultural sights are within a short distance of each other. The citizens of Brazzaville have an easier task with their well-planned capital, and many travellers find it to be a welcome escape from whatever may be transpiring across the river.

Yet Brazzaville itself is just emerging from its own troubles: pay attention to what lies beyond some rusted fences of corrugated aluminium and you will see destroyed towers, abandoned office blocks, torn-up roads, and other telltale signs of a civil war that is only barely in the past. While what occurs in Kinshasa may at times seem monumental and right in plain view of everyone, Brazzaville's problems seem forgotten and buried in the background – even by its own citizens. The city seems to have an urge to move on, and while Congo's own political problems are still very much unresolved, the capital has in many ways restored the laidback atmosphere that its reputation was founded upon.

The city has seen plenty of attention paid to formal cultural institutions, having been the epicentre of France's investments in central Africa for nearly a century. It rarely has the same level of traffic and noise as Kinshasa; crime barely exists, and a multi-culturalism is present in the city that Kinshasa has yet to master – European, Arab, Asian and African residents all go about their daily business beside one another, without armed guards and walls of razorwire between them. Families from around the world have migrated to Brazzaville, set up businesses and live in the city. It is a simpler place than Kinshasa, and better integrated in every manner.

HISTORY

Pierre Savorgnan de Brazza's treaty with the Nkuna people allowed for a town to be founded on the banks of the Congo River, near the village of N'Tamo, on 28 August 1880. After de Brazza had made his journey west to the coast, thereby allowing French map-makers to fully understand where Brazzaville was located, its relevance to the French Empire grew significantly. At the Berlin Conference of 1884, as the African continent was being carved up, de Brazza's journeys would allow all lands west of the Congo River, and north of its tributary Ubangi, to be controlled by France. Brazzaville would become the capital of Congo Français, stretching from the Congo River all the way northward to the deserts of the Sahara. De Brazza would be the first Governor-General to run the colony.

As the administrative centre of France's central African interests, Brazzaville grew quickly into a medium-sized town of tree-lined boulevards and a genuinely francophone atmosphere. Yet the city never ballooned to the size of its neighbour across the river: the planned Congo Ocean Railway was stalled for decades, and there was not nearly as much incentive for immigrants to settle in Brazzaville. The population did slowly increase, as the *concessionaires* arrived, and by 1910 Brazzaville had created designated quarters for Europeans in the city centre. Two more quarters were designated for Africans: Bacongo and Poto Poto.

It would not be until the Congo Ocean Railway began construction that Brazzaville would increase in size again, and jump in population once more as France fell to the Nazi army and those loyal to Charles de Gaulle fled their homeland to make the city their new capital of Free France. Brazzaville would remain intensely significant to France throughout World War II, an intellectual centrepoint for those opposed to Vichy rule in Europe, and a hotbed for new ideas to emerge regarding France's future plans for its colonies as the war effort raged on.

In 1944, the Brazzaville Conference was convened, which set out new rights for the African colonies of France. Charles de Gaulle and Brazzaville Governor Félix Eboué would chair the conference, and it would grant each colony a position in France's new legislature. All-too-common practices in their African holdings would be abandoned, including forced labour and polygamy. Trade union rights would be strengthened. Citizens of overseas colonies would be treated almost as equals with citizens of France.

Brazzaville would remain capital of Afrique Equatoriale Française in 1950 as Pointe Noire became the provincial administrative centre of Moyen Congo. The division between bureaucratic duties helped split the population into both centres, though both cities continued to grow rapidly. When independence arrived in 1959 Pointe Noire would lose its status as Congo's capital, as the newly independent government would bring it back to Brazzaville.

Each upheaval in government that Congo endured throughout the 1960s and 1970s was felt, mostly, in Brazzaville. The capital also helped followers of Patrice Lumumba who fled their government in Léopoldville, and the city gained prominence within Africa as a centre for socialist reform. Hosting Lumumbist rebels of Congo-Léopoldville, socialist Angolan rebels, as well as Cuban, Russian and Chinese advisors, the Cold War arrived in Africa in full force on either side of the Congo River. Portions of this large communist backing would remain even after the rise of Congo's right-wing military leader Marien Ngouabe. Brazzaville was also seeing riots, as well as soldiers flooding the streets, and protests from trade unions. The sleepy Europeanesque capital had turned into a genuine hotbed of ideological revolution, and continued to be the centrepoint of immigration across Congo – this would mean, in effect, that every tribal group had staked out their own quarters in the city, making it both a diverse and dangerous place.

Brazzaville's lines were redrawn in 1980 as the city continued to grow, allowing for seven *arrondissements* in addition to the centre of Brazzaville. With the arrival of Denis Sassou-Nguesso as head of state, Congo began to see some economic reforms, bringing about new trade and investment into the capital and across the country.

However, as the 1990s arrived and multi-party elections were planned, chaos broke loose in Brazzaville. Armed groups loyal to their tribes, and political parties aligned to them, created riots and open conflict on the streets of Brazzaville. This persisted as Sassou-Nguesso was voted out of office and replaced by Pascal Lissouba. Lissouba's reign was short-lived, though, as combat continued and Nguesso was reinstated. The rebel group of the Ninjas attacked the capital again in 2003, and were repelled by the Congolese army. They currently hold them back via a nominal front line west of the city, as Brazzaville tries to rebuild from a turbulent decade.

Further elections are planned for 2009, which could mean a return to violence; however, the city has reached a period of calm, and some renewed business interest has seen Brazzaville slowly drift away from its worst years. Most of Brazzaville's major cultural points of interest were untouched in the fighting, and on the surface, the city bears a remarkable lack of scars from conflict.

ORIENTATION

Straddling the Congo River, Brazzaville sits on the north bank just southwest of Malebo Pool. Its far western edge is along the River Djoué and the rapids which make the final leg of the Congo River impassable. Route Nationale No 2 heads north out of the city, and Route National No 1 goes west.

The most identifiable landmark is **Tour Nabemba** near the Congo River, Brazzaville's tallest tower and an excellent point of reference. On the road directly north of the tower is **Rond Point Poto Poto**, which is the heart of the very African Poto Poto neighbourhood. Further north is **Rond Point Moungali**, again the heart of the neighbourhood called Moungali. West of Tour Nabemba is the **Centre Ville**, also known as **Plaine**, which can be nominally called Brazzaville's geographical centre. The Place de la Plaine is a small open area near the **Rond Point City Centre**, where Avenue de l'Indepéndance turns off from Avenue Patrice Lumumba.

Avenue Foch is Brazzaville's true commercial heart, a small but busy street where business begins every morning in the city. **Maya-Maya Airport** indicates the northwestern limits of the town, and just south of it are several open areas comprising the zoo, athletic stadium and ministry buildings. Southeast towards Avenue Foch is **Plateau Ville**, containing plenty of interesting sights as well as numerous embassies.

GETTING THERE AND AROUND

BY AIR Maya-Maya Airport is a small, ageing, claustrophobic throwback to an era of African travel that most of the continent has abandoned. Customs processes can be maddening, luggage is slow to arrive, but security is halfway decent – yet the airport is overloaded with badge-bearing touts who are employed, in theory, to help you in your quest to get into and out of the airport (while parting with too much money to do it). There is really no reason to employ these people – if you have large amounts of luggage and are not meeting anyone, paying a porter CFA500 to take them to a taxi is more than enough. In front of the airport are numerous offices for every airline flying in and around the country, and can be a decent place to purchase air tickets. International carriers that fly into Brazzaville maintain offices in the city centre however, and getting anything done will necessitate being there instead of fighting with the crowds at Maya-Maya.

Airline offices

✈ **Aéro Service** Av Foch, Centre Ville; ☎ 81 00 26
✈ **Air France** Av Amilcar Cabral, BP 16; ☎ 81 27 19 (reservations)/82 07 98 (airport); f 81 51 35; e mail.cto.bzv@airfrance.fr
✈ **Air Gabon** Rue Félix Éboué, Centre Ville; ☎ 81 58 76
✈ **Brazza Airways** Av Foch, Centre Ville
✈ **Canadian Airways Congo** Maya-Maya Airport

✈ **Ethiopian Airlines** Av Foch, Centre Ville, BP 14125; ☎ 81 07 61/81 07 66/528 10 59; e bzvam@ethiopianairlines.com
✈ **Hewa Bora Airways** Av A Conus; ☎ 566 0104
✈ **TAAG Angolan Airlines** Rue Félix Éboué, Centre Ville; ☎ 851 6341/851 30 921
✈ **Trans Air Congo** Maya-Maya Airport, BP 2422; ☎ 81 10 46

BY TAXI In abundance across Brazzaville are green taxis. In theory it should cost CFA800 for a ride across town, but having the correct change for this endeavour often makes paying an even thousand more likely. For short trips within a

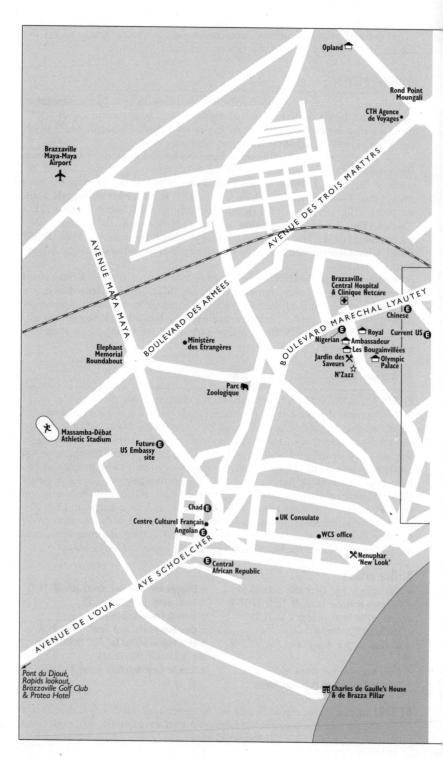

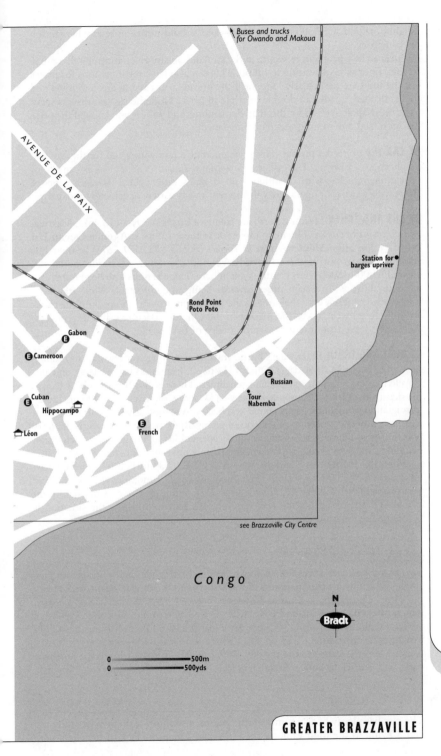

Buses and trucks
for Owando and Makoua

AVENUE DE LA PAIX

Station for
barges upriver

Rond Point
Poto Poto

Gabon

Cameroon

Russian

Cuban
Hippocampo

Tour
Nabemba

Léon

French

see Brazzaville City Centre

Congo

N

Bradt

0 ———————— 500m
0 ———————— 500yds

GREATER BRAZZAVILLE

13

neighbourhood, CFA500 is acceptable – and should not require any bargaining on your part.

Fuel can be a problem to secure in the city, and on any given morning there may be long lines of taxis waiting to fill up. This can also have repercussions for prices – if the lines are particularly long, or if the president is passing through town and fuel is needed, a ride can double or triple in price. Nonetheless taxi drivers seem to be more apologetic about this than demanding, and will let you know if the price has increased due to unforeseen circumstances.

BY CAR If you need a private vehicle, negotiating a fare with a taxi for the day will be cheapest. However, **Europcar** (*Maya-Maya Airport;* \ *83 21 48*) is capable of providing vehicles with chauffeurs on a daily rate. Camal Voyages, one of Brazzaville's two tour operators, will also rent a wide variety of vehicles for day trips.

BY BUS AND TRUCK Heading north are frequent **buses** to Oyo, Owando, Makoua, and places in between. The main purveyor of these routes is **Agence Ocean Du Nord** (*1 Rue Ango Mikalou, Av de la Tsiemé;* m *628 8833/521 7678*) at their bus station in the far northern reaches of Brazzaville – however, a taxi ride should still cost CFA1,000–2,000 from Centre Ville to here. Large **trucks** also head north and west for those with certain urges towards being uncomfortable while travelling long distances. Prices are the same as the buses, but provide an option if the buses are full. To go west, go to the market in the Quartier Bacongo, and to go north, trucks also leave from the northernmost edge of Brazzaville.

BY BOAT AND TRAIN Brazzaville's **barge station** sees a huge variety of boats heading upriver to Mossaka (four days), Ouesso (14 days), Impfondo (seven days), and also Boyele (ten days), all on intermittent schedules. There is also **'Le Beach'**, which is the departure point for Kinshasa – a *canôt rapide* across the river is US$40, including immigration formalities. Many people will be at you as soon as you depart the boat in Kinshasa; you don't need to pay anyone a penny. Right beside the beach is the ferry port for across the river, and significantly cheaper at US$10, but you'll be in charge of handling your own immigration formalities. Sometimes the extra fees are worth it.

When the **trains** come and go, they cost CFA20,000 to Pointe Noire for first class and CFA13,000 for second class. As mentioned, sometimes the 'Ninjas' can be a problem (see *Chapter 11, History*, page 231), and if they're creating significant trouble I'd advise against the train entirely. It's best to ask how the situation is before taking the train west.

LOCAL TOUR OPERATORS

Two travel agencies specialise in tours around Brazzaville, and can also arrange single- or multi-day trips to points of interest around the capital. Right across from the Hôtel Eucalyptus is **Camal Voyages** (\ *81 01 75/8;* e *camal_bzv@yahoo.fr*), which offers day trips around Brazzaville as well as renting out a wide variety of vehicles with driver from US$75 per day. Near the Rond Point Moungali is **CTH Voyages & Tourisme** (\ *81 55 39;* f *81 56 45; www.travel-congo.com*) who will likewise arrange tours around the city. Both can also organise trips to the northern parks with sufficient notice. Each has at least one person who speaks some English.

 ## WHERE TO STAY

The city has plenty of accommodation options, and most of them exist at the top end. Owing to the high value of the CFA, and a genuine lack of travellers who are not in the country professionally, finding budget accommodation can be quite a task, but not impossible: outside the city centre, and especially in the neighbourhood of Poto Poto, hotels frequented by Congolese travellers can provide an inexpensive option for someone passing through. The best advice I can give someone without too much money is simply not to spend much time in the capital.

EXPENSIVE

🏠 **Hôtel Marina** Centre Ville, BP 2129; **m** 665 8555; **f** 81 16 43; **e** hotelmarina@yahoo.fr. Near the city centre & recently renovated with a large secure car park out front. Also has 2 restaurants, a bar, pool, small conference room, internet available for an hourly fee, airport shuttle on request. All rooms have TV, AC. Accepts euros, but not credit cards. Sgl/suite $$$$$

🏠 **Le Meridien Hôtel** Centre Ville, BP 588; ↘ 81 03 02/81 03 07; **f** 81 55 49; **e** meridienbrazzaville@hotmail.com. Brazzaville's flagship international hotel – with 2 restaurants, 2 bars, a pool, tennis court, garden, nightclub, several conference rooms, TV, AC, internet connection & airport shuttle. The lobby is a little small & cluttered but has a unique atmosphere for a major hotel. Accepts euros & all major credit cards. Sgl/dbl/suite $$$$$

🏠 **Olympic Palace Hôtel** Centre Ville, BP 65; ↘ 81 34 36; **f** 81 00 30; **e** olympicreception@hotmail.com. With restaurant, bar, pool, small conference room, TV, AC, safety deposit boxes, en-suite internet (for an extra fee), & airport shuttle. Accepts euros, Visa, MasterCard. Sgl/dbl/suite $$$$$

🏠 **Protea Hôtel** In the Cité du Djoué; ↘ 81 25 20/81 46 72; **f** 81 13 45; **e** brazzavillebeach@yahoo.fr. On the top of a hill in a secluded suburb of Brazzaville. Has bar & restaurant, 2 pools, internet connection by the hour, secure parking, small conference room, fitness room, TV, AC, airport shuttle. Accepts euros, but not credit cards. Sgl/dbl/suite $$$$$

MID-RANGE

🏠 **Alizés Hôtel and Snack Bar** Pl de la Plaine; **m** 666 6670/656 5441. With a small terrace for their restaurant & spotless high-end rooms with rather flashy designs, though a little heavy on the zebra-striped carpets & pictures of women on the walls. Probably not your best bet if you're a little conservative. Discounts offered for extended stays. Sgl/dbl $$$$, suite $$$$$

🏠 **Hippocampe Hôtel** Centre Ville, BP 35; **m** 668 6068; **e** hotresthippocampe@yahoo.fr. One of Brazzaville's older hotels situated at the foot of some hills, & was used often by journalists & aid workers during the civil war. The restaurant is a pleasant enough place with good pizza. Also has a bar & secure parking. Rooms are simple but have hot running water & AC. Sgl/dbl $$$

🏠 **Hôtel Ambassadeur** Near the Olympic Palace Hôtel, BP 15377; ↘ 81 33 71. Amongst a variety of other hotels along this street the Ambassadeur is probably the best value for quality, with good clean rooms. They have AC & TV. A bar & restaurant are present as well as parking out front. Sgl $$$, suite $$$$

🏠 **Hôtel de L'Aeroport** Right in front of Maya-Maya Airport; **m** 558 1717. Nothing to write home about but it is within walking distance of the airport &

has respectable rooms for this price range – with hot running water, AC, & TV. Also present is a bar & restaurant. Accepts euros, but not credit cards. Sgl $$$$, suite $$$$$

🏠 **Hôtel du Centre** Centre Ville, BP 13353; ↘ 81 15 06; **f** 81 02 80. On the main road heading northeast towards the docks with basic rooms. AC, cold running water & TV included, along with a secure parking area. Within walking distance of Pl de la Plaine. Has a bar & restaurant, safety deposit boxes, airport shuttle on request. Sgl/dbl $$$, suite $$$$

🏠 **Hôtel Eucalyptus** Centre Ville, BP 2392; ↘ 81 25 17; **f** 82 37 90. Off the busy Av Lumumba, the rooms are good quality for this price range though beginning to show their age. Eucalyptus has weathered several decades through Brazzaville's troubles. Rooms have AC & cold running water. The attached restaurant is one of the city's best. Sgl $$$, dbl $$$$

🏠 **Hôtel Léon** Av du Colonel Bisset, BP 2111; ↘ 81 23 11; **f** 81 58 78; **e** hotel_leon@yahoo.fr. Large clean rooms with hot water, AC & cable TV. Also sports a bar & restaurant. Has been recently fixed up & there is a pleasant sitting area out front. It's in a quiet neighbourhood but still

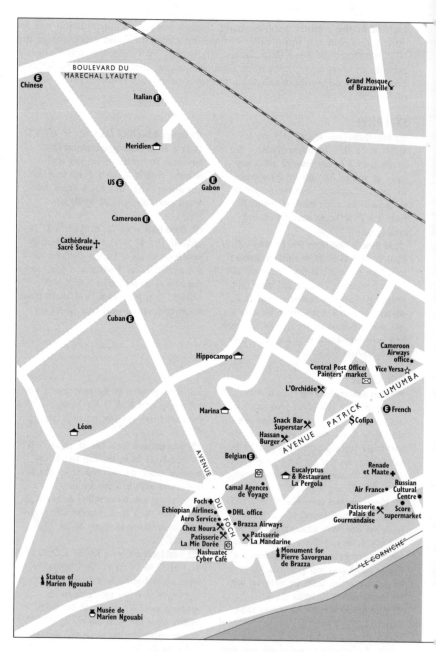

BOULEVARD DU MARECHAL LYAUTEY

Chinese

Grand Mosque of Brazzaville

Italian

Meridien

US

Gabon

Cameroon

Cathédrale Sacré Soeur

Cuban

Hippocampo

Cameroon Airways office

Central Post Office/ Painters' market

Vice Versa

L'Orchidée

Marina

Léon

AVENUE PATRICK LUMUMBA

Snack Bar Superstar

Cofipa

French

Hassan Burger

Belgian

Eucalyptus & Restaurant La Pergola

Renade et Maate

AVENUE DU FOCH

Camal Agences de Voyage

Air France

Russian Cultural Centre

Foch

Ethiopian Airlines

DHL office

Aero Service

Patisserie Palais de Gourmandaise

Score supermarket

Chez Noura

Brazza Airways

Patisserie La Mie Dorée

Patisserie La Mandarine

Nashuatec Cyber Café

Monument for Pierre Savorgnan de Brazza

"LE CORNICHE"

Statue of Marien Ngouabi

Musée de Marien Ngouabi

close to the city centre. Sgl/dbl $$$$, suite $$$$$

⌂ **Hôtel Saphir** Centre Ville, BP 1307; ☎ 81 01 25; f 81 15 35; e hotelsaphirbzv@yahoo.fr. Centrally located with a restaurant, pool, small conference room, safety deposit boxes, airport shuttle on

request. It's popular with French expatriates as their embassy is right behind it. There is a large open terrace bar. Excellent ambience — a sort of 19th-century apt block. Entrance is on a secure side street. Accepts euros, but not credit cards. Sgl/dbl $$$$

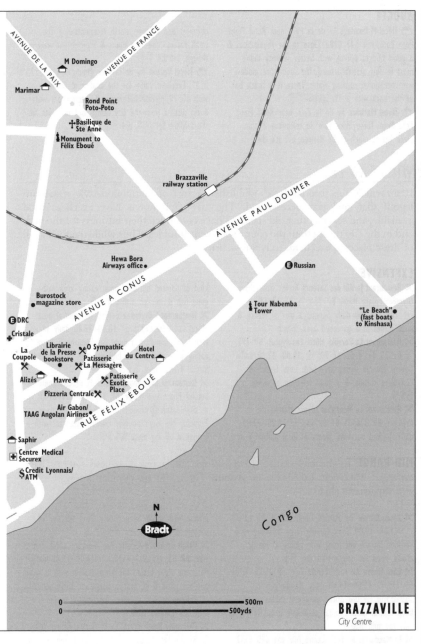

BRAZZAVILLE
City Centre

🏠 **Les Bougainvillees** Across from the Olympic
Palace Hôtel, BP 646; ✆ 81 11 56; f 81 11 81.
A large area with plenty of plants to keep it green.
Rooms have cold running water & AC. Also has a
bar & restaurant, safety deposit box, free laundry
service. Accepts euros. Sgl \$\$\$, dbl \$\$\$\$

🏠 **Royal Hôtel** Near the Olympic Palace Hôtel, BP
13939; ✆ 81 33 76. A cheaper option on this stretch
of road & often full. Not as nice as its neighbours but
it can be a good place to save some money. Rooms
have AC & occasional running water. Also has a bar.
Only accepts euros & CFA. Sgl \$\$\$, dbl \$\$\$\$

BUDGET

🏠 **Hôtel M Domingo** Av de la Paix, near Rond Point Poto Poto; m 547 0187. Close to the roundabout & a good budget option, with better security than most in this neighbourhood. The rooms are modest with occasional running water. There is a snack bar at the back with a TV. Sgl/dbl $$

🏠 **Hôtel Marimar** Av de la Paix, near Rond Point Poto Poto. These folks have no telephone & the place leaves much to be desired, but it's the cheapest bed in town worth recommending. The small rooms have thin doors & intermittent water though. Sgl/dbl $$

🏠 **Hôtel Opland** Av de la Paix, Moungali; m 527 0731. Excellent value for the quality of rooms — with AC, TV, private bathrooms & intermittent water. A bit distant from the city centre, but it's close to the airport. Sgl $$, dbl $$$

✖ WHERE TO EAT

Brazzaville's top eateries have established a sort of compound-style restaurant layout that civil war necessitated. The city's top hotels have excellent food available, and several other old standbys have continued their business for the high end in the city throughout the country's recent troubles. Thus while the food at all of these places is excellent, so is the security.

EXPENSIVE

✖ **Restaurant Jardin des Saveurs** Across from the Olympic Palace Hôtel, BP 264; ✆ 81 17 74; ⏰ 18.00–22.00 daily. Serving a mix of French & local dishes in a gardened area. $$$

✖ **Restaurant La Pergola** Hôtel Eucalyptus, BP 292; ✆ 81 25 17; f 82 37 90; ⏰ 18.00–22.00 daily. Decent enough dining area with both French & Congolese cuisine, & a good selection of wines. $$$

✖ **Restaurant Le Nenuphar** In the Marché des Artisans, BP 326; ✆ 81 09 15; ⏰ 18.00–22.00 daily. Tricked out with plenty of local paintings in a kind of pointed hut-style open eating area with good fish & chicken dishes. $$$

✖ **Restaurant L'Orchidee** Behind the central post office; m 660 6732; ⏰ 18.00–22.00 daily. In a secure compound in a quiet neighbourhood, large eating area with a very high-end feel to it. Sticks to formal French fare. $$$$

✖ **Restaurant O Sympathic** Rond Point City Centre, behind Pharmacie Mavre, BP 329; m 677 8143; e osympathic@yahoo.fr; ⏰ 18.00–22.00 daily. Probably the city's premier French restaurant with a formal AC dining area. $$$$

MID-RANGE In the city centre, pastry shops and a few Lebanese eateries have emerged. Pavement cafés exist on Avenue Foch, and are popular amongst locals and expatriates alike.

✖ **Assan Burger** Bd Patrice Lumumba; ✆ 81 17 74; ⏰ 11.00–19.00 daily. Serving large hamburgers & chicken. Terrace out front with plenty of plastic chairs, good for people-watching. $$

✖ **Chez Noura** Av Foch, Centre Ville, BP 2585; ✆ 81 55 77; ⏰ 10.00–19.00 daily. Hamburgers & shawarma for low prices, pavement tables on the busy central road. Popular as a café if La Mandarine gets too full. $$

✖ **La Mandarine** Av Foch, Centre Ville; m 660 6732; ⏰ 07.00–18.00 daily. Brazzaville's most popular patisserie with decent-priced b/fasts, fresh juices, grenadine, freshly brewed coffee (not Nescafé), & a wide variety of pastries. Very busy around midday. $$

✖ **La Mie Dorée** Av Foch, Centre Ville; m 566 6600; ⏰ 07.00–18.00 daily. Patisserie on Brazzaville's main avenue, with indoor seating only. Good selection of pastries & freshly brewed coffee. $$

✖ **Palais de Gourmandaise** Rue Amilcar Cabral, Centre Ville, BP 85; m 527 2518; ⏰ 11.00–19.00 daily. Patisserie right beside the Score Market with a large outdoor patio & AC indoor restaurant. Large selection of pastries as well as other inexpensive snacks including burgers. $$

✖ **Patisserie Exotic Place** Ex la Manne, Centre Ville; ✆ 81 25 16; ⏰ 07.00–17.00 daily. Decent selection of pastries & snacks with a small outdoor terrace. $$

✖ **Patisserie La Messagère** Near Pl de la Plaine, behind Pharmacie Mavre; ⏰ 07.00–17.00 daily. Quite similar to Exotic Place which is nearby, except with pavement tables. $$

✖ **Pizzeria Centrale** Near Pl de la Plaine, Centre Ville; ☉ 11.00–17.00 daily. Serving pizzas in the city centre, at the lower end of the price spectrum. **$$**

✖ **Restaurant La Coupole** Bd Patrice Lumumba; ☉ 16.00–22.00 daily. Large outdoor terrace in the city centre, recently renovated, with good views of the surrounding streets. A large selection of pizzas. **$$**

✖ **Snack Bar Super-Star** Bd Patrice Lumumba; m 538 0808; ☉ 11.00–19.00 daily. Similar to Assan Burger, an inexpensive place for hamburgers, chicken, & some Lebanese dishes. **$$**

ENTERTAINMENT AND NIGHTLIFE

Nightlife tends to be sparse, and limited to what the major hotels can offer. A few local discotheques operate around the city, the most notable of which is on Congo's **rapids**. Rooms are also available there for CFA12,000 if you don't fancy a trip back into the city. Other places to hang out in the evening are some inexpensive local nightclubs: **N'zazz**, across from the Olympic Palace Hôtel and **Vice Versa** along Boulevard Patrice Lumumba. The **Meridien Hôtel** has a casino and nightclub as well, and is the first stop for any expatriates in town looking for more of their kind.

SHOPPING

For any kind of groceries, the **Score Supermarket** (*Rue Félix Éboué;* ✆ *81 03 35;* ☉ *08.00–12.30 & 14.00–19.00 Mon–Sat, 08.00–13.00 Sun*) stands out as the best place to visit – similar to other upmarket supermarkets across central Africa, if it's a domestic device you require and available in the country, it should be in stock here. European foods can be found, but prices are not particularly low. The opening hours shown above are not always adhered to, but usually closing in the middle of the day and open only in the morning on Sundays.

Outside the central post office, an **Artists' Market** emerges in the afternoons with large numbers of paintings, metal sculptures and other items of interest to souvenir seekers passing through. If possible, bring a local friend who can advise you on decent prices to pay; the quality of many of these items is excellent, and a testament to Brazzaville's highly regarded painting school in Poto Poto.

For books, there are two places: **Burostock** on Avenue de l'Indépéndance across from the DR Congo embassy has a large selection of French magazines, and nearby is the **Librairie de la Presse**, a two-storey bookstore filled with more francophone literature.

PRACTICALITIES

BANKS The most important financial institution in Congo for a foreigner will be **Credit Lyonnais**, as it often deals with expatriates who need bank accounts in country – and most importantly, has the only ATM available anywhere aside from Pointe Noire. The machine is closed from 22.00 until 06.00, with posted security guards to monitor whoever goes in and out.

$ **Banque Cofipa** Av Amilcar Cabral; ✆ 81 03 73; ☉ 08.00–14.30 Mon–Fri

$ **Credit Lyonnais Congo** Av Amilcar Cabral; ✆ 81 07 15; ☉ 07.00–16.15 Mon–Fri, 08.00–12.00 Sat

FOREIGN EMBASSIES Some major embassies have their Brazzaville operation running from across the river in Kinshasa; interestingly enough, most countries have taken the political instability of Congo-Brazzaville far more seriously than Congo-Kinshasa. Of course, there is more to their reasons for not having a permanent presence in Brazzaville – this country does not have the same economic clout as their larger neighbour across the river.

Ⓔ Angola 223 Av Charles de Gaulle, BP 388 (behind the Centre Culturel Français); ☎ 81 37 03
Ⓔ Belgium Av Patrice Lumumba, Centre Ville, BP 225; ☎ 81 37 12; f 81 37 04;
e Brazzaville@diplobel.org
Ⓔ Cameroon Rue Bayardelle; ☎ 81 26 24
Ⓔ Central African Republic In Plateau Ville, off Av Schoelcher
Ⓔ Chad Av Charles de Gaulle (behind the Centre Culturel Français); ☎ 81 27 06
Ⓔ China Bd du Marechal Lyautey, BP 213; ☎ 81 11 32; f 81 11 35; e chinaemb_cg@mfa.gov.cn
Ⓔ Cuba 28 Rue Lacien Fourneaux, BP 80
Ⓔ Democratic Republic of Congo Av de l'Indépendance; ☎ 81 30 52
Ⓔ France Rue Alfassa, BP 2089; ☎ 81 55 41/81 55 42/81 55 43; e ambafrance-cg.org
Ⓔ Gabon Bd du Marechal Lyautey, Poto Poto; ☎ 81 56 20

Ⓔ Italy 2 Bd du Marechal Lyautey, BP 2484; ☎ 81 58 41; f 81 11 52; e ambitbra@congonet.cg
Ⓔ Nigeria 11 Bd du Marechal Lyautey, BP 790; ☎ 83 38 46/83 13 16/83 27 49
Ⓔ Russia Av Gouverneur General Félix Éboué (beside Tour Nabemba), BP 2132; ☎ 81 19 23; f 81 50 85; e amrussie@congonet.cg
Ⓔ South Africa Le Meridien Hôtel, Room 704; m 530 1388
Ⓔ United Kingdom (Consulate) Et-Lisa Av Foch, Plateau Ville; ☎ 62 08 93; f 83 85 43; e vorick@congonet.org. Limited services – other services available from Kinshasa; ☎ 62 08 93; f +243 838 543; e ambrit@ic.cd
Ⓔ United States Operates from Kinshasa; ☎ +243 088 43608; f +243 088 41036; temporary office in Brazzaville at 70 Rue Bayardelle; ☎ 81 14 72. New embassy due to be constructed along Av du Maya-Maya.

HOSPITALS AND EMERGENCIES The country's largest and most important hospital is along Boulevard du Maréchal Lyautey, a crowded and intimidating place that is rarely used by foreign staff. Numerous clinics cater to First World standards; among them the **Centre Medical Securex** (*33 Av Amilcar Cabral, Centre Ville;* ☎ *81 38 72;* f *81 53 84;* e *clinique.securex@brazzavillecliniquesecurex.com*) and **Clinique Netcare** (*Bd du Maréchal Lyautey, Quartier du CHU (Brazzaville Central Hospital)*); ☎ *94 38 75*).

Pharmacies are in abundance across Brazzaville, but the largest and most comprehensive is **Pharmacie Mavre** (*Pl de la Plaine, Centre Ville;* ☎ *81 18 39*), which stocks plenty of things unavailable anywhere outside Brazzaville or Pointe Noire, including Malarone (for a steep price). They also have European pharmacists who can advise and prescribe something if necessary. Other pharmacies in Centre Ville with a decent selection are **Pharmacie Foch** (*Av Foch*), and **Pharmacie Cristale** (*Av de L'Independence*), near the DR Congo embassy. Also near the French embassy and Score Supermarket is a small place called **Pharmacie Renande et Maate** (☎ *81 18 18*).

INTERNET The largest and most popular internet café is also on Avenue Foch: **Nashuatec**, charging CFA2,000 per half-hour. A cheaper option for internet access is on Avenue Patrice Lumumba, across from the Belgian embassy, at CFA1,000 per half-hour.

POST The capital's main post office is easy to find – a large structure just across from the French Embassy, in a large roundabout identified, obviously enough, as **Place de la Poste** (☎ *81 17 45;* ⊕ *07.00–14.00 Mon–Fri*). Along Avenue Foch is a **DHL** office (☎ *94 09 84/04 57 57;* ⊕ *07.30–18.00 Mon–Sat, 09.00–15.00 Sun*), which may be a more reliable option if you are sending documents of importance.

WHAT TO SEE AND DO

Congo's capital has several bona fide tourist attractions, though their condition is often not the greatest. Being something of a cultural centrepoint for francophone central Africa, a few monuments have sprung up around town and can keep the average visitor busy for a day or so.

Perhaps the most interesting sight in town is the **Congo Rapids**, at the **Pont du Djoué** that goes over the Djoué River. Interesting rock formations skirt the shoreline of the Congo River, while various people wash their clothes and bathe in the water. The **Rapids Bar and Nightclub** (*Sgl/dbl* $$, *restaurant* $) is near a lookout point and gets lively on weekend evenings. Further out from the rapids and right beside the Protea Hôtel is the **Brazzaville Golf Club**, a reasonably well-maintained and secure set of greenery where CFA2,000 will get you a set of clubs for hire for a round of golf. The views are admirable, from high on the hills and overlooking both the Congo and Djoué rivers.

Back closer to town is the famous **house built for Charles de Gaulle**, constructed for him when he resided here during World War II. In front is a **Monument to de Brazza**, with a decent lookout over the river. The house itself is the residence of France's ambassador and closed to the public.

Closer into town is the **Centre Culturel Français** (✆ *81 19 00*), a landmark in its own right and a great place to see what's going on in the environs of Brazzaville in terms of cultural events. Completed in 1994 and reopened in 2004 after the civil war, it hosts numerous art exhibitions as well as international films on selected evenings. The **Basilique de St Anne** is Brazzaville's most famous landmark, a unique-looking church with pointed stone arches, completed in 1949 by Father Moysan and right near the Rond Point Poto Poto. Directly behind the Basilique de St Anne is a **Monument to Félix Éboué**, at the entrance to a small sports field dedicated to his name. In the same area is the **Grand Mosque**, the biggest of Brazzaville's three mosques and the largest in the Congos.

Up a hill from the city centre is the **Cathédrale Sacrée Soeur**, an ornate little Catholic church with daily services. Close by is the **Statue of Marien Ngouabi**, in the middle of a park across from his **Mausoleum**, which is currently closed; it may reopen in the future. Towards the airport is a rather depressing **Zoo** (⏲ *09.00–16.00 Mon–Fri; CFA2,100 admission if you bring a camera*), and while not worth recommending, can be a reminder of the effect that the years of war have had on the region's wildlife. It is also the only one of its kind to survive in either Congo.

In the city centre, the **Memorial to Pierre Savorgnan de Brazza** is due to be completed soon, and will have a small dome structure with information on him, as well as a statue outside.

And finally, no visit to Brazzaville is complete without a walk or drive along the **Corniche** to see the looming presence of Kinshasa across the river. If you are bound for Congo's larger neighbour, seeing it from here is a good opportunity to reflect on Brazzaville's comparatively quaint and easy-going attitude.

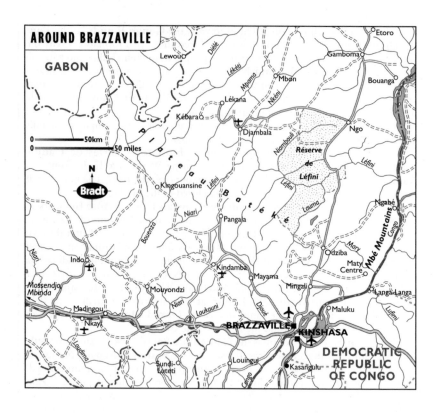

14

Around Brazzaville

Outside Congo's capital are several points of interest, though none of them is particularly simple to visit – without your own transportation, the options are either limited or non-existent. Nonetheless, with your own vehicle, getting to and from these locations should not be a big deal – however, be prepared for the unexpected and bring a spare tyre, your own food, as well as a GPS and decent country map. Be prepared to ask along the way – it's the Congolese custom, and entirely welcome. People will be happy to help.

LOUFOULAKARI FALLS AND BELA FALLS

⊕ *04°35.02 S, 14°58.28 E & 04°51.29 S, 14°45.20 E*

Two impressive waterfalls exist along the Congo River to the southwest of Brazzaville – at the confluence of two separate rivers from the Congo, the waterfalls can be an impressive sight made all the more unique by the lack of development surrounding them. Indeed, at one point in history these falls may have been a modest point of interest on the tourist radar, but now are so far off it that they can be rediscovered by those intrepid enough to visit.

The Bela Falls are on a wider river and by some accounts a more impressive sight. I'd recommend, if you are going to visit at all, to make the effort to see both as they are along the same rough road.

Anticipate a full day's trip if you visit one or both of the falls. Accommodation is non-existent, meaning the trip should be done as an early departure from Brazzaville with the intention of returning the same day – no real place to camp is available, and due to the unregulated nature of the countryside surrounding western Brazzaville, overnighting in a random spot cannot be recommended.

The falls can be reached on the road to Boko; public transport exists to the village, but not directly to either falls. If you're that keen on walking dozens of kilometres from the main road to the falls it may be possible to avoid having to secure private transport. Ask a taxi driver in Brazzaville to take you to the buses for Boko if you're interested in this option.

LAC BLEU AND THE GORILLA RESERVE ⊕ *03°18.57 S, 15°28.52 E*

Northward on Congo's Route National No 2 you begin to gain altitude into a unique area in Congo with few trees, open plains, rocky hills, and almost a Europe-like atmosphere with its paved highway winding upward through the western end of the Batéké Plateau, a rough equivalent of the Scottish highlands in Congo. About 100km north on the highway is a turn-off (⊕ *03°19.55.43 S, 15°33.47.37 E*) for the gorilla sanctuary (interchangeably called the Lesio-Louna Reserve) on the edge of the Lefini Reserve, and also on the shores of Lac Bleu. Occupying over 200km² at this point, the area used to be something of a popular destination for tourists before the war – and these days, it is still a good getaway from Brazzaville for a day or weekend. If you have a desire to see some decent wildlife and have little time in the capital, the gorilla reserve can be a good compromise. Funded by the John Aspinall Foundation (*www.totallywild.net*), the primates are usually rescued from bushmeat markets at smaller villages throughout Congo, and brought to the reserve with the ultimate aim of reintroducing them back to the wilderness in Lefini.

LEFINI RESERVE

Just north of Brazzaville is the 6,300km^2 Lefini Reserve, an important area designed to protect the habitats of animals and landscape in an area that has plenty of incursions – numerous villages are in and around the plateau region, as it has the finest soil for agriculture in Congo. This has put strains on the land and reserve; furthermore, since its inception in 1951 it has only been designated as a reserve, never having had the same protection as Congo's three national parks. Construction of a dam at the confluence of the Lefini and Congo rivers was begun several years ago, and it is unclear whether this will have any environmental effect on the reserve.

The primary interest in the reserve is the populations of gorillas, often reintroduced into the wild from the sanctuary on the edge of Lefini. Given the reserve's wide-open spaces and spectacular views from the surrounding hills, it makes viewing the primates in their natural habitat quite simple. Lefini was heavily hunted during the 20th century, but populations have begun to rebound as the civil war's legacy drifts further into history. There are also slowly growing numbers of forest buffalo, and some species of antelope. Various bird species have been spotted within the reserve including the spot-breasted ibis, Finch's francolin, black-chinned weaver, and Brazza's martin.

Entry to the reserve is done either on foot or by *pirogue*; there is a small town called **Mbouambe-Lefini** (✪ *02°54.57.83 S, 15°37.55.92 E*), straddling the river and bridge of Route National No 2, which has numerous amenities for those wishing to travel upriver into the reserve. Permits must first be obtained from the Ministry of Forest and Environment in Brazzaville for all parties wishing to enter the reserve. Things may be changing quickly, however; Lefini's tourist potential has been noted, and the addition of amenities (such as a base camp) for tourists seems imminent. The government sees this as a method to satisfy local employment, by promoting tourism; the conservation groups see this as a method to ensure that the animals and landscape are being protected by locals and political forces alike.

Organised tours tend to begin with visiting the gorilla reserve on the edge of the park, then moving with a guide into the reserve to visit the primates in their newly adopted habitat. Most of the Lefini Reserve surrounding the gorilla rehabilitation reserve is swampy, and it is quite possible you will see nothing – explaining why beginning in the sanctuary in the first place will guarantee at least a little wildlife viewing.

MADINGOU AND BOUENZA FALLS

✪ *04°09.50 S, 13°33.07 E & 03°54.06.56 S, 13°45.39.23 E*

If, for some reason you wish to do things the hard way, it is possible to catch a truck from Brazzaville to the town of Mindouli – from here you can change to another truck or minibus and continue the journey west to Madingou and Nkayi. As mentioned, the risks are high for travelling through this area – so the reward for showing up here could, perhaps, be a chance to see the Chutes de la Bouenza. They are situated amongst some of Congo's highest mountains and said to be at least as impressive as the Loufoulakari Falls, though this could in fact be debatable – being harder to reach, and so far from Brazzaville, perhaps getting there in the first place makes them seem more impressive. They are roughly 50km north of Madingou, following a road northward that turns off from the main highway just before the town. There should be one or two taxis in Madingou who will do the trip for you – bargain hard, as it should take a full day there and back.

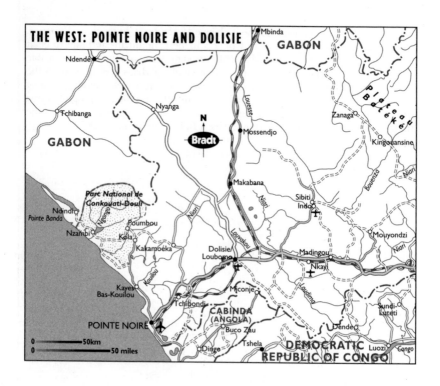

THE WEST: POINTE NOIRE AND DOLISIE

Mbinda

GABON

Ndende

Nyanga

Tchibanga

N

Bradt

Louesse

Zanaga

GABON

Mossendjo

Kingouansine

Plateaux

Makabana

Niari

Bouenza

Niari

Parc National de
Conkouati-Douli

Sibiti
Indo

Ndindo
Pointe Banda

Ngongo

Poumbou

Louvolou

Mouyondzi

Niari

Nzambi

Kola

Madingou

Kakamoéka

Dolisie
Louboma

Nkayi

Loudima

Kouilou

Kayes
Bas-Kouilou

Mconje

Tchibondi

Sundi-
Luteti

CABINDA
(ANGOLA)

POINTE NOIRE

0 ———— 50km
0 ———— 50 miles

Buco Zau

Dinge

Tshela

Dended

DEMOCRATIC
REPUBLIC OF CONGO

Luozi

Congo

15

The West: Pointe Noire and Dolisie

West of Congo's Poule region, the mountainous plateau of the country holds the bulk of the nation's industry and population – in many ways a more critical region to the country's health than Brazzaville or the north, the west has the most frequent air connections, two of Congo's largest cities, and an important park on its west coast that protects marine and animal life. In addition to the park is the Jane Goodall Chimpanzee Sanctuary, one of several across the world and one of the most active organisations promoting the protection of wildlife in Congo.

The west is home to the country's second city, Pointe Noire, which is an escape from familiar institutions in Congo in every way. It is connected by the Congo Ocean Railway which, while dilapidated after so many years of neglect, still remains a heavily used piece of infrastructure. The west has enough activities to keep casual visitors to Congo busy while not devouring too much of their time. Furthermore, Pointe Noire is by far the easiest city to live in across the entire region, and a good introduction for those new to central Africa.

POINTE NOIRE ⊕ 04°47.56 S, 11°51.05 E

A city like no other in the Congos, Pointe Noire is a strange adjustment from the usual grinding difficulties that punctuate travelling in the region. Sitting as a bustling medium-sized city on the far west coast of central Africa, it is a unique place – with beautifully paved streets, numerous towers, piles of beautifully painted mansions and more private cars, restaurants and discotheques than the rest of the country combined. It can be disconcerting to see the nation's wealth concentrated so heavily in one place, and even more so given that these people never had to endure the open combat that Congo's other two major cities, Brazzaville and Dolisie, still struggle to emerge from.

Pointe Noire and the oil wealth inherent off Congo's small stretch of Atlantic coast are the centrepoint of Congo's otherwise languid economy. The expatriates who have arrived here to work in the oil industry have brought with them the trappings that seem to follow their like across the globe: international restaurants galore, large and expensive hotels, private medical clinics and pharmacies, yacht and swimming clubs, scads of bars (and scads of prostitutes to go with them), and cavalcades of brand-new 4x4 vehicles. Touristic restaurants with *tiki* lamps, faux-wooden Chez Afrique courtyards and the glitzy theme-park stylings of a dark continent filtered down, interpreted and presented to the consumer with the crusts removed and a beat palatable to Western ears in the background, abound in Pointe Noire.

Arriving here from the hinterlands of the country, then, can be disconcerting – so much choice after spending days or weeks in the jungle, eating only canned tuna and stale bread, is a surreal experience that cannot easily be described. In the context of Congo it can feel like an entirely different world altogether. In some

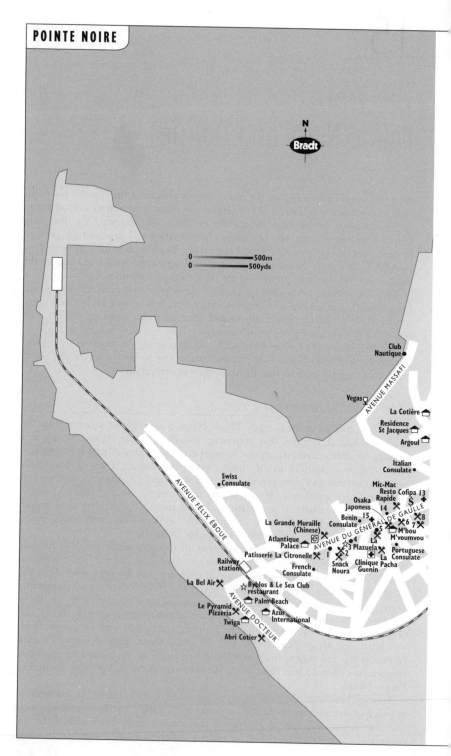

POINTE NOIRE

N

Bradt

0 ———— 500m
0 ———— 500yds

Club
Nautique

AVENUE MASSAFI

Vegas

La Cotière

Residence
St Jacques

Argoul

Italian
Consulate

Swiss
Consulate

Mic-Mac
Resto Cofipa 13
Rapide

Osaka
Japoness

14

AVENUE DU GÉNÉRAL DE GAULLE

Benin
Consulate

La Grande Muraille
(Chinese)

15

8

6 7

Atlantique
Palace

5

M'bou
M'voumvou

La

Patisserie La Citronelle

4

3 Plazuela

1 2

La
Portuguese
Consulate

Railway
station

French
Consulate

Snack
Noura

Clinique
Guenin

La
Pacha

La Bel Air

AVENUE FÉLIX EBOUE

Byblos & Le Sea Club
restaurant

Palm Beach

Le Pyramid
Pizzeria

AVENUE DOCTEUR

Azur
International

Twiga

Abri Cotier

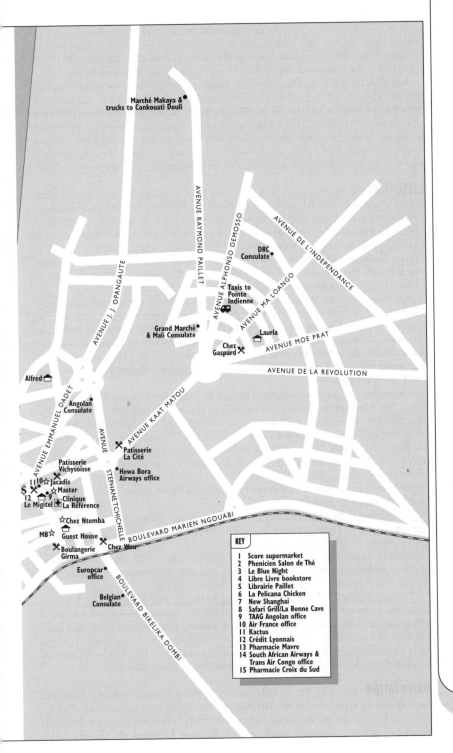

Marché Makaya &
trucks to Conkouati Douli

AVENUE RAYMOND PAILLET

AVENUE J. J. OPANGAUTE

AVENUE ALPHONSO DEMOSSO

AVENUE DE L'INDEPENDANCE

DRC
Consulate

AVENUE MA LOANGO

Taxis to
Pointe
Indienne

Grand Marché
& Mali Consulate

Lauria

Chez
Gaspard

AVENUE MOE PRAT

AVENUE DE LA REVOLUTION

Alfred

AVENUE EMMANUEL DADET

Angolan
Consulate

AVENUE KAAT MATOU

Patisserie
La Cité

Patisserie
Vichysoisse

AVENUE STEPHANE TCHICHELLE

Hewa Bora
Airways office

11 10 Jacadis

Master

$

12   9

Le Migitel

Clinique
La Référence

Chez Ntemba

MB

Guest House

Chez Wou

Boulangerie
Girma

BOULEVARD MARIEN NGOUABI

Europcar
office

BOULEVARD BIKELIKA DOMBI

Belgian
Consulate

KEY
1   Score supermarket
2   Phenicien Salon de Thé
3   Le Blue Night
4   Libre Livre bookstore
5   Librairie Paillet
6   La Pelicana Chicken
7   New Shanghai
8   Safari Grill/La Bonne Cave
9   TAAG Angolan office
10 Air France office
11 Kactus
12 Crédit Lyonnais
13 Pharmacie Mavre
14 South African Airways &
    Trans Air Congo office
15 Pharmacie Croix du Sud

The West: Pointe Noire and Dolisie   POINTE NOIRE

15

ways it is – but venture outside the expatriate bubble and you will find roadside meals, noisy spartan bars with plastic chairs, sandy pavements, and west African general stores like any other town in the nation. It is the city with the most contrasts in the entire country. It is, in many ways, a jewel in search of a crown.

It is also, by many accounts, the only town in Congo that most people manage to visit. This in itself is incredibly unfortunate – but if you are put in this position, spend some time in La Cité, in the African quarters, and you will have a glimpse of how the rest of Congo lives. Only a tiny number are as lucky as the upper crust in Pointe Noire, and only Pointe Noire was lucky enough to not have suffered during Congo's brutal civil war. However, its wealth is slowly flowing outward, and may be the saving grace for Congo's economic recovery in the years to come.

HISTORY Pierre Savorgnan de Brazza arrived on the shores of the Atlantic Ocean after a journey of several months west from the fledgling outpost of Brazzaville, encountering the point that Portuguese cartographers had mapped out centuries earlier. In the same fashion that he founded a French town on the western edge of Malebo Pool, he struck a treaty with the local African king, ceding the coast to France. Loango in particular seemed to suit his requirements for a decent harbour, but through the remainder of the 19th century the southern Atlantic coast of Congo Français would remain a scattered cluster of African villages.

It was not until the proposal for a railway was seriously considered, that Pointe Noire began to take shape. French concessionary companies, operating deep in Congo's jungles, wanted some output to the ocean. Amidst numerous proposals, the town of Loango was chosen – though just slightly south of Loango in a deeper natural harbour, at Punta Negra, Portuguese by title, as it had been designated on European maps for centuries. It would later be renamed Pointe Noire, to reflect the French interests there.

The railway began construction in earnest in 1921, and grew rapidly as a planned town. Yet it would not grow exponentially as exports slowed down in the 1930s. Nonetheless, to diversify the bureaucratic stranglehold that Brazzaville held over all of the AEF countries as well as Moyen Congo, Pointe Noire was designated capital of the colony, Moyen Congo, in 1950. Once independence was achieved in 1959, the government moved their now national capital back to Brazzaville, without any internal debate. The citizens of Pointe Noire were rightfully angered by this move, but it would later prove to have saved the city from much of the strife that would rock Brazzaville.

Continuing to be a planned city after independence, Pointe Noire would slowly appropriate the lands around it, with directives handed down from the government. Its importance to the economics of Congo would increase as oil companies began tapping proven reserves off its coast. With the Congo Ocean Railway terminating there, as well as being the only deep-water port in the area, Pointe Noire became the major economic hub for Congo.

The city avoided much of the chaos and internal strife of the 1990s; there was little interest in interrupting the cash flow of the city, as it would have such a critical effect on the well-being of the nation as a whole. Tribal politics were also non-existent, as it lacked the major factionalisation of Brazzaville. Economic interest has only increased since the turn of the millennium and, while the railway operates on a stunted schedule, the seaport and airport are more active than ever.

ORIENTATION The city sits directly on the Atlantic Ocean, with the main rail station not far from the shore. The rail line winds its way from Pointe Noire's main harbour in the northwest on a southern curve, before winding east. From the main rail station, the large boulevard of **Avenue Général de Gaulle** heads northeast towards the roundabout of **Rond Point Patrice Lumumba**. Avenue General de Gaulle is the heart of European Pointe Noire, and along its pavements are the majority of the airline offices, hotels, patisseries and shopping available in the town.

Rond Point Patrice Lumumba marks the beginning of the African city, referred to as **'La Cité'**; head further north from it and you encounter the crowded and bustling market (the **'Grand Marché'**), filled with all kinds of residents from across the continent. Directly west of the African city is the main road north out of town, **Route Nationale No 5**.

The airport is at the southern end of the city, and beside it is the smaller train station of Tie Tie – where you may first arrive if coming by rail. Right beside this rail station is the highway out of the city, in the direction of Dolisie.

The harbour is situated on the Bay of Pointe Noire, and the shores north of the city's harbour are known as **Côte Mondaine**. South of the harbour are the most popular beaches with Europeans, on **Côte Sauvage**.

GETTING THERE AND AROUND

By air Pointe Noire has a newly inaugurated airport, an impressive structure that defies the usual state of government buildings across Congo. Air France flies directly from Paris several times a week, and there are frequent flights to both Brazzaville and Dolisie. Several other airlines offer the same plane service from Brazzaville.

✈ **Aero Service** ☎ 81 34 29/82 08 38; e aerl0@ calva.com. With flights to Dolisie, Nkayi & Brazzaville.
✈ **Air France** 69 Av General de Gaulle; ☎ 81 27 19; f 94 49 50; e mail.cto.pnr@airfrance.fr. Flights direct to Paris.
✈ **Hewa Bora Airways** Southwest corner of Av General de Gaulle & Av Stéphane Tchichelle. Flights direct to Kinshasa.
✈ **Trans Air Congo** Av General de Gaulle; ☎ 94 35 69; f 94 79 12. Flies the only jet service, an ageing Boeing 737, direct to Brazzaville.

✈ **South African Airways** Av General de Gaulle; ☎ 94 33 08; f 94 35 10. The airline does not fly direct to Pointe Noire, but instead sells tickets from Brazzaville.
✈ **TAAG Angolan Airlines** 94 Av General de Gaulle; ☎ 94 54 72. Does a milk run from Luanda to Kinshasa, then Brazzaville, then to Pointe Noire; the Pointe Noire–Luanda connection should be direct.

By taxi Taxis are ubiquitous and should cost no more than CFA1,000 for a ride across town. From the airport to the city centre, it should cost no more than CFA5,000. The biggest problem in Pointe Noire is the streets – they tend to be poorly marked, and most drivers won't know the name of minor side streets. Expect a few trials of driving in circles as the driver asks passers-by in the neighbourhood where a certain road may be.

By train The train station is at the far west end of Avenue de Gaulle, and the current schedule sees an arrival and departure to Dolisie three times a week. More people choose to take the train eastward than any kind of truck; indeed, finding vehicles going to Dolisie is sometimes quite complicated.

By sea Passenger boats are rare in Pointe Noire, but the port is busy with shipping options for cargo.

WHERE TO STAY

In a city of oil expatriates, the selection of hotels is naturally excellent. As is often the case across Congo, however, it is difficult to find decent accommodation at a lower price level. If you are seeking plenty of amenities without much concern for cost, however, your options are large.

In general, the closer to the Côte Sauvage you get, the more expensive the hotels become. The Cité has the cheapest options available, but few of them can be recommended. The city's top addresses are considered to be **Azur International** and the recently opened **Atlantic Palace**.

Expensive

🏠 **Argoul Hôtel** Off Av Emmanuel Débat; m 670 9946. Cheaper option in comparison with its neighbour Residence St Jacques nearby, though lacking any good character. There is a secure parking area & bar. Rooms have AC & hot running water. Sgl $$$, dbl $$$$

🏠 **Azur International** Near the Côte Sauvage; ☎ 94 27 71/94 19 74; f 94 27 34; e congohotelazur@mtcybernet.com. This is considered Pointe Noire's premier hotel & while not on the beach, is just across the street from it. The rooms are good but not great for this price range, with a simple ambience rather than an attempt to appear too high class. Has an open grassy area with a pool, 2 bars, a high-end restaurant, a tennis court, billiard tables, internet connection, satellite telephone & fax service. Conference rooms available, shuttles available to the airport. Visa & MasterCard accepted, as well as euros. Sgl $$$$, suite $$$$$, presidential suite $$$$$

🏠 **Guest House Hôtel** 13 Av Barthelemy Boganda, Pointe Noire Centre; ☎ 94 70 61/92 79; f 94 47 28; e lestaubiere@mac.com. Has bar & restaurant, accepts credit cards & euros, shuttle available to airport. Sgl $$$, dbl/suite $$$$

🏠 **Hôtel Atlantic Palace** Av General de Gaulle; ☎ 94 10 21/94 11 37/94 12 85. A huge brand-new hotel on the main boulevard that looms over the busy street below, & perhaps is an indicator of the city Pointe Noire will become in the following decades. The lobby is a formal affair, as are the rooms, with every trapping expected. AC, satellite TV, hot running water, private refrigerators. Has an excellent restaurant, & some parking. The surrounding shops were built with the hotel & make for good shopping. Sgl/dbl/suite $$$$$

🏠 **Hôtel M'bou-M'voumvou** Av General de Gaulle; ☎ 94 90 42/94 90 66; f 94 14 64; e hotel-mboumvoumou@yahoo.fr. Large hotel with plenty of rooms without too much character, but they are well maintained & clean with AC, TV & hot running water. There is a huge area for parking out front & the hotel is popular with large groups. Has bar, restaurant, pool, tennis courts, safety deposit boxes, 2 large conference rooms, airport shuttle. Accepts euros, but not credit cards. Sgl $$$, small suite $$$$, presidential suite $$$$$

🏠 **Hôtel Palm Beach** Near the Côté Sauvage; ☎ 94 45 17/94 10 88; f 94 49 34; e palmbeachhotel2003@yahoo.fr. A very popular place for long-term expats in the city, this is a large complex right near the beach. Has secure parking, bar & restaurant, pool, safety deposit boxes, free internet connection for guests. Conference room available. International calls & faxes accepted. Credit cards not accepted. Sgl $$$$, suite $$$$$

🏠 **Hôtel Twiga** On the Côte Sauvage; m 658 4747/657 4848; e info@twigahotel.com; www.twigahotel.com. Very tourist-styled hotel right on the ocean with its own private beach, swimming pool, popular restaurant & bar. Has a sauna & fitness room, pleasant gardened area out front, & plenty of parking — while not secured by a wall, it is guarded at all hours. Accepts euros. Sgl $$$$, dbl/suite $$$$$

🏠 **Le Migitel Hôtel** 96 Av General de Gaulle, Pointe Noire Centre; ☎ 94 09 18/94 09 19/94 36 36; f 94 02 58; e migitel@yahoo.fr. Once one of Pointe Noire's better hotels, it has been overshadowed by newer accommodation constructed around the city. Has a pleasant ageing atmosphere to it, & is situated in a busy neighbourhood surrounded by nightclubs. Has bar & restaurant, safety deposit boxes, small conference room, internet connection. Parking is on the street. Accepts euros, but not credit cards. Sgl $$$, small suite $$$$, presidential suite $$$$$

🏠 **Malonda Lodge** (12 private bungalows) BP152, Pointe Noire; m 557 5151; e info@malondalodge.com; www.malondalodge.com. Situated 15km south of Pointe Noire in a secluded beach area with lots of character. The look & feel are of a tourist resort & is popular with w/ending expatriates. They have a golf course nearby as well as an equestrian field. The hotel can arrange numerous activities including fishing charters. B/fast inc. Bungalows $$$$$

🏠 **Residence St Jacques** Off Av Emmanuel Débat; ☎ 94 51 80/661 7720; f 94 15 17; e saintjacqueshotel@yahoo.fr. A very clean boutique hotel in the quiet northern suburbs. Rooms have cable TV & AC, are of modest size but well maintained. With bar, restaurant & pool. Sgl/dbl $$$$, suite $$$$$

Mid-range

⌂ **Alfred Hôtel** Off Av Emmanuel Dédat, just past Av Amilcar Cabral; m 544 2725. Excellent value for the price & recently renovated. AC rooms with private bathrooms & hot water, with TV. Small bar available, & secure parking. Sgl $$, dbl $$$, suite $$$$

⌂ **Hôtel La Côtière** Pointe Noire Centre; ☎ 94 24 16/94 27 24. Looking a little old with a not-so-tasty off-green-colour motif, but good value for its quality. Secure parking, Bar & restaurant, pool, safety deposit boxes, small conference room, internet connection. Accepts euros. Sgl $$, dbl/suite $$$$

⌂ **Hôtel Lauria** In the Cité, off Av Moe Prat; ☎ 94 70 28; f 94 70 41. Best hotel in the Cité with clean rooms & running water in a multi-storey building. The hotel sticks out like a sore thumb as a bastion of new development in an area where it seems like nothing has changed in many years. Sgl $$, dbl $$$, suite $$$$

✖ WHERE TO EAT

More than any other town in either Congo, with perhaps the exception of Kinshasa, Pointe Noire has a wide variety of excellent restaurants. Quality tends to be high, with numerous options for those with plenty of cash to go around. On the budget side of things, small snack bars and cafés provide some excellent places for cheaper eating and people-watching in the city centre.

Patisseries

✖ **La Citronelle** 7 Av General de Gaulle; ☎ 94 81 40; f 94 41 31; ⏰ 07.00–17.00 daily. Pointe Noire's oldest & busiest patisserie with an outdoor eating area & a wide selection of dishes, though the most expensive place of its kind in the city. $$$

✖ **Boulangerie Girma** Av Barthelemy Boganda; ☎ 94 93 02; ⏰ 07.00–15.00 Mon–Sat. Smaller place near the Guest House Hôtel. Popular with local Africans as opposed to expatriates, & very busy in the morning when their fresh baking comes out of the oven. $$

✖ **La Cité** Av Kaat Matou; ☎ 94 26 26/578 2626; ⏰ 07.00–17.00 daily. Large open eating area with some plasma TVs blasting TV5 at all hours. Has parking out front. Close to the Cité, but before Rond Point Lumumba. $$

✖ **La Vichysoisse** Av General de Gaulle; ⏰ 07.00–17.00 daily. Cheaper than Pointe Noire's other 2 patisseries of similar quality, though with less selection. Has a good view of Av de Gaulle & can be a bit quieter than its rivals. $$

African

✖ **Restaurant Chez Gaspard** In the Cité, Av Moe Prat No 67; ☎ 94 01 45/94 01 46; ⏰ 18.00–23.00 daily. An attraction in its own right & one of the best places to sample central African cuisine. Serves massive fish & meat dishes with fried bananas. Hugely popular with locals & expatriates alike. $$$

Asian

✖ **Osaka Restaurant Japoness** Av General de Gaulle (at Hôtel M'bou-M'voumvou); m 523 6578; ⏰ 19.00–23.00 daily. Pointe Noire's first & only Japanese restaurant, with a spotless & bright dining area & top-quality cuisine, including sushi – but at prices you would expect to find in Tokyo. $$$$

✖ **Chez Wou** Centre Ville; m 553 4455/553 1272/94 01 20; ⏰ 18.00–22.00 daily. Pointe Noire's oldest Chinese restaurant, with a large parking area in a quiet neighbourhood. Has a buffet at weekends. $$$

✖ **La Grande Muraille** Centre Ville, Av de Gaulle; ☎ 94 88 66; ⏰ 18.00–01.00 daily. Medium-priced restaurant in a shopping area near the train station with various Chinese dishes. Ambience is good & there is sometimes a place to sit out on the pavement. Also has a bar inside & becomes something of a nightspot in the evenings. $$$

✖ **New Shanghai** Off Av General de Gaulle; m 529 2204/667 2228; ⏰ 19.00–23.00 daily. Centrally located restaurant serving average Chinese fare. $$

European

✖ **Abri Cotier** Av Docteur, behind Hôtel Azur International; m 533 2319; ⏰ 18.30–midnight daily. Hôtel Azur's main restaurant, with its own private stretch of oceanside, plenty of thatch roofs, pseudo-African atmosphere, & top-notch food. $$$$

✘ **Le Sea Club** Near the Côte Sauvage; ☎ 94 12 11; ⏱ 18.30–23.30 daily. High-end French restaurant near the beach specialising in seafood, but only has a few tables so it can get crowded during dinner hours. Show up early or late. **$$$$**

✘ **Safari Grill/Restaurant La Bonne Cave** Av General de Gaulle; ☎ 94 12 01; ⏱ 19.00–midnight daily. Good selection of dinners à la carte with somewhat high prices, & a decent 2nd-storey terrace looking out onto Av de Gaulle. Also doubles as a bar & a good quiet nightspot for a drink with friends. **$$$$**

✘ **La Bel Air** Corner of Av Docteur & Av General de Gaulle; ☏ 655 6875/553 9759; ⏱ 19.00–23.00

Snack bars and other eateries

✘ **La Pacha** Behind Hotel M'bou-Mvoumvou; ☎ 94 55 55; ⏱ 18.00–23.00 daily. Lebanese restaurant with a huge selection of dishes. On the 2nd storey. **$$**

✘ **La Pelicana Chicken** Av General de Gaulle; ⏱ 12.00–21.00 daily. A fast-food fried chicken franchise from South Korea makes an appearance in Pointe Noire. A relatively new place with friendly service & clean eating area. **$$**

✘ **La Plazuela** – Across from Hôtel M'bou-M'voumvou; ☏ 541 4251; ⏱ 12.00–21.00 daily. Small but busy snack bar in the heart of town, with European dishes as well as some African specialities. **$$**

✘ **Le Kactus** Av General de Gaulle & corner of Av Emmanuel Dadet; ☎ 94 50 25/564 5025; ⏱ 17.00–midnight daily. Small but popular eatery for a bite to eat throughout the day. Wide selection

daily. On the corner of Pointe Noire's most popular stretch of beach, it emits a touristic vibe to be sure – with plenty of *tiki* lamps & thatch roofs. **$$$**

✘ **La Pyramide Pizzeria** Av Docteur, Côté Sauvage; ☎ 94 28 27; ⏱ 19.00–23.00 daily. Another beachside restaurant which, obviously, enough, specialises in pizzas. Has an open-air eating area. **$$$**

✘ **Restaurant Twiga** At Hôtel Twiga, Av Docteur; ☏ 658 4747/657 4848; ⏱ 17.00–23.30 daily. Right on the beach with a selection of Italian dishes, ice creams, & some African specialities. Has both an inside dining area & some tables along the shore, & a bar. **$$$**

of burgers & pizzas, with omelettes available for b/fast. Becomes a drinking spot later in the evening. **$$$**

✘ **Mic-Mac Resto Rapide** Av General de Gaulle; ☏ 530 1313; ⏱ 15.00–22.00 daily. A 2-storey eatery with a selection of burgers & drinks. A bona fide fast-food place with the plastic chairs that go with it. **$$**

✘ **Phenicien Salon de Thé** Near the Score Supermarket; ☎ 94 81 97; ⏱ 11.00–21.00 daily. Large outdoor terrace with drinks, burgers & pizzas. Also has an interior AC dining area. **$$**

✘ **Snack Noura** Near the Score Supermarket; ☎ 81 57 77; ⏱ 12.00–21.00 daily. A place for some cheap snacks, including Middle Eastern fare. Has an AC interior. **$$**

ENTERTAINMENT AND NIGHTLIFE Pointe Noire has garnered a reputation for its nightlife, for both locals and expatriates alike. Numerous nightclubs can keep the visitor busy deep into the evening. Most tend to play a huge selection of music, sell mid-priced drinks, and can be a decent place to chat with friends or be picked up by Pointe Noire's population of working females.

The most popular are centred on the hotels Migitel and Guest House – **MB Nightclub** (popular with expatriates) and **Chez Ntemba Nightclub** (operated by the same owner as the club in Kinshasa, catering to the upmarket African crowd) on Avenue Barthelemy Boganda, then **Nightclub Jacadis** and **Master Nightclub** on Avenue General de Gaulle. Further down is **Le Blue Night Nightclub**, close to the Score Supermarket. Near the beach is **Byblos**, an upmarket place.

Naturally, the Cité will give a more 'authentic' experience for nightlife than these nightclubs, and there are plenty of drinking spots around the Grand Marché. However, lone foreigners would be quite a rarity at these places – for the best experience, make a local friend and go with them.

SHOPPING Near Avenue Emmanuel Dadet lies a stretch of souvenir sellers who wait with bated breath for a taxi-driven foreigner to arrive. The selection is excellent, but bargaining is essential. Another decent souvenir shop is at the Hôtel Azur International, with slightly higher prices – though they'll accept credit cards.

The centre of everyday shopping is around the **Score Supermarket** (↘ *94 03 02; ⊕ 08.00–12.30 & 14.00–19.00 Mon–Fri*), with short daytime hours and a good selection of imported foods. Across the street are a few boutique shops, many of them new, thanks to the recent opening of the Hôtel Atlantic Palace. Many other items can be had in the area of Avenue General de Gaulle, including a sporting goods and clothing store further up the street.

PRACTICALITIES

Banks As in Brazzaville, Credit Lyonnais Congo is a traveller's friend – offering the only other ATM service in the country. Several foreign-exchange services dot Avenue General de Gaulle, though they will charge a modest commission. Western Union offices are abundant, and any bank will be able to make arrangements to send or receive money through them.

$ **Credit Lyonnais Congo** Av Emmanuel Dadet; ↘ 94 24 00; ⊕ 07.00–16.15 Mon–Fri, 08.00–12.00 Sat

$ **Banque Cofipa** Av General de Gaulle; ↘ 81 17 45; f 94 09 95; ⊕ 08.00–14.30 Mon–Fri

Consulates Foreign representation ebbs and flows in Pointe Noire, as economic and political interests follow their course. Rumour has it that the UK once had a consulate here, though it no longer exists; therefore if your home country has a consulate in Pointe Noire, contacting them ahead of time may confirm if they are still around. Both Angola and the DR Congo consulates are able to provide visas for travellers.

❸ **Angola** Av Stephane Tchichelle; ↘ 94 19 12/94 82 97
❸ **Belgium** Bd Bikelika Dombi; ↘ 94 59 53; f 94 59 54
❸ **Benin** Av General de Gaulle; ↘ 94 44 80
❸ **Democratic Republic of Congo** Near Marché Makaya; m 544 1414

❸ **France** 4 Allée Nicolau; ↘ 94 00 02; f 94 46 37
❸ **Italy** Av M'Bemba; ↘ 94 04 91; f 94 11 54
❸ **Mali** In the Cité, on Av Ma Loango
❸ **Portugal** Av Moet Vangoula; ↘ 94 77 74; f 94 77 73
❸ **Switzerland** Rue Massabi 5; ↘ 94 37 07; f 94 44 56; e consulsuisse@cg.celtelplus.com

Media La Maison de la Presse on Avenue de Gaulle, also known as **Libre Livre** (↘ *94 00 64; ⊕ 09.00–17.00 Mon–Fri, 10.00–17.00 Sat*) has plenty of French material; **Librairie Paillet** (↘ *94 10 62; f 94 39 36; e librairiepaillet@aol.com; ⊕ 09.00–17.00 Mon–Fri, 12.00–17.00 Sat*) further up the road has a large selection of magazines including, surprisingly enough perhaps, several English-language publications. For **television and radio**, the rules are much the same as Brazzaville. An **internet café** is just beside the Hôtel Atlantic Palace.

Medical clinics Pointe Noire has a public hospital, but anyone who can afford to will avoid it. The most popular private clinic is **Clinique Guenin** (↘ *94 17 51/94 27 42; f 94 18 86*), who offer 24-hour emergency services. Another excellent option is **Clinique La Référence** (m *523 4729*).

Numerous pharmacies dot Avenue General de Gaulle, including **Pharmacie Mavre** (↘ *94 24 29*) and **Pharmacie Croix du Sud** (↘ *94 04 47/94 30 07*).

WHAT TO SEE AND DO If you are into fishing, the **Club Nautique** (m *535 83 65*) can provide information on various boat charters off the coast, including some popular fishing. There really is no tourist infrastructure for this, however – enquiring with the expats is the best way to get access to this activity.

Most of Pointe Noire's activities are situated outside the city, a little to the north – including **Pointe Indienne**, where numerous private cabins abound along the coast. It's a popular weekend spot, with spectacular white sandy beaches. Getting there is not simple, and directions are essential – even when turning left from the highway, you will enter a winding maze of dirt roads that all lead to separate areas of the beach. If you are renting a cabin for the weekend, make sure you get exact directions. Numerous small villages sit just inland from the coast, and if you speak to the people there they should be able to offer a few of the cabins for rent. Otherwise, noticeboards advertising bungalows for rent are ubiquitous in Pointe Noire – including at the various bookstores and higher-end hotels.

Inland from Pointe Indienne is the town of **Diosso**, which includes a lookout for the spectacular **gorge** that's well worth a visit – though a gang of children has blocked off the best viewpoint and charges CFA2,000 for the privilege of passing. Also in town is the **Musée de Diosso** (m *533 6816; CFA2,000 admission*), a small place that chronicles the history of the village – Diosso is where the royalty of the ancient Loango Kingdom are said to be buried. The museum is normally only open at weekends (⏰ *10.00–15.00*), but it can be visited during the week if an appointment is made. Diosso also has an excellent **Golf Club** (m *579 9957*) which is situated on a plateau overlooking the coast. Eighteen holes will set you back CFA15,000, with an extra charge of CFA5,000 if you need your own clubs.

A short drive north of Diosso along the main highway is the **Hôtel Relais de Kouilou** (m *529 4412; sgl $$, dbl $$$, suite $$$$*), which has a private stretch of beach, as well as a nightclub, restaurant and pool. They can also arrange fishing charters.

AROUND POINTE NOIRE

JANE GOODALL CHIMPANZEE (TCHIMPOUNGA) SANCTUARY Some 50km north of Pointe Noire sits a large reserve area, the Tchimpounga Sanctuary, founded and funded by the Jane Goodall Institute. Occupying over 500km² it is the largest of its type in either Congo, and focused entirely on the protection and rehabilitation of chimpanzees for western central Africa.

Driving along a sandy road through a planned forest with row upon row of neatly planted trees, you will eventually arrive to find a modest research facility (referred to as the conservatory) at the foot of a hill. The site itself is deceiving, as it is only a small fraction of the land that the reserve occupies – around 18,000 acres in total are protected. It, however, also acts as a lookout, and in the land beyond are numerous small patches of forest in an otherwise open plain.

There are several chimps kept in captivity for research or rehabilitation, while communities of them live in the surrounding trees – the groups of chimps are free to roam the entire reserve, but always return back to the general vicinity of the research area (because, amongst other things, they know they will find food there). The research area itself is an interesting mix of playground and what could be called a dormitory, with slides and other things for them to hang off. Beside it, a smaller caged area allows researchers to isolate them – but they are released back into the larger holding area at the end of every day. The captive chimps include the world's oldest primate, Gregoire, who was rescued from the Brazzaville Zoo in 1997 after spending 46 years there. In his mid sixties, he is kept company by another surprisingly old chimp, La Vieille, born in 1968.

The sanctuary is a popular diversion for visitors to Pointe Noire, but heading out into the reserve wilderness is generally not possible. Small displays have biographies on the dozen chimps currently held in captivity for the visitor. Rangers are friendly, but speak only French – and will gladly give a tour around the research

That tiny piece of land you see between the Republic of Congo and the Democratic Republic of Congo was in fact once itself a Congo of sorts – Portuguese Congo. Long a separate colony under the Portuguese Empire, it formally ceded power from its local tribal chiefs to Portugal in 1885 with the Treaty of Simulambuco. It was a major trading post for slaves until the abolition of the practice in the mid 19th century, but would again become a hot topic with the independence of Angola in 1975.

An ongoing resistance movement against Angola has persisted since independence from Portugal in that same year – while the battle with UNITA has grabbed all of the headlines for three decades, the rebel movement FLEC, or Frente para a Libertação do Enclave de Cabinda, has fought with some brutal results against Angolan forces in the small exclave. Oil hangs in the balance as the region is rich in the resource; corporate giants such as Chevron and BP have significant interests off Cabinda's shores and human rights groups have accused them of funding Angola's government to put down the rebels as efficiently as possible.

Cabinda's rebels insist that their colony has always been a separate country from Angola, and that this was enshrined in the 1885 treaty. Cabinda proclaimed independence from Portugal and Angola on 1 August 1975, and endured an invasion from the forces of Mobutu Sésé Seko soon after – he sought to use its independence from Portugal as a chance for annexation. It was the Cuban-assisted MPLA who repelled the attack against Cabinda by driving out the Mobutu-funded FLEC from the area. Congo-Brazzaville's Marien Ngouabi and Mobutu made an agreement after this conflict to respect the territorial boundary of Cabinda, and Angola's Luanda government installed their own troops soon after.

No international body recognises this as an illegal occupation, making Cabinda's case an uphill battle. Cabinda can be construed as unsafe given the ongoing conflict, but in recent years there have been concessions and ongoing negotiations between parties from Luanda and Cabinda.

The region itself is home to only one main town, also known as Cabinda. Access is simple enough from either the Congolese or Angolan border in theory – US$100 will get you across, not including a negotiated taxi ride. However, keep in mind that the government in Angola may consider this border officially 'closed' and therefore a visit by land could be deemed to be unofficial. There are a few minor sights around the town, and one major hotel intended for oil expatriates. Tourists, in this part of the world, are an extreme rarity.

Cabinda maintains a government in exile stationed in Jamestown, St Helena Island. Saint Helena recognises some of the Republic's privately held companies, and their friendliness towards the government in exile explains a little why they're based here. For more information on their historical viewpoint, visit their website (www.cabinda.net).

facility. Entry is by donation, and a small information centre has shirts for sale as well as some statistics on the bushmeat trade that has endangered chimpanzee habitats throughout Congo.

There is no cost to visit and they are open from 09.00. Dropping in is fine, but if you want to speak directly with the researchers, it is best to make an appointment – the reserve has an office in Pointe Noire on Avenue Benoit Seize. You can also find more information on the sanctuary at the Jane Goodall website (www.janegoodall.org), as well as one of their partner organisations, the Pan African Sanctuary Alliance (www.panafricanprimates.org).

PARC NATIONAL CONKOUATI-DOULI: CONKOUATI-DOULI NATIONAL PARK

Occupying the northwestern half of Congo's coast, Conkouati-Douli has a hugely diverse landscape – encompassing not only a protected marine area for sea turtles and manatee, but also an important lagoon that is the largest of its kind in Congo. The park also boasts deep equatorial forest, and a stretch of the savanna that is found more commonly further inland in Congo. It is home to a large population of forest elephants, chimpanzees, gorillas, mandrills and even forest buffalo. It is the second-largest national park in Congo, covering around 5,000km².

The park itself was set up originally as a reserve around 1980 with the assistance of the Wildlife Conservation Society; it was not until 1999 that the reserve's status was changed to that of a full national park, and is operated as a co-operative project between WCS and the government of Congo. Yet its existence is not without problems – there are seven villages within the park's perimeter, with a total population of around 6,000, who have been asked politely to cease hunting within Conkouati-Douli's boundaries as well as limit their harvest of plants and trees. This has put some unnecessary strain on relations between researchers and the wildlife-protection organisations working to preserve the park, and the Congolese living within its boundaries. As with most parks in Congo, facilities are at a minimum – you can arrive at the small village of Conkouati and stock up on some basic supplies, but other amenities are not really available. Some bungalows have been built along the coast for visiting weekenders from Pointe Noire, but at last check they lacked electricity. Near the village of Conkouati is the base station for the park, and enquiries about travelling within the park can be made there.

In addition to the base camp, another chimpanzee-rescue organisation has operations near Conkouati: HELP Congo – Habitat Ecologique et Liberté des Primates (*www.help-primates.org*). Founded in 2001, they have been steadily reintroducing their rescued chimpanzee population back into the wild. Three small islands are in the lagoon, and the chimps are raised there before being released back into the wilderness.

The park, is unfortunately desperately understaffed – with only a few government officials and two dozen 'Ecoguards' trained by WCS to report any suspicious activities. Illegal mining has threatened various regions of the park, as well as illegal logging. Furthermore, a truck route from logging camps along the Congolese–Gabonese border runs dangerously close to the park; efforts to get these trucks using the normal highway south to Dolisie and then west to Pointe Noire have been unsuccessful, since the road is in such bad condition.

Getting there and away The base station near Conkouati takes about five hours to reach from Pointe Noire. Trucks leave from **Marché Makaya** in the north of the city three times a week, usually at a cost of CFA7,000. The road is paved up until the Kouilou River, which you must cross on a rundown ferry. Afterwards the route deteriorates dramatically. The trucks continue onwards to the Gabonese border, crossing the entire north–south length of the park, stopping at villages within Conkouati-Douli along the way.

DOLISIE ⊕ *04°12.20 S, 12°40.27 E*

Dolisie isn't a city you would go out of your way to visit, but is a true crossroads in Congo: it's the convergence of two main overland routes from Gabon, and the mid point of air and rail networks between Brazzaville and Pointe Noire. It's one of those places where any traveller will more than likely find themselves for at least a day or two while sorting out transportation for other destinations. Despite all of this, Dolisie remains the third most important city in Congo, and indeed can be a reminder of just how sparsely populated the nation is.

At just over 100,000 inhabitants, it can feel like a much smaller place: a tight, scattered town of unpaved roads and mostly single-storey buildings, it does have enough amenities for a traveller to feel comfortable – including an internet café, a few restaurants, and a vibrant town centre during the daytime. There is also an older colonial set of buildings near the **rail station** which gives the aura of a place long abandoned by the people who created it. Indeed, foreign presence is small in Dolisie, despite it being a town manufactured by the arrival of French interests.

Dolisie was founded as the Congo Ocean Railway was constructed in the 1920s; it assumed the name of Albert Dolisie, companion of Pierre Savorgnan de Brazza on his initial trek west from Brazzaville to the ocean. It was built between the Niari River and east of the Mayombé Mountains, making its location somewhat scenic. In 1975, the name of the town was changed to Loubomo, and older maps of Congo will reflect this; however, in 1991 as the political climate changed in the country, the old name of Dolisie was restored.

Its economy revolves around some modest mining and logging in the mountains, cattle farming, and as a trade centre for surrounding villages.

WHERE TO STAY AND EAT Dolisie is short on anywhere especially memorable for the traveller. The **Grand Hôtel de Dolisie** (✆ *91 01 02/91 01 03;* f *91 02 01; sgl/dbl* $$) is the town's top address, which unfortunately is not saying much – if there are officials in town, there may not be a room available. They also have a restaurant

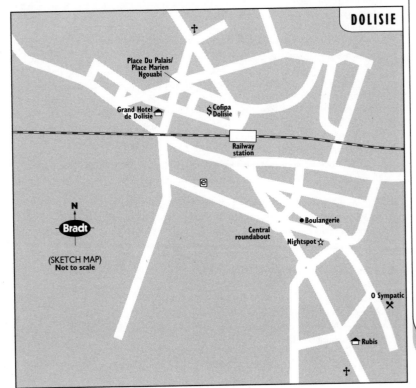

DOLISIE

Place Du Palais/
Place Marien
Ngouabi

Grand Hotel
de Dolisie

Cofipa
Dolisie

Railway
station

Boulangerie

Central
roundabout

Nightspot

O Sympatic

N

Bradt

(SKETCH MAP)
Not to scale

Rubis

The hissing of insects in the jungle was nearly deafening, and a few men emerged from the darkness. Congo's border formalities were, in fact, incredibly simple. Its officers incredibly friendly. They told me I needed to walk to the border town of Mbinda, a mere 7km. I was preparing my pack for a walk when one offered to call into town and see if someone could pick me up.

Yet sitting around a smouldering fire in the deep jungle that separates Gabon and Congo, I was reminded why I continue to travel to Africa – friends aren't hard to find, the heavy red sunsets ignite the soul, the smell of charcoal and thick foliage in the air creates an irreplaceable atmosphere. These men had no electricity, and went about their border formalities with only an oil lamp and a flashlight.

'The train leaves Tuesday, so you'll have to wait,' the police officer said. It was Saturday night – I hadn't expected this. The last information I could find on Congo-Brazzaville said trains were running every day. This was far from the truth.

There had to be another way. I found another traveller – Leroy – a Congolese who had been fleeced by the Gabonese army and then turned back with nothing, and offered to pay his way to Dolisie if he could find some transport.

We hitched a free ride a short way to a small village called Mayoko first, with a Malaysian. There were many Malaysians in this part of Congo – cutting down trees and shipping them overseas; sitting in a cab with the Malaysian was a decidedly bizarre thing after the always-gregarious if hard-to-understand banter that the average African engages in with his seatmates. He could only respond 'Yes, yes' to any questions I asked him about his business here, which perhaps meant that I shouldn't know. He dropped us off right beside our next connection – a large logging truck, a Mercedes Comilog, with the phrase *PASSAGERS INTERDIT* stencilled on its side. This would be my next ride south, for about US$15, and it would only get harder from there.

Sunset coloured the sky red as we trundled along in the logging truck, through the hilly slopes near the Congolese–Gabonese border. There was little room in the cab to sit, five of us packed tightly together, and a few more hanging off the rear of the tractor. The driver was wired up on something, more than likely a few things, and took his hands off the wheel every so often when the truck was moving in a straight line to sniff back some kind of powder into his nose. He was hired by the Malaysians to take his truck through the thick forest here, south and then west to Pointe Noire, about a week's journey.

Progress would be slow. At dusk, the rains came, and the truck stopped on a hill. There would be no way to get the vehicle moving in the heavy monsoons, and we would sit it out. I entertained the driver, and the others who had all piled into the cab to escape the rain, with information on how much truck drivers made in Canada and the States.

Once the rains ended, we exited the vehicle and watched its tyres burn slowly on the muddy hillside, gaining a few inches every few minutes. After continuous periods of digging itself into the dirt road, the truck would jar to a halt and the mechanic on board would chock the back wheel. I entertained visions in my mind of an express bus to Mbinda – yet even finding a logging truck heading south was apparently modestly good fortune.

Though in the deep evening, the truck arrived at the crest of the hill and we piled in on our way south to spend the evening in a tiny village, Moungoudou, the president's village (as they would ceaselessly remind me). Along a strip of dirt road in the middle of nowhere, the villages of Congo pop up with their thatch roofs and mud bricks, oil lamps, and idle population. The others in the truck started passing around a jerrycan of palm wine; I went to the one general store and bought a can of warm Coke.

We continued in the morning much the same: through winding roads, other logging trucks joining us in convoy, grinding slowly up and down muddy tracks. Fog set in early in the morning, and we had to wait – the driver would stand on the roadside chatting with villagers until another vehicle arrived from the opposite direction, and he would ask them about the road ahead.

In the afternoon of the second day, we finally arrived in Mossendjo – halfway between Mbinda and Dolisie. It was a modestly large town, and we were ejected from our logging truck on its outskirts – the driver went into a large compound owned by the Malaysians, and we hitched into the town with a small pickup truck. In the centre, a stretch of trucks sat on the roadside and crowds milled around aimlessly.

A bridge was out. The Malaysians were busy fixing it, but no-one was coming or going this day. In Mossendjo, then, there would be little to do but wait. I was becoming increasingly frustrated, having a schedule of cities to visit and little interest in becoming too mired in Congo-Brazzaville's various problems. We found a hotel – a jerrycan of fresh water was waiting in the bathroom, and a bucket. No running water. No electricity. We waited out the afternoon, waiting for the horns of trucks to begin blaring, a call to passengers that they needed to rush out for their transport south. The blue sky turned to red sky, then black sky. I fell fast asleep; no-one was going anywhere this day.

In the early morning, I grumbled loudly to Leroy and he quickly disappeared from my sight to find out what was going on. Minutes later he reappeared, saying he had secured transport south, in a different truck – the trucks that one sees in this part of Africa, large trucks sitting several feet off the ground, the back piled with goods and people and a cage covering it so more people and more goods can hang from the roof. Its horns blasted, we negotiated a price with the driver, and in the early morning we began roaring down the dirt road. Thirty minutes later they stopped at a small village and pulled out their tools to remove a rear wheel, drink some palm wine, and water the plants.

We were still following the rail line south – the Malaysians flitted past in a tiny rail car, tooting their horn, and the crowd of Congolese men turned from their palm wine just in time to watch them float by. I sat on a bench in the truck and watched an hour go by, until we started again, roared further down the road, and stopped at another village behind a long line of logging trucks.

Tsimba – the town had a restaurant under a thatch roof, two small general stores, and a video hut repeatedly playing *Tomb Raider* throughout the morning. Passengers migrated from the back of the truck to a small wooden cabin with benches made from palm trees; I watched the sun rise, the clouds move, and my watch tick away the hours.

But in the early afternoon, as boredom had firmly set in, the driver carried us all the way to the front lines: to the front of the logging truck's queues, to a clearing of dirt and mud, to a cement bridge and a mess of bent steel beams angling down into the river. One logging truck's payload had proven to be too much for the old steel bridge. 'C'est L'Afrique,' one man turned to me and said. 'But this bridge, it's French!' He corrected himself. I doubt the French had intended, when they built this bridge 80 years ago, that it would be used by a dozen logging trucks a day. And that the logging firm who came through would be too cheap to build a new one.

However, they had built a new one – sort of. Beside the bent mass of steel beams were four logs laid side by side, gone over once with packed mud, and large holes dropping down into the stream. The driver, his mechanic, and all of us passengers wandered out onto it and began the slow, agonising, only-in-Africa kind of discussion as to what to do.

Take the risk? That hole would devour a tyre. Pack some more mud into the holes? Wait for the Malaysians to properly repair the bridge? I stared out into space, actually over

continued overleaf

to the various planks that were hanging off of the steel beams, wondering how long it might take the two dozen passengers and other people hanging around to figure it out. Surely, I could have told them; but then I wouldn't discover as much from how these people worked. And would they listen to me? And perhaps they already knew, but still needed to go through the ritual of a lively discussion on how to fix the bridge.

Eventually, one passenger wandered over to the old bridge's wreckage. Then another. Then a half dozen, then ten of us on the old bridge to pass materials over and five more on the new bridge to pile the planks onto the new bridge. The driver was standing there, holding his keys and sporting a big grin: *'Je prends le risque!'* he shouted enthusiastically, and disappeared to the back of the trucks' line-up to grab our massive cargo vehicle.

Minutes later our repair job was done, the truck appeared at the foot of the bridge, and he revved his engine. We cleared out of the way, and seconds later it was over – he had passed through comfortably, the crowds standing around cheered and thanked God for his help, and we wandered to the top of a hill to pile into the back of our transport. We had to leave, get on with this day, and most importantly get to Dolisie.

This late afternoon, the clouds eased in and drops of rain started to come down. We passed through numerous roadside villages, swapping empty jerry cans for ones full of palm wine, working our way south along the dirt road. Other bridges we shared with the train tracks – signs on either end warned trucks to yield to trains, and slowly we were making genuine progress.

However, none of this was easy – massive pot-holes in the ground were the rule rather than the exception, and once the rains truly arrived the tarps went over the back and those hanging from the roof piled into the rear. A bare light bulb kept us illuminated in the darkness inside and outside, and my butt was getting sorely bruised from sitting on a hard bench for over six hours.

My anxiety subsided when finally we arrived in Dolisie – electric lights were the first tip-off that we had arrived into a town of some size, then shops with lights and even other vehicles could be seen. Private passenger vehicles! Motorbikes! The road here had been incredibly empty – with the exception of the logging trucks and the very rare old pickup, no real transport could be seen.

I had arrived in Dolisie, three days after leaving Mbinda. I remarked to Leroy that the train should be arriving today as well, but he countered that the train would just be arriving in Mbinda today. Once they're done loading, it will head south again.

for your perusal. Closer to the train station is a small hotel run by a European, which also has a snack bar. Probably the best value in town is a hotel on the road towards the airport, **Hôtel Rubis** (*sgl/dbl* $). Near the main **roundabout** is the town's largest **boulangerie**, where you can pick up some freshly baked bread throughout the day and even into the evening. Further along is a modestly decent restaurant, **Le Sympatic** (*13 Av de Gaulle;* m *553 4421/553 9848;* ⏰ *18.00–22.00 daily;* **$$**), which serves a small variety of chicken and fish dishes in a decidedly average environment. Otherwise, the Mauritanian general stores are well stocked for food – there are also a few night spots for drinks around the town if you have an urge to go out for some entertainment after dark.

PRACTICALITIES Also available is an **internet café** in the town centre (with an amazingly slow connection), and the single bank in town, **Banque Cofipa** (☏ *81 17 45;* m *558 9670*), is able to send and receive money via Western Union.

MOSSENDJO ✛ 02°56.24 S, 12°43.12 E

A mid-sized town of bright-red dirt roads and a small but spread-out centre, Mossendjo is seeing an increase in activity due to a large presence of Malaysians arriving here for logging. They operate a large building just outside town, a unique site as it is made entirely of rainforest lumber – a direct contrast to the old francophone stone buildings that make up the town centre.

In the middle of Mossendjo, trucks arrive and depart south for Dolisie and to points north on the way to Mbinda. The classic small-town Congo rules apply here: a general store without power selling any number of well-preserved biscuits and canned fish, a few hotels with intermittent water and power for CFA8,000–10,000. Across the street from the general store is a small bar that sells tin cups of palm wine, or a can of warm beer for the random rich traveller passing through.

Mossendjo is about a day's journey north from Dolisie, and another day's journey will get you to Mbinda. There are regular trucks and buses that do this route, and the once-weekly train passes through as well.

MBINDA ✛ 02°06.31 S, 12°52.48 E

Lying close to the Gabonese border to the north of Mossendjo and indeed the only town of its size in this region, Mbinda was once a proud outpost of logging and mining interests. Perhaps it was dreamed, long ago, that the Congo Ocean Railway would link up with the Trans-Gabonais rail line, only a few hundred kilometres to the north. Yet this never happened: continued internal strife in Congo, and a much more stable infrastructure from the deeper regions of Gabon to their own port of Libreville made such a rail line unnecessary. So, Mbinda sits as a sleepy jungle village with a wide muddy road, a small stretch of shops and a train station.

The train leaves on Thursdays, arriving the night before, but this can change at a moment's notice. Do not expect to see the train more than once a week, and it will be a slow affair as it trundles along a creaky rail line that has not seen any maintenance for decades. To pass the time while in Mbinda, there is a tiny television room in the middle of town with a few DVDs of the month being played for the entertainment of the locals. There are no restaurants. A few general stores and a few street sellers peddling the only warm food for sale from dozens of kilometres in every direction, are found along the roadside.

There is one place to stay at the north end of town, the **Catholic Mission**, offering spartan rooms for CFA3,000. They have no power or running water, but the security is good and they will offer an oil lamp.

The border with Gabon is about 7km away, an easy walk, though a few people with vehicles will offer to drive a traveller there for far too much money. Registering with the police upon arrival is necessary. There is no regular onward transport from the border to the next town in Gabon, Bakoumba, so arranging something beforehand will be essential. Note that the Gendarmerie du Gabon monitors the border, and are notoriously corrupt – expect to pay CFA20,000 in bribes, even when your paperwork is in order. You will likely have to pay even more if you are travelling with your own vehicle.

15

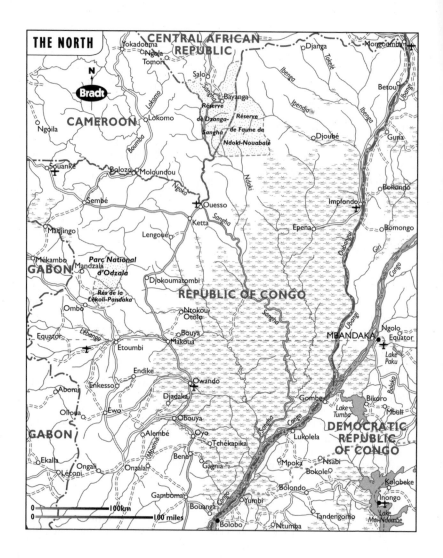

16

The North

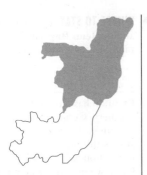

The Republic of Congo's far north is one of the least developed regions of Africa, with stretches of barely touched equatorial rainforest and wetlands stretching for hundreds of kilometres in every direction. The footprint of civilisation is small, and in some ways threatens to disappear altogether – with barely existent dirt roads connecting small villages and the looming presence of Ebola endemic throughout the area, wilderness and animal concerns take precedence over the daily lives of people. By some accounts, Congo's north is the 'last great wilderness' of Africa and attracts most tourists in the Congo to the region, especially to the Ndoki-Nouabalé National Park, yet they tend to only arrive in small numbers by aircraft.

If you can manage to travel independently through the towns of northern Congo, the local population will make any visitor feel welcome. Tourists on their own are exceedingly rare, and given how patchy transportation can be, allowing for extensive travel time is essential. Trucks can be delayed for days in any direction; boats up and downriver can sometimes take two weeks to reach Brazzaville. Furthermore, registering with the police is required when you stay overnight in any town throughout the region – in some cases the chief of police may seek a monetary reward for his troubles, but in other cases, when a foreigner goes out of their way to follow the country's laws, such hassles can be easily forgotten.

In many ways, this is the essential Congo, and the one I personally enjoy the most – a scattered network of small towns and villages, vast wilderness and exceedingly friendly people.

OYO ⊕ 00°55.41 S, 15°43.16 E

Marking roughly the halfway point between Ouesso and Brazzaville, Oyo is seeing a large amount of development in the area – from a new airport with a brand-new terminal, to French interests paving a highway towards Owando, to Chinese interests building large new stretches of apartment blocks, it's a surprising sight in a country where, outside Pointe Noire, there still remains little interest in updating the infrastructure. In fact, you will find the highway to be in excellent condition to and through Oyo – and conspicuously enough perhaps, there is a reason for this: Oyo is the home of Congo's President Denis Sassou-Nguesso. Near the north end of town past the roundabout is a large yellow mansion, his usual residence when in the country.

If he is here, you will be subject to frequent searches when both arriving in and leaving the town; this is nothing to be concerned about, though it can slow the journey down. The president has a large contingent of soldiers who will be readily visible around his mansion, and throughout the area. Aside from the mansion, which is closed to visitors anyway, there is little to recommend in Oyo, but it is well on its way to being the fourth-most important town in Congo, and your minibus will inevitably stop here for food and passengers.

WHERE TO STAY Two hotels to recommend are the **Bel Air** (☏ *91 00 10; sgl/dbl* $$) and the **Jean Baptiste** (☏ *91 00 41; sgl/dbl* $$) if you happen to need to spend the night. Buses arrive and depart around noon in both directions.

OWANDO ⊕ *00°29.01 S, 15°54.04 E*

Owando has changed drastically in the past few years – once just another town of northern Congo with dirt roads and little activity on its main boulevard, it is boasting a brand-new structure for its **central market**, as well as newly paved streets throughout. At the time of writing the entire town had been thrust into renovation, with new buildings and fresh concrete galore – courtesy of, I was told, Chinese construction companies. Owando is the largest town in northern Congo, but this statistic is deceiving – in terms of amenities, it has few to offer.

GETTING THERE AND AWAY A traveller heading north will inevitably arrive here. Buses from Brazzaville terminate in Owando every day, except in the case of the occasional direct transport to Makoua. The bus station is situated right in the 'middle' of town, for all that is worth – given that Owando, in essence, is simply a one–street town. There are no taxis in town – if you are laden down with luggage, children will transport it for you via wheelbarrow.

To get anywhere but back to Brazzaville, go down to the bridge around dawn, from where there are daily trucks towards Makoua. Down on the banks are *pirogues* that will take you upriver, and in theory it may be possible to reach Lebango and Odzala Park this way – however, it will take several days at a minimum, and it is actually quicker to go to Makoua for CFA5,000.

 WHERE TO STAY Two places will put a roof over your head for the night. The first, closest to the bus station, is the **Catholic church** (*sgl/dbl* $) which has a **hostel** on the right-hand side and offers spartan rooms with shared bathrooms. Out back they have an empty area with a few plastic tables where you can enjoy a beer, or if you prefer, there is a nightspot called **Bar Performance** to the right of the bus station. The town's best address is **Hôtel Sarah** (*5 rooms; sgl/dbl* $), further east down the road towards the bridge that crosses the river. In theory it

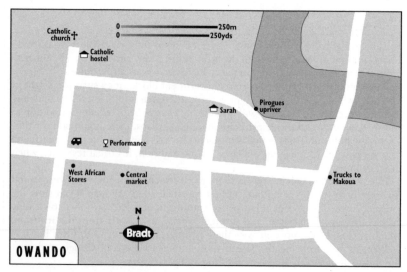

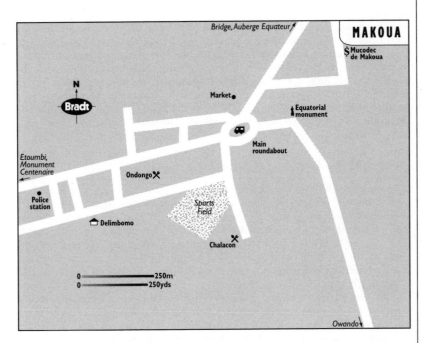

is required to register with the police, though no-one seems too concerned with this in Owando.

MAKOUA ✪ 00°00.16 S, 15°37.24 E

Makoua is directly on the Equator, and indeed has a small monument at the entrance of the town to mark this fact although it is currently incomplete, waiting for more funding to expand the small pillar into something a little more spectacular. I wouldn't bet on this happening anytime soon, though.

At the main roundabout in the town, trucks and buses head in every direction for Congo's hinterlands – north to Mambili, where you can find transport onward to Ouesso; west to Etoumbi, intermittently, where transport can be found north to Odzala Park. Makoua is also connected by a bus directly to Brazzaville three times per week, and on other days there is usually a large truck or two heading there.

Makoua's streets are sandy, its town centre sleepy. Locals while away their time walking between shady shops visiting the market in the morning, and snoozing through midday. Waiting for transport in any direction is what will bring you to Makoua, for either hours or days. If you have your own vehicle, there should be someone selling petrol from jerry cans at the roundabout.

Registering with the police is mandatory, and the chief does not charge a fee for his services.

Aside from the equatorial monument, the **Monument Centenaire** on the road west to Etoumbi is the town's other top attraction. If you are travelling here, you will undoubtedly have an afternoon to wander around – as vehicles towards Mambili or Etoumbi leave only in the morning.

WHERE TO STAY AND EAT There are two hotels in town, the better of which is at the southeast end of town, the **Residence Dahovour** (*8 rooms;* m *569 9831; sgl* $, *dbl* $$), also called **Hôtel Delimbomo**, where the rooms have fans and occasional running water, but otherwise clean private bathrooms. Closer to the bridge at the north end of town is **Auberge Equateur** ($), Makoua's second place for a bed and, while cheaper, is far more rundown – don't expect any power or running water (at least, at the other place, it's intermittent!). Near the hotel is one of the town's two restaurants, **Ondongo Bar/Restaurant** ($), serving a *plat du jour* for around CFA1,000. A short walk further east is the **Chalacon Restaurant** ($), a smaller place that sells similar food. Makoua also has a small bank, **Mucodec de Makoua**, (◷ *08.00-15.00 Mon–Fri*) though they are unable to change money – the west Africans in the town centre, near the roundabout, can do this.

PARC NATIONAL D'ODZALA: ODZALA NATIONAL PARK

Those who reach Odzala end up being impressed by its large variety of wildlife, as well as the ease of seeing it there – Odzala is unique in that in its vast area, there are numerous clearings amongst the dense jungles of northern Congo. It is also one of central Africa's oldest parks, founded in 1935 by AEF administrator St Floris. In 2001, it was expanded to encompass a much larger area of almost the entire northwest corner of the nation, but it still remains a very remote place, and the bushmeat trade that has threatened populations in the other Congolese parks is not nearly as much of a concern here.

The general layout of the park is intermixed savanna and rainforest slowly merging into the dense rainforest of the Grand Forêt that encompasses the far north of Congo. Near the park is the Lossi Gorilla Sanctuary, an area created for researchers who monitor the gorilla populations in the region. Visitors are welcome, and some gorillas there have been habituated for tourists who manage to visit.

Odzala is also a prime spot to see western lowland gorillas, and has the largest population of these creatures in the whole of Africa. Forest elephants, bongo, buffalo, sitatunga and other large mammals also make their home here. Given the high densities of all these animals within the park's boundaries, if you have one specific animal to study, guides will be able to find it for you. For birdwatchers, there have been over 400 African species spotted in the park.

The situation is not all rosy, however – the Ebola outbreaks common to the Gabonese–Congolese border have taken their toll on animal populations. Researchers have witnessed what they call a massive 'die-off' of gorillas and elephants, especially in the areas around the park. Some regions have reported up to 90% of their populations decimated by the disease; while Ebola has not intruded too far into the park, the damage has been done – if one group of gorillas is killed off by the disease, a survivor from the group will seek to join with another family. The infection perpetuates this way. The Ebola problems have also meant intermittent closures of the park to tourists, making a little investigation with WCS in Brazzaville necessary to avoid disappointment – I could only imagine the disappointment of spending so much time to reach Odzala, only to be turned away on arrival!

Most travel throughout Odzala is restricted to waterways, and there are plenty of them – making for only a few intrusive road networks. The main base camp is near an airstrip directly inside the park, with a permanent set of tents on wooden platforms. Some local staff can provide food, but independent visitors are quite rare in this respect and they may be unprepared. There are several other camps throughout the park, with basic amenities – mostly along the Mambili River heading north.

GETTING THERE AND AWAY Odzala is easily the most difficult park to reach in Congo – no regular flights go anywhere near it, thus necessitating a journey of several days by road. Begin by arriving in Makoua and asking about transportation

The remoteness of northern Congo cannot be understated, and it is driven home by the outbreaks of Ebola that have occurred there in recent years. The worst was in November 2003, when over 100 people were killed by the virus before it was brought under control.

Traditional burial rights have been the largest killer – Congolese normally touch the body of the deceased, as a way of absolving themselves of having anything to do with that person's death. With Ebola, this can be deadly again as the disease spreads rapidly through human contact.

The original theory was that the virus broke out due to a family slaughtering a local boar and eating it, thereby consuming the infected food. It is a common method of transmission for the virus. It spread quickly throughout the hinterlands between Mbomo and Lebango, and the worst infections were centred on Etoumbi. It took officials from the World Health Organization four days to reach the site of the outbreak, and begin to bring it under control. During that time local health workers became infected, and five of them eventually died.

Another outbreak occurred in the same area in May 2005, but was brought under control rather quickly. With the assistance of the World Health Organization, Congo-Brazzaville's government has established a National Co-ordination Committee in Brazzaville to deal with Ebola outbreaks as they occur in the Congo hinterlands.

For a traveller passing through these areas, vigilance is important. Avoid any foods that are not pre-packaged, drink bottled water, and inspect water sources for bathing. Being overly cautious is not entirely necessary, as most Ebola cases occur in rural areas outside towns. Always take a safer, more sanitary hotel room to rest in over a squalid one. Try to avoid crowds of people, and pay extra to sit in the front seat of a shared vehicle if travelling this way.

If you are caught in a situation where the area has been quarantined, there is little to do. If there are international staff assisting local health workers in assisting victims of the disease, ask them to ensure you are not infected and leave the area. They may or may not comply – Ebola is taken extremely seriously, and any inconvenience in your travel plans is irrelevant next to containing the virus.

---

west to **Etoumbi** (✪ *00°01.21 N, 14°53.32 E*) – there are usually trucks several times a week that do the journey, which should take a day. Getting north to **Lebango** (✪ *00°25.54 N, 14°41.54 E*) and **Mbomo** (✪ *00°33.45 N, 14°39.26 E*), the true entrance to the park, can take several more days depending on the schedules of passing trucks. Mbomo is usually reached via *pirogue* from Lebango. If you are travelling in your own vehicle, bring petrol as it can be difficult to find after Makoua. If you wish to charter an aircraft, there is an airstrip directly inside the park (✪ *00°35.53.26 N, 14°52.36.96 E*). Etoumbi and Lebango also have some very basic airstrips.

If you've discovered the village of Mambili near the river, it may be possible to hire a motorised *pirogue* from the river crossing into the park – however, the distance is still 75km, making it at least a full day's journey to the base camp. Entry to the park is free.

MAMBILI ✪ *00°18.29.35 N, 15°28.32.41 E*

The shattered overland route from Brazzaville to Ouesso becomes apparent after Makoua, and trucks ply a brutal road north to Mambili for those crazy enough to try and reach Ouesso by land. Mambili itself is nothing but a small village of mud huts with thatch roofs, but has become the staging point for the toughest part of the journey.

Quite simply, the road ends in Mambili – at one point it continued to the river of the same name, and across a bridge, but the war of 1997 obliterated the bridge and any kind of way for vehicles to reach Mindouli, another stretch of mud huts on the north bank of the river. Therefore you need to walk for roughly 8km – usually around midday under the burning sun – through jungle and open grassland, across a dozen small footbridges, and then cross the river in a wooden *pirogue* (for CFA500). Once in Mindouli, police and customs are ready for travellers to welcome them to Sangha district – for non-Congolese citizens, 'formalities' cost CFA8,000. The onward journey on a waiting truck is CFA10,000.

Progressing north from Mindouli, the plateau region of Congo descends into the lowlands of central Africa and the Grand Forêt, or the Great Rainforest – a dense mass of thick jungle abundant in animal life, and the home of the pygmy tribes. Bushmeat is abundant here, as are protections against illegal hunting – there are forest ranger checkpoints along the way, with men who will inspect any animal carcasses that your vehicle may be transporting. The road from Mindouli to Ouesso is good, and should take on average four–five hours for the journey either way. Note that they like to transport their hunting prizes live when possible, and if you're squeamish around injured mammals tied up into contorted positions and groaning for hours, you may wish to take the plane.

While Ebola is not generally endemic in this area of Congo, it is close enough to the Ebola regions that eating any bushmeat (abundant as it is) should still be avoided. Of course, if an Ebola-stricken animal happens to get thrown into the same truck that you're travelling in, there is not much you can do to avoid it – aside from ride in the front, called *la cabine*, which you should be doing anyway.

After crossing the Liouesso River and barrelling down another 75km of dirt road, you will arrive at Ouesso – a modestly large town located in the extreme north of Congo.

OUESSO ✪ *01°36.51 N, 16°02.54 E*

Though in practice it is simply a scatter of dirt roads, Ouesso has all of the amenities required for a traveller heading north or south. It's also a pygmy town of sorts – throughout the town you'll see men and women of short stature, dressed in everyday clothes that defy the normal vision of pygmies (a pygmy in a leisure suit was the strangest thing I had seen for quite some time). Many of them have integrated into Ouesso's fabric, making it even more of a multi-cultural place than usual for Congo's towns.

GETTING THERE AND AWAY To Cameroon, you head along the river in a *pirogue* to then cross by boat, starting in **Maboko** (✪ *01°45.47 N, 16°00.13 E*); from there, frequent trucks can take you to connections northward for larger towns.

Ouesso's **airport** is a busy place that sees at least one flight per day heading back to Brazzaville, but in peak times it is absolutely necessary to reserve a place beforehand. Buying a ticket at the airport is not possible – all of the offices are in town and manage all facets of air travel. Therefore the only thing to do at the airport is board the flight.

At the main roundabout in the morning, **trucks** head back south to Mindouli, leaving in the early morning. For travel upriver, there are daily **barges** north to Bomassa. South to Mossaka, there is usually at least one per week – and the journey takes four days.

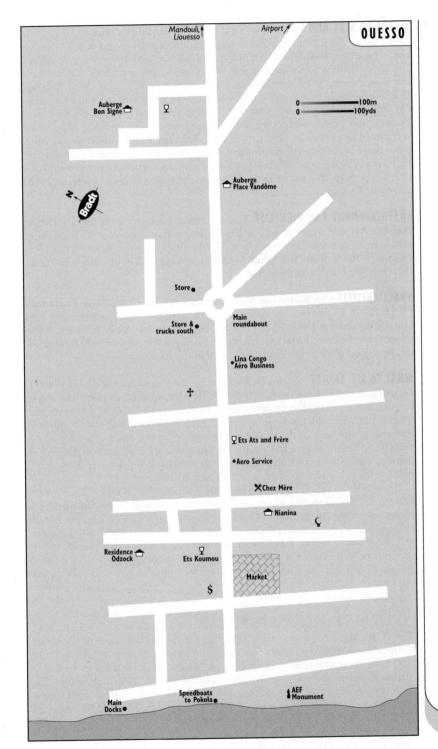

283

WHERE TO STAY AND EAT Ouesso's top address is **Hôtel Nianina** (20 73 70/76 63 75; sgl/dbl $$), with air conditioning, satellite television and regular running water. Nearby is **Residence Odzock** (sgl/dbl $$), which has hot water on request and large rooms – while cheaper than the Nianina, they are a little rundown and not the cleanest. At the northern end of town is a popular spot called **Auberge Bon Signe** (m 521 0519; sgl/dbl $$), which has the town's most popular restaurant ($), as well as basic rooms with fan, satellite television (really only TV5 from France), and private bathrooms with running water. The cheapest place worth recommending is nearby on the main road, **Auberge Place Vandôme** ($) where water and electricity seem intermittent. They are more accustomed to renting out their rooms by the hour. It is best to plan ahead if arriving in Ouesso on a weekend, as it is a popular spot for locals from around the region to book rooms on Friday and Saturday nights.

ENTERTAINMENT AND NIGHTLIFE There are several decent bars in town, including **Bar Ets Ats and Frère** as well as **Ets Koumou Bar** nearby on the main street; across from Auberge Bon Signe is a popular drinking spot. Across from Hôtel Nianina is **Restaurant/Bar Chez Mère** ($), serving food in the early evening and then nothing but drinks thereafter.

PRACTICALITIES Ouesso has one bank near the river, **La Congolaise de Banque** (81 10 30; 08.00–17.00 Mon–Fri), open during Congo's intermittent bank hours – however, it can send and receive Western Union money transfers. Across the street is the town's **market**, which has a covered structure of mild interest and can be a good place to get inexpensive food in the mornings.

WHAT TO SEE AND DO Ouesso itself cannot be said to have a great deal of things to keep the traveller busy – though the **AEF Monument**, marking the town's location and the date of its founding along the Sangha River can be a pleasant place to spend an afternoon on the shore. The church in the centre of town is modestly interesting, and west of the main roundabout are several relics of a colonial past that give Ouesso a unique feel – some ancient, rundown mansions on the roadside point to a long-departed European presence. Otherwise Ouesso is a sleepy transit point nestling between the river and the Great Rainforest.

If you want to visit the pygmies, there are a fair number of their villages around Ouesso. Getting to them is not nearly as difficult as it would seem – independently, taking one of the trucks west to Mindouli, stating that your purpose is to find the villages, should be all that is necessary. Any of the Bantu villagers along the road will know where to find the pygmies, and will lead you there for a small sum. I'd recommend bringing some sort of gift – some food, palm wine, even a domestic animal if you can get one. Make sure whoever guides you approves of your offering.

NATIONAL PARC NDOKI-NOUABALÉ

This is quickly becoming a prime attraction for visitors to Congo, bringing tour groups directly into the Pokola base camp and on guided tours from there in. In 1990, it began as an extension of the Dzanga-Sangha Special Reserve in the Central African Republic and was initially simply a faunal reserve; as a result of the efforts from conservation groups worldwide, it has since become a fully fledged national park. On occasion this area is referred to as the Sangha Tri-National Reserves, with the Lobeke National Park in Cameroon further extending the protected area. WCS Congo has hired several dozen Ecoguards to monitor the entire reserve and in so doing reducing the frequency of illegal hunting and logging when compared with other reserves and parks throughout either Congo. The guards work closely with the Ministry of Forest and Environment in Brazzaville, and the ministry has ensured that the park remains a protected region.

All of this means that Ndoki-Nouabalé is quickly becoming a very popular place to witness one of the last undeveloped wilderness regions on the African continent. It has several villages within its boundaries, including pygmy settlements, and these people have also been enlisted by conservation groups to protect the landscape. Large mammals are generally undisturbed in the area, and due to a well-maintained airstrip directly on the edge of the park in addition to regular commercial flights from Brazzaville, it has become easily accessible for those interested in visiting.

Pokola is the closest town to the park, and the inhabitants' primary employers are a wide variety of logging concession companies in the region – the entire area between the Lac Tele Reserve and the Ndoki-Nouabalé National Park is criss-crossed with dirt roads for this purpose. If you are arriving with your own vehicle, having guidance is essential. From Pokola you first need to reach Bomassa, on the edge of the park, and the actual headquarters of Ndoki-Nouabalé – it is here that you should be able to gather all relevant information of where, and how, to get around the area, as well as registering yourself and employing a local guide if one is available. From Bomassa you continue by road to Wali Bai, and then by foot and *pirogue* to the main camp of the park, Mbeli Bai, a large clearing where a variety of animals can be seen on a regular basis. There are numerous viewing platforms available. For other animals, heading deeper into the park is necessary; this is usually done by foot or *pirogue*. The park has no road network beyond the entrance. Entrance to the park is free.

AROUND NDOKI-NOUABALÉ

POKALA (⊕ 02°03.08 N, 16°05.16 E) Pokala is 35km north of Ouesso, an hour by motorboat (and CFA4,000 for the privilege); flights from Brazzaville are also stopping here once weekly, catering to a new generation of organised tours heading into the park. If you are travelling to the park independently you will need to make a stop here to register yourself and get some information on what is permitted; and it is more than likely you will be asked to have some sort of escort throughout the reserve (and indeed this is a good idea, given the size of the place – the rangers can provide transport to common sights to see wild animals). The park is still a stretch north from Pokala, however – it is better to head directly to **Bomassa** (⊕ 02°12.11 N, 16°11.11 E), where a number of tour operators embark for the park. Boats from Ouesso to Bomassa leave in the early morning, or a motorised *pirogue* from Pokola can get there in about two hours.

MOSSAKA (⊕ 01°13.36 S, 16°47.46 E) Mossaka is the crossroads for boats heading upriver along the Congo and Oubangui to Impfondo and Bangui, or upriver along the Sangha to Ouesso. Due to unusually high occurrences of sleeping sickness in the region, a few NGOs have made their base here to assist surrounding villages, and some very basic services have sprung up in their wake. However, beyond that it is a remote place, without any direct road access. An airport is nearby in the village of Likouléla, and sometimes both towns are referred to as Mossaka-Likouléla. Furthermore, it is possible to travel eastward by road from Oyo: find transport to the small village of **Tongo** (⊕ 01°23.18 S, 16°18.29 E) and hire a *pirogue* upriver to Mossaka, which should cut down on the four-day barge ride from Brazzaville.

A prominent story that has developed over centuries of European exploration throughout the northern stretches of Congo concerns the possibility of a primeval beast that still exists in the region; call it the African version of the Loch Ness Monster if you will, yet its existence has never been called into doubt as much as its Scottish partner. It is undoubtedly based on a dinosaur, a four-legged herbivore, and explorers have recorded its existence in the far reaches of Congo for centuries.

French missionaries would record finding strange tracks in 1776, and after consulting with pygmy tribes of the region, knew that they were not from an elephant. Several other explorers in the swampy outer limits of civilisation also recorded something large and massive living under water – in 1913, a German explorer recorded stories from the pygmies of a huge creature, and in 1932 a British scientist wrote of a frightening experience seeing a serpent-like head emerge from the water.

There is little doubt that it is a dinosaur of sorts, described to be something similar to a brontosaurus – over 20m long and 5m tall, a massive thing indeed; yet no-one has managed to encounter it up close and verify it, aside from the pygmies.

Pygmy tribes in the area speak of building a wall in the 1960s to keep the beast away from their village, and spearing one to death. A victory feast was planned, and all who ate the meat later died from it. More research was done on the creature and an American by the name of James Powell travelled to Gabon in 1976 to explore these myths. Pygmies told him of a large creature they called N'yamala. A subsequent expedition to Impfondo in 1979 by two biologists brought stories of the Mokele-Mbembe, as they called it, living somewhere in the vast swamps north of the town.

The 'living dinosaur' has caught the imaginations of numerous explorers. Over a dozen expeditions have been launched into the Likouala swamp north of Impfondo in searched of the mythical beast, yet curiously enough for a massive dinosaur, it has never been found. Yet several snippets of photo and video taken over the past decades point to something unknown living in the vast wetlands, a swamp which is mostly undeveloped and unexplored. It is a huge area, and local tribes have repeatedly confirmed that something similar to the dinosaur pictures they have been shown exists in the area. Biologist William J Gibbons continued research on the Mokele-Mbembe in 2002, this time approaching the region from southern Cameroon, with a film crew in tow. Local people there made statements consistent with the Pygmies of northern Congo. However, when shown a picture of a rhinoceros, the locals became extremely excited, proclaiming it to be the dinosaur. Some speculation exists that Pygmies in these areas use the same terminology for both creatures; or, perhaps, they have only heard of the animal through oral histories and the similarities in descriptions makes differentiating the two creatures impossible for them. Either way, research from this expedition was ultimately inconclusive, and to this day no-one has managed to capture concrete evidence of the creature's existence.

IMPFONDO (✈ *01°36.23 N, 18°03.42 E*) Historically called Desbordesville and the largest town in the Likouala district of northeast Congo, Impfondo is either your jumping-off point to reach the Lac Tele Reserve or a stopping point on the way to Bangui by barge. There is little to recommend otherwise in the town – it is a frontier kind of place, the last vestige of what could be called civilisation in an area overwhelmed by dense forest swamps and small villages. Rumours abound of a police force and set of soldiers more corrupt than in other parts of Congo – be prepared for some procedural hassles. Perhaps this is simply because of the area's remoteness, in addition to being so close to the DR Congo across the river; soldiers from the other Congo have been known to cross and harass the population on occasion, making many people here more on edge than usual. The entire western side of the Congo River in Likouala is also home to numerous refugee camps, though as conflict in the DR Congo subsides, they should be making their way back across the river.

How long you spend in Impfondo will be highly dependent on when transportation out can be found – it is intermittent in every direction. Barges go north to Bangui, and if not directly then you should aim to reach **Boyele** (✥ *02°30.40 N, 18°13.11 E*), where there are more frequent boats northward. There is a highly undeveloped dirt trail heading north along the river into the Central African Republic – and if you brought your own vehicle by barge, as well as all of your own supplies, it may be worth a whirl.

RESERVE DE LAC TELE (LAKE TELE RESERVE)

While not yet a park, the Lac Tele Reserve west of Impfondo has become an important area to preserve the species of Congo's most remote region. It is centred on the easily identifiable Lac Tele, an almost perfectly circular lake situated in the middle of lowlands and swamp. Around 17,000 people in over two dozen villages live within the reserve's boundaries, and there are ongoing projects to manage the lives of these people in conjunction with the wildlife. The community is important to the preservation of the reserve – it is with their assistance that it can even exist, and hunting is kept at sustainable levels. This is why the area is often called the Lac Tele Community Reserve.

Large mammals are still found across the reserve, including lowland gorillas, hippos, forest elephants, crocodiles and monkeys. Indeed, one of the challenges of conservationists in the region is cutting down on illegal hunting both inside and outside the reserve – as elephants and gorillas especially often travel outside of its boundaries, where they have even less protection against poachers. The wetlands are also home to several hundred bird species, numerous snake species, and many as-yet-undiscovered aspects of the region – for example, how lowland gorillas live in the swampy forests of the reserve has not yet been fully established. Congo's wetlands are mostly unexplored, and the large majority of outsiders to visit Lac Tele are researchers.

GETTING THERE AND AWAY From Impfondo, you travel 70km southwest along a paved road to the town of **Epena** (✥ *01°21.14 N, 17°26.58 E*). The main research camp for the reserve is near the town, and should not be difficult to find if you ask a few residents. Keep in mind that onward from Epena, there are no services or means to get around: you must bring with you everything you may need to use. On occasion there are research teams going about their business on the reserve, but dropping by unexpectedly is no guarantee of being invited along. Be sure to arrange your visit beforehand – like all reserves in Congo, a permit from the Ministry of Forest and Environment in Brazzaville (*Bd des Armées*) is required for a visit. Further permits are required (also from the ministry) to actually carry out research in the park..

Appendix I

WILDLIFE GUIDE with Mike Unwin

MAMMALS Mammals as a class (Mammalia) are distinguished by having hairy bodies, among other anatomical traits, and by their habit of suckling their young. The Congos are especially rich in mammals, with upwards of 400 species. These range from such 'megafauna' as gorillas and elephants, to a multitude of lesser known rodents, bats and other smaller creatures of the night.

Ungulates and other herbivores
Ungulates, or hoofed mammals, can be divided into two principal groups: the even-toed ungulates (order Artiodactyla), which have two or four toes, and include antelope, cattle, pigs, giraffes and hippos; and the odd-toed ungulates (order Perissodactyla), which have one or three toes, and include horses and rhinos. All ungulates are herbivores, grazing or browsing on a wide range of shrubs, grass and herbs across their range. Other large herbivores include the elephants, which belong to a separate order: Proboscidae.

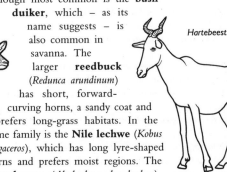

Antelope The antelope family (Bovidae) is well represented in the Congos, with a wide variety of species, each of which occupies a different habitat niche in the region. **Duikers** (*Cephalophus* spp.), are small to medium-sized antelope with short horns and rounded backs. Approximately 17 species occur in the region. The majority are adapted to forest habitats, where they take refuge in thick undergrowth when disturbed, though most common is the **bush duiker**, which – as its name suggests – is also common in savanna. The larger **reedbuck** (*Redunca arundinum*) has short, forward-curving horns, a sandy coat and prefers long-grass habitats. In the same family is the **Nile lechwe** (*Kobus megaceros*), which has long lyre-shaped horns and prefers moist regions. The **hartebeest** (*Alcelaphus buselaphus*)

Common duiker

Reedbuck

Lechwe

Hartebeest

belongs to a different antelope tribe. It has short twisted horns, a long narrow snout and long legs that allow a loping, energy-efficient gait.

The spiral-horned antelope (*Tragelaphini* spp.) are more closely related to cattle than to other antelope. The **bongo** (*Tragelaphus euryceros*) is a forest species, with a stocky, chestnut body emblazoned with white stripes, and sturdy, twisted horns. The similar but smaller **bushbuck** (*Tragelaphus scriptus*) is much more common, and can be distinguished by the white spotting along its flanks. The **sitatunga** (*Tragelaphus spekeii*) has shaggier fur and longer horns than a bushbuck and is restricted to marshy habitats, where its unusually long, splayed hooves are an adaptation for moving across wet ground. The **greater kudu** (*Tragelaphus strepsiceros*) is a tall, elegant species of dry bush country, with spectacular spiral horns in the male that can reach a length of over 1.5m. Even larger is **Derby's eland** (*Taurotragus derbianus*), which has a square, ox-like build, straight horns and a prominent dewlap, and can reach a weight of nearly 1,000kg. It is the only member of this group in which the female, as well as the male, carries horns.

Bushbuck

Greater kudu

Sitatunga

African buffalo (*Syncerus caffer*) The buffalo belongs to the same family as antelope and is Africa's only true ox. Two races inhabit the region, with the forest race being redder in colour than the savanna race. These sociable animals may gather in herds of hundreds or even thousands. Both sexes carry impressive horns, though the larger males can be distinguished from females by the heavier 'boss' or bony plate on top of the head.

African buffalo

Wild pigs (Suidae) The **warthog** (*Phacocherus africanus*) is the best known of Africa's wild pigs. It prefers lightly wooded country, where it is easily identified by its bare, grey skin and large curling tusks. More common in woodland and forested areas is the hairier, shorter-tusked **bush pig** (*Potamochoerus larvatus*), which is strictly nocturnal, and digs for roots and tubers along forest trails. The **red river hog** (*Potamochoerus porcus*) is a rainforest species, and has a rich red coat, bold white face markings and long tasselled ears. The **giant forest hog** is the largest of the family, with males sometimes exceeding 250kg. This rare species has a long black coat, stout tusks and occurs patchily in forests at up to 3,800m.

Warthog

Hippopotamus (*Hippopotamus amphibius*) Hippos are unmistakable, with their great size, rotund body, huge teeth and, most of all, their habit – unique among ungulates – of spending the daylight hours submerged in water. They frequent shallow lakes, rivers and swamplands, emerging at night to graze on waterside grassland. An adult may weigh over 2,500kg and requires about 60kg of food per night.

Okapi (*Okapia johnstoni*) Giraffes are now virtually extinct in the Congo region. However, the okapi is also a member of the giraffe family (Giraffidae), and has been a curiosity since it was first discovered at the beginning of the 20th century. This bizarre-looking animal has a longish neck, long ears, short horns and an exceptionally long tongue, used for plucking leaves from overhead branches. Its chocolate to purplish-brown coat is patterned with white face markings and white zebra-like stripes on the legs. Okapis are extremely shy, living only in deep rainforests, where they prefer low river valleys but migrate to higher ground in the rainy season.

White rhinoceros (*Ceratotherium simun*) Rhinos (Rhinocerotidae) are odd-toed ungulates, closely related to horses. These massive, thick-skinned animals have stout legs with three toes on each foot, and two distinctive horns on top of the head. Two species occur in Africa, of which only the larger white rhino remains in the Congos and is now reduced to a handful of individuals in Garamba National Park. This animal can exceed 2,500kg in weight, making it the second largest African mammal after the elephant, and prefers open woodland and grassland habitats. It is distinguished from the smaller **black rhino** (*Diceros bicornis*) by a hump on its neck, as well as by its longer head and broader mouth, the latter an adaptation for grazing.

White rhinoceros

Common zebra (*Equus Zebra*) The zebra is a member of the horse family, with one large hoof on each foot, and is rendered quite unmistakable by its pattern of black and white stripes. It travels in small family groups of up to 30, preferring open plains with good grazing and easy access to water. Although common in eastern and southern Africa, zebras have a very limited range in the Congos.

Common zebra

African elephant

African elephant (*Loxodonta Africana*) The African elephant is the largest land mammal on the planet. It is divided into two subspecies, the forest elephant (*L. a. cyclotis*) and bush elephant (*L. a. africana*), now considered by many authorities to be separate species. Forest elephants are the smaller of the two and distinguished by their downward-pointing tusks. They are also the more widespread race in the Congos. Elephants are highly gregarious creatures with complex social structures and a sophisticated range of communication techniques. They tend to move in family groups, led by a dominant older female, or matriarch, but may form larger herds in times of migration and drought.

Carnivores A wide spectrum of carnivores (order Carnivora) is found in the Congos, including cats, dogs and hyenas, as well as several smaller groups. Carnivores are specialised meat-eaters, with teeth and claws adapted to their predatory way of life. A few species, however, also include some plant matter in their diet.

Cats (Felidae) Cats are perhaps the most specialised of all carnivores. Most species are solitary and nocturnal, and have retractile claws with which to capture and despatch prey.

Lion (*Panthera leo*) The lion is both Africa's largest feline and its largest carnivore, famous for its far-carrying roar and the flowing mane of hair carried by adult males. It hunts medium-sized to large game up to the size of buffalo, but will take smaller prey if nothing else is available. Lions are the most sociable of all cats, with groups – known as `prides`– numbering anything from five to more than thirty individuals, depending upon the availability of prey. They are primarily nocturnal and prefer open bush, though they have been found in all habitats except deep equatorial rainforest. Lions occur in the eastern half of the DR Congo, and a small population also exists in northwestern Congo.

Leopard (*Panthera pardus*) The leopard is about half the weight of a lion, and its distinctive coat of black spots on a tawny to yellow background provides excellent camouflage. It is a secretive, solitary hunter, and uses stealth and cover to ambush its prey. Leopards are extremely versatile, occurring in all habitats from rainforest to desert, and are the most abundant big cat in the Congos. They feed on anything from medium-sized antelopes to small mammals, frogs and birds.

Leopard

Cheetah (*Acinonyx jubatus*) The cheetah is the fastest of all land mammals. It is the size of a leopard, but slimmer, with a smaller head, longer legs and small solid spots rather than rosettes. Cheetahs need open country in which to hunt their medium-sized to small antelope prey, running them down at exceptional speeds of up to 112km/h. They are threatened throughout Africa and rare in the Congos.

Cheetah

Cheetah

Smaller cats Smaller cats include the **golden cat** (*Felis aurata*), a powerful forest dweller that ambushes prey up to the size of duiker, and the long-legged, spotted **serval** (*Felis serval*), which uses expert hearing to locate its rodent prey in long grass and marshlands.

Serval

Other carnivores

Spotted hyena

The **spotted hyena** (*Crocuta crocuta*) is the largest member of the hyena family (Hyenidae). This sociable predator is an expert scavenger, with powerful, bone-crunching jaws, but also a proficient hunter capable of tackling prey as large as zebra. It prefers open habitats and is absent from deep forest. The **side-striped jackal** (*Canis adustus*) is the most abundant member of the dog family in the Congos, and flourishes around villages and small towns. Its omnivorous diet includes anything from small antelope to berries.

Lower down the carnivore scale, the weasel family (Mustelidae) is represented by a variety of species, varying from the widespread **honey badger** (*Mellivora capensis*), a specialist raider of bee nests, to the **swamp otter** (*Aonyx congica*), one of three otter species that use their excellent swimming skills to catch fish in the region's lakes and rivers.

Honey badger

The genet and civet family (Viverridae) comprises a number of long-tailed, low-slung species, most of which are arboreal, including the **central African linsang** (*Poiana leightoni*), which has a lithe, spotted body and hunts small prey in the tree canopy, and the **African palm civet** (*Nandinia binotata*), which feeds primarily on fruit and often frequents cultivated areas. The closely related mongooses (family Herpestidae) are small to medium-sized, short-legged carnivores. Some, such as the crab-eating **marsh mongoose** (*Atalix paludinosus*) are largely solitary and nocturnal; others, such as the smaller **banded mongoose** (*Mungos mungo*) are sociable and forage by daylight.

Banded mongoose

Primates The Congo region, with its huge tracts of forest, has the greatest variety of primate species (order Primates) in Africa. These fall into two main subdivisions: the apes and Old World monkeys (Catarrhini); and the more primitive bushbabies and pottos (Strepsirrhini), collectively known as prosimians.

Apes Apes are our closest living relatives. They are distinguished from monkeys by, among other things, their lack of a tail.

Gorilla (*Gorilla gorilla*) The gorilla is the world's largest primate. Scientists currently recognise three main subspecies: the western lowland gorilla (*Gorilla gorilla gorilla*), eastern lowland gorilla (*Gorilla beringei graueri*) and mountain gorilla (*Gorilla beringei beringei*). Further research may add more, specifically the gorillas of Mount Tshiaberimu (*Gorilla gorilla tshiaberimuensis*). By far the most numerous is the western lowland race. The eastern lowland race has slightly shorter fur and is the largest of the three. The mountain gorilla is easily recognisable by its long black fur, an adaptation to its cold, high-altitude habitat. Gorillas are herbivores and forage within their range during the day for leaves, bamboo shoots and other plant matter. They form groups of ten to thirty, presided over by a dominant male identified by his saddle of grey fur and known, consequently, as a `silverback`.

Chimpanzee

Chimpanzees (*Pan troglodytes*) Chimpanzees are smaller than gorillas but are more closely related to humans. They inhabit deep rainforests, where they feed largely on fruit in the canopy of large trees, but may also frequent low mountain forests and savanna. Their omnivorous diet includes meat, and they are capable hunters, sometimes using organised ambushes to capture monkeys or small antelope. Chimpanzee groups may number up to 120 and are strongly territorial. Individuals build nests in trees with twigs and branches, preferring areas as high as possible from the ground.

Bonobo (*Pan paniscus*) The bonobo, once thought to be a subspecies of chimpanzee, has a complex social system, in which sexuality plays a prominent role. It is also known for its habitat of often walking nearly upright. Its hair is shorter than that of the other apes, and it has an entirely hairless face and usually a bare chest. Bonobos are confined to the DRC, where they frequent swampy habitats and jungle, and seldom travel far from their home range. They eat mostly plant matter and fruit, and, like chimps, may use items as tools to retrieve their food.

Monkeys Monkeys are generally smaller than apes. Most species have long tails and dextrous limbs, allowing them great agility among the branches.

Baboons (*Papio* spp.) Baboons are large, sociable monkeys that feed mostly on the ground and roost in trees. They have distinctly bushy hair, and a long dog-like muzzle – most pronounced in the male. The two subspecies found in the Congos are the olive baboon (*Papio anubis*) and the yellow baboon (*Papio cynocephalus*), the latter being distinguished by its darker, thicker fur, including a heavy mane around the neck. Baboons are quite adaptable to human

Studies of bonobo behaviour have revealed that sex is integral to their society. These amorous apes use sexual intercourse as a means of greeting, conflict resolution and post-conflict reconciliation. Females even offer sex in exchange for food. Other than humans, bonobos are the only primates known to practise tongue kissing and oral sex. They also frequently engage in face-to-face genital sex – i.e. the 'missionary position'. There is little discrimination between partners: same-sex couplings are commonplace, as is sex within the family, including between adults and children, with the only apparent taboo being sexual intercourse between mothers and their adult sons. An outburst of communal sexual activity often accompanies an exciting new event, such as the discovery of a new food source, and is thought under these circumstances to decrease tension and allow for peaceful interaction. In fact, bonobo society tends to be much less aggressive and fractious than that of the common chimpanzee. And this – many scientists believe – is largely due to sex.

The government has established the new Sankuru Nature Reserve to try and protect bonobo populations from the commercial bush meat trade.

settlements and often become a nuisance in farmlands by raiding crops. They inhabit mostly bush and savannah regions, and are among the most abundant and approachable animals in many game parks, where they occur in large groups, dominated by one or more adult males. The related **mandrill** (*Mandrillus sphinx*) is best known for the striking red and blue face markings of the formidable male. This threatened species is now restricted to primary rainforest along the Atlantic coast.

Guereza monkey

Colobus monkeys (family Colobinae) Several species of colobus occur in the Congos. These long-legged, arboreal monkeys feed on leaves and are found mostly in rainforest, where they make spectacular leaps through the canopy. Most abundant is the **Tshuapa red colobus** (*Piliocolobus tholloni*), which has red-brown fur and a long face. The similar but larger **central African red colobus** (*Piliocolobus foai*) has a more easterly range and distinctly thicker fur. The **Angola pied colobus** (*Colobus angolensis*) has thick ruffs of white fur on the face, shoulders and tail, which contrast with its otherwise all-black coat. The similar **guereza colobus** (*Colobus guereza*) has a longer white cape and tends to occur at higher elevations.

Other monkeys Other monkeys found in the Congos include the **grey-cheeked mangabey** (*Lophocebus albigena*), which has long limbs, a ragged tail and frequents swamp forest; the common and versatile **tantalus monkey** (*Cercopithecus aethiops tantalus*), which has a distinct white trim around its dark face and is commonly found in cultivated areas; and **De Brazza's monkey** (*Cercopithecus neglectus*), which is a shy inhabitant of riverine forest and sports a distinctive combination of orange brow and white beard.

Prosimians Several small, primitive primates, known collectively as prosimians, inhabit the forests of the Congos. These only come out at night, so are seldom seen, although a spotlight might pick up their eyes in the tree canopy. **Bushbabies** or (*Galago* spp) are squirrel-sized, agile little creatures, with big ears, saucer eyes and piercing cries – hence the name. The slightly larger **potto** (*Perodicticus potto*) is a slower-moving, sloth-like primate that spends the night foraging upside down from branches.

Bushbaby

Other mammals In addition to the better known mammals described above, the Congos are home to a great many others, most of which are small, nocturnal and seldom seen by the average visitor. These include such prolific groups as bats (Chiroptera), rodents (Rodentia) and insectivores (Insectivora), as well as oddities such as pangolins and hyraxes. A few species warrant a brief mention here.

Pangolin

The **giant pangolin** (*Manis gigantea*) has a scaly body, resembling a giant pine cone, set off by a long tail and long, narrow snout. Unlike other pangolins in the region it feeds primarily on the ground, where it uses powerful claws to break into termite mounds. The **hammer bat** (*Hypsignathus monstrosus*), the largest of the region's many fruit bats, forms large roosts in lowland forests and is identified by its bizarre, hammer-shaped head. The **African giant squirrel** (*Protoxerus stangeri*) is the largest squirrel in the region, with a distinctive ringed tail, and feeds on fruits high in the rainforest canopy. **Lord Derby's anomalure** (*Anomalurus derbianus*) is a fine-furred, nocturnal rodent that make prodigious glides from tree to tree using a thin membrane stretched between its extended limbs. The **brush-tailed porcupine** (*Atherurus africanus*) is a rainforest porcupine, with a low-slung body and sharp quills along its back and tail. The **giant otter shrew** (*Potamogale velox*) is an aquatic insectivore closely related to the tenrecs of Madagascar, which uses its flattened tail for swimming and its bristly snout to capture prey such as crabs and frogs. The **western tree hyrax** (*Dendrohyrax dorsalis*) has evolutionary affinities with elephants, despite looking like a fat furry rodent, and inhabits evergreen forests, where its eerie wailing calls carry some distance at night.

Manatee Known endearingly as a sea cow, the **African manatee** (*Trichechus senegalensis*) is a large aquatic mammal, with seal-like front flippers and a broad paddle-like tail. It lives in warm, shallow coastal waters and mangroves, where it moves slowly across the sea bed, grazing on algae and seagrass, as well as the leaves of mangroves.

BIRDS The Congo region has Africa's greatest variety of birds, with over 600 species recorded in Republic of Congo and an amazing 1,139 species recorded in the Democratic Republic of Congo – the latter being the highest count for any single African country. It is impossible here to do justice to this staggering richness. The following brief account mentions a few of the better known and more obvious species to look out for, and lists the endemic and near-endemic birds – i.e. those species found only or virtually only in the Congo region – which are of particular interest to serious birdwatchers.

Water birds Lakes and other water bodies often hold a wealth of water birds. **Pink-backed pelicans** (*Pelecanus rufescens*) are expert fish catchers, as is the dagger-beaked **African darter** (*Anhinga melanogaster*), which has a characteristic habit of swimming with only its neck protruding above the surface. Among a variety of herons are the enormous **goliath heron** (*Ardea goliath*) and much smaller **black egret** (*Egretta ardesiaca*), the latter making a shady canopy with its wings to lure unsuspecting fish. Storks include the stately **saddle-billed stork** (*Ephippiorhynchus senegalensis*), with its bold red-and-yellow beak, and the massive, carrion-eating **marabou stork** (*Lepotilos crumeniferus*). Among others are the unique **hamerkop** (*Scopus umbretta*), which builds an enormous nest in an overhanging waterside branch; the **African spoonbill** (*Platalea alba*), which sweeps the shallows with its spatulate beak to filter out aquatic invertebrates; and the **sacred ibis** (*Threskiornis aethiopica*), which probes swampy ground with its long curved bill. Meanwhile the attractive **African jacana** (*Actophilornis Africana*) explores the swampy vegetation of lake fringes on its huge toes.

Ground birds Among a variety of game birds are the partridge-like **francolins** (*Francolinus* spp.) and the ubiquitous **helmeted guineafowl** (*Numida meleagris*), all of which have

AI

raucous ear-splitting calls. Open grassland habitats are home to a variety of other ground-nesting birds, including the striking **crowned lapwing** (*Vanellus coronatus*), the elegant **black-bellied bustard** (*Lissotis melanogaster*) and – in more moist areas – the **grey crowned crane** (*Balearica regulorum*), with its beautiful golden crest.

Birds of prey An abundance of prey ensures plenty of raptors: the formidable **crowned eagle** (*Stephanoaetus coronatus*) is the nemesis of monkeys in the rainforest canopy; the **long-crested eagle** (*Lophaetus occpitalis*) watches for rodents from its roadside perches; and the striking **African fish eagle** (*Haliaetus vocifer*) stakes out lakes and rivers for its fishy prey. Vultures range from the huge **lappet-faced vulture** (*Aegypius tracheliotos*) to the smaller **hooded vulture** (*Necrosyrtes monachus*), the latter often found around settlements, and even includes one vegetarian species, the widespread **palmnut vulture** (*Gypohierax angolensis*). Other raptors include the imperious **secretary bird**, which stalks grasslands for reptiles and small mammals, the scavenging and migratory **black kite** (*Milvus migrans*), and the **African harrier hawk** (*Polyboroides typus*), which winkles out prey from tree holes using double-jointed legs. When darkness falls, the owls take over, ranging in size from the giant **Verreaux's eagle owl** (*Bubo lacteus*) to the diminutive **pearl-spotted owlet** (*Glaucidium perlatum*), and including the impressive ochre-coloured **Pel's fishing owl** (*Scotopelia peli*), which hunts like a nocturnal fish eagle.

Fruit-eaters and hole-nesters Fruiting forest trees draw a variety of colourful fruit eaters. These include turacos, such as the huge **great blue turaco** (*Corythaeola cristata*); hornbills, such as the massive-beaked **black-and-white casqued hornbill** (*Bycanistes brevis*); parrots, such as the vociferous **African grey parrot** (*Psittacus erithacus*); and barbets, such as the boldly patterned **double-toothed barbet** (*Lybius bidentatus*). The **African green pigeon** (*Treron calva*), a striking member of the region's large pigeon family, has also adapted to a fruit diet.

Other colourful birds include a variety of bee-eaters, such as the stunning **red-throated bee-eater** (*Merops bulocki*), and rollers, such as the **broad-billed roller**, (*Eurostymos glaucurus*) which flashes dazzling azure wings in its display flight. These birds, like hornbills, nest in holes, as do members of the kingfisher family, such as the jewel-like **malachite kingfisher** (*Alcedo criststa*), found in waterside vegetation, or the crow-sized **giant kingfisher** (*Mageceryle maxima*), fond of quiet backwaters.

Passerines The largest order of birds is the passerines (Passeriformes), also known as perching birds. This diverse assemblage comprises about half the species in the region, including such families as the jewel-like **sunbirds** (*Nectariania* spp.), whose curved bills are adapted to sipping nectar from flowers; the industrious **weavers** (*Ploceus* spp.), which fashion an extraordinary variety of hanging nests; and the exquisite **waxbills** (*Estrilda* spp.), which feed on or near the ground in small twittering parties. Many passerines, including numerous similar cisticolas, babblers, greenbuls and other 'small brown jobs', defy identification by any but the most experienced birdwatcher. But more striking and obvious species include the melodious **white-browed robin-chat** (*Cossypha heugleni*), the dazzling **African paradise flycatcher** (*Tersiphone viridis*), the brilliant **black-headed gonolek** (*Lanarius erythogaster*), the ubiquitous **common bulbul** (*Pycnonotus barbatus*) and the spirited **fork-tailed drongo** (*Dicrurus absimiis*).

Endemic birds The following species are found only in the Congos. Many have evolved in isolation in such hotspots of endemism as the Albertine Rift or Itombwe Mountains. The **Congo peacock** (*Afropavo congensis*) inhabits deep rainforests in the Congo River region, around Maiko and Salonga. It is a colourful, green-winged member of the guinea-fowl family that feeds on the forest floor, although little research has been done on this species. The **Bedford`s paradise flycatcher** (*Terpsiphone bedfordi*) is the only all-grey member of the paradise flycatcher family and, at 20cm, the largest. It prefers low-lying rainforest and can be seen in Kahuzi-Biega park and Mount Hoyo Reserve. The **Golden-naped weaver** (*Ploceus aureonucha*) is a medium-sized weaver, almost entirely black except for a red-brown patch on its head and bright orange-yellow collar with yellow along the spine. Found only in Ituri, if at all. The **Congo bay owl** (*Phodilus prigoginei*) is a small owl found only in the Albertine Rift, with a smooth facial area and dark brown wings. The **Neumann's coucal** (*Centropus leucogaster neumanni*) is distinguished from most other coucals by its black throat and smaller size. Prefers vines on forest edges and is found near rivers in northern DR Congo. The **Prigogine's nightjar** (*Caprimulgus prigoginei*) is an extremely rare variation of the nightjar from the Itombwe Mountains. It's smaller than other nightjars, with all-brown plumage and small spots. The **Scarce swift** (*Schoutedenapus myoptilus*) and **Schouteden's swift** (*S. schoutedeni*) are both typical swifts, dark in colour with curved, pointed wings. Schouteden's swift has a more distinctly forked tail. The **Yellow-crested helmetshrike** (*Prionops alberti*) is a dark-brown to black bird, easily recognised by its bright yellow crown.

Near-endemic birds The following species occur only in the Congos and in the nearby surrounding regions. The **Hartlaub's duck** (*Pteronetta hartlaubii*) is the only truly forest-dwelling African duck and it can be found anywhere north of Katanga. It has a brown body, blue-grey wings and some white on the male's head. The **Long-tailed hawk** (*Urotriorchis macrourus*) is Africa's largest hawk. It has a long V-shaped tail with black and white markings, and a spotted or white belly. The **Bare-cheeked trogon** (*Apaloderma aequatoriale*) has bright yellow patches of skin near its beak, a bright-green rump and a red to yellow belly. The **Chocolate-backed kingfisher** (*Halcyon badia*) has a bright red bill, brown head, and blue on its wings and tail. Its call is loud and distinctive and it can be found anywhere north of Katanga. The **Red-fronted antpecker** (*Parmoptila rubrifrons*) is found in equatorial forests.The male has a bright red patch on its crown and a bright-brown belly, with a more common white belly on the female. Often confused with the red-headed antpecker, which has a red face but brown crown. The **Rockefeller's sunbird** (*Cinnyris rockefelleri*) has a broad red band across the breast with a small purple band above it. It's bill is longer than most sunbirds. It can be found among the Itombwe Mountains.

Apalises Kabobo apalis (*Apalis kaboboensis*), **chestnut-throated apalis** (*Apalis porphyrolaema*), **Kungwe apalis** (*Apalis argentea*) and **buff-throated apalis** (*Apalis rufogularis*) are all small birds with a white belly, a red or dark-brown neck, and black wings. Range: Albertine Rift, common in Virunga.

Mountain babblers Chapin's mountain babbler (*Kupeornis chapini*) has uniform smooth brown plumage, whereas **red-collared mountain babbler** (*Kupeornis rufocinctus*) has bright-orange markings on the neck and near the tail. Range: Albertine Rift.

Crombecs Green crombec (*Sylvietta virens*), **white-browed crombec** (*Sylvietta leucophrys*) and **Chapin's crombec** (*Sylvietta leucophrys chapini*) are all tiny birds with a brown crown, white belly and green wings. Range: Albertine Rift

Waxbills Most widespread is the **orange-cheeked waxbill** (*Estrilda melpoda*), which has a bright-orange face. The **black-faced waxbill** (*Estrilda nigriloris*) has a black face and black-and-white plumage, and occurs only in the Albertine Rift.

REPTILES AND AMPHIBIANS The Congos are home to more than 300 species of reptile and 200 of amphibian. The former, which include snakes, lizards, crocodiles and turtles, are distinguished from the latter by their dry scaly skin. There is no space here to do justice to the many species of frog that dominate the region's amphibian fauna, but the visitor will not be able to avoid their ubiquitous night-time chorus.

Snakes The Congos are home to a number of venomous snakes whose fearsome reputation precedes them. These include several species of cobra, such as the **forest cobra** (*Naja melanoleuca*), which rear and spread a hood when threatened, and mambas, such as **Jameson's mamba** (*Dendroaspis jamesoni*), which are swift hunters of birds and other prey in the tree canopy. In reality, however, the danger of snakebite is greatly exaggerated and even these impressive-looking species will avoid people if at all possible. More of a danger is the sluggish but quick-striking **puff adder** (*Bitis arietans*), of open country, which has a fat body and distinctive camouflage pattern. Even better camouflaged is the beautiful **gaboon viper** (*Bitis gabonica*), a forest floor resident, which has the longest fangs of any snake. Many more snakes are non-venomous. These include the **African rock python** (*Python sebae*), Africa's longest snake, which can capture and swallow prey up to the size of small antelope. Also notable are the remarkable **egg-eaters** (*Dasypeltis* spp.), which can unhinge their jaws wide enough to swallow a hen's egg several times larger than their own head.

Lizards Largest among the lizards are the giant **monitor lizards** (*Varanus* spp.). These powerful predators may exceed 2m in length, and are often seen scrambling nosily for the water when disturbed along a riverside path. Other lizards commonly encountered include smooth-bodied, long-tailed **skinks** (*Mabuya* spp.), often seen sunning themselves around buildings; **tropical house geckos** (*Hemidactylus* spp.), which use adhesive pads on their toes to clamber around ceilings at night in search of insect prey; and **agamas** (*Agama* spp.), which have rough, spiny bodies and nod their big colourful heads in striking courtship displays. Most bizarre, however, are the many species of **chameleon** (family Chamaeleonidae), which camouflage themselves among leaves and capture insects by striking with a tongue longer than their own body.

Other reptiles Two other outsized reptiles deserve a mention. The **Nile crocodile** (*Crocodylus niloticus*) is the largest of three crocodiles found in the Congos. This massive animal can exceed 5m in length and live for over 100 years. It is the supreme predator in most low-lying freshwater systems, capable of capturing prey as large as buffalo, but has declined considerably in the face of relentless persecution. Along the Congo coast the **leatherback turtle** (*Dermochelys coriacea*) hauls ashore to lay its eggs, sometimes on the beaches of Conkouati-Douli. This species is the largest of the world's sea turtles, reaching over 800kg in weight, and feeds primarily on jellyfish. It spends most of its life far out to sea.

INSECTS AND OTHER INVERTEBRATES The Congo region, in particular its rainforests, is home to an incalculable abundance of insect and other invertebrate life, with many species yet to be described by science. It includes well over a thousand species of butterfly and moth, among which the **swallowtail butterflies** (Papilionidae) and **emperor moths** (Saturniidae) are among the larger and more spectacular. Even more numerous in terms of species are the beetles, with the enormous **goliath beetles** (*Goliathus* spp) being the bulkiest insects on earth. Other notable insects include the many species of predatory **preying mantis** and herbivorous **stick insect** and **leaf insect**, which have evolved an uncanny likeness to the plants on which they live, and the columns of **driver ants** (Dorylinae) that march inexorably through the forest undergrowth, devouring anything edible in their path. Common **termites** (Termitidae family) leave impressive monuments to their industry in the form of towering termite mounds (termitaria) scattered across grasslands, while the *Anopholes* **mosquito** continues to have a deadly and debilitating impact on human populations by transmitting the parasite that causes malaria.

Among other invertebrates to look out for are some impressive spiders, including the **golden orb-web spiders** (*Nephila* spp), whose tiny males are dwarfed by the large females as they sit in the middle of a remarkably robust web strung across a clearing; giant **African land snails** (*Achatina* spp), whose fist-sized shells are often found in the bush; and **millipedes** (order Juliformia), often seen trundling along after rains on their forest of twinkling legs.

Appendix 2

LANGUAGE

FRENCH Tenses and pronunciation can be a problem for the beginner in French – but making errors with regard to these does not mean people will misunderstand you. Especially in the Congos, locals are far less picky about how people speak French than in other francophone countries. They themselves will often throw in certain tribal words when the mood hits them, meaning that they can only expect a foreigner to speak the language differently.

The letter 's' is often seen at the end of words but pronounced softly, if at all, unless the next word starts with a vowel.. This goes the same with 'x' and 'z', for example *'veux'* is pronounced 'veu' and *'Allez'* is said as 'Allay' as the 'ez' ending on a word is said as an 'ay' sound.

Accents are common in written French, with the acute accent (*l'accent aigu*) (angling upwards from left to right, as in 'é') and the grave accent (*l'accent grave*) (angling downwards from left to right, as in 'è') being most common. The *aigu* is pronounced with an 'ay' sound so *café* is pronounced 'caf-ay'. *Grave* accents lengthen the sound of the accented 'e', so for example *mère* rhymes with *chair*.

Two other accents are quite common, the first being the circumflex (*l'accent circonflexe*), such as in *forêt*, which is intended as meaning that an s-sound (and therefore silent) would follow the circumflexed letter. In this case *forêt* would be pronounced 'for-ay'. The ending '-er' on a word is also pronounced with an 'ay' sound. The circumflex can also act as a stress on a letter – *arête* is pronounced 'arette' with special stress on the 't'. Again, though, this is not usually critical for the non-fluent speaker to know.

The cedilla (*la cédille*) is a little curve below letter c, such as in *Français*, and simply means that the 'c' should be given an 's' sound. So *Français* is pronounced 'Fran-says'. Without the cedilla, 'c' is hard before 'a' (café), hard before 'o' (Congo), hard before 'u' (cuisine), and soft (so an 's' sound) before 'e', 'i' and 'y'.

Negation of a verb or other word is preceded by a *ne* and followed by a *pas*. So while one would say *je mange* to say 'I eat' the negative would be *je ne mange pas* for 'I don't eat'.

Finally, there are minor variations between the French spoken in Congo-Brazzaville and Congo-Kinshasa. Coming from the histories of France and Belgium, the most distinctive variations are the words for 70 (*soixante-dix* in France, *septante* in Belgium) and 90 (*quatre-vingt-dix* in France, *nonante* in Belgium).

Greetings/salutations

Hello	*Bonjour*	What is your	*Comment vous*
How are you?	*Comment ça va?*	name? (informal)	*appellez-vous?*
I am fine	*Je suis/vais bien*	What is your	*Comment t'appellez-*
Thank you	*Merci*	name? (formal)	*vous?*
Thank you very	*Merci beaucoup*	My name is...	*Je m'appelle...*
much		Excuse me	*Excusez-moi/Je m'excuse*
You're welcome	*Je vous en prie* (formal)	Yes	*Oui*
	Je t'en prie (informal)	No	*Non*

Common phrases

How much?	*Combien?*	Where are you going?	*Vous allez où?*
I don't understand	*Je ne comprends pas*	Let's go!	*Allons!*
Where is...	*Où est...*	I think...	*Je pense...*
I would like…	*Je voudrais...*	I know/	*Je connais/*
I want/	*Je veux/*	I don't know	*je ne connais pas*
I do not want	*je ne veux pas*	I don't have	*Je n'ai pas*
I like/I don't like	*J'aime /je n'aime pas*	When?	*Quand?*
It's possible/	*C'est possible/*		
it's not possible	*ce n'est pas possible*		

Common words

airport	*aeroport*	hôtel	*hôtel*
animals	*animaux*	hunting	*chasse*
arrested	*arrêté*	jail	*prison*
bananas	*bananes*	juice/orange juice	*jus/jus d'orange*
beef	*viande*	lake	*lac*
beer	*bière*	lunch	*dîner*
bill/receipt	*facture*	man/woman	*homme/femme*
bird	*oiseau*	market	*marché*
boat	*bâteau*	medication	*médicaments*
border	*frontière*	money/change	*argent/monnaie*
breakfast	*petit déjeuner*	moon	*lune*
bridge	*pont*	mosquitoes	*moustiques*
bus	*l'autobus*	motorcycle	*motocyclette*
car	*voiture*	mountain	*montagne*
cave	*grotte*	nausea/vomiting	*nausée/vomissement*
chicken	*poulet*	park	*parc*
church	*eglise*	passport	*passport*
cliff	*falaise*	police	*police*
coffee	*café*	rain	*pluie*
country	*pays*	river	*fleuve*
cow	*vache*	road	*la rue*
diarrhoea	*diarhée*	route	*la route*
dinner	*souper*	security	*sécurité*
doctor	*docteur*	sick/ill	*mal/malade*
embassy	*ambassade*	springs	*eau de source*
expensive/	*cher/*	store	*magasin*
inexpensive	*pas cher*	sun	*soleil*
fever	*fièvre*	taxi	*taxi*
fish	*poisson*	tea	*thé*
forbidden	*interdit*	ticket	*billet*
4x4 truck	*quatre par quatre*	toilet	*toilette*
friend/my friend	*ami/mon ami*	truck	*camion*
gorilla	*gorille*	vaccination card	*carte des vaccinations*
health	*santé*	war	*guerre*
hill	*colline*	water	*l'eau*
hospital	*hôpital*	waterfall	*chute*

Numbers

0	*zéro*	3	*trois*
1	*un*	4	*quatre*
2	*deux*	5	*cinq*

6	*six*	20	*vingt*
7	*sept*	30	*trente*
8	*huit*	40	*quarante*
9	*neuf*	50	*cinquante*
10	*dix*	60	*soixante*
11	*onze*	70	*soixante-dix/septante*
12	*douze*	80	*quatre-vingt*
13	*treize*	90	*quatre-vingt-dix/nonante*
14	*quatorze*	100	*cent*
15	*quinze*	500	*cinq-cent*
16	*seize*	1,000	*mille*
17	*dix-sept*	10,000	*dix mille*
18	*dix-huit*	$^1/_2$	*moitié*
19	*dix-neuf*	$^1/_4$	*quartier*

Time and dates

Monday	*Lundi*	Friday	*Vendredi*
Tuesday	*Mardi*	Saturday	*Samedi*
Wednesday	*Mercredi*	Sunday	*Dimanche*
Thursday	*Jeudi*		

morning	*matin*	later/late	*plus tard/en retard*
noon	*midi*	day	*jour*
afternoon	*apres midi*	week	*semaine*
evening	*soir*	month	*mois*
today	*aujourd'hui*	hour	*heure*
tomorrow	*demain*	What time is it?	*quelle heure est-il?*
yesterday	*hier*	five o'clock	*cinq heures*
now	*maintenant*	next week	*la semaine prochaine*

Countries

Australia	*Australie*	France	*France*
Austria	*Autriche*	Germany	*Allemagne*
Canada	*Canada*	Ireland	*Irlande*
Central African Republic	*République Centrafricaine*	Japan	*Japon*
		New Zealand	*Nouvelle Zélande*
Congo Republic	*République Du Congo*	Portugal	*Portugal*
DRC	*République Démocratique Du Congo*	South Africa	*Afrique Du Sud*
		Spain	*Espagne*
		Uganda	*Ouganda*
England	*Angleterre*	United States	*États-Unis*

AFRICAN LANGUAGES Please note that words in the African language vocabulary list have been split with hyphens to indicate where stress should be placed when speaking.

Lingala Lingala was originally seen as a 'military' language, or rather one that was used only by officials of Belgian Congo. Over time, it became the lingua franca along the major banks of the Congo River, where there was no common tongue between tribes. There are various dialects dependent on region and country, with slight variations between what one finds in Congo-Kinshasa and Congo-Brazzaville. However, media from both countries still broadcast a 'common' version of the language, and to an idle listener they are mostly indistinguishable. As Lingala has developed, numerous words that did not exist in Lingala have been introduced with French, or even Portuguese, equivalents.

Swahili The same Swahili used across east Africa will work fine in eastern Congo, with very little in the way of local words or accents. Plenty of interchange between visitors has made the language reasonably uniform the closer one gets to the eastern border. However, in the central DR Congo Swahili is not absolute and can be jumbled with words from Lingala or Tshiluba, along with anything in French that might come to mind faster than Swahili.

Kituba/Kikongo Kituba is an extension of the ancient Kikongo language, the original language of the Kongo Kingdom. While Kituba is spoken in the regions of Congo-Brazzaville, the provinces of Congo-Kinshasa tend to adhere more to the original Kikongo language. Therefore, there are numerous similarities; I include the Kituba word first, followed by the Kikongo word. Some words are shared by both languages.

Tshiluba The two cities where Tshiluba is mainly spoken are Kananga and Mubji-Mayi, with minor variations between the dialects. I have included the versions normally used in Mbuji-Mayi, the largest Tshiluba-speaking city.

Kinyarwanda Words in Kinyarwanda are spelled phonetically here, to make their pronunciation easy. The letters 'r' and 'l' (and their sounds) are often interchanged, also sometimes 'b', 'v' and 'w'. When a word ends in 'e', pronounce it as the French 'é'. Pronounce 'i' as 'ee' rather than 'eye'.

AFRICAN LANGUAGE VOCABULARY

English	Lingala	Swahili	Kituba/Kikongo	Tshiluba	Kinyarwanda
Greetings/salutations					
Hello	M-bo-tay	Jam-bo	M-bo-teng-gay/M-bo-tay	Mo-yee	Muraho
Goodbye	Ken-de-kay Ma-la-mu	Kwa-he-ree	Bee-ka Na M-bo-tay/ Koo-en-da M-bo-tay	Noo-sha-la M-bee-pa	Muriliwe
How are you?	San-go Nee-nee?	Ha-bar-ee?	Wa-fa-song?/Yin-ka Moo-tin-doo?	Ma-loo Kay?	Amakuru?/biitese?
I am fine	Ma-la-mu, Mu-le-see	Nu-zuri	Moo-kay M-bo-tay/ Bay-to Kay M-bo-tay	Bim-pa, Tiwa-sa Kee-dee-la	Amakuru/meza/égo
Please	Pa-la-do	Ta-fa-da-lee	Sa-dee-sa/Lem-voo-ka	Oo-fwee-la Loo-say	Mubishoboye
Thank you	Mee-lee-see	A-san-tay	Ma-ton-do	Tiwa-sa Kee-dee-la	Murakoze
You're welcome	Lee-kam-bo-tay	Ka-ree-bu	Voo-too-la Ma-ton-do/Kee-ma Vé	Ka-kway-na Bwa-loo	—
Yes	Ee-yo	N-dee-yo	Ee/In-ga	Ee-yo	Yégo
No	Tay	Ha-pa-na	Vé/N-ka-too	To	Oya

Common phrases					
How much?	Bo-nee?	N-ga-pee?	nTa-loo Ee-kwa?/In-kwa?	In-ga?	Angahe?
I don't understand	Na-Yo-Kee-Tay	See-fa-ha-mu	Yá M-pa-see Yá Koo-ba-kee-sa/ Moo-noo Ba-koo-sa Vé	Tshay-na Hgoo-voo-a To	—
Where is...	Wa-pee?	Wa-pee?	Wa-pee See-ka?/Wa-pee Kee-see-ka?	N-ten-ee?	Hehe?
When?	Tayn-go?	Lee-nee?	Wa-pee nTay-ngo/In-kee nTay-ngo	Dee-ba Kay-ee?	Ryali?
foreigner	mon-de-lay	mu-zun-gu			—

Numbers					
0	zee-ro	se-fu-ree	zay-lo/nee pa-va-la	ee-nee-zay-oo-goo	—
1	mo-ko	mo-Ja	mo-see	oo-moy	—
2	mee-ba-lay	m-bee-lee	zo-lay	ee-bee-dee	—
3	mee-sa-to	ta-too	ta-too	ee-sa-too	—
4	mee-nay	n-nay	ee-ya	ee-na-yee	—

English	Lingala	Swahili	Kituba/Kikongo	Tshiluba	Kinyarwanda
5	mee-ta-no	ta-no	ta-noo	ee-ta-noo	
6	mo-to-ba	see-ta	sam-ba-noo	ee-sam-bom-bo	
7	n-sam-bo	sa-ba	sam-bwa-dee/ni-sam-bwa-dee	moo-an-da moo-tay-kay-ta	
8	mo-am-bee	na-nay	na-na	moo-an-da moo-koo-loo	
9	lee-bwa	tee-sa	eev-wa	tshee-tay-ma	
10	zo-mee	ku-mee	koo-mee	dee-tay-ma	
11	zo-mee na mo-ko	ku-mee na mo-jo	koo-mee mo-see	dee-koo-mee n-oo-moy	
12	zo-mee na mee-ba-lay	ku-mee na m-bee-lee	koo-mee zo-lay	dee-koo-mee n-ee-bee-dee	
13	zo-mee na mee-sa-to	ku-mee na ta-too	koo-mee ta-too	dee-koo-mee n-ee-sa-too	
14	zo-mee na mee-nay	ku-mee na n-nay	koo-mee ee-ya	dee-koo-mee n-ee-na-yee	
15	zo-mee na mee-ta-no	ku-mee na ta-no	koo-mee ta-noo	dee-koo-mee n-ee-ta-noo	
16	zo-mee na mo-to-ba	ku-mee na see-ta		dee-koo-mee n-ee-sam-bom-bo	
17	zo-mee na n-sam-bo	ku-mee na sa-ba	koo-mee sam-bwa-dee	dee-koo-mee moo-an-da moo-tay-kay-ta	
18	zo-mee na mo-am-bee	ku-mee na na-nay	koo-mee na-na	dee-koo-mee moo-an-da moo-koo-loo	
19	zo-mee na lee-bwa	ku-mee na tee-sa	koo-mee eev-wa	dee-koo-mee nee tshee-tay-ma	
20	n-too-koo mee-ba-lay	ish-ir-in-ee	ma-koo-mee zo-lay	dee-koo-mee moo-an-da moo-an-da moo-koo-loo	
30	n-too-koo mee-sa-to	thay-la-thee-nee	ma-koo-mee ta-too	dee-koo-mee nee tshee-tay-ma	
40	n-too-koo mee-nay	a-ro-bay-nee	ma-koo-mee ee-ya	ma-koo-mee a boo-dee	
50	n-too-koo mee-ta-no	ham-see-nee	ma-koo-mee ta-noo	ma-koo-mee a sa-to	
60	n-too-koo mo-to-ba	see-tee-nee	ma-koo-mee sam-ba-noo	ma-koo-mee a na-yee	
70	n-too-koo n-sam-bo	sa-bee-nee septianet	ma-koo-mee sam-bwa-dee	ma-koo-mee a ta-no	
80	n-too-koo mo-am-bee	the-ma-nee-nee	ma-koo-mee na-na	ma-koo-mee a sam-bom-bo	
90	n-too-koo lee-bwa	tee-see-nee	ma-koo-mee eev-wa	ma-koo-mee nee moo-an-da moo-tay-kay-ta	
100	n-ka-ma mo-ko	mee-ya	n-ka-ma mo-see/n-ka-ma	ma-koo-mee nee moo-an-da moo-koo-loo	
500	n-ka-ma mee-ta-no	mee-ya ta-no	n-ka-ma ta-noo	loo-ka-ma	
1,000	n-ko-to mo-ko	el-foo	dee-fun-da mo-see	ka-ma ee-ta-noo	
10,000	n-ko-to zo-mee	ku-mee el-foo	ma-foon-da koo-mee / kee-tee-nee mo-see na zo-lay	tshee-hoo-noo	

English	Lingala	Swahili	Kituba/Kikongo	Tshiluba	Kinyarwanda
Time and dates					
Monday	Mo-sa-la Mo-ko	Joo-ma-ta-too	Kee-loom-boo Yá Loo-ndee	Mu Dee-moy-ee	Ku wa mbere
Tuesday	Mee-sa-la Mee-ba-lay	Joo-mau	Kee-loom-boo Yá Zo-lay	Mu Dee-bee-dee	Ku wa kabili
Wednesday	Mee-sa-la Mee-sa-to	Joo-ma-ta-no	Kee-loom-boo Yá Ta-too	Mu Dee-sa-too	Ku wa gatatu
Thursday	Mee-sa-la Mee-nay	Al-ham-ee-see	Kee-loom-boo Yá Ee-ya	Mu Dee-na-yee	Ku wa kane
Friday	Mee-sa-la Mee-ta-no	El-joo-ma	Kee-loom-boo Yá Ta-noo	Mu Dee-ta-noo	Ku wa gatanu
Saturday	Mo-ko-lo Mwa M-pu-so	Joo-ma-mo-see	Kee-loom-boo Yá mPo-so/	Mu Dee-sam-bom-bo	ku wa gatandatu
			Kee-loom-boo Yá Sa-ba-la		
Sunday	Ee-yen-ga	Joo-ma-pil-ee	Kee-loom-boo Yá Loo-min-goo	Mu Dia-loo-min-goo	Ku cyumweru
today	le-lo	le-o	ya boo-boo/loo-boo	lay-loo	none
tomorrow	lo-bee	ke-sho	m-ba-see	ma-la-ba	ejo hazaza
yesterday	lo-bee	ja-na	ma-zo-no	ma-kay-lay-la	ejo hashize
now	see-ko-yo	pa-pa	may-loo may-loo	m-pee-djay-oo	ubu/nonaha

Appendix 3

GLOSSARY OF NAMES AND ACRONYMS

GLOSSARY OF NAMES

Albert Dolisie	Military colonel and companion of Pierre Savorgnan de Brazza during a trek west to Loango and Pointe Noire.
Albertville	Former colonial name for Kalemie.
Alphonse Massamba-Débat	First prime minister of the Marxist-Leninist Congo party, the MNR.
Amicale	Pro-unionist organisation in Moyen Congo; partial precursor to Matsouanism.
André Matsoua	Catholic priest in Congo-Brazzaville who merged animist and Catholic traditions. Had a large loyal following, the Matsouanists.
Antoine Gizenga	Leader of the rebel government in Stanleyville in 1961; also prime minister from 1960 to 1961.
Avikat	Aviation Katangaise, air force and air cargo company of independent Katanga state from 1960–61.
Bakwanga	Former colonial name for Mbuji-Mayi.
Bantu	General ethnic group to which most tribes in central Africa belong.
Banyamulenge	Tutsis who settled in eastern Congo. Though ethnically the same, they are differentiated from Rwandan Tutsis.
Bernard Kolélas	Anti-socialist politician and leader of MCDDI, backed by Ninja militias.
Cabinda	Small exclave of Angola wedged between the two Congos.
Christoph Gbenye	President of the Lumumbist-loyal government of Stanleyville, 1965–67.
Cobras	Militia loyal to Denis Sassou-Nguesso in Congo, dispersed in 1998.
Concessionaires	French companies granted territory in the late 19th century across French Congo.
Congo Reform Association	First humanitarian organisation to protest against the atrocities in Congo Free State, 1898–1906.
Coquilhatville	Former colonial name for Mbandaka.
Costermansville	Former colonial name for Bukavu.
Cyrille Adoula	Founder of the MNC; Prime Minister of Congo-Léopoldville 1961–64.
Denis Sassou-Nguesso	Current head of state of Congo-Brazzaville, also head of state between 1979 and 1992.
Diego Cão	Portuguese explorer and the first European to encounter the mouth of the Congo River.
Dona Beatriz	See *Kimpa Vita* below.
Edgar de Larminat	High Commissary of Free French Africa, instrumental in creating the government of Free France.

Elisabethville	Former colonial name for Lubumbashi.
Ernest Wamba Dia Wamba	Politician who led splinter group of the RCD called RCD-ML, based in Kisangani.
Etienne Tshisekedi	Leader of Zairian opposition party the UDPS. Prime Minister under Mobutu Sésé Seko and Laurent Kabila.
Eufor R D Congo	European force established April 2006 to monitor the electoral process in the DR Congo.
Eupol Kinshasa	European Union police force assistance based in Kinshasa.
Eusec R D Congo	European Union army assistance programme for FARDC.
Évolué	Belgian programme of assimilation for the Congolese, whereby they were rewarded for becoming more European.
Federal State of South Kasai	Secessionist region of the DR Congo, with capital at Mbuji-Mayi. Independent from 1960 to 1961.
Félix Eboué	Governor of the AEF 1940–44; first black governor of a European colony.
Gaston Émile Soumialot	Political leader of the Simbas from 1965 to 1967.
Gécamines	State-owned mining corporation of the DR Congo, formerly UMHK.
George Washington Williams	African-American historian who first documented atrocities against the Congolese by Belgians.
Henry Morton Stanley	American explorer who first traversed the Congo River.
HMS *Congo*	First steam-powered warship commissioned to navigate up the Congo River.
Interahamwe	Extremist Hutu militias aimed at murdering Tutsis. Fled into eastern DR Congo from Rwanda in 1994.
Jadotville	Former colonial name for Likasi.
James Kingston Tuckey	British explorer who made first attempt to navigate up the Congo River, in 1816.
Joseph Kabila	Son of assassinated Laurent Kabila and current head of state for the DR Congo.
Joseph Kasa-Vubu	First president of the Congo Republic (Léopoldville) from 1960 to 1965.
Katanga	Province of the DR Congo, independent from 1960 to 1963. Further fracture from 1960 to1961 as North Katanga seceded.
Kimbangouists	Religious following in Belgian Congo from 1940 to 1960.
Kimpa Vita	'Congolese Joan of Arc'; reunited Kongo Kingdom in 1700. Also referred to as Dona Beatriz.
King Léopold II	Belgian monarch who engineered the creation of Congo Free State.
Kongo Kingdom	Nation that dominated the Congo regions from 1400 to1665.
Laurent Desirée Kabila	Rwandan- and Ugandan-backed leader of the AFDL and head of state of the DR Congo from 1997 to 2001.
Laurent Nkunda	Rebel general of RCD-Goma faction operating in the North Kivu region.
Léopoldville	Former colonial name for Kinshasa.
Loango	Ancient African kingdom. Also name of an old African village. Pointe Noire founded nearby.
Luluaborg	Former colonial name for the city of Kananga.
Lusaka Peace Accord	1999 peace agreement aimed at ending the Second Congo War (see *Chapter 3*, page 72).
manioc	Starchy root, staple food of Congo regions.
Marien Ngouabi	Army general and head of state of Congo-Brazzaville 1968–1977.
Matsouanists	Religious group in Moyen Congo from 1940 to 1960; founded based on principles of André Matsoua.

A3

Mayi-Mayi	Jungle rebel group that opposes all foreign occupation in the eastern DR Congo.
Mbanza Kongo	Original capital of Kongo Kingdom, in present-day Angola. Renamed to Sãao Salvador by the Portuguese.
Mike Hoare	European mercenary who participated in and led several campaigns across Congo-Léopoldville.
Mobutu Sésé Seko	Head of state of the DR Congo from 1965 to 1997.
Mokele-Mbembe	Four-legged dinosaur rumoured to live in the swamps north of Impfondo.
Moise Tshombe	Leader of secessionist Katanga state from 1960–63. Later appointed Prime Minister of Congo-Léopoldville.
Nicolas Olenga	Military leader of the Simbas from 1965 to 1967.
Ninjas	Rebel group that operates in the Poule region of Congo-Brazzaville between Madingo and Brazzaville.
Nouvelle-Anvers	Former colonial name for Makanza.
Nyiragongo	Large volcano near Goma, which last erupted in 2002.
okapi	Rare animal found only in the northeastern DR Congo, a cross between a giraffe and a zebra.
Operation ARTEMIS	European force that arrived in Ituri Province between May and September 2003.
Pascal Lissouba	Premier of the Congo from 1963 to 1968, head of state of Congo 1993–97. Outrage over rigged elections drove him from power and his followers plunged Congo into civil war.
palm wine	Common alcoholic drink of Congo-Brazzaville.
Patrice Lumumba	First Prime Minister of the Congo Republic in 1960.
Paul Carlson	American missionary executed by Simbas during their 1965 occupation of Stanleyville.
Paulis	Former colonial name for Isiro.
Pierre Savorgnan de Brazza	Italian who explored Congo-Brazzaville for the French.
Ponthierville	Former colonial name for Ubundu.
Port Francqui	Former colonial name for Llebo.
Portuguese Congo	Former colonial name for Cabinda.
Primus	Famous beer found in both Congos, but a different brand in either country.
pygmy	Non-Bantu tribes living in traditional villages in Congo rainforests.
São Salvador	See *Mbanza Kongo* above
Shaba	Traditional name for Katanga Province; name used in Mobutu's Zaire from 1969 to 1997.
Simbas	Socialist rebels in eastern Congo during the mid 1960s.
South Kasai	Secessionist province of Congo-Léopoldville from 1960–61. Folded back into Congo-Léopoldville and divided into two modern-day provinces, Kasai Occidental and Kasai Orientale.
Stanley Falls	Former colonial name for Boyoma Falls (near Kisangani).
Stanley Pool	Former colonial name for Malebo Pool (shores of Kinshasa and Brazzaville).
Stanleyville	Former colonial name for Kisangani.
Thysville	Former colonial name for Mbanza-Ngungu.
Tippu Tip	Arab-African trading magnate of the 19th century who assisted Henry Morton Stanley in his explorations of eastern Congo. Claimed eastern Congo from 1884 to 1887.
William Henry Sheppard	African-American missionary who documented atrocities against the Congolese people at the end of the 19th century.

NAMES AND ACRONYMS FOR CONGO-KINSHASA

DRC, Democratic Republic of the Congo, République Democratique Du Congo, RDC, RD Congo, DR Congo, Congo-Kinshasa

Obsolete names: Congo Free State, Belgian Congo, Colonie Belge Du Congo, Congo Belge et Ruanda Urundi, Congo-Léopoldville, People's Republic of the Congo, Republic of the Congo, Zaire

NAMES AND ACRONYMS FOR CONGO-BRAZZAVILLE

Congo-Brazzaville, Congo Republic, République Du Congo, Republic of the Congo

Obsolete names: Congo Français, French Congo, AEF, Afrique Équatoriale Française, French Equatorial Africa, Middle Congo, Moyen Congo, People's Republic of the Congo

GLOSSARY OF ACRONYMS

ABAKO	Association Des Bakongo. First political party to form in Belgian Congo, led by Joseph Kasa-Vubu.
ADF	Allied Democratic Front. Ugandan rebel group that was used as Uganda's reason to invade eastern DR Congo in 1998.
AEF	Afrique Equatoriale Française. Brazzaville-controlled colonies of central Africa to 1958.
AEC	African Economic Community. Successor to OAU, succeeded by AU.
AFDL	Alliance des Forces Démocratiques pour la Libération du Congo-Zaïre, or Alliance of Democratic Forces for the Liberation of Congo-Zaire. Laurent Kabila's Rwanda and Uganda-backed rebellion that marched on Kinshasa in 1997.
AIA	Association Internationale Africaine. Humanitarian organisation created by King Léopold for the African people.
AIC	Association Internationale du Congo. Private holding company created by King Léopold for securing assets in Congo under his name.
AMP	Alliance pour la Majorité Présidentielle, or Alliance for the Presidential Majority. Kabila's political party and current ruling party of the DR Congo.
ANC	Armée Nationale Congolais. Reformed army of 1960s Congo-Léopoldville.
AU	African Union. Formerly called AEC.
CNL	Conseil National de Libération. Lumumbist party that took Stanleyville in 1964; engineered the Kwilu Uprising.
CNR	Conseil National de la Revolution. Congo-Brazzaville Council of Revolution to plan transition from capitalism to socialism.
ECZ	Eglise du Christ au Zaïre. Overseeing body for Protestant church groups in the DR Congo.
FARDC	Forces Armées RD Congo. Current name of national army in the DR Congo.
FAZ	Forces Armées Zaïroises. Mobutu Sésé Seko's regular army forces.
FDLR	Forces Democratie de Liberation du Rwanda. Rwandan Hutus based in eastern DR Congo who fought against the Rwandan-backed RCD.
FLEC	Frente para a Libertação do Enclave de Cabinda. Separatist organisation in Cabinda enclave.
ICCN	Institut Congolais pour la Conservation de la Nature. Congolese parks management board.
IDP	Internally displaced person.
JMNR	Jeunesse Mouvement National de la Révolution. Youth corps wing of MNR in socialist Congo-Brazzaville.

LRA	Lord's Resistance Army. Fundamentalist rebels fighting against the Ugandan government with rear bases in northeastern DR Congo.
MCDDI	Mouvement congolais pour la démocratie et le développement intégral. Anti-Marxist party in Congo led by Bernard Kolélas.
MLC	Mouvement de Libération Congolais. Ugandan-backed group in the northern DR Congo that fought against Kinshasa in the Second Congo War. Now a political party.
MNC	Mouvement National Congolais. Political party in 1950s Belgian Congo, led by Patrice Lumumba.
MNR	Mouvement National de la Révolution. Sole political party in 1960s Congo-Brazzaville. Had numerous wings, most importantly the JMNR.
MONUC	Mission de l' Organisation des Nations-Unies en République démocratique du Congo, or Mission of the UN in Congo. Second UN mission in Congo from 2000 to present.
MPLA	Movimento Popular de Libertação de Angola, or Popular Movement for Liberation of Angola. Had training camps in Congo-Brazzaville throughout the 1960s.
MSA	Mouvement Socialiste Africain. Left-leaning opposition party of Moyen Congo, led by Jacques Opangault.
NGO	Non-governmental organisation.
OAU	Organisation of African Unity. Renamed to AU.
ONU	Organisation Nations-Unies. French acronym for the UN.
ONUC	Operation des Nations-Unies au Congo. Operation of the UN in Congo. First UN mission in Congo, from 1960 to 1964.
PCT	Parti Congolais du Travail. New left-wing party of Congo-Brazzaville created by Marien Ngouabi in the 1970s.
PPC	Parti Progressiste Congolais. First political party in Moyen Congo, led by Félix Tchicaya.
RCD	Rassemblement Congolais pour la Démocratie, or Rally for Congolese Democracy. Broke into three factions: RCD-Goma; RCD-K/ML (based in Kisangani); and RCD-National. Dispersed at the end of 2003.
RPF	Rwandese Patriotic Front. National army of Rwanda that invaded eastern Congo.
UDDIA	Union Démocratique pour la Défense d'Intérêts Africains. First political party to come to power in Republic of Congo-Brazzaville.
UDPS	Union pour la Démocratie et le Progrès Social. First opposition party permitted in Zaire, led by Etienne Tshisekedi.
UMHK	Union Minière du Haut Katanga. Belgian mining company that operated in Katanga Province from 1906 to 1966, then nationalised and renamed Gécamines.
UN	Union des Nationalists, or Union of Nationalists. Political party of Jean-Pierre Bemba and official opposition in the DR Congo.
UN/UNHCR/ UNICEF	United Nations/United Nations Humanitarian Commission for Refugees/United Nations International Children's Emergency Fund.
UNITA	União Nacional para a Independência Total de Angola. Angolan rebels who held rear bases along the Angolan–DR Congo border. Largely eliminated after the assassination of their leader Jonas Savimbi in 2002.
UPADS	Union Panafricaine Pour la Démocratie Sociale. Political party of Pascal Lissouba.
UPDF	Ugandan People's Defence Force. Ugandan regular army that invaded eastern Congo.
WCS	Wildlife Conservation Society. New York-based conservation group heavily influential in Congo-Brazzaville.

Appendix 4

FURTHER INFORMATION

BOOKS

DR Congo

History There is no shortage of books on Zaire and the DR Congo, and many of them illustrate wonderfully the coloured and often brutal history of the country.

Edgerton, Robert *The Troubled Heart of Africa: A History of the Congo* St Martin's Press, 2002. A simpler account of the Congolese timeline, and probably an easier read on bumpy dirt roads.

Gourevitch, Philip *We Wish to Inform You That Tomorrow We Will be Killed With Our Families: Stories from Rwanda* Picador, 1999. So much of what happened in the country at its transformation from Zaire to the DR Congo was a direct result of what occurred in Rwanda. Even now in the Kivu provinces with Interahamwe, understanding the battle between Hutus and Tutsis is critical to understanding why the eastern part of the country continues to be in turmoil. This book does a fine job in explaining the Rwandan Genocide.

Hochschild, Adam *King Leopold's Ghost* Mariner Books, 1999. Perhaps most famous amongst the books on the DR Congo, and most pertinent to understanding the long-running conundrums of the country. It documents the early decades of the Congo Free State, how such an unimaginable place began to form and later exist under the Belgian monarch's rule.

Lewis, Jerome *The Batwa Pygmies of the Great Lakes Region* Minority Rights Group International, 2000. Lewis describes the history of the Batwa pygmies in the Great Lakes region of eastern DR Congo, Uganda, Burundi and Rwanda, and the pressures faced today by what are believed to be the region's earliest inhabitants. An informative 32-page report, also available as a Pdf from www.minorityrights.org.

Liebowitz, Daniel and Pearson, Charles *The Last Expedition: Stanley's Mad Journey through the Congo* W W Norton, 2006. This book does a great job of chronicling Stanley's last voyage up the Congo River to Sudan.

Kennedy, Pagan *Black Livingstone: A True Tale of Adventure in the Nineteenth Century Congo* Penguin, 2002. Chronicling the life and times of William Henry Sheppard.

Nzongola-Ntalaja, Georges *The Congo: From Leopold to Kabila* Zed Books, 2002. At the more academic end of things is this fine account delving deeper into the details of the DR Congo's history. If you need solid clarification of cause and effect throughout the country's history, this book is where to find it.

Stanley, Henry Morton *Through the Dark Continent: Volume 2* Dover Publications, 1988. On the same theme covering the scramble for Africa. Stanley's accounts – his direct writings of this time, uncoloured by present knowledge – of the journey heading down the Congo River are an interesting look at the exploration of a region where no other European had visited.

Turnbull, Colin M *The Forest People* Jonathan Cape, 1961 (and later reprints by different publishers). A compassionate and absorbing account of the time the author spent among the pygmies of the Congo's Ituri Forest. He describes the history, background, lives, families, hunting, illnesses, quarrels, love affairs, music and traditional ceremonies of these ancient people, first mentioned in the *Iliad* and by Aristotle.

Wrong, Michela *In the Footsteps of Mr Kurtz* Harper Perennial, 2002. For a fine documentation of the final years of Mobutu's regime, written in an easy-to-read style it provides a good account of how Zaire's vast riches were shuttled away by an African dictator while the people of this vast and rich nation were left, again, to fend for themselves. Highly recommended.

Miscellaneous

Butcher, Tim *Blood River: A Journey to Africa's Broken Heart* Random House, 2007. A modern-day journalist follows Henry Morton Stanley's original overland voyage to Boma.

Conrad, Joseph *Heart of Darkness* Penguin Books, 2000. For fiction, no-one should visit the Congo without having read this famous account of Conrad's own journey down the Congo River. It is often cited as the first great literary work of the 20th century.

Herge *Tintin in the Congo* Egmont Children's, 2005. On a lighter note is this book, a great read, if not entirely politically correct, and he is still the most famous cartoon character to visit the Congo.

Stewart, Gary *Rumba on the River: A History of the Popular Music of the Two Congos* Verso, 2004. A full exploration of the roots of Congo music can be found in this book, an excellent reference for music past and present that best defines the 'Congo' sound.

Republic of Congo

The stack of books for Congo-Brazzaville, on the other hand, is much smaller – especially in the English language.

Forbath, Peter *The River Congo: The Discovery, Exploration and Exploitation of the World's Most Dramatic River* Houghton Mifflin, 1991. To learn all about the river, this book unravels the yarn of European exploration surrounding the river from day one.

O'Hanlon, Redmond *Congo Journey* Gardners Books, 1997. A wonderful account of a journey up into the wilds of the northern Congo. He paints a wonderful picture of Congo's culture and superstitions, and the fight to get anything useful done when navigating through a semi-Marxist bureaucracy.

West, Richard *Brazza of the Congo: European Exploration and Exploitation in French Equatorial Africa* Cape, 1972. A highly readable account. West does a fine job of chronicling the French scramble for central Africa and goes into great detail of de Brazza's journeys; one of the best books on the subject in the English language.

Che Guevara in Congo

Camiller, Patrick (trans) *The African Dream: The Diaries of the Revolutionary War in the Congo* Grove Press, 2001. As a primary source, his diaries have been translated into English in this book.

Galvez, William *Che in Africa: Che Guevara's Congo Diary* Ocean Press, 1999. Easier to read, this book chronicles his time in eastern Congo and how he got there.

Gleijeses, Piero *Conflicting Missions: Havana, Washington, and Africa, 1959–1976* University of North Carolina Press, 2002. If you're at all fascinated by Che Guevara's lost years in the Congo you'll want to read several books on the subject. Most detailed historically is this book, which is heavy on Cuba's involvement with Angola but indispensable reading for the finer details of Che Guevara and Cuba's power plays across both Congos in the 1960s.

Wildlife guides

Kingdon, Jonathan *The Kingdon Field Guide to African Mammals* Christopher Helm Publishers, 2003. For detailed descriptions on mammals seek out this excellent book. A little bit obsessive with smaller mammals, which is perhaps good, but unlikely one will get the chance to observe these creatures up close too often in the Congos. Nonetheless it's one of the best English-language field guides for wildlife enthusiasts. It's a bit unwieldy and perhaps a better choice for travelling with is the shorter version, *The Kingdon Pocket Guide to African Mammals* (Princeton University Press, 2005).

Sinclair, Ian *Birds of Africa South of the Sahara* Princeton University Press, 2004. This birding guide comes highly recommended and covers all the species that can be seen in central Africa. It includes a representative drawing of every bird species recorded on the continent along with diagrams of their migratory range.

Stuart, Chris and Stuart, Tilde *Southern, Central, and East African Mammals* New Holland Publishers, 1992. With information on where to find common species within the confines of 'Zaire', meaning it's a little outdated these days but still a solid resource for those looking for wildlife in the Congos. Congo-Brazzaville is not covered.

Survival guides If you're working for an extended period of time in the Congos and don't have any training or experience in a rather volatile tropical region, I definitely recommend first of all attending a basic survival course for tropical wilderness. As well, having a few books around to refresh your memory is always handy.

Pelton, Robert Young *Come Back Alive* Doubleday, 1999 A solid and entertaining read on the subject which covers pretty much everything one may encounter on Congolese soil, if only in basic detail.

Randall, Jeff and Perrin, Mike *Adventure Travel in the Third World: Everything You Need To Know to Survive in Remote and Hostile Destinations* Paladin Press, 2003. More robust details on Third World survival skills such as bribery and hiring armed guards can be found in this detailed guide.

Werner, David *Where There Is No Doctor* Macmillan Education, 1993. An excellent medical field guide which has easy-to-read instructions on basic medical care when facilities don't exist, how to recognise symptoms, and provide treatment in remote regions.

Travel guides
Briggs, Philip and Booth, Janice *Rwanda* (3rd edition) Bradt Travel Guides, 2006.
Briggs, Philip *Uganda* (5th edition) Bradt Travel Guides, 2007.
Clammer, Paul *Sudan* (1st edition and subsequent reprints) Bradt Travel Guides, 2007.
McIntyre, Chris *Zambia* (4th edition) Bradt Travel Guides, 2008.
Pritchard-Jones, Sian and Gibbons, Bob *Africa Overland: 4x4, Motorbike, Bicycle, Truck* Bradt Travel Guides, 2005.
Wilson-Howarth, Dr Jane and Ellis, Dr Matthew *Your Child Abroad: A Travel Health Guide* Bradt Travel Guides, 2005.
Wilson-Howarth, Dr Jane *Bugs, Bites & Bowels* Cadogan, 2006.

Books mentioned elsewhere in this guide
Burton, Richard Francis *Two Trips to Gorilla Land and the Cataracts of the Congo*. Volume 2. S. Low, Marston, Low, and Searle, 1876. Available online at www.gutenberg.org/etext/5761.
Dann, Douglas *The Largest Tigerfish in the World: The Goliath*. Brussels: Bugzer Europe SA, 2003.
Douville, J B *Voyage au Congo et dans l'Intérieur de l'Afrique Equinoxiale fait dans les années 1828, 1829, et 1830...* Paris, J Renouard, 1832.
Duffy, Kevin *Children of the Forest: Africa's Mbuti Pygmies* Waveland Press, 1995.
Fatau, Abdel and Fayemi, Kayode (ed) *Mercenaries: An African Security Dilemma* London, Pluto Press, 2000.
Findlay, Trevor *The Blue Helmets' First War? Use of Force by the UN in the Congo, 1960-64* Canadian Peacekeeping Press, 1999.
Flintham, Victor *Air Wars and Aircraft: A Detailed Record of Air Combat, 1945 to the Present* Facts on File, 1990.
Fossey, Dian *Gorillas in the Mist* Phoenix Press, 2001.
Hayes, T P *The Dark Romance of Dian Fossey* Touchstone Books, 1991.
Hepburn, Katharine *The Making of The African Queen: Or, How I Went to Africa With Bogart, Bacall and Huston and Almost Lost My Mind* Alfred A. Knopf, 1987.

Herodotus, and Rawlinson, George (trans) *The Histories of Herodotus.* Available online at www.classics.mit.edu/Herodotus/history.html.

Hoare, Mike *Congo Mercenary* Robert Hale Ltd, 1991.

Hoare, Mike *Congo Warriors* Robert Hale Ltd, 1991.

Hoare, Mike *The Road to Kalamata: A Congo Mercenary's Personal Memoir* Lexington Books, 1989.

Mailer, Norman *The Fight* New York, Vintage, 1997.

Malonga, Jean *Coeur d'Aryenne* Paris, Présence Africaine, 1953.

Manning, Olivia *The Remarkable Expedition* New York, Atheneum, 1995.

Osmaston, Henry *Guide to the Rwenzori: Mountains of the Moon* Rwenzori Trust, 2006.

Packham, Eric S *Success or Failure: The UN Intervention in the Congo After Independence* Nova Science Publishers, 1998.

Stanley, Henry Morton *In Darkest Africa: Or the Quest, Rescue and Retreat of Emin Governor of Equatoria*, Volumes 1 & 2 Stackpole Books, 2001.

Thornton, John Kelly *The Kongolese Saint Anthony: Dona Beatriz Kimpa Vita and the Antonian Movement, 1684–1706* Cambridge University Press, 1998.

Tuckey, James Kingston *Narrative of an expedition to explore the river Zaire, usually called the Congo, in South Africa, in 1816, under the direction of Captain J K Tuckey...* London, J Murray, 1818.

WEBSITES

www.crisisweb.org International Crisis Group. Decent summary of the DR Congo conflict, with ongoing analysis and reports.

www.hrw.org Human Rights Watch. Numerous operatives on the ground make their reports well researched and highly illuminating. They have provided continuous coverage on atrocities across the eastern DR Congo.

www.globalsecurity.org Global Security. Well-maintained site that provides a decent breakdown of the continuing conflict in DR Congo, with a large amount of background information available.

www.allafrica.com All Africa. Collects all online press releases for African nations, sorted by country.

www.africa-confidential.com Africa Confidential. Well-researched analysis and reporting on African politics. Some articles by subscription.

www.congo-site.net Official information site of Congo-Brazzaville. Government-funded website to provide basic information on the country. In French only.

www.wikipedia.org and **fr.wikipedia.org** . Wikipedia has numerous detailed articles on all aspects of the DR Congo especially, including some of the most recent background on continuing political developments. Their bibliographies, at the bottom of each page, provide excellent starting points to find primary information.

FILMS

Lumumba (2000) Raoul Peck, Director. French drama exploring the murder of Patrice Lumumba.

When We Were Kings (1996) Leon Gast, Director. Detailed documentary of 'The Rumble In The Jungle', Muhammad Ali and George Foreman's Kinshasa fight in 1974.

Congo (1995) Frank Marshall, Director. Fictional movie of greed and jungle diamonds set in the Congo, based on the novel of the same name by Michael Crichton.

Mountains of the Moon (1989) Bob Rafelson, Director. Chronicles the story of Richard Francis Burton and Jonathan Speke as they search for the source of the Nile, and encounter the Ruwenzori Mountains.

Gorillas in the Mist (1988) Michael Apted, Director. Starring Sigourney Weaver. Fictional retelling of the life and times of Dian Fossey, with her initial difficulties of researching mountain gorillas in the Congo.

The Mercenaries (1968) Jack Cardiff, Director. A fictional account of the mercenary teams hired to fight the UN during Congo's 1960s upheavals.

The Nun's Story (1959) Fred Zinneman, Director. American film starring Audrey Hepburn, concerning the fictional account of a Belgian nun working in the Congo.

Masters of the Congo Jungle (1959) Henry Brandt, Director. Documentary depicting the struggles inherent in the Belgian Congo. Portions narrated by Orson Welles.

The African Queen (1951) John Huston, Director. Starring Humphrey Bogart and Katharine Hepburn. Tells the story of two missionaries in central Africa during World War I. Bogart won his only Oscar for the performance, and the Africa scenes were shot entirely near Ubundu, just south of modern-day Kisangani.

Bradt Travel Guides

www.bradtguides.com

Africa

Africa Overland	£15.99
Algeria	£15.99
Benin	£14.99
Botswana: Okavango, Chobe, Northern Kalahari	£15.99
Burkina Faso	£14.99
Cape Verde Islands	£13.99
Canary Islands	£13.95
Cameroon	£13.95
Congo	£14.99
Eritrea	£15.99
Ethiopia	£15.99
Gabon, São Tomé, Príncipe	£13.95
Gambia, The	£13.99
Ghana	£15.99
Johannesburg	£6.99
Kenya	£14.95
Madagascar	£15.99
Malawi	£13.99
Mali	£13.95
Mauritius, Rodrigues & Réunion	£13.99
Mozambique	£13.99
Namibia	£15.99
Niger	£14.99
Nigeria	£15.99
Rwanda	£14.99
Seychelles	£14.99
Sudan	£13.95
Tanzania, Northern	£13.99
Tanzania	£16.99
Uganda	£15.99
Zambia	£15.95
Zanzibar	£12.99

Britain and Europe

Albania	£13.99
Armenia, Nagorno Karabagh	£14.99
Azores	£12.99
Baltic Capitals: Tallinn, Riga, Vilnius, Kaliningrad	£12.99
Belarus	£14.99
Belgrade	£6.99
Bosnia & Herzegovina	£13.99
Bratislava	£6.99
Budapest	£8.99
Bulgaria	£13.99
Cork	£6.99
Croatia	£13.99
Cyprus see North Cyprus	

Czech Republic	£13.99
Dresden	£7.99
Dubrovnik	£6.99
Estonia	£13.99
Faroe Islands	£13.95
Georgia	£14.99
Helsinki	£7.99
Hungary	£14.99
Iceland	£14.99
Kiev	£7.95
Kosovo	£14.99
Krakow	£7.99
Lapland	£13.99
Latvia	£13.99
Lille	£6.99
Lithuania	£13.99
Ljubljana	£7.99
Macedonia	£14.99
Montenegro	£13.99
North Cyprus	£12.99
Paris, Lille & Brussels	£11.95
Riga	£6.95
River Thames, In the Footsteps of the Famous	£10.95
Serbia	£14.99
Slovakia	£14.99
Slovenia	£12.99
Spitsbergen	£14.99
Switzerland: Rail, Road, Lake	£13.99
Tallinn	£6.99
Ukraine	£14.99
Vilnius	£6.99
Zagreb	£6.99

Middle East, Asia and Australasia

China: Yunnan Province	£13.99
Great Wall of China	£13.99
Iran	£14.99
Iraq	£14.95
Iraq: Then & Now	£15.99
Kyrgyzstan	£15.99
Maldives	£13.99
Mongolia	£14.95
North Korea	£13.95
Oman	£13.99
Sri Lanka	£13.99
Syria	£14.99
Tibet	£13.99
Turkmenistan	£14.99
Yemen	£14.99

The Americas and the Caribbean

Amazon, The	£14.99
Argentina	£15.99
Bolivia	£14.99
Cayman Islands	£12.95
Colombia	£15.99
Costa Rica	£13.99
Chile	£16.95
Dominica	£14.99
Falkland Islands	£13.95
Guyana	£14.99
Panama	£13.95
Peru & Bolivia: Backpacking and Trekking	£12.95
St Helena	£14.99
USA by Rail	£13.99

Wildlife

100 Animals to See Before They Die	£16.99
Antarctica: Guide to the Wildlife	£14.95
Arctic: Guide to the Wildlife	£15.99
Central & Eastern European Wildlife	£15.99
Chinese Wildlife	£16.99
East African Wildlife	£19.99
Galápagos Wildlife	£15.99
Madagascar Wildlife	£14.95
Peruvian Wildlife	£15.99
Southern African Wildlife	£18.95
Sri Lankan Wildlife	£15.99

Eccentric Guides

Eccentric America	£13.95
Eccentric Australia	£12.99
Eccentric Britain	£13.99
Eccentric California	£13.99
Eccentric Cambridge	£6.99
Eccentric Edinburgh	£5.95
Eccentric France	£12.95
Eccentric London	£13.99
Eccentric Oxford	£5.95

Others

Your Child Abroad: A Travel Health Guide	£10.95
Something Different for the Weekend	£12.99

WIN £100 CASH!
READER QUESTIONNAIRE

Send in your completed questionnaire for the chance to win £100 cash in our regular draw

All respondents may order a Bradt guide at half the UK retail price – please complete the order form overleaf.

(Entries may be posted or faxed to us, or scanned and emailed.)

We are interested in getting feedback from our readers to help us plan future Bradt guides. Please answer ALL the questions below and return the form to us in order to qualify for an entry in our regular draw.

Have you used any other Bradt guides? If so, which titles? . . . .
. . . .
What other publishers' travel guides do you use regularly? . . . .
. . . .
Where did you buy this guidebook? . . . .
What was the main purpose of your trip to Congo (or for what other reason did you read our guide)? eg: holiday/business/charity etc.. . . . .
. . . .
What other destinations would you like to see covered by a Bradt guide?
. . . .
Would you like to receive our catalogue/newsletters?
YES / NO (If yes, please complete details on reverse)
If yes – by post or email? . . . .
Age (circle relevant category) 16–25   26–45   46–60   60+
Male/Female (delete as appropriate)
Home country . . . .
Please send us any comments about our guide to Congo or other Bradt Travel Guides. . . . .
. . . .
. . . .
. . . .

Bradt Travel Guides
23 High Street, Chalfont St Peter, Bucks SL9 9QE, UK
☏ +44 (0)1753 893444 **f** +44 (0)1753 892333
e info@bradtguides.com
www.bradtguides.com

CLAIM YOUR HALF-PRICE BRADT GUIDE!

Order Form

To order your half-price copy of a Bradt guide, and to enter our prize draw to win £100 (see overleaf), please fill in the order form below, complete the questionnaire overleaf, and send it to Bradt Travel Guides by post, fax or email.

Please send me one copy of the following guide at half the UK retail price

Title	Retail price	Half price
. . .	. . . . . .	. . . . . .

Please send the following additional guides at full UK retail price

No	Title	Retail price	Total
. . .	. . . .	. . . . . .	. . . . . .
. . .	. . . .	. . . . . .	. . . . . .
. . .	. . . .	. . . . . .	. . . . . .

Sub total . . . . . .
Post & packing . . . . . .
(£1 per book UK; £2 per book Europe; £3 per book rest of world)
Total . . . . . .

Name . . . .

Address . . . .

Tel . . . .   Email . . . .

☐ I enclose a cheque for £ . . . . made payable to Bradt Travel Guides Ltd

☐ I would like to pay by credit card. Number: . . . .

   Expiry date: . . . / . . .   3-digit security code (on reverse of card) . . . . .

   Issue no (debit cards only) . . . . .

☐ Please add my name to your catalogue mailing list.

☐ I would be happy for you to use my name and comments in Bradt marketing material.

Send your order on this form, with the completed questionnaire, to:

Bradt Travel Guides CON1
23 High Street, Chalfont St Peter, Bucks SL9 9QE
☏ +44 (0)1753 893444   f +44 (0)1753 892333
e info@bradtguides.com   www.bradtguides.com

NOTES

NOTES

NOTES

NOTES

Index

Page numbers in **bold** indicate major entries; those in *italics* indicate maps